Bloom's Shakespeare Through the Ages

MUCH ADO ABOUT NOTHING

Edited and with an introduction by
Harold Bloom
Sterling Professor of the Humanities
Yale University

Volume Editor
Michael G. Cornelius

BLOOM'S
LITERARY CRITICISM
An imprint of Infobase Publishing

Bloom's Shakespeare Through the Ages: Much Ado about Nothing
Copyright © 2010 by Infobase Publishing
Introduction © 2010 by Harold Bloom

Bloom's Literary Criticism
An imprint of Infobase Publishing
132 West 31st Street
New York NY 10001

Library of Congress Cataloging-in-Publication Data
Much ado about nothing / edited and with an introduction by Harold Bloom ; volume
editor, Michael G. Cornelius.
     p. cm.—(Bloom's Shakespeare through the ages)
   Includes bibliographical references and index.
   ISBN 978-1-60413-706-4 (acid-free paper)   1. Shakespeare, William, 1564–1616.
Much ado about nothing.   I. Bloom, Harold.   II. Cornelius, Michael G.
   PR2828.M82 2010
   822.3'3—dc22
                                        2009043771

Bloom's Literary Criticism books are available at special discounts when purchased in
bulk quantities for businesses, associations, institutions, or sales promotions. Please call
our Special Sales Department in New York at (212) 967-8800 or (800) 322-8755.

You can find Bloom's Literary Criticism on the World Wide Web at
http://www.chelseahouse.com

Text design by Erika A. Arroyo
Cover design by Ben Peterson
Composition by IBT Global, Inc., Troy NY
Cover printed by IBT Global, Inc., Troy NY
Book printed and bound by IBT Global, Inc., Troy NY
Date printed: March 2010
Printed in the United States of America

10 9 8 7 6 5 4 3 2 1

This book is printed on acid-free paper.

All links and Web addresses were checked and verified to be correct at the time of
publication. Because of the dynamic nature of the Web, some addresses and links
may have changed since publication and may no longer be valid.

CONTENTS

❧

❖ *Much Ado about Nothing* in the Twentieth and Twenty-first Centuries **157**

Series Introduction

Shakespeare Through the Ages presents not the most current of Shakespeare criticism, but the best of Shakespeare criticism, from the seventeenth century to today. In the process, each volume also charts the flow over time of critical discussion of a particular play. Other useful and fascinating collections of historical Shakespearean criticism exist, but no collection that we know of contains such a range of commentary on each of Shakespeare's greatest plays and at the same time emphasizes the greatest critics in our literary tradition: from John Dryden in the seventeenth century, to Samuel Johnson in the eighteenth century, to William Hazlitt and Samuel Coleridge in the nineteenth century, to A. C. Bradley and William Empson in the twentieth century, to the most perceptive critics of our own day. This canon of Shakespearean criticism emphasizes aesthetic rather than political or social analysis.

Some of the pieces included here are full-length essays; others are excerpts designed to present a key point. Much (but not all) of the earliest criticism consists only of brief mentions of specific plays. In addition to the classics of criticism, some pieces of mainly historical importance have been included, often to provide background for important reactions from future critics.

These volumes are intended for students, particularly those just beginning their explorations of Shakespeare. We have therefore also included basic materials designed to provide a solid grounding in each play: a biography of Shakespeare, a synopsis of the play, a list of characters, and an explication of key passages. In addition, each selection of the criticism of a particular century begins with an introductory essay discussing the general nature of that century's commentary and the particular issues and controversies addressed by critics presented in the volume.

Shakespeare was "not of an age, but for all time," but much Shakespeare criticism is decidedly for its own age, of lasting importance only to the scholar who wrote it. Students today read the criticism most readily available to them, which means essays printed in recent books and journals, especially those journals made available on the Internet. Older criticism is too often buried in out-of-print books on forgotten shelves of libraries or in defunct periodicals. Therefore, many students, particularly younger students, have no way of knowing that some of the most profound criticism of Shakespeare's plays was written decades or centuries

ago. We hope this series remedies that problem, and more importantly, we hope
it infuses students with the enthusiasm of the critics in these volumes for the
beauty and power of Shakespeare's plays.

INTRODUCTION BY
HAROLD BLOOM

A. P. Rossiter found the essence of the Beatrice-Benedick relationship in misprision or mutual misreading by those two fierce wits:

> Benedick and Beatrice misapprehend both each other *and* themselves: each misprizes the other sex, and misapprehends the possibility of a complete agreement between them, as individuals, on what causes that misprision: love of freedom and a superior conceit of themselves as "wise" where others are fools; as "free" and untied; and as having a right to enjoy kicking over other people's traces.

That is an interestingly dark view of Beatrice and Benedick and is akin to Harold Goddard's judgment when he wrote of "antiromantic and intellectual egotism in Beatrice and Benedick" as being an aspect of the "egotism of youth." Both Rossiter and Goddar were among the double handful of critics who stood out among earlier modern Shakespearean expositors, but I have never been easy with the stance either adopted toward Beatrice and Benedick. Why moralize in regard to this couple, of all couples? Do they not represent, in *Much Ado about Nothing,* a freedom that misinterprets precisely because it *is* the freedom to misinterpret? And is such freedom, as represented by them, merely a youthful egotism?

If these questions are answerable, then it may be that the answers turn on change, and the representation of change, in Beatrice and Benedick. Comedy is, of course, a much more difficult genre in which to depict change than is tragedy or history, but one of Shakespeare's uncanniest gifts was to abolish genre and not just in what we have agreed to call his "problem plays." Here are Beatrice and Benedick in their full splendor:

Benedick: Thou and I are too wise to woo peaceably.
Beatrice: It appears not in this confession; there not one wise man among twenty that will praise himself.
Benedick: An old, an old instance, Beatrice, that liv'd in the time of good neighbors. If a man do not erect in this age his own tomb ere he

dies, he shall live no longer in monument than the bell rings and the
widow weeps.
Beatrice: And how long is that, thank you?
Benedick: Question: why, an hour in clamour and a quarter in rheum;
therefore is it most expedient for the wise, in Don Worm (his
conscience) find no impediment to the contrary, to be the trumpet of his
own virtues, as I am to myself.

Do they misinterpret each other or themselves? We must acknowledge that,
like all great wits, they are self-conscious and self-congratulatory, failings (if those
are failings) present also in Falstaff, Rosalind, and Hamlet. I think that *Much Ado
about Nothing* generates its highest humor, properly performed, precisely because
Beatrice and Benedick understand their rituals all too well. Nor will age wither
their youthful egotism; mutually supportive, it will last out their lives together.
Shakespeare represents them as changing but only into stronger versions of their
initial selves. Anne Barton usefully compares them to Katherina and Petruchio
in *The Taming of the Shrew,* another "unconventional couple who arrive at love
and understanding by way of insult and aggression." Her characterization is
closer to those earlier lovers than to Beatrice and Benedick, who understand
(and probably love) each other from the start or even before the start.

Rossiter thought that *Much Ado about Nothing* was "a fantasy of equivocal
appearances in a glittering world of amiable fools of all sorts." It is certainly
the most amiably nihilistic play ever written and is most appropriately titled.
Beatrice and Benedick are Nietzscheans before Nietzsche, just as they are
Congreveans before Congreve. The abyss glitters in every exchange between
the fencing lovers, whose mutual wit does not so much defend against other
selves as it defends against meaninglessness. You make much ado about nothing
because nothing will come of nothing. Emersonians also before Emerson,
Beatrice and Benedick confront and pass the pragmatic test, the experiential
law of compensation, that nothing is got for nothing. When they totally accept
that, the play can end, because by then they have changed altogether into the
strongest version of their own selves:

Benedick: Do not you love me?
Beatrice: Why, no, no more than reason.
Benedick: Why then your uncle and the Prince and Claudio
Have been deceived. They swore you did.
Beatrice: Do not you love me?
Benedick: Troth, no, no more than reason.
Beatrice: Why then my cousin, Margaret, and Ursula
Are much deceiv'd, for they did swear you did.
Benedick: They swore that you were almost sick for me.

Beatrice: They swore that you were well-nigh dead for me.
Benedick: 'Tis no such matter. Then you do not love me?
Beatrice: No, truly, but in friendly recompense.
Leonato: Come, cousin, I am sure you love this gentleman.
Claudio: And I'll be sworn upon't that he loves her,
For here's a paper written in his hand,
A halting sonnet of his own pure brain,
Fashion'd to Beatrice.
Hero: And here's another
Writ in my cousin's hand, stol'n from her pocket,
Containing her affection unto Benedick.
Benedick: A miracle! Here's our own hands against our
hearts. Come, I will have thee, but by this light, I take thee for pity.
Beatrice: I would not deny you, but by this good day, I yield upon great
persuasion, and partly to save your life, for I was told you were in a
consumption.
[Benedick]: Peace, I will stop your mouth.
                        [*Kissing her.*]

BIOGRAPHY OF
WILLIAM SHAKESPEARE
✌☙

WILLIAM SHAKESPEARE was born in Stratford-on-Avon in April 1564 into a family of some prominence. His father, John Shakespeare, was a glover and merchant of leather goods, who earned enough to marry the daughter of his father's landlord, Mary Arden, in 1557. John Shakespeare was a prominent citizen in Stratford, and at one point, he served as an alderman and bailiff.

Shakespeare presumably attended the Stratford grammar school, where he would have received an education in Latin, but he did not go on to either Oxford or Cambridge universities. Little is recorded about Shakespeare's early life; indeed, the first record of his life after his christening is of his marriage to Anne Hathaway in 1582 in the church at Temple Grafton, near Stratford. He would have been required to obtain a special license from the bishop as security that there was no impediment to the marriage. Peter Alexander states in his book *Shakespeare's Life and Art* that marriage at this time in England required neither a church nor a priest or, for that matter, even a document—only a declaration of the contracting parties in the presence of witnesses. Thus, it was customary, though not mandatory, to follow the marriage with a church ceremony.

Little is known about William and Anne Shakespeare's marriage. Their first child, Susanna, was born in May 1583, and twins, Hamnet and Judith Shakespeare, in 1585. Later on, Susanna married Dr. John Hall, but the younger daughter, Judith, remained unmarried. When Hamnet died in Stratford in 1596, the boy was only eleven years old.

We have no record of Shakespeare's activities for the seven years after the birth of his twins, but by 1592 he was in London working as an actor. He was also apparently well known as a playwright, for reference is made of him by his contemporary, Robert Greene, in *A Groatsworth of Wit*, as "an upstart crow."

Several companies of actors were in London at this time. Shakespeare may have had connection with one or more of them before 1592, but we have no record that tells us definitely. However, we do know of his long association with the most famous and successful troupe, the Lord Chamberlain's Men. (When James I came to the throne in 1603, after Elizabeth's death, the troupe's name changed to the King's Men.) In 1599, the Lord Chamberlain's Men provided the financial backing for the construction of their own theater, the Globe.

The Globe was begun by a carpenter named James Burbage and finished by his two sons, Cuthbert and Robert. To escape the jurisdiction of the Corporation of London, which was composed of conservative Puritans who opposed the theater's "licentiousness," James Burbage built the Globe just outside London, in the Liberty of Holywell, beside Finsbury Fields. This also meant that the Globe was safer from the threats that lurked in London's crowded streets, like plague and other diseases, as well as rioting mobs. When James Burbage died in 1597, his sons completed the Globe's construction. Shakespeare played a vital role, financially and otherwise, in the construction of the theater, which was finally occupied some time before May 16, 1599.

Shakespeare not only acted with the Globe's company of actors, he was also a shareholder and eventually became the troupe's most important playwright. The company included London's most famous actors, who inspired the creation of some of Shakespeare's best-known characters, such as Hamlet and Lear, as well as his clowns and fools.

In his early years, however, Shakespeare did not confine himself to the theater. He also composed some mythological-erotic poetry, such as *Venus and Adonis* and *The Rape of Lucrece*, both of which were dedicated to the earl of Southampton. Shakespeare was successful enough that in 1597 he was able to purchase his own home in Stratford, which he called New Place. He could even call himself a gentleman, for his father had been granted a coat of arms.

By 1598 Shakespeare had written some of his most famous works, *Romeo and Juliet*, *The Comedy of Errors*, *A Midsummer Night's Dream*, *The Merchant of Venice*, *Two Gentlemen of Verona*, and *Love's Labour's Lost*, as well as his historical plays *Richard II*, *Richard III*, *Henry IV*, and *King John*. Somewhere around the turn of the century, Shakespeare wrote his romantic comedies, *As You Like It*, *Twelfth Night*, and *Much Ado about Nothing*, as well as *Henry V*, the last of his history plays in the Prince Hal series. During the next ten years he wrote his great tragedies, *Hamlet*, *Macbeth*, *Othello*, *King Lear*, and *Antony and Cleopatra*.

At this time, the theater was burgeoning in London; the public took an avid interest in drama, the audiences were large, the plays demonstrated an enormous range of subjects, and playwrights competed for approval. By 1613, however, the rising tide of Puritanism had changed the theater. With the desertion of the theaters by the middle classes, the acting companies were compelled to depend more on the aristocracy, which also meant that they now had to cater to a more sophisticated audience.

Perhaps this change in London's artistic atmosphere contributed to Shakespeare's reasons for leaving London after 1612. His retirement from the theater is sometimes thought to be evidence that his artistic skills were waning. During this time, however, he wrote *The Tempest* and *Henry VIII*. He also wrote the "tragicomedies," *Pericles*, *Cymbeline*, and *The Winter's Tale*. These were thought to be inspired by Shakespeare's personal problems, and have sometimes been considered proof of his greatly diminished abilities.

However, so far as biographical facts indicate, the circumstances of his life at this time do not imply any personal problems. He was in good health, financially secure, and enjoyed an excellent reputation. Indeed, although he was settled in Stratford at this time, he made frequent visits to London, enjoying and participating in events at the royal court, directing rehearsals, and attending to other business matters.

In addition to his brilliant and enormous contributions to the theater, Shakespeare remained a poetic genius throughout the years, publishing a renowned and critically acclaimed sonnet cycle in 1609 (most of the sonnets were written many years earlier). Shakespeare's contribution to this popular poetic genre are all the more amazing in his break with contemporary notions of subject matter. Shakespeare idealized the beauty of man as an object of praise and devotion (rather than the Petrarchan tradition of the idealized, unattainable woman). In the same spirit of breaking with tradition, Shakespeare also treated themes that hitherto had been considered off limits—the dark, sexual side of a woman as opposed to the Petrarchan ideal of a chaste and remote love object. He also expanded the sonnet's emotional range, including such emotions as delight, pride, shame, disgust, sadness, and fear.

When Shakespeare died in 1616, no collected edition of his works had ever been published, although some of his plays had been printed in separate unauthorized editions. (Some of these were taken from his manuscripts, some from the actors' prompt books, and others were reconstructed from memory by actors or spectators.) In 1623, two members of the King's Men, John Hemings and Henry Condell, published a collection of all the plays they considered to be authentic, the First Folio.

Included in the First Folio is a poem by Shakespeare's contemporary Ben Jonson, an outstanding playwright and critic in his own right. Jonson paid tribute to Shakespeare's genius, proclaiming his superiority to what previously had been held as the models for literary excellence—the Greek and Latin writers. "Triumph, my Britain, thou hast one to show / To whom all scenes of Europe homage owe. / He was not of an age, but for all time!"

Jonson was the first to state what has been said so many times since. Having captured what is permanent and universal to all human beings at all times, Shakespeare's genius continues to inspire us—and the critical debate about his works never ceases.

SUMMARY OF
MUCH ADO ABOUT NOTHING
🙂

Act 1

Much Ado about Nothing begins with an ending—a messenger arrives in Messina to spread the news that the recent military conflict between Don Pedro, Prince of Aragon, and his half brother Don John is resolved, with Don Pedro claiming victory. This success comes as good news to Leonato, the governor of Messina, and the members of his household, who are told to expect the arrival of the victorious Don Pedro shortly. Leonato notes that, in his letter, Don Pedro heaps high praise on a young Florentine count named Claudio, while Beatrice, Leonato's niece, asks the messenger about the return of "Signior Mountanto," a scathing reference to a nobleman named Benedick from Padua. In the ensuing conversation, the messenger replies to Beatrice's witty, biting questions with great puzzlement, until Leonato explains that "There is a kind of merry war betwixt Signior Benedick and her [Beatrice]: they never meet but there's a skirmish of wit between them." The messenger also informs the crowd that Benedick and Claudio have become sworn companions, to which Beatrice replies, "God help the noble Claudio! If he have caught the Benedick, it will cost him a thousand pound ere a' be cured." Don Pedro then enters, along with Claudio, Benedick, Balthasar, and Don John. After greeting one another warmly, Don Pedro and Leonato exchange friendly barbs; when Benedick inserts himself into the exchange, Beatrice likewise interjects, commencing the first "merry war" of wit between the two that we witness in the play. This particular conversation ends with Benedick gaining the upper hand; Beatrice's rejoinder, "You always end with a jade's trick: I know you of old," suggests a deeper relationship between the two than previously suspected.

Leonato then welcomes Don John, who is now reconciled with his brother and likewise traveling in his company. All then exit except for Benedick and Claudio, who is eager to ask his companion about Leonato's daughter, Hero. Benedick replies to Claudio's sincere questions ("Is she not a modest young lady?") with jokes and quips; a "professed tyrant to their sex," Benedick has earlier told us he would never deign to marry. Yet his jokes fall on deaf ears, as the young count is clearly smitten with the maid. When Don Pedro re-enters,

5

seeking his companions, Benedick, exasperated, tells him that Claudio is in love
with "Hero, Leonato's short daughter." Don Pedro is overjoyed, for he believes
Hero to be "very well worthy" of Claudio's affections. Surprisingly, Claudio is
suspicious of Don Pedro's approval ("You speak this to fetch me in, my lord"),
but Don Pedro assures him that he spoke in earnest. The exasperated Benedick
declares again that he will "live a bachelor." His companions jest that he, too,
will someday fall in love and wed. The three go on to exchange several jokes
about horns ("If this should ever happen, thou wouldst be horn-mad."). Horn
jokes are common throughout *Much Ado about Nothing* and are references to
cuckoldry, to the male fear of female infidelity. Earlier, Benedick had joked to
Leonato about the parentage of Hero:

> *Don Pedro*: I think this is your daughter.
> *Leonato*: Her mother hath many times told me so.
> *Benedick*: Were you in doubt, sir, that you asked her?

These constant joking references to female sexual fidelity reflect a current of
tension that permeates the play and foreshadow what will occur later in act 4.

When Benedick departs, Don Pedro and Claudio become more serious about
the prospect of Claudio's forthcoming engagement. Claudio first asks about the
possibility of Leonato having a son and is told by Don Pedro that Hero is his
only child and thus his only heir. Don Pedro asks Claudio if this is important,
and he replies:

> When you went onward on this ended action,
> I look'd upon her with a soldier's eye,
> That liked, but had a rougher task in hand
> Than to drive liking to the name of love:
> But now I am return'd and that war-thoughts
> Have left their places vacant, in their rooms
> Come thronging soft and delicate desires,
> All prompting me how fair young Hero is,
> Saying, I liked her ere I went to wars.

Nonetheless, his posing the question is significant enough; clearly, the match
is ideal for Claudio from both a romantic and economic perspective. The scene
ends with Don Pedro promising to woo Hero in Claudio's guise, a needlessly
complicated process that portends future trouble.

Scene 2 introduces the audience to Antonio, Leonato's brother, who tells Leonato
that he has overheard a conversation between the Prince and Claudio and suggests
that it is Don Pedro who will be asking for Hero's hand. This is good news for
Leonato, who would then be allied by marriage to the royal house of Aragon.

In scene 3, the audience is introduced more fully to Don John. Despite his recent crushing defeat and reconciliation with his brother, from his speech, it is evident that Don John will emerge as the play's villain:

> I had rather be a canker in a hedge than a rose in his grace, and it better fits my blood to be disdained of all than to fashion a carriage to rob love from any: in this, though I cannot be said to be a flattering honest man, it must not be denied but I am a plain-dealing villain. I am trusted with a muzzle and enfranchised with a clog; therefore I have decreed not to sing in my cage. If I had my mouth, I would bite; if I had my liberty, I would do my liking: in the meantime let me be that I am and seek not to alter me.

One of Don John's retainers, Borachio, then enters. As in scene 2, he has also heard of the upcoming engagement, but unlike Antonio, Borachio's fellow has his information correct: Don Pedro will woo in Claudio's name. This news excites Don John, who senses an opportunity to create mischief among the proceedings: "this may prove food to my displeasure. That young start-up hath all the glory of my overthrow: if I can cross him any way, I bless myself every way." Assured that he has the assistance of his men, Borachio and Conrade, he goes off to feast.

Act 2

Scene 1 opens at the feast, a masquerade ball to celebrate Don Pedro's victory and return to Messina. Leonato and his family enter first, speaking of Don John and his "melancholy disposition." The conversation quickly turns to love and, more specifically, to Beatrice's pledge never to wed. She describes her ideal man to the others, a figure who does not exist within the confines of the play, and jokes about spending her afterlife among the bachelors in heaven, where she will live "as merry as the day is long." Hero's duty, however, is much more clear, and her father tells her that if the Prince asks to marry her, she knows how to answer him. Beatrice tries to foment a mild rebellion in Hero, telling her, "Yes, faith; it is my cousin's duty to make curtsy and say 'Father, as it please you.' But yet for all that, cousin, let him be a handsome fellow, or else make another curtsy and say 'Father, as it please me.'" Hero, however, is a dutiful daughter; she says nothing to her father, noting her own acquiescence. Hero reflects the ideal Renaissance virtues of silence, obedience, and chastity in a woman; this is a stark contrast to Beatrice, whose chastity is never called into question but who is unmistakably not silent.

A masked Don Pedro begins the dancing by taking Hero as his partner. Other couples follow suit: first Balthasar and Margaret, Hero's attendant, and then Antonio and Ursula, another lady's maid to Hero. Benedick goes to Beatrice in disguise, telling her that some unknown individual has slandered her. Beatrice is not fooled by Benedick's trick and turns the tables on him, insulting Benedick directly to his face while forcing him to pretend he is someone else. Meanwhile, Don John and Borachio approach Claudio. Under the pretense that they believe him to be Benedick, they tell him the Prince is wooing Hero for himself and urge him to intercede, as Hero is too far below Don Pedro's station. Claudio's response to this clumsy subterfuge is telling:

> Thus answer I in the name of Benedick,
> But hear these ill news with the ears of Claudio.
> 'Tis certain so; the prince wooes for himself.
> Friendship is constant in all other things
> Save in the office and affairs of love.

Claudio believes that Don Pedro has deceived him and has wooed Hero for himself. In his subsequent conversation with Benedick, he is petulant and aggrieved, lashing out at Benedick before storming off. Benedick has his own troubles; he is upset over Beatrice's trick. He says: "But that my Lady Beatrice should know me, and not know me!" indicating not only his displeasure over Beatrice's jibe but also of the fact that she has formed such a low opinion of him. When the Prince enters, he recounts Claudio's earlier reaction. When Don Pedro tells him that "The Lady Beatrice hath a quarrel to you: the gentleman that danced with her told her she is much wronged by you," Benedick responds vociferously: "O, she misused me past the endurance of a block!" Beatrice suddenly appears, and Benedick requests a posting far away from her. When Don Pedro says he has none, Benedick, like Claudio, storms off. Don Pedro says to Beatrice, "Come, lady, come; you have lost the heart of Signior Benedick," to which her response is significant: "Indeed, my lord, he lent it me awhile; and I gave / him use for it, a double heart for his single one." This, coupled with her earlier line of "I know you of old," suggests some type of past relationship between that two that went awry, a prior history that would explain both their sniping toward each other and their attitudes about love. Shakespeare, however, does not give any fuller description of the pair's past, leaving it deliberately ambiguous.

Beatrice has brought Claudio to Don Pedro, who has come begrudgingly. When Don Pedro tells him, however, that he has wooed Hero for him and that Leonato has given his permission for the marriage, his countenance changes. He says little, noting that "Silence is the perfectest herald of joy." Thus Claudio and Hero are happily united. Beatrice, watching the proceedings, notes, "Good Lord, for alliance! Thus goes every one to the world but I, and I am sunburnt; I may sit in a corner and cry heigh-ho for a husband!" These sentiments go against her previous railings against marriage; yet when Don Pedro offers his own hand to Beatrice, she gently rebuffs him, noting, "I was born to speak all mirth and no matter." She leaves, and Don Pedro suggests that Beatrice and Benedick would be a perfect match for each other. The others laugh at the notion. Leonato quips, "O Lord, my lord, if they were but a week married, they would talk themselves mad." Still, Don Pedro persists, and in the time leading up to Claudio and Hero's wedding the Prince proposes that the assembled groups conceive of a way to trick Benedick and Beatrice into falling in love.

Scene 1 is one of the longest, and certainly the most action-packed, scenes in the play. Much of the proceedings foretell graver issues to come: the forthcoming deception of Claudio by Don John and his retainers, and Claudio's angry reaction; the coming together of Beatrice and Benedick through deception, mirroring Don Pedro's wooing of Hero in Claudio's name; Beatrice's cunning turnabout in regard to Benedick, reflecting not only the way the two will eventually come together but highlighting the important role deception and masks will play throughout the comedy. Dissembling is a key art in *Much Ado about Nothing*. Except for Dogberry and Verges, each of the characters in the play either practices deception or is deceived by others. This scene also indicates the reasons Shakespeare titled the work *Much Ado about Nothing*. Much of the tension created in the scene is based on matters of misinterpretation or of little consequence. Claudio's intense reaction to Don John's slight bit of villainy best reflects this; ultimately, we learn that he has reacted over nothing. Similarly, most of the deceptions are perpetrated for someone's amusement, whether in a relatively harmless manner (such as Beatrice insulting Benedick to his masked face) or a manner designed to harm (as in Don John's villainy toward Claudio). Shakespeare indicates that all of these deceptions and machinations, though important in their moment, will ultimately amount to nothing and be of no great consequence in the end.

Scene 2 extends the theme of deception, when Borachio tells Don John that he knows of a way to impede Claudio's forthcoming nuptials. He tells Don John that he is a favorite of Hero's gentlewoman, Margaret, and that at an appointed hour he will "court" Margaret at Hero's window, referring to her by Hero's name as she calls him by Claudio's. If Don John were to bring Claudio and Don Pedro to the window at the correct time, the impending wedding would be prevented. Don John agrees to the plan; the main villainy of *Much Ado about Nothing* is thus set to wend its course.

Scene 3 engenders even more deception, all in the attempt to bring Benedick and Beatrice together in marriage. The scene opens with Benedick, ruminating on marriage yet again. Here Benedick, as Beatrice did in scene 1, describes his ideal woman, painting a portrait of a figure who is bound not to exist in all of Italy. When Claudio, Don Pedro, and Leonato enter, Benedick hides, not wishing to hear anymore crowing from Claudio, whom he labels "Monsieur Love." The three men know that Benedick is there, however, and prepare their trap. Don Pedro begins by asking Balthasar to sing a love song, and a significant exchange occurs between them:

Balthasar: Note this before my notes;
There's not a note of mine that's worth the noting.
Don Pedro: Why, these are very crotchets that he speaks;
Note, notes, forsooth, and nothing.

The connection between "noting" (observing, watching, scrutinizing, listening) and "nothing" are key here, again indicating the meaning behind the work's title. Once Balthasar has finished his song, Don Pedro sets out his bait: "What was it you told me of to-day, that your niece Beatrice was in love with Signior Benedick?" The three men discuss Beatrice's great "love" for Benedick, so strong that Leonato fears Beatrice "will do a desperate outrage to herself." Of course, they argue, Beatrice can never tell Benedick how she feels: "Hero thinks surely she will die; for she says she will die, if he love her not, and she will die, ere she make her love known, and she will die, if he woo her, rather than she will bate one breath of her accustomed crossness." The trap well set, the three rush off, but not before plotting to send Beatrice to summon Benedick to dinner.

Benedick, emerging from hiding, is astounded by what he hears but believes that "This can be no trick: the conference was sadly borne. They have the truth of this from Hero." He happily declares he will requite Beatrice's love, pausing only to worry about how he himself may be chided for going against all of his previous condemnations of marriage. Still, he reasons, "the world must be peopled. When I said I would die a bachelor, I did not think I should live till I were married." Beatrice then enters, come to get Benedick for dinner. She is prepared for another "merry war" of words, and Benedick's fawning reactions puzzle her. Benedick, of course, is more convinced than ever that Beatrice's insults harbor deep passion: "'Against my will I am sent to bid you come in to dinner;' there's a double meaning in that."

Act 3

The action in the first scene of the act runs seamlessly with the concluding action of act 2, scene 3. Beatrice, lured into the garden, overhears Hero, Margaret, and Ursula discussing her: "she is too disdainful; / I know her spirits are as coy and wild / As haggerds of the rock." As in the previous scene, the three are soon discussing the great love Benedick holds for Beatrice. The scene is structured exactly like the preceding one: Benedick is praised while Beatrice is derided. Ursula urges that Beatrice be told of Benedick's great love, but Hero says no: "Nature never framed a woman's heart / Of prouder stuff than that of Beatrice." Likewise, when they are done, they believe the trap to have worked effectively: "If it proves so, then loving goes by haps: / Some Cupid kills with arrows, some with traps." When they depart, Beatrice's reaction is similar to Benedick's:

What fire is in mine ears? Can this be true?
Stand I condemn'd for pride and scorn so much?
Contempt, farewell! and maiden pride, adieu!
No glory lives behind the back of such.
And, Benedick, love on; I will requite thee,
Taming my wild heart to thy loving hand.

With both traps seemingly well set, Beatrice and Benedick appear on course for a happy ending.

The first half of scene 2 features Don Pedro, Claudio, and Leonato chiding Benedick for his newfound disposition and the changes he has made to his physical appearance—shaving his beard, wearing cologne—in order to woo Beatrice. For his part, Benedick is mostly silent, apparently confused by their jibing; he asks Leonato to "walk aside" with him, and the others suspect it is to "to break with him about Beatrice." The jocular mood of the scene dissipates, however, when Don John appears. He tells Claudio and Don Pedro that he has important news for the groom: that his "lady is disloyal." Both men react in amazement, wondering "May this be so?," though neither states that he believes it wholly out of the question. Don John tells Claudio and Don Pedro to accompany him tonight to Hero's window, to witness her "disloyalty" for themselves. Though as of yet Claudio has been presented with no proof of Hero's dishonor, he is already planning her recompense: "If I see any thing to-night why I should not marry her to-morrow in the congregation, where I should wed, there will I shame her." Don Pedro agrees to join him in shaming the woman he has wooed for his companion. With Claudio's exhortation of "O mischief strangely thwarting!" the scene ends.

Scene 3 introduces Dogberry, a constable of Messina; Verges, a "headborough" who acts in accord with Dogberry; and the Prince's watchmen. Dogberry is a high comic figure, who speaks almost wholly in riddles and misunderstandings; as such, he is a kind of fool figure, common in Shakespeare, though Dogberry is played almost solely for laughs, offering none of the wisdom Feste professes in *Twelfth Night*, for example. In this scene, Dogberry directs the watchmen, and his simple command becomes needlessly muddled by his obfuscated speech and hopelessly jumbled directions

When Dogberry and Verges leave, Borachio and Conrade enter. The watch is concealed, so a drunken Borachio delights in telling Conrade that "I have to-night wooed Margaret, the Lady Hero's gentlewoman, by the name of Hero." He further crows that he has deceived Claudio and Don Pedro by this action and that Hero will be mercilessly shamed tomorrow in front of everyone at the wedding ceremony because of his own villainous deeds. At this admission, the watch springs forth and arrests both men, taking them to Dogberry for questioning.

Scene 4 opens on the morning of the wedding with a nervous Hero talking with Margaret about her wedding apparel. It is understandable that Hero, about to be married, is anxious and peevish. When Beatrice enters, however, the scene mirrors the actions of the first half of scene 2, with Hero and Margaret chiding Beatrice for her blissful state, brought on by her love for Benedick. Beatrice says that "I am out of all other tune, methinks," and Hero and Margaret tease her with musical quips and other such barbs. Like Benedick before, Beatrice is confused by their words, since she is unaware of the role they played in joining the couple. Ursula then enters, telling the group that the Prince and Claudio have arrived and that the wedding will begin shortly.

In the final scene of act 3, Dogberry and Verges come to Leonato to inform him that the night watch "ha' ta'en a couple of as arrant knaves as any in Messina" and that they require Leonato's presence for the interrogation. Of course, with Dogberry being the bearer of the news, it is difficult for Leonato to extract this information from him. Numerous times Leonato expresses a mild exasperation with the constable and his aide: "Neighbours, you are tedious," he states before finally exclaiming, "I would fain know what you have to say." Once he learns of the substance of their errand, he tells Dogberry to conduct the interrogation himself, as he has other matters that are currently more pressing.

Act 4

Scene 1 of the act is perhaps the seminal scene in the entire play—the first wedding scene. Most of the characters are assembled, and tension is apparent in the countenances of Claudio, Don Pedro, and Don John. When the Friar asks Claudio, "You come hither, my lord, to marry this lady," he curtly replies, "No." The moment is quickly smoothed over when Leonato, believing that Claudio is still joking, says, "To be married to her: friar, you come to marry her." Claudio, however, soon reveals why he has really come to the wedding: "Not to be married, / Not to knit my soul to an approved wanton." He further explains:

> Give not this rotten orange to your friend;
> She's but the sign and semblance of her honour.
> Behold how like a maid she blushes here!
> O, what authority and show of truth
> Can cunning sin cover itself withal!
> Comes not that blood as modest evidence
> To witness simple virtue? Would you not swear,
> All you that see her, that she were a maid,
> By these exterior shows? But she is none:
> She knows the heat of a luxurious bed;
> Her blush is guiltiness, not modesty.

The reaction to these charges is immediate. A stumbling Leonato at first believes that it is Claudio who has had sexual relations with Hero, charges Claudio denies: "I never tempted her with word too large; / But, as a brother to his sister, show'd / Bashful sincerity and comely love." Don Pedro further explains by describing what he believes he and Claudio witnessed the previous night. Hero denies the allegation, then swoons and faints. Leonato's reaction is just as severe: "Hath no man's dagger here a point for me?" Don Pedro and Claudio, spurred by Don John, leave. The rest of the wedding party stands around the prostrate Hero in amazement. Beatrice worries that Hero may have actually died, but Leonato argues that death would be preferable to the shame she has caused him. Benedick's only response is that he is so confounded, he is unsure what has happened. Only Beatrice defends her cousin's honor: "O, on my soul, my cousin is belied!" Leonato, however, will not hear of it: "Would the two princes lie, and Claudio lie, / Who loved her so, that, speaking of her foulness, / Wash'd it with tears? Hence from her! let her die." The Friar speaks out in defense of Hero, however, noting that her "thousand blushing apparitions" belie her innocence. Still, Leonato is not wholly convinced, even when Hero revives and insists on her innocence. Benedick rightly points out that

> Two of them have the very bent of honour;
> And if their wisdoms be misled in this,
> The practise of it lives in John the bastard,
> Whose spirits toil in frame of villanies.

Leonato is still unconvinced: "I know not. If they speak but truth of her, / These hands shall tear her; if they wrong her honour, / The proudest of them shall well hear of it." Finally, the Friar advises the group that they should pretend that Hero has indeed died as a result of the slander, so that when Claudio

> shall hear she died upon his words,
> The idea of her life shall sweetly creep
> Into his study of imagination,
> And every lovely organ of her life
> Shall come apparell'd in more precious habit,
> More moving-delicate and full of life,
> Into the eye and prospect of his soul,
> Than when she lived indeed; then shall he mourn,
> If ever love had interest in his liver,
> And wish he had not so accused her,
> No, though he thought his accusation true.

Benedick persuades Leonato to heed the Friar's advice.

The group exits, leaving Beatrice and Benedick. Now that they are alone, he notices that she has been weeping. He tells her that he believes her cousin has been wronged, and she replies, "how much might the man deserve of me that would right her!" Though it is perhaps an odd time for such a disclosure, Benedick finally confesses, "I do love nothing in the world so well as you." Beatrice is momentarily startled by this, but she eventually confesses her own feelings for him as well. Happy, Benedick exhorts Beatrice to "Come, bid me do any thing for thee," and she stonily replies, "Kill Claudio." Benedick is taken aback and refuses. Beatrice tells him his love for her is false. When Benedick asks Beatrice if Claudio is really her enemy, she replies:

> Is he not approved in the height a villain, that hath slandered, scorned, dishonoured my kinswoman? O that I were a man! What, bear her in hand until they come to take hands; and then, with public accusation, uncovered slander, unmitigated rancour,—O God, that I were a man! I would eat his heart in the market-place.

She ultimately convinces Benedick, who pledges to challenge Claudio.

Act 4, scene 1 is a rich, complex scene, buffeted by Claudio's rejection of Hero and Benedick's declaration of love for Beatrice. The impact of Hero's rebuff is lessened for the audience by the events of act 3, scene 3, since the audience is aware that the watch has uncovered the truth of Hero's innocence and that such news will soon be delivered to the others. Still, Claudio's actions and the uproar that ensues suggest that this is the "much ado" that is made of "nothing." "Nothing" is here implied by the accusation against Hero, since it is false. The "much ado" associated with Claudio and Don Pedro's actions, however, is made all the more extensive and impactful by the fallacy of their claims. Thankfully, this rough scene is balanced by Beatrice and Benedick's happy discovery of each other's affection, though this joy, too, is tempered by Beatrice's exhortation to Benedick to "Kill Claudio." Her argument convincing Benedick to challenge Claudio has fractured another coupling—that of two good friends—a reality that tempers the only light moment in the entire scene.

Scene 2 revives the comic workings of Dogberry and Verges, who are busy interrogating Borachio and Conrade. Again, Dogberry's flair for employing language in unusual ways is highlighted here, and his constant misunderstanding of words confuses both the Sexton and his captives. Thankfully, the watchmen manage to tell what they overheard to the Sexton, who tells the group that everything the watch has overheard has, indeed, come to pass. He rushes off to inform Leonato of what he has uncovered. After his departure, Shakespeare gives us one of the play's comic highlights when Conrade calls Dogberry an "ass." Dogberry is incensed that the Sexton is not there to write the offense down and exhorts everyone to "remember that I am an ass; though it be not written down, yet forget not that I am an ass."

Act 5

Scene 1 opens with Leonato conversing with his brother, Antonio, about the events at the wedding. Having had time to carefully consider the matter, Leonato believes that, "My soul doth tell me Hero is belied." Spying the Prince and Claudio, the two men confront them. "Thou hast so wrong'd mine innocent child and me!" Leonato cries, telling the two that Hero has died from the slander done to her. Antonio echoes his claim: "God knows I loved my niece; / And she is dead, slander'd to death by villains." Don Pedro refuses to heed their words, however, and the two leave swearing that they will be heard.

Benedick enters, the individual Don Pedro and Claudio had been seeking. They tell him of the confrontation and ask him to "use thy wit" to lighten their moods. Benedick, however, refuses, and mirroring earlier scenes in which one character is uncivil while the others jocular, he responds to their attempts at humor with terse, derisive answers. Confronting Claudio directly, he challenges him before discharging himself from Don Pedro's service: "I must discontinue your company: your brother the bastard is fled from Messina: you have among you killed a sweet and innocent lady." He then leaves, and both Don Pedro and Claudio are astounded by his earnest challenge. They blame this change in attitude on his love for Beatrice, however, and Don Pedro notes, "What a pretty thing man is when he goes in his doublet and hose and leaves off his wit!" The Prince then wonders what the news of his brother's departure means, but before Claudio can reply, Dogberry, Verges, Conrade, Borachio and the watch enter. Dogberry's speech confounds Don Pedro, who then states to the prisoners, "This learned constable is too cunning to be understood: what's your offence?" A forlorn Borachio confesses the plot to Don Pedro and Claudio. The impact of Borachio's words is immediate: "Runs not this speech like iron through your blood?" Don Pedro intones. Leonato enters, having been informed of the discovery by the Sexton, and confronts Borachio: "Art thou the slave that with thy breath hast kill'd / Mine innocent child?" Borachio replies that yes, it was he alone, and Leonato retorts:

> No, not so, villain; thou beliest thyself:
> Here stand a pair of honourable men;
> A third is fled, that had a hand in it.
> I thank you, princes, for my daughter's death:
> Record it with your high and worthy deeds:
> 'Twas bravely done, if you bethink you of it.

Claudio begs Leonato's forgiveness, telling him to "Choose your revenge yourself." Don Pedro parrots this sentiment. Yet, despite the fact that Hero is now proved innocent, Leonato still continues the charade. He urges the two to

"Possess the people in Messina here / How innocent she died; and if your love / Can labour ought in sad invention, / Hang her an epitaph upon her tomb." He then tells Claudio that he will now be wed to his brother Antonio's daughter, who is now heir to them both, and "so dies my revenge." Leonato talks of confronting Margaret about her role in the affair, but Borachio pleads for her innocence, saying that she did not know of the plan. He then discharges the prisoners, before pledging that he will see Claudio and Don Pedro to solemnize the wedding ceremony tomorrow.

Scene 2 returns to the story of Beatrice and Benedick and opens with Benedick and Margaret exchanging witticisms. There is a change in Benedick's wit, however; while previously it was barbed and pointed, in this scene his jibes are gentle and almost praising of his female companion. Margaret leaves to get Beatrice, and while he waits, Benedick unsuccessfully attempts to compose a love sonnet to her, though he ultimately concludes that he "was not born under a rhyming planet." Beatrice enters, and the two spar wittily again, though as with Margaret, the "merry war" has become a gentler, more romantic skirmish. Beatrice asks Benedick what has happened between him and Claudio, and Benedick replies, "Only foul words; and thereupon I will kiss thee." Beatrice says he will remain unkissed, but then Benedick tells her he is awaiting word about his challenge. He then turns to talk of love, asking Beatrice, "for which of my bad parts didst thou first fall in love with me?" She replies in kind, and the two speak about their hearts before Benedick gives a silly speech on the value of self-promotion. Ursula's entrance concludes the love talk, and she brings with her the good news that Hero has been proved innocent.

In Scene 3, Claudio sings his dirge to Hero's tomb, pledging to continue the ritual yearly until he dies. He and Don Pedro then leave to prepare for the wedding ceremony the next day.

Scene 4 begins with Leonato and the Friar discussing Hero's innocence, stating that the only true fault lies with the villainous Don John. Leonato then sends Hero, Beatrice, Margaret, and Ursula off to put on veils before making their appearance. Benedick then pulls the Friar aside, asking for his help in marrying Beatrice. He is puzzled by Leonato's rejoinder that Benedick has learned of his feelings for her from him, the Prince, and Claudio—and Beatrice from Hero—but they all pledge to help and support him win her hand. Don Pedro and Claudio enter and once again jokingly spar with Benedick, including another cuckold joke referencing horns: "I think he thinks upon the savage bull. / Tush, fear not, man; we'll tip thy horns with gold / And all Europa shall rejoice at thee." Antonio then enters with the four women, all masked. Claudio asks to see the face of his bride, and Leonato says he cannot until Claudio has pledged before the Friar to marry the maid. When Claudio agrees, she takes off her mask to reveal the face of Hero. Both Claudio and Don Pedro are amazed, and Leonato explains, "She died, my lord, but whiles her slander lived." Hero adds:

"One Hero died defiled, but I do live, / And surely as I live, I am a maid." The Friar tells them he will explain it all once the wedding is concluded, but before anyone can act Benedick speaks up, asking which of the maids is Beatrice. She emerges and unmasks herself, but when Benedick asks her in such a public forum if she loves him, she demurs, and replies, "Why, no; no more than reason." Benedick gives nearly the same response to her question, and the two realize the plot against them. They pledge friendship only, but Claudio and Hero produce sonnets that each had written to the other, professing their love. They agree to wed, though not without their usual banter, before Benedick finally says, "Peace! I will stop your mouth," and publicly kisses Beatrice for the first time. Turning to the Prince, Benedick tells him, "man is a giddy thing, and this is my conclusion," perhaps the best line in the play indicating the "much ado" that had ultimately been made over "nothing." He relinquishes Claudio from his challenge and calls for a dance before the wedding ceremony. At that moment a messenger appears, heralding news of Don John's capture, who materializes moments thereafter. Benedick tells Don Pedro to "Think not on him till to-morrow: I'll devise thee brave punishments for him" before exhorting "Strike up, pipers" and leading everyone in a dance to conclude the play.

Key Passages in
Much Ado about Nothing
❦

Act 1, 1, 112–41

Benedick: If Signior Leonato be her father, she would not have his head on her shoulders for all Messina, as like him as she is.

Beatrice: I wonder that you will still be talking, Signior Benedick: nobody marks you.

Benedick: What, my dear Lady Disdain! are you yet living?

Beatrice: Is it possible disdain should die while she hath such meet food to feed it as Signior Benedick? Courtesy itself must convert to disdain, if you come in her presence.

Benedick: Then is courtesy a turncoat. But it is certain I am loved of all ladies, only you excepted: and I would I could find in my heart that I had not a hard heart; for, truly, I love none.

Beatrice: A dear happiness to women: they would else have been troubled with a pernicious suitor. I thank God and my cold blood, I am of your humour for that: I had rather hear my dog bark at a crow than a man swear he loves me.

Benedick: God keep your ladyship still in that mind! so some gentleman or other shall 'scape a predestinate scratched face.

Beatrice: Scratching could not make it worse, an 'twere such a face as yours were.

Benedick: Well, you are a rare parrot-teacher.

Beatrice: A bird of my tongue is better than a beast of yours.

Benedick: I would my horse had the speed of your tongue, and so good a continuer. But keep your way, i' God's name; I have done.

Beatrice: You always end with a jade's trick: I know you of old.

This passage represents the first "merry war" of words that Beatrice and Benedick will wage in the text. As with all of their duels of wit, however, their quips tend to contain references to larger themes and ideas at work in the play.

Benedick's opening salvo is actually given in response to Don Pedro, who has been exchanging jibes with Leonato over the parentage of his daughter, Hero.

These seemingly lighthearted, comical remarks about fidelity and the threat of female sexuality belie the concern that the men in the play continually—if humorously—express over the matter. Much of the male tension in the play, whether real or imagined, is prompted by concerns about female sexuality.

Inserting herself into this tension, and into the male game, is Beatrice. Since the first performances of *Much Ado about Nothing*, many critics have responded enthusiastically to the comedy in the interchanges between Beatrice and Benedick. It is hardly surprising why; though occasionally crude, their witty banter and back-and-forth verbal sparring demonstrate some of the most successful, expertly realized humor in all of Shakespeare. This "merry war" also reflects an inherent conflict that seems to be waged between the characters onstage—the very "much ado about nothing" suggested in the title. Many critics have made much over the role of gender in the larger dynamics of the text. Claudio's swift decision to turn against Hero—not once, but twice—hints at a larger male distrust of women. It is significant that it is not only Claudio who instantly believes the worst about Hero, as Don Pedro and her own father likewise voice their distrust of her. Benedick speaks of his amazement at what he has seen but does not immediately defend Hero either. Only Beatrice does so; hers is the first voice that argues for Hero's innocence.

Thus the tendency of the men to turn on women over what is, ultimately, "nothing," is telling. Beatrice, however, remains unaffected by this, and part of the reason is her aggressive speech posturing and patterns as depicted in this scene. Strangely enough, by taking on the men directly, by engaging with them at their own game and at their own level, Beatrice is seen as being less mysterious, and thus less threatening, than the other woman in the play. It is, ultimately, her willingness to engage Benedick in this "merry war" that preserves her from a fate similar to Hero's.

The scene itself also illustrates both characters' views toward marriage, the first (though not the last) time these opinions are shared. Though both profess themselves to be wholly against the concept, the audience is not fooled, and neither are the rest of the play's characters, as soon, they will seize on the notion of bringing the two squabbling figures together. Beatrice's last line of the exchange, "You always end with a jade's trick: I know you of old," also suggests a prior relationship between the two that perhaps did not end well. There is further evidence of this relationship as well (2.1.275–79), though Shakespeare ultimately never completes the picture of what the nature of this relationship might have been.

Act 2, 1, 170–80

Claudio: Thus answer I in the name of Benedick,
But hear these ill news with the ears of Claudio.
'Tis certain so; the prince wooes for himself.

Friendship is constant in all other things
Save in the office and affairs of love:
Therefore, all hearts in love use their own tongues;
Let every eye negotiate for itself
And trust no agent; for beauty is a witch
Against whose charms faith melteth into blood.
This is an accident of hourly proof,
Which I mistrusted not. Farewell, therefore, Hero!

and

Act 4, 1, 29–41

Claudio: Sweet prince, you learn me noble thankfulness.
There, Leonato, take her back again:
Give not this rotten orange to your friend;
She's but the sign and semblance of her honour.
Behold how like a maid she blushes here!
O, what authority and show of truth
Can cunning sin cover itself withal!
Comes not that blood as modest evidence
To witness simple virtue? Would you not swear,
All you that see her, that she were a maid,
By these exterior shows? But she is none:
She knows the heat of a luxurious bed;
Her blush is guiltiness, not modesty.

These two passages demonstrate Claudio's reactions to Don John's two main deceptions in the play: the first occurring during the masquerade scene of act 2, the latter during the wedding scene in act 4. Both reveal the swiftness with which Claudio turns on his betrothed, thus indicating an inherent propensity to instinctively distrust the woman he professes to love.

In the first scene, Claudio, speaking in soliloquy, responds to the falsely reported news that Don Pedro has wooed Hero for himself. Though the evidence is scant to support such an accusation, Claudio believes it wholly, saying, "Friendship is constant in all other things / Save in the office and affairs of love." Here Claudio readily demonstrates his belief that Don Pedro's earlier promise to secure Hero's favor for Claudio meant nothing to him. The second and more damning speech is presented in front of the entire wedding ensemble; there, Claudio viciously turns on Hero. In suggesting she is "but the sign and semblance of her honour," Claudio asserts that Hero only appears to be the idealized Elizabethan female—silent, obedient, and chaste; in this scene, Claudio calls into question her chastity, shaming her in front of the assembled group. The importance of outward appearances ("exterior shows") is highlighted in this speech; Hero's blushing response to the accusation is viewed by Claudio as proof of her duplicity and wantonness: "She knows the heat of a luxurious bed."

Critics have long remarked about the ferocity of this response and Claudio's quick propensity to believe the word of Don John, a proven villain. Even before he witnesses what he believes is Hero in the arms of another man at her bedroom window, Claudio has plotted his revenge (3.2.119–21). Yet Claudio's reaction in the first scene is also highly indicative of some instinct within his character to mistrust both Hero and his lord, Don Pedro. The condemnation in the first speech is for both Don Pedro, whom Claudio calls inconstant, and Hero, whom Claudio labels a witch who has bedeviled Don Pedro with her beauty. Critics have long been divided as to whether these scenes reveal Claudio's general inexperience with life and his naiveté (both plans by Don John defy logic and are so incredulous that seemingly only a man as young and foolish as Claudio could be gulled twice by them) or something more inborn to his character that is instinctively and perhaps pathologically fearful, and thus vengeful, toward women in general. Both scenes nonetheless demonstrate that Claudio's professed love for Hero is the true inconstant factor in the play, and that, in him, overtures of love too easily give way to expressions of rancor.

<hr />

Act 2, 3, 43–57

Don Pedro: Come, Balthasar, we'll hear that song again.
Balthasar: O, good my lord, tax not so bad a voice
To slander music any more than once.
Don Pedro: It is the witness still of excellency
To put a strange face on his own perfection.
I pray thee, sing, and let me woo no more.
Balthasar: Because you talk of wooing, I will sing;
Since many a wooer doth commence his suit
To her he thinks not worthy, yet he wooes,
Yet will he swear he loves.
Don Pedro: Now, pray thee, come;
Or, if thou wilt hold longer argument,
Do it in notes.
Balthasar: Note this before my notes;
There's not a note of mine that's worth the noting.
Don Pedro: Why, these are very crotchets that he speaks;
Note, notes, forsooth, and nothing.

Much has been made of perception and the act of perceiving in *Much Ado about Nothing*. What the characters both hear and see is often called into question, if not by them, then at least by the audience. Many critics have pointed out that the action in *Much Ado about Nothing* hinges on deception and being deceived; whether the deception is intended as harmful (such as Don John deceiving Claudio and Don Pedro into believing Hero is unfaithful) or relatively harmless (as when Beatrice and Benedick are tricked into falling in love), the action and drama of the play are built around misperceptions and misunderstandings.

The word *nothing* comes significantly into play in the work. The scene from which this exchange is taken is ostensibly about a song and the singer who is modestly reluctant to sing it. Yet the scene reveals much about the underlying condition and theme of the play, as encapsulated in the title of the work itself. In Don Pedro's final line, the word *nothing* would have actually been pronounced as "noting," helping to create one last play on words before Balthasar sings. Yet the meaning of the word *noting* is key here to understanding the subtle underpinnings of the text. *Note* has more usage in the scene than just its musical context; the verb *to note* also suggests to observe something or to mark it. These observations generally occur with the sense of sight (to observe, whether openly or covertly) or the sense of hearing (to hear or, as is often the case in *Much Ado about Nothing*, to overhear). The scene is constructed on a precept of overhearing and being stealthily observed, as Don Pedro, Leonato, and Claudio are preparing a false conversation for the benefit of Benedick, to convince him of Beatrice's great love for him.

The last three lines of the dialogue are most important. When Don Pedro urges Balthasar to "Do it in notes," he is not only commenting on the music but also making a pun on the word *notes* itself, suggesting that if Balthasar wishes to continue arguing with Don Pedro over the quality of his voice, he should do it "in notes," in writing or in hints. Balthasar's reply takes up the pun and extends it, asking that the listeners "Note this before my notes," or regard this word of advice before he sings; "There's not a note of mine that's worth the noting," he says, indicating that his music is not worthy of the Prince's praise or attention. Yet the line also reads as a conceit on the word *notes*, an extended metaphor and pun. By suggesting, "There's not a note of mine that's worth the noting," Balthasar insists that nothing he says is worth paying attention to. In the larger thematic landscape of the play, this advice holds sway for many, as much of what is being said is based on deception, subterfuge, and lies. Don John's character, for example, is based on presenting a false reconciled face before his brother and the others who have rendered his defeat. Still, almost every character in the play deceives. Don Pedro, Claudio, Leonato, Hero, Margaret, and Ursula are all involved in the scheme to unite Beatrice and Benedick; Don Pedro and Claudio concoct the plan to have the Prince woo Hero in disguise at the masquerade; Don John, Borachio, and Conrade are all involved in deceiving Claudio at the masquerade and, later, on the night before his wedding; Claudio and Don Pedro come to the wedding with the intention of shaming Hero, not celebrating a solemn marriage; Margaret is involved (though indirectly) in the plot to slander Hero's name and ruin Claudio's marriage; the Friar, Leonato, Beatrice, Benedick, Antonio, and Hero all dissemble about Hero's demise; the same grouping, plus Margaret and Ursula, are all involved in the plan to pledge Claudio to Leonato's "niece" before revealing the truth of Hero's "resurrection." The only characters that are not actively involved in crafting deception are Dogberry, Verges, and the watch, though their roles in bringing to light the truth behind these deceptions reveals their important role in "noting" and observing in the play as well. Thus when Balthasar says that nothing he speaks is worth noting, the same may be said for most of the play, when what much of the characters speak, hear, and do is based on falsehoods and lies. Don Pedro sums it aptly when he suggests, "Note, notes, forsooth, and nothing," indicating that much of the action of the play really will be "much ado about" what is ultimately "nothing."

Act 2, 3, 216–42

Benedick: [Coming forward] This can be no trick: the conference was sadly borne. They have the truth of this from Hero. They seem to pity the lady: it seems her affections have their full bent. Love me! why, it must be requited. I hear how I am censured: they say I will bear myself proudly, if I perceive the love come from her; they say too that she will rather die than give any sign of affection. I did never think to marry: I must not seem proud: happy are they that hear their detractions and can put them to mending. They say the lady is fair; 'tis a truth, I can bear them witness; and virtuous; 'tis so, I cannot reprove it; and wise, but for loving me; by my troth, it is no addition to her wit, nor no great argument of her folly, for I will be horribly in love with her. I may chance have some odd quirks and remnants of wit broken on me, because I have railed so long against marriage: but doth not the appetite alter? a man loves the meat in his youth that he cannot endure in his age. Shall quips and sentences and these paper bullets of the brain awe a man from the career of his humour? No, the world must be peopled. When I said I would die a bachelor, I did not think I should live till I were married.

and

Act 3, 1, 107–16

Beatrice: [Coming forward]
What fire is in mine ears? Can this be true?
Stand I condemn'd for pride and scorn so much?

Contempt, farewell! And maiden pride, adieu!
No glory lives behind the back of such.
And, Benedick, love on; I will requite thee,
Taming my wild heart to thy loving hand:
If thou dost love, my kindness shall incite thee
To bind our loves up in a holy band;
For others say thou dost deserve, and I
Believe it better than reportingly.

These scenes show the reactions of Benedick and Beatrice, respectively, to the false reports that each is madly in love with the other. Their swift and wholly accepting response to the news—both pledge to requite the other with little fuss—demonstrates that the news was likely neither unwelcome nor unexpected. Their responses suggest both interesting similarities and unique divergences about each character.

In the first, Benedick is initially concerned about how his companions will perceive him if he displays any sign of love for Beatrice, since he has spent so much time railing against it. This gives way to an evaluation of Beatrice's finer qualities (her beauty, her virtue, her wit) before Benedick again returns to his worries over how he will be viewed by his male peers. His arguments in favor of changing his mind range from the sensible, if not crude ("doth not the appetite alter? a man loves the meat in his youth that he cannot endure in his age") to the utterly ridiculous ("the world must be peopled"). Still, the audience begins to believe that these considerations and evaluations are meant to convince him as much as anyone else, and the sincerity of feeling behind the insincere logic of these somewhat ridiculous arguments is not lost on the audience.

Beatrice's response is perhaps more direct than Benedick's; she seems less surprised than Benedick by what she has overheard, though the news of how others (Hero and Ursula) perceive her has somewhat taken her aback. In casting off her old self, Beatrice pledges to alter her previously proud ways, and when she promises to love Benedick ("Taming my wild heart to thy loving hand"), there is also an inherent promise to change her behavior toward him as well. Benedick made no similar promise to alter his essential character; though he worried how his male companions would perceive his sudden change in attitude, he does not suggest altering any of his characteristics to suit Beatrice or match her more appropriately. This difference may reflect Elizabethan gender dynamics, that the expected role of the woman would be to conform to her husband's precepts of behavior (certainly Shakespeare examines this concept in *The Taming of the Shrew*). Beatrice's pledge is also somewhat diminished by the fact that her subsequent appearances suggest little actual change to her own self-fashioning; she may be "tamed," but she is hardly domesticated. Many critics have suggested that it is actually Benedick's character that undergoes a greater transformation toward the end of the play, and that these changes occur because of Beatrice. Thus, while she pledges to change, she, in truth, changes little, while Benedick, who makes no such promise, undergoes the greater alteration of character.

Another key difference between the two speeches is that Beatrice's is in verse and contains one of the few instances of rhymed poetry in the play; Benedick's is in prose. Shakespeare may have associated the lineated verse speech with the feminine, but it also allows for a great difference of character when the two speeches are examined side by side, perhaps allowing Beatrice to retain more of her essential, individual self than a speech that would parrot the structure, intention, and style of Benedick's earlier discourse.

Act 4, 1, 254–333

Benedick: Lady Beatrice, have you wept all this while?

Beatrice: Yea, and I will weep a while longer.

Benedick: I will not desire that.

Beatrice: You have no reason; I do it freely.

Benedick: Surely I do believe your fair cousin is wronged.

Beatrice: Ah, how much might the man deserve of me that would right her!

Benedick: Is there any way to show such friendship?

Beatrice: A very even way, but no such friend.

Benedick: May a man do it?

Beatrice: It is a man's office, but not yours.

Benedick: I do love nothing in the world so well as you: is not that strange?

Beatrice: As strange as the thing I know not. It were as possible for me to say I loved nothing so well as you: but believe me not; and yet I lie not; I confess nothing, nor I deny nothing. I am sorry for my cousin.

Benedick: By my sword, Beatrice, thou lovest me.

Beatrice: Do not swear, and eat it.

Benedick: I will swear by it that you love me; and I will make him eat it that says I love not you.

Beatrice: Will you not eat your word?

Benedick: With no sauce that can be devised to it. I protest I love thee.

Beatrice: Why, then, God forgive me!

Benedick: What offence, sweet Beatrice?

Beatrice: You have stayed me in a happy hour: I was about to protest I loved you.

Benedick: And do it with all thy heart.

Beatrice: I love you with so much of my heart that none is left to protest.

Benedick: Come, bid me do any thing for thee.

Beatrice: Kill Claudio.

Benedick: Ha! not for the wide world.

Beatrice: You kill me to deny it. Farewell.

Benedick: Tarry, sweet Beatrice.

Beatrice: I am gone, though I am here: there is no love in you: nay, I pray you, let me go.

Benedick: Beatrice,—

Beatrice: In faith, I will go.

Benedick: We'll be friends first.

Beatrice: You dare easier be friends with me than fight with mine enemy.

Benedick: Is Claudio thine enemy?

Beatrice: Is he not approved in the height a villain, that hath slandered, scorned, dishonoured my kinswoman? O that I were a man! What, bear her in hand until they come to take hands; and then, with public accusation, uncovered slander, unmitigated rancour,—O God, that I were a man! I would eat his heart in the market-place.

Benedick: Hear me, Beatrice,—

Beatrice: Talk with a man out at a window! A proper saying!

Benedick: Nay, but, Beatrice,—

Beatrice: Sweet Hero! She is wronged, she is slandered, she is undone.

Benedick: Beat—

Beatrice: Princes and counties! Surely, a princely testimony, a goodly count, Count Comfect; a sweet gallant, surely! O that I were a man for his sake! or that I had any friend would be a man for my sake! But manhood is melted into courtesies, valour into compliment, and men are only turned into tongue, and trim ones too: he is now as valiant as Hercules that only tells a lie and swears it. I cannot be a man with wishing, therefore I will die a woman with grieving.

Benedick: Tarry, good Beatrice. By this hand, I love thee.

Beatrice: Use it for my love some other way than swearing by it.

Benedick: Think you in your soul the Count Claudio hath wronged Hero?

Beatrice: Yea, as sure as I have a thought or a soul.

Benedick: Enough, I am engaged; I will challenge him. I will kiss your hand, and so I leave you. By this hand, Claudio shall render me a dear account. As you hear of me, so think of me. Go, comfort your cousin: I must say she is dead: and so, farewell.

This extensive but key scene runs the gamut from great sadness to spontaneous confessions of love to unmitigated (though wholly justified) female rancor, all of which results in the joining of two individuals who had previously professed never to love or marry anyone. This scene occurs after the public castigation of Hero at the wedding; Beatrice, the first and most vociferous of her cousin's defenders to this point, has gone off to weep alone. Benedick, showing concern for the woman whom he loves and who, he has been told, loves him, clumsily follows her, a desire to comfort and care for her gently buffeted by his own inexperience in matters of pathos and love. When Benedick says that "Surely I do believe your fair cousin is wronged," it is the first time in the play he expresses this sentiment so directly; earlier he had expressed his amazement and averred to the possibility of Hero's innocence, but here, and perhaps for Beatrice's sake, he openly says so for the first time. Beatrice's rejoinders are evasive; she clearly has something in mind but refuses to openly say what it is.

Benedick's expression of love for her is spontaneous and, given the circumstances of the moment, perhaps ill timed. Yet in the grief of what both the characters and the audience have just witnessed, it seems perfectly suited. Beatrice, initially flustered, soon responds in kind, and a happy moment, one long awaited by the audience, surfaces; Benedick's spontaneous exhortation that Beatrice "Come, bid me do any thing for thee" is a joyful expression of his love. Beatrice's reply, "Kill Claudio," is clearly something neither he nor the audience expected to hear.

Many critics have commented on the jarring nature of Beatrice's rejoinder here, but the request hardly comes as a surprise, considering the earlier part of their conversation. In actuality, the line perfectly melds the two prior conversations into one. Clearly, Beatrice still has Hero's castigation in mind; when she says there is "no such friend" who can do her the favor she refers to, and that "It is a man's office, but not yours," it is evident that Hero's matters weigh heavily on her mind. When Benedick declares his love, Beatrice's thinking shifts from "no such friend" to "one" such friend. The nature of Beatrice's request for Benedick to "Kill Claudio" is significant; in her mind, this action, more than their previous declarations of love, joins the pair. Far more than merely professing their emotions (something, after all, that Claudio did to Hero on numerous occasions), Beatrice merges with Benedick into a single force; one's actions thus reflect the other's; their passions are each other's passions, their causes the cause of the other. Beatrice is also possibly manipulating the scene to incur such a reaction from Benedick, to find a champion for Hero; however, her reaction to Benedick's declaration of love—and the spontaneity of the gesture—belies this. Benedick has most likely tapped into a great hope Beatrice had secretly possessed, when he asks her to "Come, bid me do any thing for thee." In doing so, he has not fallen into a skillful manipulator's hands; rather, he has taken on the position of lover and hero that Beatrice was only moments ago lamenting she lacked.

Benedick's hesitation here is understandable; not only does the challenge mean becoming involved in a potentially lethal duel with his friend, it also means wholly allying himself to Beatrice, joining himself to her in a real and significant way. He tries to reason with Beatrice ("Is Claudio thine enemy?") but this line of questioning bears no results, especially when he is confronted by the full force of Beatrice's emotions: "O God, that I were a man! I would eat his heart in the market-place." Her mournful rejoinder that "I cannot be a man with wishing, therefore I will die a woman with grieving" seems enough to remind Benedick of the strength of his love and the position he has placed himself in. Now firmly by Beatrice's side, he accepts the challenge.

The manner in which both Hero and Claudio and Beatrice and Benedick pursue their respective relationships has long been discussed in critical circles. The former are traditional lovers: Claudio first spied his chosen bride from a distance, while he prepared for war; Hero responded favorably to his glances, but their courting never went beyond this mutual admiration until his return from the military action against Don John. After his return, Claudio uncomfortably discloses his feelings to his companions, but to none other, and it is Don Pedro who arranges to court Hero in Claudio's name. The match is thus made by a third party, not atypical in Elizabethan times; its fragility is perhaps due in no small part to how little Hero and Claudio truly know each other. Beatrice and Benedick, on the other hand, are quite familiar with each other; Shakespeare hints in several moments in the play about a past between them and their "merry war" of words and continual long-distance posturing (such as seen in act 1, scene 1, when Beatrice jokingly accosts the messenger about Benedick) only adds to the attraction between them. Both are quite willing to share what is on their minds, so it is perhaps no surprise that they are also quite willing to share what is in their hearts as well.

Yet, the scenes in which each couple faces hardship are perhaps more telling than their courting scenes. Claudio has been led to believe Hero is deceiving him; rather than confronting her alone, in private, or in the presence of her father, he chooses to publicly humiliate her. He never asks her for an explanation of what he had seen, never seeks to hear her side of the story. Even when evidence is given that shows his understanding of events is not complete or accurate, and Don John's story is at least partially false (the idea that Hero has had numerous sexual partners is disputed by Beatrice's testimony that she had shared a bed with Hero every night, except for the sole evening in question), Claudio refuses to relent or listen to reason. The crisis—manufactured as it is—is enough to wholly destroy the nuptials, at least the first time around.

Beatrice and Benedick, on the other hand, face a similar and much more real crisis. Beatrice asks Benedick to choose her honor and her feelings over his close companions. Understandably, he balks, but he also listens to her persuasions. In the end, he sides with his love, not just because he loves her (as is later supposed by Don Pedro and Claudio), but because he believes her. Thus, the complex nature of this rich scene—and the range of emotions it contains and portrays—reflects more capably than any other scene the intricate and at times complicated nature of successful relationships in the play. What starts with excess of speech ultimately results in a surfeit of trust, loyalty, and true emotion. In the end, critical and audience reaction to *Much Ado about Nothing* has demonstrated Beatrice and Benedick to be the more discussed, respected, renowned, and elevated pair in the play; this scene demonstrates why.

List of Characters in *Much Ado about Nothing*

Don Pedro is the prince of Aragon, which makes him the highest-ranked individual in the play. In action that occurs prior to the opening scenes of *Much Ado about Nothing*, he completed a successful military campaign against usurping forces led by his own half brother, Don John. In the play, Don Pedro conceives the plans to woo Hero for Claudio and to unite Beatrice and Benedick. He is also key in Hero's castigation in the wedding scene of act 4. Unmarried, Don Pedro asks Beatrice to be his bride. When she tells him no, he conceives of the plan to unite her with Benedick.

Don John is referred to as the bastard brother of Don Pedro; they share the same father but different mothers. Before the events the play presents, Don John led some type of revolt against his father; the scope of this action is unknown, but the fact that his brother quelled the uprising with minimal loss of men suggests that it was not a significant threat. As the play opens, Don John is publicly reconciled to his brother and travels in his company, but he privately looks for any opportunity to cross those who brought about his downfall. The chief villain of the play, Don John is behind the two deceptions that are intended to disrupt Claudio's impending wedding: the first, minor deception at the masquerade and the second, major deception prior to the actual wedding. Don John flees after Hero is reported dead but is eventually brought back for "brave punishments" at the play's end.

Claudio is a young count from Florence. His age is unknown, but Benedick's reference to him as "Lord Lackbeard" suggests he is at least slightly younger than the other men in the Prince's retinue. During the military action against Don John, Claudio distinguished himself and is given much of the glory and credit for Don John's defeat, which explains the latter's intense dislike for him. After returning from war, Claudio is even more enamored of Leonato's daughter, Hero, whom he had first noticed prior to the conflict. Claudio is an idealist and a romantic, but his naiveté and inexperience with life in general and women in particular allow him to be easily ensnared by Don John's schemes.

His extreme reactions in both the masquerade scene (act 2, scene 1) and the marriage scene (act 4, scene 1) suggest his youthful folly and inexperience in believing that his love would so readily betray him.

Benedick is a young lord from Padua in service to Don Pedro. Benedick likewise served in the military action against Don John; though he is not reputed to have distinguished himself as much as Claudio, his service is remarked on admirably. He is described as being Claudio's closest companion, though the two have a falling out when Claudio publicly castigates Hero at their wedding. Benedick is likely older than Claudio; he is more assured and experienced, and the presence of his beard (though he shaves it off in order to please Beatrice) likewise suggests his maturity. Benedick is adept at quips, and his wit is only matched in the play by Beatrice's; more than once, Don Pedro or Claudio come to Benedick to seek amusing conversation. When Benedick grows more serious with the pair after the wedding scene, it takes some time for them to recognize his earnestness. From the beginning of the play, Benedick engages in a "merry war" of words with Beatrice, though their sniping seems to belie deeper emotions that are easily brought to the forefront. Though he is a professed "tyrant" against women and pledges numerous times never to marry, the others have little trouble convincing him of his love for Beatrice.

Leonato is the governor of Messina and father to Hero. Probably the oldest of the high-ranking men in the play, Leonato serves as a father figure in multiple ways throughout the play. He dotes on his daughter, his only child, and hopes for a marriage between her and Don Pedro. When Don Pedro woos Hero for Claudio instead, however, Leonato does not challenge the match. When Hero is publicly scorned by Claudio and the Prince, Leonato initially turns on his daughter, believing the word of the two men over his own child. His fury at her is truly frightening. Eventually his rage gives way to confusion, as Beatrice, Benedick, and the Friar all suggest Hero's possible innocence. Ultimately, Leonato believes his daughter, and he confronts Don Pedro and Claudio prior to uncovering evidence that proves Hero's innocence. Once it is established, he concocts a scheme to ensure all of Messina is aware of Hero's virtue and further punishes Claudio by continuing to pretend Hero is dead until after Claudio has pledged to wed the woman he believes is her cousin.

Antonio, Leonato's younger brother (though still called an "old man" in the text), works mainly to support his brother in both his desire to pursue an alliance with the royal house of Aragon and, later, in defending his niece against the charges brought by Claudio and Don Pedro. His defense of Hero in act 5, scene 1 is passionate and admirable. It is revealed in act 1, scene 2 that he has a son, but this character makes no other appearance and is not referenced again. Later in the play, Leonato says that Antonio has only one child, a daughter, but this may be part of his subterfuge when he tells Claudio that he will have to marry this niece now that Hero is dead.

Balthasar is a retainer in the service of Don Pedro. He sings for the Prince in act 2, scene 3 and woos Margaret, a gentlewoman attending Hero, in the masquerade scene.

Borachio is an attendant to Don John and the chief architect of the main scheme against Claudio and Hero. Borachio instigates the first deception of Claudio in the masquerade scene by bringing to Don John and Conrade the news of Claudio's impending marriage. Later, he devises the plan to lure Claudio and Don Pedro to Hero's window where he will court Margaret, Hero's attendant, in her name. He is paid well for these services, but his later boasting to Conrade over what he has done is overheard by the watch. The news of Hero's demise seems to deflate his braggadocio, and he later confesses to Don Pedro, Claudio, and Leonato what he has done.

Conrade is a gentleman in service to Don John. He has no role in planning either scheme against Claudio, though he is the one to whom Borachio boasts of his success in the false courting of Hero the night before the wedding. Conrade is captured along with Borachio by the watch and later snobbishly insists he is a gentleman when questioned by Dogberry and the Sexton.

Friar Francis is the holy man brought to marry Hero and Claudio. Later, after Hero's public humiliation, it is Friar Francis who urges that the news of Hero's death be spread, hoping that Claudio will prove so remorseful over her demise that he will regret his harsh actions at the wedding. This does not come to light, but the news of her death allows for the watch to bring forth the evidence of her innocence.

Dogberry is a master constable of Messina and the chief comic figure in the play. Dogberry speaks in constant doggerel, making his speech difficult for the other characters to understand and potentially highly amusing for the audience or reader. Dogberry's speech is best marked by his unusual use of words, often substituting a word that sounds similar to another or misunderstanding the meaning of a common word to an amusing degree. His speech patterns render him incomprehensible to both Leonato and Don Pedro, who must receive his news, as "translated" by others, before understanding it. Nonetheless, Dogberry plays a key role in bringing Hero's innocence to light.

Verges is a headborough, the term given to the officer who is subordinate to the constable. Thus, Verges acts as Dogberry's assistant. He is the only one who seems capable of understanding Dogberry, though his speech, while not as incomprehensible as his partner's, is often quite obfuscated as well.

A **Sexton** is a minor church official, usually charged with the upkeep of church facilities and grounds, including the graveyard. In the play, it is the Sexton who records the testimony of the watch and takes the news of Hero's innocence to Leonato, which suggests that his official duties may include more than groundskeeping.

Hero is the daughter of Leonato and betrothed to Claudio. She is Leonato's only child and thus his only heir. The ideal portrait of a dutiful Elizabethan woman, Hero espouses the virtues of silence, obedience, and chastity. Hero is often so silent that she says nothing, even in situations when speech seems necessary. She says little to defend herself, for example, when she is accused of infidelity in the wedding scene of act 4. At the end of the play, when she reveals to Claudio she is alive, she insists that she is indeed virginal; though her innocence had already been firmly established, her insistence demonstrates the importance of her virtue to her.

Beatrice is Hero's cousin and niece to Leonato (though she is not Antonio's daughter). Beatrice is parentless, which may explain the freedom she feels to possess perhaps the sharpest and quickest tongue in the play. Her wit is legendary in Messina, and no character in the play escapes it. Nonetheless, she is highly admired by the men in *Much Ado about Nothing* and is considered virtuous, fair, pleasant, and wise. Don Pedro even asks for her hand before deciding that she would be the perfect match for Benedick. Beatrice gently turns the Prince down, having stated on numerous occasions that she would never deign to marry. Nonetheless, upon hearing that Benedick loves her, she quickly changes her mind. This may be on account of a previous relationship between them; Shakespeare hints at it (1.1.140, 2.1.275–79) but provides no substantial details as to its nature. Later, after Hero's public castigation at the hands of Claudio and Don Pedro, Beatrice is the first and most vociferous defender of her cousin's honor; her passionate speech raging against Claudio ("O God, that I were a man! I would eat his heart in the market-place") suggests the inner strength she possesses. Beatrice cannot challenge Claudio herself, but she eventually persuades Benedick to do so. Beatrice's boisterous personality is perhaps why the men respond to her so warmly, for there seems to be little doubt she speaks what is on her mind.

Margaret is a gentlewoman attending Hero. During the play, she is pursued by Balthasar, and is later involved—indirectly—in the plot against Hero, since she favors Borachio and is "courted" by him at Hero's window, assuming her mistress's name.

Ursula is a gentlewoman attending Hero who plays a key role in convincing Beatrice that Benedick loves her.

CRITICISM
THROUGH THE AGES

MUCH ADO ABOUT NOTHING IN THE SEVENTEENTH AND EIGHTEENTH CENTURIES

ॐ

Critically speaking, individual Shakespearean comedies received little attention in the seventeenth and eighteenth centuries. Those that were cited in the varying sources of the day, whether artistic or scholarly, were usually distinguished by some identifying characteristic that made them readily discernible from the other plays Shakespeare had crafted in the same style or genre. *The Taming of the Shrew*, for example, with its popular and highly stereotyped figure of Katharina, became a common work for later artists and critics to reflect on; sequels were written to this play, including *The Woman's Prize, or The Tamer Tamed* by John Fletcher (ca. 1611), a work that examines the treatment of Katharina by Petruchio and the other men in the play as flawed and allowing the "shrew" to subject some of her own "taming" on others. Other comedies, such as the problem play *Measure for Measure*, stood out because of the text's complicated relationship to the genre and themes it espoused; critics were sometimes puzzled by the inherent message of the work or debated whether it truly fit into its designated genre, sparking debate that resonated in the artistic pages and tomes of the day.

Much Ado about Nothing, by its very nature, may arguably represent the zenith of Shakespearean comedy (many critics have asserted it is the best pure representation of the genre by Shakespeare), but as a work there is nothing that is, on the surface, ostensibly peculiar about it. It does not feature a controversial figure like Katharina that offers some insight and commentary into a great public debate of the time, nor does it represent a problematic relationship to the comedic genre like *Measure for Measure*. *Much Ado about Nothing* may be a sublime work, a pinnacle achievement in a career marked by many such achievements, but it stands out because of its merits, not because of its anomalies. As such, discussion of the individual work was infrequent in critical circles essentially until the nineteenth century. This is not to say that the work did not excite interest among the public; *Much Ado about Nothing* has always been one of the most popular of Shakespeare's works to stage. Its bright plotlines, happy ending, beautiful wordplay, and, most of all, unforgettable characterizations of Beatrice and Benedick (and to a lesser extent Dogberry) have always been extraordinarily popular if not fashionable with audiences (there is some evidence to suggest that *Much Ado about Nothing* was less popular in the seventeenth century than in subsequent years, but productions of the play still ran in London and elsewhere). Several times in the seventeenth and eighteenth centuries, the work was adapted by other playwrights in varying forms, including Sir William Davenant (1673) and James Miller (1737) (both excerpted in this section), and was used by authors such as Charles Johnson (1679–1748), who included text from *Much Ado about Nothing* in his play *Love in a Forest* (1723), which centered on *As You Like It* and included dialogue from five other Shakespeare plays. Yet as one can see by the examples proffered here, the work excited relatively little critical interest in the seventeenth and eighteenth centuries.

Perhaps another reason for the dearth of critical representation of *Much Ado about Nothing* is its relationship to its original source material. Unlike most of Shakespeare's plays, *Much Ado about Nothing* is largely an original work. The main plotline, the story of Claudio and Hero, originates in the story of Ariodante and Ginevra in Ludovico Ariosto's *Orlando Furioso*. The tale had been translated into English at least four times prior to Shakespeare's version of it, the first in 1565–66 by Peter Beverly, with subsequent versions by George Tuberville, Edmund Spenser (in part of his *Faerie Queene*), and in an anonymous play, *A History of Ariodante and Geneuora*. However, based on Shakespeare's rendering, it is likely that his original source material was Matteo Bandello's version of Ariosto's work, which had been previously translated into French by François de Belleforest in his *Histoires Tragiques* (a source Shakespeare used for other works besides *Much Ado about Nothing*, including *Hamlet*). In Belleforest's translation, we find Messina, the characters of Don Pedro and Leonato, the narrative of the courting by proxy, and the treachery by a jealous third party determined to upset the happy nuptials. The story, however, diverges in many distinct ways: the names of the lovers are Timbreo and Fenicia, not Claudio and Hero; the villain, Girondo, is spurred on not by his jealously over Timbreo/Claudio's role in his defeat but because he is a spurned suitor of Fenicia/Hero; and the rumor of the lady's death is enough to convince the villain to confess, whereas in *Much Ado about Nothing*, Don John and his accomplices are captured, their treachery brought to light through other means.

As is evident, Shakespeare's relationship to his source required a deft view of interpretation; the best aspects of the play, including Beatrice, Benedick, and Dogberry and the watch, have largely been viewed solely as inventions of Shakespeare himself (some critics have contended that there are antecedents in earlier literature for these characters, and certainly squabbling lovers like Beatrice and Benedick were not uncommon in the literary canon of Elizabethan England; nonetheless, there remains no direct source for them, unlike the other major plotline in the text). Because of the many original elements Shakespeare incorporated into *Much Ado about Nothing*, then, there is little work needed in comparing the play to its source material, and until the nineteenth century, almost no work in examining the relationship between the play and other possible sources exists beyond Gerard Langbaine's (1691) excellent commentary on the subject in *An Account of the English Dramatick Poets*.

The one aspect of *Much Ado about Nothing* that always stood out to critics, however, was the characterizations within the play, especially with the figures of Beatrice and Benedick. Most of the characters warranted debate within critical circles over the merits of individual figures and their actions within the world of the play. This characterizes literary criticism of its type until the nineteenth century, when critics were largely evaluative of the main work being criticized. In other words, they explored the merits of particular aspects of a work—a plotline, a character, the wordplay inherent in the text—and dissected features of the particular aspect in question as largely positive or negative. In discussing a character like Claudio, for example, early critics might examine his actions in the play and wonder whether such a course of activity is reasonable or merited. They might also assess what aspersions these actions may constitute upon his character and speculate about his motivations or possible future actions based on what transpired in the play. These critical renderings often suggested larger points about the work or Shakespeare as a whole that likewise resulted in the critic evaluating the play or the aspect in question as either good or bad, comparing it to similar figures in additional works by the author or others. The seeming end result of this type of evaluative criticism is to render a type of judgment, one way or the other, on the figure or literary aspect being debated. As such, this approach to literary criticism is an amalgamation of contemporary scholarly criticism, which is more analytical in its intent, and performance-based criticism, which evaluates the merits of a work from the perspective of whether or not it is worth attention. Criticism of *Much Ado about Nothing* prior to the nineteenth century muddled those two distinct goals, as is seen in the works excerpted in this section.

It may be heartening to contemporary audiences that characters such as Claudio and Don Pedro receive disapproving judgments from the critics of the seventeenth and eighteenth centuries, as Charles Gildon (1710) notes. The general reaction to the Claudio/Hero storyline ranged from mild repudiation to outright shock, but for the most part, critics came down harshly against Claudio for how easily he is duped by Don John and how callously he reacts in publicly castigating Hero in the wedding scene that begins act 4. Though Claudio would eventually have his few defenders, throughout the initial centuries he was largely looked on with sentiments ranging from dismay to disgust; though he is not always faulted, it was not uncommon for critics to speculate on how truly happy a marriage that had such a rocky start may be.

More critics, however, focused on the happier storyline of Beatrice and Benedick. These two squabbling lovers were viewed as the antithesis of Claudio and Hero, the breath of fresh air that truly dominated the spirit of the play.

Beatrice especially has long excited critical interest in *Much Ado about Nothing*, and while not all of it is positively slanted toward her, throughout the seventeenth and eighteenth centuries, she was largely viewed as a witty figure and zealous defender of her cousin and her gender. Nicholas Rowe's (1710) reaction to the pair is fairly typical for the time period; clearly, he delights in them both. Gildon likewise relishes the comedy the duo bring to the page, while Margaret Cavendish (1664) considers Beatrice a strong, relatable female creation of Shakespeare's, high praise indeed.

Dogberry was another character who excited interest among critics; William Warburton (1733), for one, railed against the foolishness of the figure. It seems as if critics have long been puzzled by Dogberry's presence in the play. Surely he is a comic figure, but what sort of comic figure does he represent? Is he designed to mock the serious post he has—if so, why is it Dogberry and the watch who save the day by uncovering Don John's true scheme, despite how clumsily they do? Is Dogberry's language designed to poke fun at a particular strain of speech common to Elizabethan society? If so, which? Does Shakespeare mock a particular social class in Dogberry? Or does he praise it? Of all of Shakespeare's figures in *Much Ado about Nothing*, it is Dogberry that has excited the most questions in regard to his purpose and origin; early on, critics took a rather dimmer view of his character than later commentators, as is evident here.

Generally, though, critical reception to *Much Ado about Nothing* in the seventeenth and eighteenth centuries was largely effusive and praise filled. *Much Ado about Nothing* is a middle comedy (it is, in fact, exactly in the middle of Shakespeare's great surge of comedic writing). As such, Shakespeare has seemingly ironed out the kinks of the previous comedies and yet not delved into the complications of some of the latter ones. The result is a smooth, seamless text that has long been one of the author's most popular to produce onstage. The critical reception to the work included in this section reflects these ideas; the evaluations of the play reveal it was highly regarded as a robust, rich work of comedic expression and one of the most popularly performed Shakespeare texts of the day.

1600—William Shakespeare. *Much adoe about nothing*

Much adoe about | Nothing. | *As it hath been sundrie times publickely* | acted by the right honourable, the Lord | Chamberlaine his seruants. | *Written by William Shakespeare.* | London | Printed by V. S. for Andrew Wise, and | William Aspley. | 1600.

1640—Leonard Digges. From
Poems: Written by Wil. Shakespeare, Gent.

Leonard Digges (1588–1635) was a well-known poet and translator in his day. The son of a well-connected family, Digges's stepfather, Thomas Russell, was one of the men who administered Shakespeare's will. The following is a commendatory poem, a work of praise, from John Benson's 1640 edition of Shakespeare's poems titled *Poems: Written by Wil. Shakespeare, Gent.* In it, Digges mentions a few of Shakespeare's most famous figures, including Beatrice and Benedick.

Vpon Master W ILLIAM S H A K E S P E A R E,
the Deceased Authour, and his P O E M S .

Poets are borne not made, when I would prove
This truth, the glad rememberance I must love
Of never dying Shakespeare, who alone,
Is argument enough to make that one.
First, that he was a Poet none would doubt,
That heard th'applause of what he sees set out
Imprinted; where thou hast (I will not say
Reader his Workes for to contrive a Play:
To him twas none) the patterne of all wit,
Art without Art unparaleld as yet.
Next Nature onely helpt him, for looke thorow
This whole Booke, thou shalt find he doth not borrow,
One phrase from Greekes, nor Latines imitate,
Nor once from vulgar Languages Translate,
Nor Plagiari-like from others gleane,
Nor begges he from each witty friend a Scene
To peece his Acts with, all that he doth write,
Is pure his owne, plot, language exquisite,
But oh ! what praise more powerfull can we give
The dead, then that by him the Kings men live,
His Players, which should they but have shar'd the Fate,
All else expir'd within the short Termes date;
How could the Globe have prospered, since through want
Of change, the Plaies and Poems had growne scant.
But happy Verse thou shalt be sung and heard,
When hungry quills shall be such honour bard.
Then vanish upstart Writers to each Stage,

You needy Poetasters of this Age,
Where Shakespeare liv'd or spake, Vermine forbeare,
Least with your froth you spot them, come not neere;
But if you needs must write, if poverty
So pinch, that otherwise you starve and die,
On Gods name may the Bull or Cockpit have
Your lame blancke Verse, to keepe you from the grave:
Or let new Fortunes younger brethren see,
What they can picke from your leane industry.
I doe not wonder when you offer at
Blacke-Friers, that you suffer : tis the fate
Of richer veines, prime judgements that have far'd
The worse, with this deceased man compar'd.
So have I seene, when Cesar would appeare,
And on the Stage at half-sword parley were,
Brutus and Cassius : oh how the Audience,
Were ravish'd, with what wonder they went thence,
When some new day they would not brooke a line,
Of tedious (though well laboured) Catilines;
Sejanus too was irksome, they priz'de more
Honest Iago, or the jealous Moore.
And though the Fox and subtill Alchimist,
Long intermitted could not quite be mist,
Though these have sham'd all the Ancients, and might raise,
Their Authours merit with a crowne of Bayes.
Yet these sometimes, even at a friends desire
Acted, have scarce defrai'd the Seacoale fire
And doore-keepers : when let but Falstaffe come,
Hall, Poines, the rest you scarce shall have a roome
All is so pester'd : let but Beatrice
And Benedicke be seene, loe in a trice
The Cockpit Galleries, Boxes, all are full
To heare Maluoglio that crosse garter'd Gull.
Briefe, there is nothing in his wit fraught Booke,
Whose sound we would not heare, on whose worth looke
Like old coyned gold, whose lines in every page,
Shall passe true currant to succeeding age.
But why doe I dead Sheakspeares praise recite,
Some second Shakespeare must of Shakespeare write;
For me tis needlesse, since an host of men,
Will pay to clap his praise, to free my Pen.

1662—Thomas Fuller. From *The History of the Worthies of England*

The English theological historian Thomas Fuller (1608–61) was also a renowned author, clergyman, and orator, famous for his sermons and his wit. He is best remembered today as the author of the book *History of the Worthies of England*.

Plautus, who was an exact Comaedian, yet never any Scholar, as our *Shake-speare* (if alive) would confess himself. Adde to all these, that though his Genius generally was *jocular*, and inclining him to *festivity*, yet he could (when so disposed) be *solemn* and *serious*, as appears by his Tragedies, so that *Heraclitus* himself (I mean if secret and unseen) might afford to smile at his Comedies, they were so *merry*, and *Democritus* scarce forbear to sigh at his Tragedies they were so *mournfull*.

He was an eminent instance of the truth of that Rule, *Poeta non fit, sed nascitur*, one is not *made*, but *born* a Poet. Indeed his Learning was very little, so that as *Cornish diamonds* are not polished by any Lapidary, but are pointed and smoothed even as they are taken out of the Earth, so *nature* it self was all the *art* which was used upon him.

1664—Margaret Cavendish. From *Sociable Letters*

The Duchess of Newcastle, Margaret Cavendish (1623–73) wrote on a wide range of topics and produced nineteen plays, poetry, and memoirs about her and her husband. Though often viewed as an eccentric in her day, her surviving work demonstrates she possessed a sharp mind and flair for prose and was one of the keenest observers of her own society and its social mores. In one of her *Sociable Letters*, a series of essays addressed to female correspondents, Cavendish describes Shakespeare's ability to write strong, relatable female characters, including Beatrice.

So well he hath expressed in his plays all sorts of persons, as one would think he had been transformed into every one of those persons he hath described; and as sometimes one would think he was really himself the clown or jester he feigns, so one would think, he was also the King and Privy Counsellor . . . nay, one would think he had been metamorphosed from a man to a woman, for who could describe Cleopatra better than he hath done, and many other females of his own creating, as Nan Page, Mrs Page, Mrs Ford, the Doctor's Maid, Beatrice, Mrs Quickly, Doll Tearsheet, and others, too many to relate?

1673—William Davenant. From *The Law Against Lovers*

Sir William Davenant (1606–68) was an early Restoration era playwright and adaptor of Renaissance text. In *The Law Against Lovers*, perhaps his most unusual work, Davenant adapted the main plotline of Shakespeare's *Measure for Measure* and infused it with the Beatrice and Benedick storyline from *Much Ado about Nothing*. In Davenant's hybridized work, Beatrice is a ward of Angelo, the Duke's second in command in *Measure for Measure*, while Benedick is Angelo's brother. Besides engaging in their continuing merry wars, the two work in the play against Angelo to help the original lovers of *Measure for Measure*, Julietta and Claudio, in a plot device that resembles (though not too closely) the duo's machinations against Claudio in *Much Ado about Nothing*. Balthazar is also imported from *Much Ado about Nothing* as a companion for Benedick, while Beatrice is given a sister, Viola.

Initially, Davenant utilizes the early scenes between Beatrice and Benedick in his new play, including Beatrice's tête-à-tête with the messenger and their exchange in act 1, scene 1. However, Davenant soon begins to craft his own exchanges for the two, as is necessary to fit the plot of this new work. His own "merry wars" are not nearly as deft and humorous as Shakespeare's, though they do not lack for a certain clumsy panache, as the scene below, from act 3, scene 1 of *The Law Against Lovers*, demonstrates. Readers will detect glimpses of Beatrice's dialogue from act 2, scene 1 of *Much Ado about Nothing*, though in that instance she is speaking to Leonato, Antonio, and Hero and not Benedick.

Benedick: I was told, Lady, you would speak with me.
Beatrice: I would, and I would not.
Benedick: Then I'll stay, or I will not stay;
'Tis all one to me.
Beatrice: Nay, I know you are but an indifferent man:
Yet now by chance, I rather am inclin'd
That you should stay.
Benedick: And 'tis a greater chance
That our inclinations should so soon meet;

For I will stay.
Beatrice: Your Brother is a proper Prince, he rules
With a Rod in's hand instead of s Scepter,
Like a Country School-Master in a Church;
He keeps a large Palace with no Attendants,
And is fit to have none but Boys for his Subjects.
Benedick: As ill as he governs (if my
Design thrive against the Fetters of marriage,
As his rule does against the liberty of Lovers)
His rule may last till the end of the world;
For there will be no next Generation.
Beatrice: Would I might trust you Benedick.
Benedick: Madam, you believe me to have some honour.
If you have most secretly invented
A new Dressing, can you think I'll reveal
The Fashion, before you wear it?
Beatrice: Notwithstanding your seeming indisposition
To inventions of Fashions, yet there be
Those in *Turin*, who have intercepted
Packets between you and Taylors of *Paris*.
Well, though those are but light correspondents,
Yet I would trust you in matter of weight.
Benedick: I hope, Lady, you have no plot upon me.
I'll marry no woman.
Beatrice: I did not think you had been so well natur'd,
As to prevent the having any of
Your breed. Marry you? what should I do with you?
Dress you in my old Gown, and make you my
Waiting Woman?
Benedick: A waiting Woman with a Beard?
Beatrice: I shall ne'er endure a Husband with a Beard.
I had rather lye in woolen.
Benedick: Though you disfigure matrimonial pretensions,
With pretty scorn, yet I am glad I have
A Beard for my own defence. And though fashion
Makes me shave much (and yet you believe me
A lover of fashions) yet mine shall grow
To a very bush, for my greater security.
But, pray proceed to your matter of weight.
Beatrice: I will trust you; not as a man of love,
But a man of Arms.
Benedick: At your own peril.

And more t'encourage you, I will declare
That though I'm very loth to come within
The narrow compass of a Wedding Ring;
Yet I owe every fair Lady a good turn.
But to the business.
Beatrice: In brief you must
Renew familiarity with your Brother;
And steal the use of his Signet to seal
Julietta's pardon and her liberty,
And *Claudio's* too; this done, they shall practice
Their escape, I'll endeavour mine; and you
Signior may shift for your self.
Benedick: This is but betraying an ill Brother,
For a good purpose; I'll do't if I can.
Beatrice: You shall give me the Signet, for I'll have
All in my own management.
Benedick: No, though I rob my Brother of the Signet;
You shall not rob me of the danger.
Beatrice: Then I'll proceed no further.
Benedick: That as you please.
Beatrice: You would have the honour of the business.
Benedick: 'Tis due to my Sex.
Beatrice: Fare you will Sir—yet you
May come again an hour hence, to receive
An ill look.
Benedick: That will not fright me much; for you can look
No better than you use to do.

1691—Gerard Langbaine. From
An Account of the English Dramatick Poets

Gerard Langbaine (1656-92) is often considered the first theater historian in England. Langbaine's scholarship on the theatrical works of Renaissance and Restoration England laid the groundwork for all future scholarship. In his lifetime, Langbaine published three texts cataloguing the source material for English plays and, in the last one, *An Account of the English Dramatick Poets*, a biography of each author as well. The following excerpt, from that work, mentions a possible source for some scenes in *Much Ado about Nothing*.

Sir William Davenant . . . the mercurial Son of a saturnine Father . . . Poet *Laureat* to Twoo Kings . . . During this Honour, of which his Wit and Parts rendered his Worthy, he writ . . . his Dramatick Pieces . . . with good applause, and . . . like success in Print. *Law against Lovers,* a Tragi-Comedy made up of two Plays written by Mr. *Shakespear, viz. Measure for Measure,* and *Much Ado about Nothing.* Tho' not only the Characters, but the Language of the whole Play almost he borrow'd from *Shakespear :* yet where the Language is rough or obsolete, our Author has taken care to polish it. Honest *Shakespear* was not in those days acquainted with those great Wits, *Scudery, Calprenede, Scarron, Corneille &c . . . Shakespear's Measure for Measure,* how ever despis'd by Mr. *Dryden,* with his *Much Ado about Nothing,* were believ'd by Sr. *William Davenant,* (who I presume had as much judgment as *Sir Positive At-all*) to have wit enough in them to make one good Play &c . . . if Mr. *Shakespear's* Plots are more irredular than those of Mr. *Dryden's* (which by some will not be allow'd) 'tis because he never read *Aristotle,* or *Rapin* . . . In the Comedy call'd *Much Ado about Nothing* the Bastard accuses *Hero* of Disloyalty before the Prince, and *Claudio* her Lover: who (as surpris'd at the News) asks Who! *Hero? Bast.* Even she, *Leonato's Hero,* your *Hero,* every Mans *Hero.* In this Play [*All for Love* Act IV.] on the like occasion, where *Ventidius* accuses *Cleopatra, Antony* says, Not *Cleopatra! Ven.* Even she my Lord! *Ant.* My *Cleopatra? Ven.* Your *Cleopatra ; Dollabella's Cleopatra :* Every Mans *Cleopatra . . . Much Ado about Nothing,* a Comedy. I have already spake of Sir *William Davenant's* use of this Comedy. All that I have to remark is, That the contrivance of *Borachio,* in behalf of *John* the Bastard to make *Claudio* jealous of *Hero,* by the Assistance of her Waiting Woman *Margaret,* is borrowed from *Arioso's Orlando Furioso :* see Book the fifth in the story of *Lurcanio, and Genevza :* the like story is in *Spenser's Fairy Queen,* Book 2, Canto 4.

1710—Nicholas Rowe. From "Some Account of the Life &c. of Mr. William Shakespear"

A poet and renowned tragedian of his day, Nicholas Rowe (1674–1718) was the author of several popular plays and well-received poems. In 1715, he was named poet laureate of England. Rowe was also the first modern editor of Shakespeare's work, and some of his plays were written in a Shakespearean style. In the following selection, Rowe praises Shakespeare's comedies, including *Much Ado about Nothing,* focusing on the popular characterizations of Beatrice and Benedick that critics delighted in in the eighteenth century.

His Plays are properly to be distinguish'd only into Comedies and Tragedies.
Those which are called Histories, and even some of his Comedies, are really
Tragedies, with a run or mixture of Comedy amongst 'em. That way of Trage-
Comedy was the common Mistake of that Age, and is indeed become so
agreeable to the *English* Tast, that tho' the severer Critiques among us cannot
bear it, yet the generality of our Audiences seem to be better pleas'd with
it than with an exact Tragedy. *The Merry Wives* of Windsor, *The Comedy of
Errors*, and *The Taming of the Shrew* are all pure Comedy; the rest, however
they are call'd have something of both Kinds. 'Tis not very easie to determine
which way of Writing he was most Excellent in. There is certainly a great deal
of Entertainment in his Comical Humours; and tho' they did not then strike
at all Ranks of People, as the Satyr of the present Age has taken the Liberty to
do, yet there is a pleasing and a well-distinguish'd Variety in those Characters
which he thought fit to meddle with. *Falstaff* is allow'd by every body to be
a Master-piece; the Character is always well-sustain'd, tho' drawn out into
the length of three Plays; and even the Account of his Death, given by his
Old Landlady Mrs. *Quickly*, in the first Act of *Henry V.* tho' it be extremely
Natural, is yet as diverting as any Part of his Life. If there be any Fault in the
Draught he has made of this lewd old Fellow, it is, that tho' he has made him
a Thief, Lying, Cowardly, Vain-glorious, and in short every way Vicious, yet
he has given him so much Wit as to make him almost too agreeable; and I
don't know whether some People have not, in remembrance of the Diversion
he had formerly afforded 'em, been sorry to see his Friend *Hal* use him so
scurvily, when he comes to the Crown in the End of the Second Part of *Henry*
the Fourth. Amongst other Extravagances, in *The Merry Wives* of Windsor,
he has made him a Deer-stealer, that he might at the same time remember
his *Warwickshire* Prosecutor, under the Name of Justice *Shallow*; he has given
him very near the same Coat of Arms which *Dugdale*, in his Antiquities of
that County, describes for a Family there, and makes the *Welsh* Parson descant very pleasantly upon 'em. That whole Play is admirable; the Humours
are various and well oppos'd; the main Design, which is to cure *Ford* of his
unreasonable Jealousie, is extremely well conducted. *Falstaff's Billet-doux*, and
Master *Slender's*

　　Ah! Sweet Ann Page!

are very good Expressions of Love in their Way. In *Twelfth-Night* there is something singularly Ridiculous and Pleasant in the fantastical Steward *Malvolio*.
The Parasite and the Vain-glorious in *Parolles*, in *All's Well that ends Well*, is as
good as any thing of that Kind in *Plautus* or *Terence*. *Petruchio*, in *The Taming of
the Shrew*, is an uncommon Piece of Humour. The Conversation of *Benedick* and
Beatrice, in *Much ado about Nothing*, and of *Rosalind* in *As you like it*, have much
Wit and Sprightliness all along.

1710—Charles Gildon. "The Argument of *Much Ado About Nothing*" from *The Works of Mr. William Shakespear*

Charles Gildon (ca. 1665-1724) was a prolific English writer best known for his many biographies of figures contemporary to his day. The subject of biting satirical works by Alexander Pope, Gildon's work is often viewed unfavorably today, but in many instances his biographies of the men of his time stand as the only extant record of their lives. In the following excerpt, Gildon remarks on some of the more tragic elements of the play, especially the repudiation of Hero, and he berates Claudio and Don Pedro for the role they played in it. Like many critics of his time, Gildon casts a more favorable eye on Beatrice and Benedick, admiring the comic nature of their relationship and considering that the high mark of the text.

The scene lies at Messina in Sicily and in and near the house of Leonato. Don Pedro of Aragon with his favorite Claudio, and Benedick a gay young cavalier of Padua, and Don John the bastard brother of Don Pedro, come to Leonato's, the Governor of Messina. Claudio is in love with Hero, Leonato's daughter, whom Don Pedro obtains for him, and while they wait the wedding day, they consult how to make Benedick and Beatrice, the niece of Leonato, in love with each other, both being gay and easy and averse to love and like great talkers, railing always at each other. However, by letting them overhear their discourse they persuade them that they are in love with each other. In the meantime Don John, the very soul of envy and mischief, contrived how to break the match betwixt Claudio and Hero, and to this purpose, by his engines, Conrade and Borachio, they make Claudio and the Prince believe that Hero is a wanton and put a plausible cheat on them to confirm the suspicion by having Borachio talk to Hero's maid, Margaret, at the chamber window at midnight, as if she were Hero. Convinced by this fallacy, Claudio and Don Pedro disgrace her in the church where he went to marry her, rejecting her, and accusing her of wantonness with another. Hero swoons away, and the priest interposing and, joining in the attestation she makes of her virtue, she is privately conveyed away and reported dead. The rogue Borachio being taken by the watch, as he was telling the advaenture of his comrade, discovers the villainy and clears Hero; but Don John is fled. Her innocence being known, her father is satisfied with Claudio, that he hang verses on her tomb that night and marry a niece of his the next morning without seeing her face, which he agrees to and performs, and then it is discovered that it is Hero whom he married and so the play ends with an account of Don John's being taken.

This fable is as full of absurdities as the writing is full of beauties: the first I leave to the reader to find out by the rules I have laid down; the second I shall endeavor to show and point out some few of the many that are contained in the play. Shakespear indeed had the misfortune which other of our poets have since had of laying his scene in a warm climate where the manners of the people are very different from ours, and yet he has made them talk and act generally like men of a colder country; *Marriage à la Mode* has the same fault.

This play we must call a comedy, though some of the incidents and discourses too are more in a tragic strain; and that of the accusation of Hero is too shocking for either tragedy or comedy; nor could it have come off in nature, if we regard the country, without the death of more than Hero. The imposition on the Prince and Claudio seems very lame, and Claudio's conduct to the woman he loved highly contrary to the very nature of love, to expose her in so barbarous a manner and with so little concern and struggle, and on such weak grounds without a farther examination into the matter, yet the passions this produces in the old father make a wonderful amends for the fault. Besides which there is such a pleasing variety of characters in the play, and those perfectly maintained, as well as distinguished, that you lose the absurdities of the conduct in the excellence of the manners, sentiments, diction, and topics. Benedick and Beatrice are two sprightly, witty, talkative characters, and, though of the same nature, yet perfectly distinguished, and you have no need to read the names to know who speaks. As they differ from each other, though so near akin, so do they from that of Lucio in *Measure for Measure,* who is likewise a very talkative person; but there is a gross abusiveness, calumny, lying, and lewdness in Lucio, which Benedick is free from. One is a rake's mirth and tattle; the other that of a gentleman and a man of spirit and wit.

The stratagem of the Prince on Benedick and Beatrice is managed with that nicety and address that we are very well pleased with the success and think it very reasonable and just.

The character of Don John the Bastard is admirably distinguished, his manners are well marked, and everywhere convenient or agreeable. Being a sour, melancholy, saturnine, envious, selfish, malicious temper—manners necessary to produce these villainous events they did—these were productive of the catastrophe, for he was not a person brought in to fill up the number only, because without him the fable could not have gone on.

To quote all the comic excellencies of this play would be to transcribe three parts of it. For all that passes betwixt Benedick and Beatice is admirable. His discourse against love and marriage in the later end of the second act is very pleasant and witty, and that which Beatrice says of wooing, wedding, and repenting. And the aversion that the poet gives Benedick and Beatrice for each other in their discourse heightens the jest of making them in love with one another. Nay, the variety and natural distinction of the vulgar humors of this play are remarkable.

The scenes of this play are something obscure, for you can scarce tell where the place is in the two first acts, though the scenes in them seem pretty entire and unbroken. But those are things we ought not to look much for in Shakespear. But whilst he is out in the dramatic imitation of the fable, he always draws men and women so perfectly that when we read, we can scarce persuade ourselves but that the discourse is real and no fiction.

1733—William Warburton. From the notes to Lewis Theobald's *The Works of Shakespeare*

Named bishop of Gloucester in 1760, William Warburton (1698–1779) was a well-regarded writer on philosophy, theology, and literature. In the selection included here, Warburton rails against the foolishness of the constable Dogberry, based on a description referenced in act 5, scene 1 of the play.

There could not be a more agreeable Ridicule upon the *Fashion* than the Constable's Descant upon his own Blunder. One of the most fantastical Modes of that Time was the indulging a *favourite Lock* of Hair, and suffering it to grow much longer than all its Fellows; which they always brought *before* (as we do the Knots of a Tye-Wig), ty'd with Ribbands or Jewels. King *Charles* the 1st wore One of those favourite Locks, as his Historians take Notice, and as his Pictures by *Vandike* prove; and whoever has been conversant with the Faces of that Painter must have observ'd a great many drawn in that Fashion. In Lord CLARENDON's *History compleated* (a Book in *Octavo*), being a Collection of Heads engrav'd from the Paintings of *Vandike*, we may see this Mode in the Prints of the Duke of *Buckingham*, Earl of *Dorset*, Lord *Goring*, &c., all great Courtiers.—As to the *Key* in the *Ear* and the *Lock* hanging by it, there may be a Joak in the Ambiguity of the Terms. But whether we think that *Shakespeare* meant to ridicule the *Fashion* in the abstracted Sense; or whether he sneer'd at the Courtiers, the Parents of it, we shall find the Description equally satirical. The *Key* in the *Ear* might be suppos'd literally: for they wore Rings, Lockets, and Ribbands in a Hole made in the Ear; and sometimes Rings one within another. But it might be likewise allegorically understood, to signify the great Readiness the Courtiers had in giving Ear to or going into new Follies or Fashions. As for *borrowing Money* and *never paying*, that is an old *Common Place* against the Court and Followers of Fashions. (I, 476)

⸺⚬⚬⚬⸺ ⸺⚬⚬⚬⸺ ⸺⚬⚬⚬⸺

1737—James Miller. From *The Universal Passion*

James Miller (1703–44) was a prominent playwright and poet and
also the first translator of Molière into English. Miller's play *The
Universal Passion* combined much of the material from *Much Ado about
Nothing* (though character names are changed) with parts of other
Shakespearean comedies, including *Twelfth Night* and *As You Like It*,
and Molière's *Princess d'Elide*. Much of the play would be familiar to
those intimate with *Much Ado about Nothing*, as the following scene
demonstrates. Here, Miller combines the conversations between
Beatrice and Benedick (named Liberia and Protheus in the play)
from act 4, scene 1 and act 5, scene 2 into one scene; in doing so,
he needed to compose a bridge between the two scenes, which is
excerpted here. The scene commences with the conclusion of act 4,
scene 1, in which Beatrice/Liberia has convinced Benedick/Protheus
to challenge Claudio (named Bellario in *The Universal Passion*), and
continues until it moves into the dialogue in act 5, scene 2, in which
the two lovers discuss the qualities they most prefer in the other.
Miller's bridge is thus designed to link two very disparate scenes, and
the additional dialogue has often been described as out of character
for both figures.

Protheus: Sweet *Liberia* stay; by this Hand I love thee.
Liberia: Use it for my Love, then, some other way than swearing by it.
Protheus: Do you think in your Soul that *Bellario* has wrong'd your
Cousin?
Liberia: As sure as I have either Thought or Soul.
Protheus: Enough, I'm engag'd—He shall render me strict Account for
this Behaviour: Go, fair Lady, comfort your Cousin, and tell her who's
her champion. As you hear of me, so think of me.
Liberia: Right, now you say somewhat, Lord *Protheus*—when you talk
like a Man you talk like what a Woman values. If ever I change my Life
for any one, it shall be for one who would venture his own for me.
Protheus: That sentence has whetted my Sword; I'll make *Bellario*, within
this half Hour, either forswear all he has said, or he shall never be able to
say or swear any thing again: But before we part, lest we should never meet
again, pray tell me for which of my *bad* Parts you first fell in love with me?

Liberia: Fell in love with you!

Protheus: Yes, fell in love with me, for that you are in love with, fair *Liberia*, is out of the Question—I would therefore fain know which of my *bad* Parts was the Occasion of it.

Liberia: All of 'em together, which contain so close a Union of Evil that they'll admit no good Part to mingle with 'em.

1748—Peter Whalley. From *An Enquiry into the Learning of Shakespeare, with Remarks on Several Passages of his Plays.*

Peter Whalley (1722–91) was an English academic and teacher who published on both Shakespeare and Ben Jonson. Whalley was particularly interested in Shakespeare's education, believing that Shakespeare, while perhaps not as formally educated as some of his peers, did have a strong knowledge of the classics, and that many classical ideas came through in his works. The excerpt included here shows a connection between a scene in *Much Ado about Nothing* and sentiment expressed in Plautus arguing that humans only realize their blessings when they have lost them.

Shakespeare wrote with greater Exactness than the Generality of his Readers may imagine, who seldom consider how nice and accurate a Painter he was, as well as the universal Master of Nature, and that he did not render great Subjects more elevated and surprizing by the Magnificence and Sublimity of his Descriptions than he made common and little ones agreeable by his Likeness and Propriety.

If all the Instances, continued *Eugenius*, which I shall hereafter mention do not come fully up to the Point which we propose to settle yet they will convince us at least that *Shakespeare* could not think like the Ancients, and express himself with an equal Simplicity: for I do not pretend to determine that he had his Eye in every Particular upon some ancient Author. I have placed here the Volumes all before me, with some Strictures which I have made from Antiquity, and shall begin with pointing out a Passage in the *Tempest* where the Sentiment is full in the Spirit of *Homer*. It is *Prospero's* Answer to his Daughter.

> *Be collected*:
> *No more Amazement; tell your piteous Heart,*
> *There's no Harm done.* [1.2.13ff.]

Would not you think that the Poet was imitating those Places in the other, where his Heroes are rouzing up their Courage to take Heart of Grace, and begin with a

Tetlathi de kradie[1]

We may observe also in the same Play a remarkable Example of his Knowledge in the Ancient Poetic Story, when *Ceres* in the Masque speaks thus to *Iris* upon the Approach of *Juno*:

> *High Queen of State,*
> Great Juno *comes; I know her by her Gait.* [4.1.101f.]

Here methinks now is no small Mark of the Judgment of our Author in selecting this peculiar Circumstance for the Discovery of *Juno*. And was *Virgil* himself to have described her Motion he would have done it in the same manner, for probably the *Divûm incedo Regina*[2] of that Author might furnish *Shakespeare* with the Hint; and his *Decorum* of the Character is perfectly consistent, and her Attendance upon the Wedding intirely agreeable to her Office.

Let us turn now to the next Play, where a Passage stops us at the very Beginning. *Theseus* complains thus of the Tardiness of Time;

> *Oh, methinks, how slow*
> *This old Moon wanes! she lingers my Desires*
> *Like to a Stepdame, or a Dowager*
> *Long withering out a young Man's Revenue.*
>
>   [*A Midsummer Night's Dream* 1.1.3ff.]

Suppose we were to put this into a *Latin* Dress, could any Words express it more exactly than these of *Horace*:

> *Ut piger Annus*
> *Pupillis, quos dura premit custodia matrum,*
> *Sic mihi tarda fluunt, ingrataque tempora.*[3]
>
>   L. I. Ep. 1. v. 21, & seq.

Pass we on from these to *Measure for Measure*, where in the second Scene of the third Act *Claudio* gives us such an image of the intermediate State after Death as bears a great Resemblance to the *Platonic* Purgations described by *Virgil*.

> *Ay, but to die, and go we know not where; . . .*
> *. . . the delighted Spirit*
> *To bathe in fiery Floods, or to reside*

In thrilling Regions of thick-ribbed Ice,
To be imprison'd in the viewless Winds,
And blown with restless Violence round about
The pendant World, &c. [3.1.119ff.]

Ergo exercentur poenis, veterumque malorum
Supplicia expendunt. Aliae panduntur inanes
Suspensae ad ventos: aliis sub gurgite vasto
Infectum eluitur scelus, aut exuritur igni.[4]

    Aeneid, L. VI. 739, & seq.

The next Instance which I have observed to demand our Notice occurs in *Much ado about Nothing,* where the Thought is very natural and obvious, founded on a Failing common to Human Nature.

    What we have we prize not to its worth
While we enjoy it; but being lack'd and lost,
Why, then we rack the Value; then we find
The Virtue that Possession would not shew us
Whilst it was ours. [4.1.218ff.]

You may have seen, perhaps, the same Sentiment in many Classic Authors; but the most analogous, and which would almost tempt one to believe the Poet had it directly before him, is the following from *Plautus*:

Tum denique homines nostra intelligimus bona,
Quom quae in potestate habuimus, ea amisimus.[5]

    Captiv. Act I. Sc. II. v. 29.

Shakespeare's Translation of these Verses, if I may take the Liberty to call it so, tho' something diffused and paraphrastical exceeds, in my humble Opinion, the Original; for the Proposition being diversified so agreeably makes a deeper Impression on the Mind and Memory.

If we compare the Description of the wounded Stag in *As you like it* with *Virgil's* Relation of the Death of the same Creature, we shall find that *Shakespeare's* is as highly finished and as masterly as the other:

The wretched Animal heav'd forth such Groans,
That their Discharge did stretch his Leathern Coat
Almost to bursting; and the big round Tears
Cours'd one another down his innocent Cheeks
In piteous Chase. [2.1.36ff.]

What an exquisite Image this of dumb Distress, and of a wounded Animal languishing in the Agonies of Pain! I cannot help thinking that the Lines of *Virgil* do not reach it altogether so perfectly.

[Quotes *Aeneid* 7.500ff.: 'But the wounded creature fled under the familiar roof, and moaning crept into his stall, where, bleeding and suppliant-like, he filled all the house with his plaints.']

NOTES

1. *Odyssey*, 20.18: 'Bear up, my heart.'
2. *Aeneid*, 1.46: 'I, who move as queen of gods.'
3. 'As the year lags forwards held in check by their mother's strict guardianship: so slow and thankless flow for me the hours which defer my hope . . . '
4. 'Therefore are they schooled with penalties, and for older sins pay punishment: some are hung stretched out to the empty winds; from some the stain of guilt is washed away under swirling floods or burned out in fire.'
5. 142f.: 'Ah, we mortals realise the value of our blessings only when we have lost them.'

1754—Charlotte Lennox. From *Shakespear Illustrated*

Charlotte Lennox (1720–1804), best known for her satirical novel *The Female Quixote*, was a well-respected author and translator. The following commentary, from her text *Shakespear Illustrated*, begins by examining the source material for *Much Ado about Nothing*, largely parroting what Langbaine had written more than sixty years earlier. However, Lennox then delves into the differences between the two works, especially in the characterizations of the main antagonists, ultimately praising Shakespeare for his "want of Judgment" while lamenting his "Poverty of Invention."

This Fable, absurd and ridiculous as it is, was drawn from the foregoing Story of *Genevra* in *Ariosto's Orlando Furioso*, a Fiction which, as it is managed by the Epic Poet, is neither improbable nor unnatural; but by *Shakespeare* mangled and defaced, full of Inconsistencies, Contradictions and Blunders. . . . by changing the Persons, altering some of the Circumstances and inventing others has made the whole an improbable Contrivance, borrowed just enough to shew his Poverty of Invention, and added enough to prove his want of Judgment.

The Scheme for ruining the Lady in the Original is formed and executed by a rejected Lover who sees a Rival, his inferior in Rank and Fortune, preferred before him, and loses at once the Object of his Wishes and the Prospect of increased Honours by that Preference. Ambition and the Desire of Revenge are

Passions strong enough in a Mind not very virtuous to produce Acts of Baseness and Villainy. *Polynesso*, urged by those powerful Incentives, contrives to blacken *Genevra*'s Fame, which produces a Separation between her and her Lover and prevents a Stranger from marrying this Princess, and consequently enjoying those Honours he so ardently desired himself.

Don *John* in the Play is a Villain merely through the Love of Villainy, and having entertained a capricious Dislike to *Claudio* closes eagerly with his Confident's horrid Scheme for breaking off his Marriage with *Hero*.

To prevent the multiplying such outrageously wicked and therefore unnatural Characters, Don *John* himself might have been the Proposer of that black Contrivance against the innocent *Hero*, and *Borachio*, for the sake of the thousand Ducats that was afterwards given him by Don *John*, be induced to execute it. But here we have two Villains equally bad, . . . only distinguished from each other by their Names. . . .

Claudio only is the Object of Don *John*'s Hatred, yet the chief Force of the intended Injury is to fall on *Hero* and *Leonato* her Father, towards whom he has no Malice; and he is made to engage in this wicked Enterprize to procure the Ruin and Death of two Persons he hates not, to give a little Vexation to one he does. These Absurdities have their Rise from the injudicious Change of the Characters. The Contrivance to slander *Hero* is not less ridiculous, and this also is occasioned by the Poet's having deviated from the Original to introduce his own wild Conceits.

Borachio tells Don *John* that he is highly favoured by *Margaret*, *Hero*'s waiting Woman; that he will persuade her to dress in her Lady's Cloaths, assume her Name, and talk to him out of her Chamber-window, all which Don *Pedro* and *Claudio* being Witnesses of would effectually convince them that *Hero* was dishonoured.

But . . . *Margaret* is all along represented as faithful to her Mistress; it was not likely she would engage in a Plot that seemed to have a Tendency to ruin *Hero*'s Reputation unless she had been imposed on by some very plausible Pretences, what those Pretences were we are left to guess, which is indeed so difficult to do that we must reasonably suppose the Poet himself was as much at a Loss here as his Readers, and equally incapable of solving the difficulty he had raised. . . .

Margaret having done her Part towards defaming her Mistress, without knowing any Thing of the Matter, though her Discourse with *Borachio* was calculated to raise the most injurious Suspicions; assists her next Morning to dress for her Wedding, attends her to the Church, hears the designed Bridegroom refuse her Hand, proclaim her a Wanton, and urge her last Night's loose Discourse with *Borachio* from her Chamber Window as a Proof: Yet all the while she appears wholly insensible of what had happened, . . . Thus supernaturally (if what is out Nature may be called above it) is the Plot brought to perfection, nor is the unravelling of it less happily imagined. . . . Such is *Borachio*'s extreme eagerness to tell his wicked Exploit, that he never thinks of carrying his Friend to his own Lodgings, where he may boast in Safety, but in a rainy Night stands in the Street, close to the Door of the Man whose Daughter he had injured, and there at his leisure relates the whole treacherous Contrivance.

However, all this happens exactly right, because the Watch who is posted about *Leonato*'s House, hear every Syllable, that is spoken, . . . they seize the two Wretches with an Intent to bring them before *Leonato*, not that same Night to prevent the Lady's Disgrace, but the next Morning, when all was over, to discover her Innocence.

Two or three absolute Ideots, are here very artfully introduced for Constable and Watchmen, for had they the least Ray of Reason to direct them, they must have conceived that it was absolutely necessary to acquaint *Leonato* immediately with the Treason, . . . This Method of protracting the Discovery, is not indeed very ingenious, but the Poet's Occasions are answered by it, and that is sufficient. . . . the Lady is shamefully refused, hence arise two or three new Contrivances. . . . These Incidents, were they ever so natural, cannot affect the Readers either with Pity or Surprize, since they are let into the Secret beforehand: and can anticipate the Catastrophe.

. . . *Ariodant* and *Claudio*, . . . alike . . . are represented as passionate Lovers, . . . prevailed upon . . . through the Treachery of a Villain; but *Ariodant* yields only to the strongest Conviction, *Claudio* to the grossest Artifice. *Ariodant*'s . . . Despair . . . prompts him to lay violent Hands on his own Life. *Claudio* is actuated by a Desire of Revenge, and that of the meanest Sort, for he suffers the supposed Gallant to escape, and only mediates the Ruin of the Lady.

There is a great deal of true wit and humour in the comic scenes of this play; the characters of *Benedick* and *Beatrice* are properly marked, and beautifully distinguished.

1757—Arthur Murphy. From the
London Chronicle: or Universal Evening Post

Arthur Murphy (1727–1805) was an Irish theater critic for the *London Chronicle: or Universal Evening Post* as well as a prolific playwright. He also wrote three biographies, including one of David Garrick, the actor mentioned in the following review of a 1757 production of *Much Ado about Nothing* at the Drury Lane Theater.

Shakespeare's Comedy, called *Much Ado About Nothing*, was performed this Evening. Benedick is one of Mr Garrick's best Parts in Comedy. All thro' the Part his Pleasantry is inimitable, and if he had no other Merit in it would sufficiently recompence his Auditors in the Speech where he first deliberates whether he shall marry Beatrice. His Manner of coming forth from the Arbour, and the Tone of his Voice when he says 'This is no Trick,' &c. [2.3.201] is diverting in the highest Degree. His Arguments to reason himself out of his former youthful Resolutions against Marriage are exquisitely humourous; and they are quite agreeable to the Practice of Mankind in general, who seldom want delusive Fallacies to urge in Behalf of their Passions when once they are become fond of any Object whatever. Many of the Scenes in this Comedy are both interesting and entertaining, and particularly when Mr Garrick resolves to give the Challenge, his Performance is perhaps equal to any Thing we have seen from this masterly Actor. (279)

1795—Charles Dibdin. From *A Complete History of the Stage*

An English musician, actor, and writer, Charles Dibdin (ca. 1745–1814) was best known for his operettas and compositions for the stage. In *A Complete History of the Stage*, Dibdin expresses his admiration for *Much Ado about Nothing.*

This play is so witty so playful, so abundant in strong writing, and rich humour, that it has always attracted universal applause. The beauties it contains are innumerable, they are a cluster, and are set so thick that they scarcely afford one another relief, and yet the best critic would find it difficult to say which of them ought to be displaced.

MUCH ADO ABOUT NOTHING IN THE NINETEENTH CENTURY

&

The nineteenth century saw an explosion of interpretive interest in *Much Ado about Nothing* as both a text and a source of critical inquiry. As in the previous century, much of the focus on the play examined the juxtaposition between the main storyline of Hero and Claudio and the secondary storyline of Beatrice and Benedick, and as before, the latter was generally the more celebrated of the two. Still, the questions raised about these two differing sections pushed the nature of critical inquiry surrounding the play further than in the previous century. One commonly debated perspective, for example, examined the nature of genre in the play itself. Many critics, such as William Hazlitt (1817), questioned the role of comedy in the play, especially if the characters of Beatrice and Benedick are removed from the proceedings. The Hero/Claudio narrative is certainly the more serious one, perhaps bordering on the tragic (except, of course, for its "happy" ending); critics questioned the real "comedy" inherent in the machinations of Don John or in the public repudiation of Hero. For a comedy, they reasoned, *Much Ado about Nothing* seemingly had more than its share of dark, disturbing moments. This contrasted sharply to a work like *The Taming of the Shrew*, perhaps the Shakespearean play most often compared to *Much Ado about Nothing*, thanks to the perceived similarities between the two main female characters (though G. G. Gervinus and others would challenge that). Yet in *Shrew*, even the most troubling moments, such as Petruchio's "taming" of Katharina, are still laced with some notion of Elizabethan comedy; whereas in *Much Ado about Nothing*, the repudiation of Hero, the villainy of Don John, the misperceived wooing of Hero by Don Pedro, and numerous other scenes surrounding the main storyline reveal no comedy at all. It is usually the presence of Beatrice and/or Benedick that signals the comedic elements of the play; in this sense, critics realized the work perhaps compared more favorably to plays like *Measure for Measure*, which is today perceived of as a "problem" play for its ambiguous stance in regard to genre.

This juxtaposition in character remained the dominant perspective in critical inquiry throughout the nineteenth century. Critics who espoused this view argued that the richness of Beatrice and Benedick, as compared to the rest of the characters in the play, is part of Shakespeare's design; by creating them so fully formed, the two balance the more superficial figures found in the rest of the play, who dominate by force of plot and strength of scene. The audience is hardly likely to match the rancor and shock in the scene of Hero's repudiation with any other moment in the play—except perhaps for the second half of that scene, when the two favorite characters, Beatrice and Benedick, declare their love and promise revenge against those who have wronged Beatrice's cousin. Her famous lines of "Kill Claudio" and "O God, that I were a man! I would eat his heart in the market-place" resonate in the audience's mind as sharply as the vicious castigation they have just witnessed. Nineteenth-century critics noted that the two storylines resonate with differing emphases; the main plotline of Hero and Claudio is heavily dependent on plot and machination, while the secondary plotline of Beatrice and Benedick depends on character and wordplay. The former is heavy, ponderous, and largely tragic; the latter is lighter, more engaging, and thus more fondly remembered. Occasionally, adaptations of the tale would omit the Hero/Claudio storyline altogether in favor of the other pair, most famously in Hector Berlioz's 1862 comic opera *Béatrice et Bénédict*.

Beatrice remained the character who received the bulwark of critical attention, though certainly all of the characters in the play began to receive their due; nonetheless, it was this particular figure that sparked the imagination of nineteenth-century critics. Most critics admired Beatrice—Henry Giles (1868) considers her "*the* wit" and the pinnacle among Shakespeare's comedic women—though a few, such as Henrietta Lee Palmer (1859), found fault with her, and one, Thomas Campbell (1838), reviled her. Many subsequent scholars took offense at Campbell's depiction of Beatrice, but his work demonstrated the wide range of opinion that sprang up about Shakespeare's most noted figure in the play. In some ways, the critical reception of Beatrice in the nineteenth century seemed inspired by the burgeoning women's rights movement, which was sparked by the appearance of Mary Wollstonecraft's *A Vindication of the Rights of Woman* in 1792. Beatrice was often viewed as an early model of an educated woman who speaks her mind, expresses her will, and is still generally admired by the people around her.

Perhaps surprisingly, the other character who received the most critical attention was not Benedick or Dogberry, who had been so noted in the previous century, but Claudio. The young count was generally reviled in the nineteenth century, as critics pondered his character to determine why he does what he does in the play. They debated his ready belief in Don John's ridiculous lies (often noting that even before Claudio has seen any supposed "proof" of Hero's infidelity, he is plotting his revenge) and the fury behind the public repudiation of act 4. Typical among the Claudio-focused criticism are the works of Roderich Benedix (1873) and Mary Cowden Clarke (1850), who consider Claudio a "vain coxcomb, with no will of his own" and a "heartless fellow," respectively. Heinrich

Bulthaupt (1884) questions the entire Hero/Claudio storyline and laments that Hero could seemingly so readily forgive Claudio at the end of the play for his actions. Still, a few critics choose to defend Claudio, including F. Kreyssig (1862), who believes that the character's youth and general innocence explain, if not excuse, his behavior in the play, and Wilhelm Wetz (1890), who argues that Claudio's "deep hurt" is the cause of his actions.

Perhaps the most noteworthy critical advancement in regard to *Much Ado about Nothing* in the nineteenth century is the work done on the construct of "noting" and the significance of the title of the play. This scrutiny laid the foundation for twentieth-century criticism of the play. Elizabeth Inchbald (1806–09) was the first to underscore the significance of "noting"—as she labels it, the actions of "many unwarrantable listeners," or eavesdroppers—and how the passive activity of listening and overhearing is essential to the text. Highlighting an idea that W. H. Auden and others would take up in the next century, Inchbald pinpoints the construct of "nothingness" that overshadows the text—that throughout the play, "much ado," or much excitement and upheaval, is created over what is essentially "nothing": misunderstandings, misinterpretations, and lies. Hudson and Frederick S. Boas (1986) would likewise pick up this theme, examining the play from the perspective of it making "much ado about nothing," questioning what the role of "nothing" is in the text, how it is defined, and what ultimately will become of it.

Above all, nineteenth-century criticism of *Much Ado about Nothing* is dominated by fresh, in-depth examinations of the characters of Shakespeare's play. From Beatrice to Claudio, from Dogberry to Don John, critics provided new insights into the world of *Much Ado about Nothing* by exploring these characters and their larger roles in the context of the world of the play and the Shakespearean canon overall. In doing so, these critics not only reflected the interests of the play's audiences, who have always responded to the bickering romance of Beatrice and Benedick and the tragic circumstances of Hero and Claudio's engagement, they also established a solid foundational base for twentieth-century critical inquiry of the play, which would further these character studies while delving more deeply into the themes inherent to the play's plotting and language structure as well.

1806–09—Elizabeth Inchbald. From *The British Theatre*

Elizabeth Inchbald (1753–1821) began her career as an actress but later became a writer, producing plays, novels, and articles for *The Edinburgh Review*. Her plays were successful in her day, and her later fiction proved even more popular. In this brief selection, Inchbald focuses on listening as a key aspect to the action of the play, especially in regard to Beatrice

and Benedick, lamenting the "many unwarrantable listeners" or eaves-
droppers in the play. She also notes that, not only are these characters
essential to the action, but Beatrice and Benedick are so worthy of
esteem that the audience can happily overlook this fact as they cheer
the two on toward their natural conclusion—marriage to each other.

Those persons, for whom the hearts of the audience are most engaged, have
scarce one event to aid their personal interest; every occurrence which befalls
them depends solely on the pitiful act of private listening. If Benedick and
Beatrice had possessed perfect good manners, or just notions of honour and
delicacy, so as to have refused to become eaves-droppers, the action of the play
must have stood still, or some better method have been contrived,—a worse
hardly could,—to have imposed on their mutual credulity. But this willingness
to overhear conversations, the reader will find to be the reigning fashion with
the *dramatis personae* of this play; for there are nearly as many unwarrantable
listeners, as there are characters in it. But, in whatever failings the ill-bred custom of Messina may have involved Benedick and Beatrice, they are both highly
entertaining and most respectable personages. They are so witty, so jocund, so
free from care, and yet so sensible of care in others, that the best possible reward
is conferred on their merit,—marriage with each other.

1809—August Wilhelm Schlegel. From *Lectures on Dramatic Art and Literature*

August Wilhelm Schlegel (1767–1845) was a German poet and critic
who is often considered a leader in the German romanticism movement. Schlegel was an important translator of Shakespeare into
German. Like many pre-twentieth-century critics of the play, Schlegel
believes the work's success lies in the irresistible bickering of Beatrice
and Benedick, though he does point out that two dramatic moments of
"theatrical effect" occur during the wedding scene in act 4, when Hero
is repudiated by Claudio, and in the reconciliation scene in act 5, when
Claudio discovers that Hero is not dead after all.

The main plot in *Much Ado About Nothing* is the same as the story of *Ariodante
and Ginevra* in Ariosto; but the secondary circumstances and development
are very different. The mode in which the innocent Hero before the altar at
the moment of the wedding, and in the presence of her family and many witnesses, is put to shame by the most degrading charge, false indeed, yet clothed
with every appearance of truth, is a grand piece of theatrical effect in the true

and justifiable sense. The impression would have been too tragical had not Shakespeare carefully softened it in order to prepare for a fortunate catastrophe. The discovery of the plot against Hero has been already partly made, though not by the persons interested; and the poet has contrived, by means of the blundering simplicity of a couple of constables and watchmen, to convert the arrest and examination of the guilty individuals into scenes full of the most delightful amusement. There is also a second piece of theatrical effect not inferior to the first, where Claudio, now convinced of his error, and in obedience to the penance laid on his fault, thinking to give his hand to a relation of his injured bride, whom he supposes dead, discovers on her unmasking, Hero herself. The extraordinary success of this play in Shakespeare's own time, and long afterward, is, however, to be ascribed more particularly to the parts of Benedick and Beatrice, two fun-loving cynics, who incessantly attack each other with all the resources of raillery. Avowed rebels to love, they are both entangled in its net by a merry plot of their friends to make them believe that each is the object of the secret passion of the other. Objection has been made to the same artifice being twice used in entrapping them; the drollery, however, lies in the very symmetry of deception. Their friends attribute the whole effect to their own device; but the exclusive direction of their raillery against each other is in itself a proof of a growing inclination. Their wit and vivacity does not even abandon them in the avowal of love; and their behavior only assumes a serious appearance for the purpose of defending the slandered Hero. This is exceedingly well imagined; the lovers of jesting must fix a point beyond which they are not to indulge their humor, if they would not be mistaken for buffoons by trade.

1817—William Hazlitt. From
Characters of Shakespear's Plays

One of the greatest English literary critics of the nineteenth century, William Hazlitt (1778–1830) also wrote on art, politics, and history. A renowned intellect and essayist, Hazlitt was keenly interested in Shakespeare. In his reading of *Much Ado about Nothing*, Hazlitt juxtaposes the "serious part" of the play, the story of Claudio and Hero, with the "principal comic characters" of Benedick and Beatrice.

THIS admirable comedy used to be frequently acted till of late years. Mr. Garrick's Benedick was one of his most celebrated characters; and Mrs. Jordan, we have understood, played Beatrice very delightfully. The serious part is still the most prominent here, as in other instances that we have noticed. Hero is the principal figure in the piece, and leaves an indelible impression on the mind by her beauty, her tenderness, and the hard trial of her love. The passage in which Claudio first makes a confession of his affection towards her conveys as pleasing an image of the entrance of love into a youthful bosom as can well be imagined.

> "Oh, my lord,
> When you went onward with this ended action,
> I look'd upon her with a soldier's eye,
> That lik'd, but had a rougher task in hand
> Than to drive liking to the name of love;
> But now I am return'd, and that war-thoughts
> Have left their places vacant; in their rooms
> Come thronging soft and delicate desires,
> All prompting me how fair young Hero is,
> Saying, I lik'd her ere I went to wars."

In the scene at the altar, when Claudio, urged on by the villain Don John, brings the charge of incontinence against her, and as it were divorces her in the very marriage-ceremony, her appeals to her own conscious innocence and honour are made with the most affecting simplicity.

> "*Claudio.* No, Leonato,
> I never tempted her with word too large,
> But, as a brother to his sister, shew'd
> Bashful sincerity, and comely love.
>   *Hero.* And seem'd I ever otherwise to you?
>   *Claudio.* Out on thy seeming, I will write against it:
> You seem to me as Dian in her orb,
> As chaste as is the bud ere it be blown;
> But you are more intemperate in your blood
> Than Venus, or those pamper'd animals
> That rage in savage sensuality.
>   *Hero.* Is my lord well, that he doth speak so wide?
>   *Leonato.* Are these things spoken, or do I but dream?
>   *John.* Sir, they are spoken, and these things are true.
>   *Benedick.* This looks not like a nuptial.
>   *Hero.* True! O God!"—

The justification of Hero in the end, and her restoration to the confidence and arms of her lover, is brought about by one of those temporary consignments to the grave of which Shakespear seems to have been fond. He has perhaps explained the theory of this predilection in the following lines:—

Friar. She dying, as it must be so maintain'd,
Upon the instant that she was accus'd,
Shall be lamented, pity'd, and excus'd,
Of every hearer: for it so falls out,
That what we have we prize not to the worth,
While we enjoy it; but being lack'd and lost,
Why then we rack the value; then we find
The virtue, that possession would not shew us
Whilst it was ours.—So will it fare with Claudio:
When he shall hear she dy'd upon his words,
The idea of her love shall sweetly creep
Into his study of imagination;
And every lovely organ of her life
Shall come apparel'd in more precious habit,
More moving, delicate, and full of life,
Into the eye and prospect of his soul,
Than when she liv'd indeed."

The principal comic characters in MUCH ADO ABOUT NOTHING, Benedick and Beatrice, are both essences in their kind. His character as a woman-hater is admirably supported, and his conversion to matrimony is no less happily effected by the pretended story of Beatrice's love for him. It is hard to say which of the two scenes is the best, that of the trick which is thus practiced on Benedick, or that in which Beatrice is prevailed on to take pity on him by over hearing her cousin and her maid declare (which they do on purpose) that he is dying of love for her. There is something delightfully picturesque in the manner in which Beatrice is described as coming to hear the plot which is contrived against herself—

"For look where Beatrice, like a lapwing, runs
Close by the ground, to hear our conference."

In consequence of what she hears (not a word of which is true) she exclaims when these good natured informants are gone,

"What fire is in mine ears? Can this be true?
  Stand I condemn'd for pride and scorn so much?
Contempt, farewel! and maiden pride adieu!
  No glory lives behind the back of such.
And, Benedick, love on, I will requite thee;
  Taming my wild heart to thy loving hand;
If thou dost love, my kindness shall incite thee

> To bind our loves up in an holy band:
> For others say thou dost deserve; and I
> Believe it better than reportingly."

And Benedick, on his part, is equally sincere in his repentance with equal reason, after he has heard the grey-beard, Leonato, and his friend, "Monsieur Love," discourse of the desperate state of his supposed inamorata.

> "This can be no trick; the conference was sadly borne.—They have the truth of this from Hero. They seem to pity the lady; it seems her affections have the full bent. Love me! why, it must be requited. I hear how I am censur'd: they say, I will bear myself proudly, if I perceive the love come from her; they say too, that she will rather die than give any sign of affection.—I did never think to marry: I must not seem proud:—happy are they that hear their detractions, and can put them to mending. They say, the lady is fair; 'tis a truth, I can bear them witness: and virtuous;—'tis so, I cannot reprove it: and wise—but for loving me:—by my troth it is no addition to her wit;—nor no great argument of her folly, for I will be horribly in love with her.—I may chance to have some odd quirks and remnants of wit broken on me, because I have rail'd so long against marriage: but doth not the appetite alter? A man loves the meat in his youth, that he cannot endure in his age.—Shad quips, and sentences, and these paper bullets of the brain, awe a man from the career of his humour? No: the world must be peopled. When I said, I would die a bachelor, I did not think I should live till I were marry'd.—Here comes Beatrice: by this day, she's a fair lady: I do spy some marks of love in her."

The beauty of all this arises from the characters of the persons so entrapped. Benedick is a professed and staunch enemy to marriage, and gives very plausible reasons for the faith that is in him. And as to Beatrice, she persecutes him all day with her jests (so that he could hardly think of being troubled with them at night) she not only turns him but all other things into jest, and is proof against every thing serious.

> "*Hero.* Disdain and scorn ride sparkling in her eyes,
> Misprising what they look on; and her wit
> Values itself so highly, that to her
> All matter else seems weak: she cannot love,
> Nor take no shape nor project of affection,
> She is so self-endeared.
>   *Ursula.* Sure, I think so;
> And therefore, certainly, it were not good
> She knew his love, lest she make sport at it.

Hero. Why, you speak truth: I never yet saw man,
How wise, how noble, young, how rarely featur'd,
But she would spell him backward: if fair-fac'd,
She'd swear the gentleman should be her sister;
If black, why, nature, drawing of an antick,
Made a foul blot: if tall, a lance ill-headed;
If low, an agate very vilely cut:
If speaking, why, a vane blown with all winds;
If silent, why, a block moved with none.
So turns she every man the wrong side out;
And never gives to truth and virtue that
Which simpleness and merit purchaseth."

These were happy materials for Shakespear to work on, and he has made a happy use of them. Perhaps that middle point of comedy was never more nicely hit in which the ludicrous blends with the tender, and our follies, turning round against themselves in support of our affections, retain nothing but their humanity.

Dogberry and Verges in this play are inimitable specimens of quaint blundering and misprisions of meaning; and are a standing record of that formal gravity of pretension and total want of common understanding, which Shakespear no doubt copied from real life, and which in the course of two hundred years appear to have ascended from the lowest to the highest offices in the state.

1818—Samuel Taylor Coleridge. From
Lectures and Notes on Shakspere

One of the most significant authors and critics of his time, Samuel Taylor Coleridge (1772-1834) is perhaps best known today for his epic poems *Kubla Khan* and *The Rime of the Ancient Mariner*. In this excerpt from his *Lectures and Notes on Shakspere*, Coleridge notes the interconnectedness of plot and character in the play.

The interest in the plot is always in fact on account of the characters, not *vice versa*, as in almost all other writers; the plot is a mere canvas and no more. Hence arises the true justification of the same stratagem being used in regard to Benedick and Beatrice,—the vanity in each being alike. Take away from the "Much Ado About Nothing" all that which is not indispensable to the plot, either as having little to do with it, or, at best, like Dogberry and his comrades, forced into the service, when any other less ingeniously absurd watchmen and night-constables would have answered the mere necessities of the action,—take away Benedick, Beatrice, Dogberry, and the reaction of the former on the character of Hero,—and what will remain? In other writers the main agent of the plot is always the prominent character; in Shakspere it is so, or is not so, as the character is in itself calculated, or not calculated, to form the plot. Don John is the main-spring of the plot of this play, but he is merely shown and then withdrawn.

1832—Anna Brownell Jameson.
From *Characteristics of Women*

Famed as an art historian, travel writer, and feminist pioneer, Anna Brownell Jameson (1794–1860) wrote the popular, two-volume work *The Loves of the Poets*, which explored the lives of the women who were loved and celebrated by great poets throughout time. In the following selection, Jameson comments on the character of Beatrice. Unlike many critics of her time, Jameson finds no disconnection between Beatrice's aggressive behavior and her station in life as a woman of the genteel class; indeed, Jameson ultimately believes that, with Beatrice, it is not what she says that is of great importance, but rather who she is, "the soul of wit, and the spirit of gayety."

Shakspeare has exhibited in Beatrice a spirited and faithful portrait of the fine lady of his own time. The deportment, language, manners, and allusions are those of a particular class in a particular age; but the individual and dramatic character which forms the groundwork is strongly discriminated, and being taken from general nature, belongs to every age. In Beatrice, high intellect and high animal spirits meet, and excite each other like fire and air. In her wit (which is brilliant without being imaginative) there is a touch of insolence, not unfrequent in women when the wit predominates over reflection and imagination. In her temper, too, there is a slight infusion of the termagant; and her satirical humour plays with such an unrespective levity over all subjects alike that it required a profound knowledge of women to bring such a character within the pale of our sympathy. But Beatrice, though wilful, is not wayward; she is volatile, not unfeeling. She has not only an exuberance of wit and gayety, but of heart and soul and energy of spirit; and is no more like the fine ladies of modern comedy—whose wit consists in a temporary allusion, or a play upon words, and whose petulance is displayed in a toss of the head, a flirt of the fan, or a flourish of the pocket-handkerchief—than one of our modern dandies is like Sir Philip Sidney.

In Beatrice, Shakspeare has contrived that the poetry of the character shall not only soften, but heighten its comic effect. We are not only inclined to forgive Beatrice all her scornful airs, all her biting jests, all her assumption of superiority; but they amuse and delight us the more when we find her, with all the headlong simplicity of a child, falling at once into the snare laid for her affections; when we see *her* who thought a man of God's making not good enough for her, who disdained to be o'ermastered by "a piece of valiant dust," stooping like the rest of her sex, vailing her proud spirit and taming her wild heart to the loving hand of him whom she had scorned, flouted, and misused "past the endurance of a block." And we are yet more completely won by her generous enthusiastic attachment to her cousin. When the father of Hero believes the tale of her guilt; when Claudio, her lover, without remorse or a lingering doubt, consigns her to shame; when the Friar remains silent, and the generous Benedick himself knows not what to say, Beatrice, confident in her affections, and guided only by the impulses of her own feminine heart, sees through the inconsistency, the impossibility of the charge, and exclaims, without a moment's hesitation,

"O, on my soul, my cousin is belied!"

Schlegel, in his remarks on the play, has given us an amusing instance of that sense of reality with which we are impressed by Shakspeare's characters. He says of Benedick and Beatrice, as if he had known them personally, that the exclusive direction of their pointed raillery against each other "is a proof of a growing inclination." This is not unlikely; and the same inference would lead us to suppose that this mutual inclination had commenced before the opening of the play. The very first words uttered by Beatrice are an inquiry after Benedick, though expressed with her usual arch impertinence:—

"I pray you, is Signior Montanto returned from the wars, or no?"
"I pray you, how many hath he killed and eaten in these wars? But how many hath he killed? for indeed I promised to eat all of his killing."

And in the unprovoked hostility with which she falls upon him in his absence, in the pertinacity and bitterness of her satire, there is certainly great argument that he occupies much more of her thoughts than she would have been willing to confess, even to herself. In the same manner Benedick betrays a lurking partiality for his fascinating enemy; he shows that he has looked upon her with no careless eye when he says,

"There's her cousin [meaning Beatrice], an she were not possessed with a fury, excels her as much in beauty as the first of May does the last of December."

Infinite skill, as well as humour, is shown in making this pair of airy beings the exact counterpart of each other; but of the two portraits, that of Benedick is by far the most pleasing, because "the independence and gay indifference of temper. The laughing defiance of love and marriage, the satirical freedom of expression, common to both, are more becoming to the masculine than to the feminine character. Any woman might love such a cavalier as Benedick, and be proud of his affection; his valour, his wit, and his gayety sit so gracefully upon him! and his light scoffs against the power of love are but just sufficient to render more piquant the conquest of this "heretic in despite of beauty." But a man might well be pardoned who should shrink from encountering such a spirit as that of Beatrice unless, indeed, he had "served an apprenticeship to the taming-school." The wit of Beatrice is less good-humoured than that of Benedick; or, from the difference of sex, appears so. It is observable that the power is throughout on her side, and the sympathy and interest on his: which, by reversing the usual order of things, seems to excite us *against the grain*, if I may use such an expression. In all their encounters she constantly gets the better of him, and the gentleman's wits go off halting, if he is not himself fairly *hors de combat*. Beatrice, woman-like, generally has the first word, and will have the last. . . .

In the midst of all this tilting and sparring of their nimble and fiery wits, we find them infinitely anxious for the good opinion of each other, and secretly impatient of each other's scorn; but Beatrice is the most truly indifferent of the two—the most assured of herself. The comic effect produced by their mutual attachment, which, however natural and expected, comes upon us with all the force of a surprise, cannot be surpassed: and how exquisitely characteristic the mutual avowal! . . .

The character of Hero is well contrasted with that of Beatrice, and their mutual attachment is very beautiful and natural. When they are both on the scene together, Hero has but little to say for herself: Beatrice asserts the rule of a master spirit, eclipses her by her mental superiority, abashes her by her raillery, dictates to her, answers for her, and would fain inspire her gentle-hearted cousin with some of her own assurance.

> "Yes, faith; it is my cousin's duty to make curtsy and say 'Father, as it please you.'—But yet for all that, cousin, let him be a handsome fellow, or else make another curtsy and say 'Father, as it please me.'"

But Shakspeare knew well how to make one character subordinate to another, without sacrificing the slightest portion of its effect; and Hero, added to her grace and softness, and all the interest which attaches to her as the sentimental heroine of the play, possesses an intellectual beauty of her own. When she has Beatrice at an advantage, she repays her with interest, in the severe but most animated and elegant picture she draws of her cousin's imperious character and unbridled levity of tongue. The portrait is a little overcharged, because administered as a corrective, and intended to be overheard:

> "But nature never fram'd a woman's heart
> Of prouder stuff than that of Beatrice:
> Disdain and scorn ride sparkling in her eyes," etc.

Beatrice never appears to greater advantage than in her soliloquy after leaving her concealment "in the pleached bower where honeysuckles, ripened by the sun, forbid the sun to enter;" she exclaims, after listening to this tirade against herself,—

> "What fire is in mine ears? Can this be true?
> Stand I condemn'd for pride and scorn so much?"

The sense of wounded vanity is lost in better feelings, and she is infinitely more struck by what is said in praise of Benedick, and the history of his supposed love for her, than by the dispraise of herself. The immediate success of the trick is a most natural consequence of the self-assurance and magnanimity of her character; she is so accustomed to assert dominion over the spirits of others that she cannot suspect the possibility of a plot laid against herself. . . .

It is remarkable that, notwithstanding the point and vivacity of the dialogue, few of the speeches of Beatrice are capable of a general application, or engrave themselves distinctly on the memory; they contain more mirth than matter; and though wit be the predominant feature in the dramatic portrait, Beatrice more charms and dazzles us by what she is than by what she *says*. It is not merely her sparkling repartees and saucy jests, it is the soul of wit, and the spirit of gayety informing the whole character—looking out from her brilliant eyes, and laughing on the full lips that pout with scorn—which we have before us, moving and full of life. On the whole, we dismiss Benedick and Beatrice to their matrimonial bonds rather with a sense of amusement than a feeling of congratulation or sympathy; rather with an acknowledgment that they are well-matched and worthy of each other, than with any well-founded expectation of their domestic tranquillity. If, as Benedick asserts, they are both "too wise to woo peaceably," it may be added that both are too wise, too witty, and too wilful to live peaceably together. We have some misgivings about Beatrice—some apprehensions that poor Benedick will not escape the "predestinated scratched face," which he had foretold to him who should win and wear this quick-witted and pleasant-spirited lady; yet when we recollect that to the wit and imperious temper of Beatrice is united a magnanimity of spirit which would naturally place her far above all selfishness, and all paltry struggles for power—when we perceive, in the midst of her sarcastic levity and volubility of tongue, so much of generous affection, and such a high sense of female virtue and honour, we are inclined to hope the best. We think it possible that though the gentleman may now and then swear, and the lady scold, the native good-humour of the one, the really fine understanding of the other, and the value they so evidently attach to each other's esteem, will insure them a tolerable portion of domestic felicity; and in this hope we leave them.

NOTE BY THE EDITOR.—The poet Campbell, in his introduction to the play, remarks: "Mrs. Jameson, in her characters of Shakespeare, concludes with hoping that Beatrice will live happy with Benedick, but I have no such hope; and my final anticipation in reading the play is the certainty that Beatrice will provoke her Benedick to give her much and just conjugal castigation. She is an odious woman. Her own cousin says of her—

'Disdain and scorn ride sparkling in her eyes,
Misprising what they look on, and her wit
Values itself so highly that to her
All matter else seems weak: she cannot love,
Nor take no shape nor project of affection,
She is so self-endeared.'

I once knew such a pair; the lady was a perfect Beatrice; she railed hypocritically at wedlock before her marriage, and with bitter sincerity after it. She and her Benedick now live apart, but with entire reciprocity of sentiments, each devoutly wishing that the other may soon pass into a better world. Beatrice is not to be compared, but contrasted, with Rosalind, who is equally witty; but the sparkling sayings of Rosalind are like gems upon her head at court, and like dew-drops on her bright hair in the woodland forest."

Verplanck, after quoting this passage, comments upon it as follows: "We extract this last criticism, partly in deference to Campbell's general exquisite taste and reverent appreciation of Shakespeare's genius, and partly as an example of the manner in which accidental personal associations influence taste and opinion. The critical poet seems to have unhappily suffered under the caprices or insolence of some accomplished but fantastical female wit, whose resemblance he thinks he recognizes in Beatrice; and then vents the offences of the belle of Edinburgh or London upon her prototype of Messina, or more probably of the court of Queen Elizabeth. Those who, without encountering any such unlucky cause of personal prejudice, have looked long enough upon the rapidly passing generations of wits and beauties in the gay world to have noted their characters as they first appeared, and subsequently developed themselves in after-life, will pronounce a very different judgment. Beatrice's faults are such as ordinarily spring from the consciousness of talent and beauty, accompanied with the high spirits of youth and health, and the play of a lively fancy. Her brilliant intellectual qualities are associated with strong and generous feelings, high confidence in female truth and virtue, warm attachment to her friends, and quick, undisguised indignation at wrong and injustice. There is the rich material, which the experience and the sorrows of maturer life, the affection and the duties of the wife and the mother, can gradually shape into the noblest forms of matronly excellence; and such, we doubt not, was the result shown in the married life of Beatrice."

We may add what Mr. Furnivall says on the same subject: "Beatrice is the sauciest, most piquant, sparkling, madcap girl that Shakspere ever drew, and yet a loving, deep-natured, true woman too. . . . She gives her heart to Benedick. . . . The two understand one another. We all know what it means. The brightest, sunniest married life, comfort in sorrow, doubling of joy. . . . The poet Campbell's story of his pair was an utter mistake: he never knew a Beatrice."

See also the extract from Gervinus, p. 18 above.

1838—Thomas Campbell. From
The Dramatic Works of William Shakespeare.
With Remarks on His Life by Thomas Campbell

Thomas Campbell (1777–1844) was a renowned Scottish poet best known for his sentimental verse, including *The Pleasures of Hope* and *Epistle to Three Ladies*. Campbell was also an important editor of Shakespeare's, whose edition was titled *The Dramatic Works of William Shakespeare. With Remarks on His Life by Thomas Campbell*. The most noteworthy aspect of Campbell's criticism of Shakespeare presented here is his disdain for the character of Beatrice, whom he finds "odious" and "not a pleasing representative of her sex." Several later critics took issue with Campbell's work, indicating its prominence among Shakespearean scholars.

I fully agree with the admirers of this play in their opinion as to the most of its striking merits. The scene of the young and guiltless heroine struck speechless by the accusation of her lover, and swooning at the foot of the nuptial altar, is deeply touching. . . . At this crisis, the exclamation of Beatrice, the sole believer in her innocence, 'O, on my soul, my cousin is belied,' is a relieving and glad voice in the wilderness, which almost reconciles me to Beatrice's otherwise disagreeable character. . . . Who, but Shakespeare, could dry our tears of interest for Hero, by so laughable an agent as the immortal Dogberry? . . . yet Shakespeare, after pouncing this ridiculous prey, springs up, forthwith, to high dramatic effect in making Claudio, who had mistakenly accused Hero, so repentant as to consentingly marry another woman, her supposed cousin, under a veil, which, when it is lifted, displays his own vindicated bride.

At the same time, if Shakespeare were looking over my shoulder, I could not disguise some objections to this comedy, . . . debarring it from ranking among our Poet's most enchanting dramas. . . . Our fanciful faith is misused, when it is spurred and impelled to believe that Don John, without one particle of love for Hero, but out of mere personal spite to Claudio, should contrive the infernal treachery which made the latter *assuredly* jealous. Moreover, during one-half of the play, we have a disagreeable female character in that of Beatrice. Her portrait, I may be told, is deeply drawn, and minutely finished. It is; and so is that of Benedick, who is entirely her counterpart, except that he is less disagreeable. But the best-drawn portraits by the finest masters may be admirable in execution, though unpleasant to contemplate, and Beatrice's portrait is in this category. She is a tartar, . . . and, if a natural woman, is not a pleasing representative of the sex. In befriending Hero, she almost reconciles us to her, but not entirely; for a good heart, that shows itself only on extraordinary occasions, is no sufficient atonement for a bad temper, which Beatrice evidently shows. . . . my final anticipation in reading the play is the certainty that Beatrice will provoke her Benedick to give her much and just conjugal castigation. She is an odious woman.

1839—Hermann Ulrici. From *Shakespeare's Dramatic Art*

A prominent German philosopher, Hermann Ulrici (1806–84) was a professor of philosophy in Halle and a famed theist scholar whose later works were often designed to prove the existence of God. Here, Ulrici places the character of Dogberry into the larger pantheon of Shakespearean fools, suggesting that he plays the same role in *Much Ado about Nothing* that the Fool in *Twelfth Night* and similar comic foils in other Shakespeare's works play.

Most delightful is the contradiction between appearance and reality, between subjective conception and objective reality, as we have it exhibited in the Clown of the piece, the dutiful constable Dogberry, who considers his position so very important and maintains it so zealously, but who is always uttering contradictory maxims and precepts; who is so presumptuous and yet so modest; who looks at things with so correct an eye and yet pronounces such foolish judgements; talks so much and yet says so little, in fact, perpetually contradicts himself, giving orders for what he advises to be left undone, entreating to be registered an ass, and yet is the very one to discover the *nothing* which is the cause of the *much ado*. He is the chief representative of that view of life upon which the whole is based, inasmuch as its comic power is exhibited most strongly and most directly in him. For this contrast, which, in accordance with its nature, usually appears divided between its two poles, is, so to say, individualised in him, that is, united in the one individual and fully reflected in his inconsistent and ever contradictory doings and resolves, thoughts, and sayings. Dogberry personifies, if we may say so, the spirit and meaning of the whole, and, therefore, plays essentially the same part as the Fool in *Twelfth Night*, Touchstone in *As You Like It*, Launce in *The Two Gentlemen of Verona*, and the majority of the clowns in Shakespeare's comedies.

1849—G. G. Gervinus. From *Shakespeare Commentaries*

Georg Gottfried Gervinus (1805-71) was a renowned German literary historian who authored numerous works, including a four-volume study of Shakespeare. In the following excerpt, Gervinus responds to popular conventions that the coupling of Beatrice and Benedick will ultimately prove to be an unhappy one. Gervinus argues that the perceived flaws and quarrels of the two characters are only minor ones, reflecting the rather simplistic nature of problems that occur in most of Shakespeare's comedies. Gervinus argues that rather than connecting Beatrice to early, shrewish characters like Katharina from *The Taming of the Shrew*, she is more truly aligned to later, more fully defined women like Silvia from *The Two Gentlemen of Verona*. Gervinus thus discusses these two distinct classes of women he believes are present in Shakespeare, believing that his views of women evolved along with his writing.

Mrs Jameson has but little hope for the domestic felicity of the pair, whose wooing has been so stormy; Campbell goes so far as to call Beatrice *an odious woman*. We will not take occasion here to enlarge upon the significance of these expressions, we will merely make two general remarks which seem in place with regard to the actual excellence of Shakespeare's humourous characters: we must not be misled by the versatility and quickness of their wit, or by their intellectual equipment to draw any conclusion as to their moral and general human value in the eyes of the Poet himself. We have too often had occasion to mention this to think it necessary to dwell upon it here. As for the characters in his comedies, we must remember, once for all, that we are introduced to a social circle in which Shakespeare never illustrated profound natures or violent passions. This is not the soil for grand and lofty virtues or for depths of crime; they are to be found in the plays which we have designated as dramas rather than comedies, in *The Merchant of Venice*, in *Cymbeline*, in *Measure for Measure*. Here, in *Much Ado*, only minor faults and minor virtues disfigure or distinguish the characters, and the greatest distinction achieved by the most prominent among them must always be understood as comparative. Here are no tragic struggles with intense passions, no encounters with the dark powers that rule the destiny of mankind, no deeds of unusual self-sacrifice and force of will;—they would injure the character of the comedy, which is developed from the weaknesses of human nature along the smooth pathways of social intercourse, among men of the commoner sort. If, thus considered, we find Beatrice and Benedick not to be compared with Katharine and Petruchio, and moreover lacking in the ideal grace of Rosalind and Orlando, we are right. Yet, taken in Shakespeare's sense, we must not under-rate these blunt, practical natures, nor must we, taking them in his sense over-estimate them. If we would discover the Poet's own actual estimate of Beatrice, and of women of her stamp, a close examination will show us that it was probably different at different periods of his life. We have elsewhere called attention to the fact that there is a striking number of disagreeable women in the Plays of the first period; the Poet's own experience seems to have impressed him with an unfavourable view of the feminine character. Another type of woman prevails in the second period. There is doubtless a certain family resemblance in Silvia in *The Two Gentlemen of Verona*, in Rosaline and her companions, in Portia and Nerissa, Rosalind, and Beatrice. All show in different degrees a vein of wit, which makes them mistresses of the art of conversation, and which, however true they may be at heart, sometimes makes the tongue speak falsely; they nearly all possess a preponderating culture of the understanding, and are gifted to such a degree with intellectual and mental force that at times it seems to transcend the bounds of feminine capacity. They all have more or less of something unfemi-ninely forward in their composition, something domineering and arrogant, and consequently the men associated with them either play a subordinate part, or are obliged to take pains to keep pace with the ladies of their choice. Shakespeare must have learned to know in London, in the higher circles to which he was there introduced, ladies who transformed into enthusiastic admiration his previ-ous estimate of women. In Portia he has given us a feminine ideal that borders on perfection; she yields to no man in force of will and self-control, in wit, and scope of intellect. In his later plays Shakespeare rather dropped this style of woman. A closer intimacy with feminine nature led him to take more pleasure in its emo-tional side, and he then painted with but few strokes those sensitive creatures whose sphere is that of instinct, so peculiarly woman's own, who avoid license of speech as well as license of action, and who in the purity of their emotions wield a far greater power than belonged to Shakespeare's earlier and wittier darlings. In that earlier period Shakespeare never would have declared with such emphasis as he did in *Lear* that a low voice is an *excellent thing in woman*. He did indeed then create modestly retiring women, the gentle figures of a Bianca, a Hero, a Julia, but he kept them in the background. His Juliet stands on middle ground, between the two classes of which we speak. Afterwards Viola, Desdemona, Perdita, Ophelia, Cordelia, Miranda advance to the front, and Imogen, loveliest of all, who in her sphere contests the palm with Portia in hers. Thus Shakespeare advanced, clarifying his knowledge of the sex, and his feminine creations gain in spiritual beauty and moral worth in proportion as they lose in superficial brilliancy and keenness of intellect. Which class of women Shakespeare preferred is learned from the fact that the earlier type appears only in his comedies, while the latter class is brought forward in his tragedies, wherein we find revealed the most profound emotions of either sex.

1850—Mary Cowden Clarke. "On Shakspeare's Individuality in his Characters: Shakspeare's Lovers"

Mary Cowden Clarke (1809–98) was a renowned Shakespearean authority who created the first concordance of Shakespeare in 1844. Here, Clarke disparages the character of Claudio, calling him a "heartless fellow" and considering his love of Hero motivated by "what she is worth to him, not for what she is herself."

It is marvellous how consistently the poet has drawn this character of Claudio. He has made him throughout a heartless fellow, with a constant eye to his own advantage; and yet so artistically as well as consistently is he drawn, that he passes for a gallant young soldier, a pleasant companion, a gentleman, and a LOVER! We are made to hear of his bravery in the wars, we are made to see that his friends like him, and we find him polished in manner and accomplished in speech. But on scrutinizing his character, we discover his nature to be radically mean and selfish. . . . [He] is, in fact, a type of a large class of men who rank as lovers in the world. He loves the woman for his own sake, not for hers; for what she is worth to him, not for what she is herself. . . . That is quite the act of a worldly man, Claudio's asking Benedick, in the first instance, his opinion of Hero. A worldly man is apt to judge his mistress—or aught else he would appropriate—through the eyes of others. A worldly man likes to know the general estimate of a woman or a purchase he seeks to make his own. He rates them by the market-price of public opinion. If he discover that they stand high in the judgment of the world, they immediately rise in his own idea. To find that the lady he admires is thought a fine woman, is toasted as a beauty, is the prize sought by many suitors,—find that the horse he has thought of for his own riding has several other bidders,—to find that the lease of the house he has some notion of renting is likely to fall into other hands;—gives suddenly to each cent. per cent. additional value in his eyes, and excites his desire to become their possessor.

1851—Hartley Coleridge. From *Essays and Marginalia*

The son of Samuel Taylor Coleridge, Hartley Coleridge (1796–1849) was a minor writer who never lived up to the promise and expectations his father placed on him. Coleridge was more known for his literary journalism and criticism, placing essays and poems in several popular magazines of the day and publishing one biographical work in his lifetime. Coleridge is one of the few prominent critics in his day who did not find *Much Ado about Nothing* wholly admirable, suggesting that it lacks "the truth of ideal nature"—a quality in Shakespeare's works that for Coleridge reflected the veracity of the human condition—that was present in Shakespeare's best dramas.

There is, alas! but too much nature in this sulky rascal. Men who are inly conscious of being despicable take it for granted that all their fellow-creatures despise them, and hate the whole human race by anticipation. . . .

Beatrice and Benedict are, without owning it to themselves, mutually in love; and the somewhat clumsy and twice-repeated stratagem is not the real cause of their attachment, but its apparent justification. . . .

This play is one of Shakspeare's few essays at what may be called genteel comedy, and proves that neither genius, wit, humour, nor gentility will serve to produce excellence in that kind. It wants that truth of ideal nature which was Shakspeare's *forte*, and does not present enough of the truth of real life and manners to compensate for the deficiency. The more impassioned scenes are scarcely in place. Tragi-comedy is one thing, comi-tragedy is another. Where pathos is predominant, it often may derive an increase of power from lighter scenes; but where the ground-work is comic, it is vain to work in flowers of sombre hue. The tale, too, is improbable, without being romantic. Still it is Shakspeare—delightful in each part, but unsatisfactory in the effect of the whole.

P.S. I never censure Shakspeare without finding reason to eat my words.

1859—Henrietta Lee Palmer. "Beatrice" and "Hero" from *The Stratford Gallery; or the Shakespeare Sisterhood*

A southern American author and translator, Henrietta Lee Palmer published two books, including *The Stratford Gallery; or the Shakespeare*

Sisterhood in 1859. The book comprises forty-five character studies of the main female characters in each of Shakespeare's plays; the excerpts included here focus on Beatrice and Hero. Palmer both praises and scorns Beatrice, admiring her intellect and wit though suggesting that each is limited by Beatrice's desire for a quick retort. According to Palmer, it is Beatrice's impassioned defense of her cousin, even in the face of disbelieving males, that redeems her.

If this sharp-tongued young lady serve no better purpose to the humanity of this day and generation, at least she saves it from one graceless distinction, by proving in her own person that the "fast" woman is by no means a modern "institution:" not that we would detract from the perfected specimens of our own time, by comparison with this rudimentary example; but we contend that she possesses all the qualities necessary to a successful assumption of the character—her education, and the manners of the time, alone impede her.

Beatrice, like many another woman before and since, is the slave of a pert tongue; her intellect, though quick, is not strong enough to keep her vanity in subjection, and the consciousness of possessing in a ready wit the power of discomfiting others, proves a successful snare for her good taste and all the graceful effects of her gentle breeding. It is only in situations so inspiring as to compel her for the moment to forget her flippant affectations, that she appears as Nature made her—a spirited, generous, clever woman. . . .

The wit of Beatrice, brilliant as it is, is but the dazzle of words—it has no imaginative element, none of the half-playful pathos which renders that of Rosalind so charming; the two compare as the cold, artificial glitter of a diamond with the cordial warmth of sunshine. To use Benedick's own words—and he, as chief sufferer, should be excellent authority—Beatrice "speaks poignards, and every word stabs" [II.i.247–8], while, in the poetic simile of Mrs. Jameson, "the wit of Rosalind bubbles up and sparkles like the living fountain, refreshing all around" [I.80].

Beatrice has none of Rosalind's romantic susceptibility, no passion; her love for Benedick we can never regard as more than an experimental freak; though, to do her justice, her soliloquy in the garden, where, concealed, she has overheard that Benedick loves her [III.i.107–16], is creditable alike to her heart and her good sense. . . .

But however the gratuitous impertinence and unseemly forwardness of Beatrice may jar with one's fine ideas of a lady, she nobly redeems herself by her chivalrous defence of her cousin Hero, on the occasion of her cruel disgrace; her hearty, clear-headed

Oh, on my soul, my cousin is belied! [IV.i.148]

in the face of her uncle's conviction of his daughter's shame, and Benedick's amazed suspicion, is worth whole volleys of her murderous wit.

Hero

In point of romantic interest and dramatic situation, Hero is undoubtedly the leading character in *Much Ado about Nothing*, although, adopting the popular appreciation, we have conferred the distinction of "first lady" on her cousin Beatrice—not the first time, by the by, that loud and persistent vanity has succeeded in usurping the honorable place belonging to modest, graceful excellence.

A rare chasteness of thought and person is plainly the trait in Hero's character which expresses itself most distinctly in the affairs of her daily life; and in this particular she affords a lively contrast to her cousin's inherent vulgarity. Her emotions are as still as they are deep—her words few; yet, that she can express herself well on occasion, is attested by her conversation with Ursula, designed to be overheard by Beatrice, in which her caustic description of that flippant young woman is quite equal to many of her renowned sallies; no wonder that Beatrice issues from her concealment with "fire in her ears" [III.i.107] . . .

It is noticeable that in the repartee—coarse even for the women of Shakspeare's time—bandied by the less fastidious tongues of her rattle-brain cousin and her gentlewoman, she never takes part, unless to repel some direct attack upon herself, with a

Fye upon thee! Art not ashamed? [III.iv.28]

and that, too, with no affectation of prudery; her delicacy is as virgin as Desdemona's, that very snow-drop among women.

1862—F. Kreyssig. From *Vorlesungen ueber Shakespeare*

Friedrich Alexander Theodor Kreyssig (1818–79) was a German scholar of literature and literary thought and author of several books on the subject. His work on Shakespeare was especially noted. Here, Kreyssig castigates the character of Claudio, considering him "Arrogant, faint-hearted, liable to hasty change of mood, and in anger capable of heartless cruelty." Kreyssig lingers on the masquerade scene, suggesting that it presages Claudio's lack of faith in those around him—not only in Hero, but also in Don Pedro, who promised to woo in Claudio's name. Though many prior critics had similarly discussed Claudio's shortcomings and flaws, few have done so as eloquently or didactically as Kreyssig, and his attention to the masquerade scene is particularly useful here. Yet Kreyssig also points out that the fault is not to be placed entirely on the character of Claudio but rather on his youth and general inexperience. The critic argues that Claudio has truly experienced little of the world and even less of women, and that if his reactions in both the masquerade scene and later, in the wedding scene, seem juvenile and childish, it is because they spring from a man who, until very recently, was viewed as a child by the society around him. Kreyssig also detects an innocence in Claudio that reflects how easily he comes to feel betrayed; and while these aspects of the character may not be enough to outright excuse his reprehensible behavior, they at least do much in helping us understand it.

The repulsive traits in Claudio's character have been frequently indicated. Arrogant, faint-hearted, liable to hasty change of mood, and in anger capable of heartless cruelty, he repeatedly brings into question his qualification to be the hero of the Play, the fortunate lover. His reply to Benedick, when he first tells of his love for Hero is ominous: 'If my passion change not shortly, God forbid it should be otherwise.' How poorly this spoiled favourite of fortune is endowed with energy, endurance, and strength of character is evident all too soon. I refer to the interlude of the masked ball, which is introduced to prepare us in some measure for the catastrophe. Don Pedro has but just discussed Claudio's suit with Claudio, in whose breast there has been no suspicion of treachery on the part of Don Pedro, and yet a clumsy slander by a villain suffices to fill his proudly-swelling little heart with vacillating doubt, to change gratitude and confiding devotion to his generous patron into desperate distrust. And look what depth of worldly wisdom the first shadow of disappointment extorts from this petted darling of fortune [II, i, 168–175]. Such is the result of this profound wisdom. Without an attempt to see for himself, without an effort to recover what seems lost, his love and his friend are instantly given up. And the equally clumsy slanderers find him equally fickle. Verily the commonest regard for a blameless lady,—let alone the love of a happy bridegroom for so dainty a presentment of the charm and freshness of maidenhood as the Poet gives us in Hero,—should have prompted him to receive with the greatest caution any accusation on the part of the sullen malcontent, who has but just become reconciled with the prince. . . . A silly farce enacted in the darkness of night by a low villain and a waiting maid, is sufficient proof in the blinded eyes of this hot-head to condemn the first lady in Messina, a model of propriety, and his own betrothed. . . . And the way in which he shows his regained composure, and his subsequent repentance is scarcely more to his credit. What in the world are we to think of a man, who after such terrible experiences, feels the need of amusement, and incites a friend to jest to drive away his *high-proof* melancholy? What sort of a sense of honour is that which permits a man in the very height of his grief for the death,—not to say murder,—of his falsely-slandered bride, to declare himself ready for another marriage to be arranged by the outraged father?

All these, to speak mildly, unattractive features,—certainly not qualified to command esteem,—are part of Claudio's character; indeed the Poet was obliged thus to endow him if the plot in its developement was to be probable, or even conceivable. All the more admirable is the art with which Shakespeare has contrived, without in the least falsifying or weakening the effect of these disagreeable traits in detail, essentially to modify the painful impression of the whole play. It is precisely the complete personality of the fickle Count with its affluence of vitality, which necessarily creates an extenuating perspective for his conduct as a whole. The worst aberrations become tolerable as soon as the observer can detect, in their source, the soil favourable for their developement. Here it is youth, endowed with unusual vitality, but totally inexperienced, and spoiled by fortune, that pleads for forbearance, and where could a better advocate for transgression be found? Claudio is first presented to us as a young hero, 'doing the feats of a lion in the figure of a lamb.' The rays of princely favour, and of the future favour of women, each in itself strong enough to melt much harder stuff, are the fiercest tests for the ductile metal of his yet unformed character. If flaws appear,—very ugly flaws,—the better, honester metal beneath cannot but be perceived. Above all, this youth with his lack of experience of good, is equally a stranger in the school of vice. Claudio is vain, arrogant, inconsiderate, and fickle, but he is never vulgar; the canker of debauchery has not eaten away his bloom. How admirable is his reception of Benedick's banter when he is brooding over the suspected treachery of his princely friend. Not a word of remonstrance does his provoking comrade extort from him. I cannot understand how commentators, otherwise sensible enough, can attach to the bitter, pregnant words: 'I wish him joy of her' the same significance in all seriousness lent them by Benedick in jest: 'So they sell bullocks.' One must certainly be long past all experience of the *grande passion* not to perceive the intense bitterness that manly pride, and love betrayed, can express in such a congratulation. That the extravagance of youthful arrogance and of a passionate temperament has unhinged for a time an essentially noble nature is shown in Claudio's behaviour toward the angry old Leonato. . . . This delicate sense of honour, with the conscious vitality of youth, has given a certain license to the Count's errors and follies before the tribunal of poetic justice, which has not been without result, if we attach any weight to the public verdict of three centuries.

1866—E. W. Sievers. From *William Shakespeare*

A renowned German Shakespearean scholar, Eduard Wilhelm Sievers (1820–94) was a professor at the university in Gotha, Germany. In the following text, Sievers argues that the crux to understanding *Much Ado about Nothing* lies in reading the play as a paean on vulnerability and how the vulnerable aspects of an individual's character allow for that person to be altered, completed, manipulated, or fulfilled: "Shakespeare tells us plainly enough: it lies in every human being's temperament, that no self-poise, no steadfastness, can come from vulnerability in some one spot." Sievers sees this vulnerability especially in the actions of Beatrice and Benedick, who give up their steadfast refusal to ever endure love to fulfill their heart's desire and be with each other. Sievers argues that Don Pedro only needs to nudge the two characters toward each other to make them fall in love, indicating, indeed, that this response fulfills some deep-seated need that had previously made them vulnerable, necessitating their shedding of their rough exterior personas before assuming the role of husband and wife.

Four or five years have elapsed since Shakespeare wrote his *Midsummer Night's Dream*, and, in addition to his greatest comedy of this period, *The Merchant of Venice*, he had completed his first two tragedies, *Romeo and Juliet*, and *Hamlet*; we find him now again at odds with human nature, and this time it is our temperament which he makes his target, the vital foundation of our being, upon which the inner world of the spirit rests. The ancient complaint that man, to whatever heights he may attain, must still be vulnerable,—the complaint to which the two most intellectual races of the world, the Greek, and the Indo-Germanic, have given such marvellously accordant expression in Achilles and Siegfried, we now hear from Shakespeare in *Much Ado about Nothing*, wherein he attacks human temperament. In it he recognizes the Achilles-heel of mankind, that which, by whatever name it may be called, makes all vulnerable, dragging down to the sphere of chance, and to finite warfare those who by rights, should soar to divine heights, and partake of divine delights. No human being,—he says in effect,—exists, who cannot be thrown off of his balance if assailed through his temperament, as there has never been a philosopher, 'That could endure the toothache patiently. However they have writ the style of gods And made a push at chance and sufferance.' This is the point of view from which Shakespeare composed his comedy, *Much Ado about Nothing*. . . .

Thus it is with Benedick and immediately afterward with Beatrice. Both fall into the trap set for them, or to quote Hero, [sic] 'devour greedily the treacherous bait.' But where lies the reason for this rapid and total rout of these two persons, who are, to all appearance, so steadfast and invulnerable? Shakespeare tells us plainly enough: it lies in every human being's temperament, that no self-poise, no steadfastness, can save from vulnerability in some one spot. If his temperament be normal, and not degenerate, man must always *be susceptible to the joy of being beloved*. Beatrice and Benedick make shipwreck upon this characteristic of human personality; it is the corner-stone of Don Pedro's *treacherous* scheme which causes them to belie their former selves, a scheme devised with extreme subtlety and knowledge of mankind. It is most interesting to note the lever which Don Pedro employs to put in motion this characteristic. We here meet with a profound psychological conception, one which can be traced in subtle windings throughout the play, making it a remarkable contrast to the *Midsummer Night's Dream*, in which Shakespeare influences his characters through the *eye*; in *Much Ado about Nothing* he does it through the *ear*. When we speak of possessing a man's ear it is equivalent to saying that we have him, himself, that we control him, and modern psychology recognizes the profound mental significance of the ear. It is this significance that Shakespeare illustrates here for the first time in Benedick and Beatrice.

Let us study Don Pedro's tactics more closely still. How does he contrive to influence the antagonistic personalities of the twain, and, although their attitude hitherto has been almost hostile, to make lovers of them? He contrives it by forcing them to *overhear*. By this one stroke of Art, at the very outset, he robs them of all their peculiar advantages. Their wit, their readiness of tongue, all their mental dexterity, and volubility, in short every offensive and defensive weapon of which they have hitherto made use to ward off the danger of any deep impression, is useless to them; they are condemned to complete, absolute *passivity*, forced, contrary to all their use and wont, to play the part of silent listeners. . . .

As the result of our study, the view of mankind which Shakespeare illustrates in this play may be summed up thus: Man, in spite of all his boast of freedom and independence, is but the impotent creature of his temperament,—this is the force that controls his personality, and its developement; in accord with this view, while on one hand there must be no more talk of freedom of will, and self-mastery, on the other there needs only a certain temperament to force us to succumb to evil. . . .

Of course Dogberry is somewhat vain; in fact he is tenderly in love with himself! and hitherto no one has ventured to disturb his self-complacency. But on a sudden he hears a rascal call him an ass, and in an instant he is as if metamorphosed, his calm self-satisfaction is overthrown, and he, who until now has been entirely peaceable, invokes the majesty of the law to bear witness that he *is* an ass;—now what is it that makes him so sensitive to this insult, if it be not his unassailable conviction of the inviolability of human individuality which he represents so solemnly, and whence he derives *pathos*, in the fullest sense of the word?

———ⁱⁱⁱ⁔⁔⁔⁔ ———⁔⁔⁔⁔ ———⁔⁔⁔⁔———

1868—Henry Giles. From *Human Life of Shakespeare*

Henry Giles (1809-1882) was an English Unitarian minister and well-known orator. After moving to the United States in 1840, Giles penned several volumes of literary criticism, including the *Human Life of Shakespeare*. In comparing Beatrice to the rest of Shakespeare's comedic women, Giles argues that Beatrice is "*the* wit": "she is resistless in the sphere of the ridiculous; and there is nothing that she cannot place within that sphere." He also writes of Dogberry, another "wit" in the play, speculating that only an ample figure could hide a man so full of "tranquil self-consequence."

As with many of the author's plays, a part of the plot and story of *Much Ado* was borrowed. But the same matter had been so often borrowed before, and run into so many variations, that we cannot affirm with certainty to what source Shakespeare was immediately indebted. Mrs. Lenox, an uncommonly deep person, instructs us that the Poet here "borrowed just enough to show his poverty of invention, and added enough to prove his want of judgment"; a piece of criticism so choice and happy, that it ought by all means to be kept alive; though it is indeed just possible that the Poet can better afford to have such things said of him than the sayer can to have them repeated.

So much of the story as relates to Hero, Claudio, and John, bears a strong resemblance to the tale of Ariodante and Ginevra in Ariosto's *Orlando Furioso*. The Princess Ginevra, the heroine of the tale, rejects the love-suit of Duke Polinesso, and pledges her hand to Ariodante. Thereupon Polinesso engages her attendant Dalinda to personate the Princess on a balcony by moonlight, while he ascends to her chamber by a ladder of ropes; Ariodante being by previous arrangement stationed near the spot, so as to witness the supposed infidelity of his betrothed. This brings on a false charge against Ginevra, who is doomed to die unless within a month a true knight comes to do battle for her honour. Ariodante betakes himself to flight, and is reported to have perished. Polinesso now appears secure in his treachery. But Dalinda, seized with remorse for her part in the affair, and flying from her guilty paramour, meets with Rinaldo, and declares to him the truth. Then comes on the fight, in which Polinesso is slain by the champion of innocence; which done, the lover reappears, to be made happy with his Princess.

Here, of course, the wicked Duke answers to the John of the play. But there is this important difference, that the motive of the former in vilifying the lady is to drive away her lover, that he may have her to himself; whereas the latter acts from a spontaneous malignity of temper, that takes a sort of disinterested pleasure in blasting the happiness of others.

A translation, by Peter Beverly, of the part of Ariosto's poem which contains this tale, was licensed for the press in 1565; and Warton says it was reprinted in 1600. And an English version of the whole poem, by Sir John Harrington, came out in 1591; but the play discovers no special marks of borrowing from this source. And indeed the fixing of any obligations in this quarter is the more difficult, inasmuch as the matter seems to have been borrowed by Ariosto himself. For the story of a lady betrayed to peril and disgrace by the personation of her waiting-woman was an old European tradition; it has been traced to Spain; and Ariosto interwove it with the adventures of Rinaldo, as yielding an apt occasion for his chivalrous heroism. Neither does the play show any traces of obligation to Spenser, who wrought the same tale into the variegated structure of his great poem. The story of Phedon, relating the treachery of his false friend Philemon, is in Book ii., canto 4, of the *Faerie Queene*; which Book was first published in 1590.

The connection between the play and one of Bandello's novels is much more evident, from the close similarity both of incidents and of names. Fenicia, the daughter of Lionato, a gentleman of Messina, is betrothed to Timbreo de Cardona, a friend of Piero d'Arragona. Girondo, a disappointed lover of the lady, goes to work to prevent the marriage. He insinuates to Timbreo that she is disloyal, and then to make good the charge arranges to have his own hired servant in the dress of a gentleman ascend a ladder and enter the house of Lionato at night, Timbreo being placed so as to witness the proceeding. The next morning Timbreo accuses the lady to her father, and rejects the alliance. Fenicia sinks down in a swoon; a dangerous illness follows; and, to prevent the shame of her alleged trespass, Lionato has it given out that she is dead, and a public funeral is held in confirmation of that report. Thereupon Girondo becomes so harrowed with remorse, that he confesses his villainy to Timbreo, and they both throw themselves on the mercy of the lady's family. Timbreo is easily forgiven, and the reconciliation is soon followed by the discovery that the lady is still alive, and by the marriage of the parties. Here the only particular wherein the play differs from the novel, and agrees with Ariosto's plan of the story, is, that the lady's waiting-woman personates her mistress when the villain scales her chamber-window.

It does not well appear how the Poet could have come to a knowledge of Bandello's novel, unless through the original; no translation of that time having been preserved. But the Italian was then the most generally-studied language in Europe; educated Englishmen were probably quite as apt to be familiar with it as they are with the French in our day; Shakespeare, at the time of writing this play, was thirty-five years old; and we have other indications that he knew enough of Italian to be able to read such a story as Bandello's in that language.

The foregoing account may serve to show, what is equally plain in many other cases, that Shakespeare preferred, for the material of his plots, such stories as were most commonly known, that he might have some tie of popular association and interest to work in aid of his purpose. It is to be observed, further, that the parts of Benedick and Beatrice, of Dogberry and Verges, and of several other persons, are altogether original with him; so that he stands responsible for all the wit and humour, and for nearly all the character, of the play. Then too, as is usual with him, the added portions are so made to knit in with the borrowed matter by mutual participation and interaction as to give a new life and meaning to the whole.

So that in this case, as in others, we have the soul of originality consisting in something far deeper and more essential than any mere sorting or linking of incidents so as to form an attractive story. The vital workings of nature in the development of individual character,—it is on these, and not on any thing so superficial or mechanical as a mere framework of incident, that the real life of the piece depends. On this point I probably cannot do better than by quoting the following remarks from Coleridge:

"The interest in the plot is on account of the characters, not *vice versa*, as in almost all other writers: the plot is a mere canvas, and no more. Take away from *Much Ado about Nothing* all that is not indispensable to the plot, either as having little to do with it, or, like Dogberry and his comrades, forced into the service, when any other less ingeniously-absurd watchmen and night-constables would have answered the mere necessities of the action; take away Benedick, Beatrice, Dogberry, and the reaction of the former on the character of Hero,—and what will remain? In other writers the main agent of the plot is always the prominent character: John is the main-spring of the plot in this play; but he is merely shown, and then withdrawn."

The style and diction of this play has little that calls for special remark. In this respect the workmanship is of about the same cast and grain with that of *As You Like It*; sustained and equal; easy, natural, and modest in dress and bearing; everywhere alive indeed with the exhilarations of wit or humour or poetry, but without the laboured smoothness of the Poet's earlier plays, or the penetrating energy and quick, sinewy movement of his later ones. Compared with some of its predecessors, the play shows a decided growth in what may be termed virility of mind: a wider scope, a higher reach, a firmer grasp, have been attained: the Poet has come to read Nature less through "the spectacles of books," and does not hesitate to meet her face to face, and to trust and try himself alone with her. The result of all which appears in a greater freshness and reality of delineation. Here the persons have nothing of a dim, equivocal hearsay air about them, such as marks in some measure his earlier efforts in comedy. The characters indeed are not pitched in so high a key, nor conceived in so much breadth and vigour, as in several of the plays written at earlier dates: the plan of the work did not require this, or even admit of it; nevertheless the workmanship on the whole discovers more ripeness of art and faculty than even in *The Merchant of Venice*.

One of the Poet's methods was, apparently, first to mark out or else to adopt a given course of action, and then to conceive and work out his characters accordingly, making them such as would naturally cohere with and sustain the action, so that we feel an inward, vital, and essential relation between what they are and what they do. Thus there is nothing arbitrary or mechanical in the sorting together of persons and actions: the two stand together under a living law of human transpiration, instead of being gathered into a mere formal and outward juxtaposition. That is to say, the persons act so because they *are* so, and not because the author *willed* to put them through such a course of action: what comes from them is truly rooted in them, and is *generated* vitally out of the nature within them; so that their deeds are the veritable pulsations of their hearts. And so it is in this play. The course of action, as we have seen, was partly borrowed. But there was no borrowing in the characteristic matter. The personal figures in the old tale are in themselves unmeaning and characterless. The actions ascribed to them have no ground or reason in any thing that they are: what they do, or rather *seem* to do,—for there is no real doing in the case,—proceeds not at all from their own natures or wills, but purely because the author chose to have it so. So that the persons and incidents are to all intents and purposes put together arbitrarily, and not under any vital law of human nature. Any other set of actions might just as well be tacked on to the same persons; any other persons might as well be put through the same course of action. This merely outward and formal connection between the incidents and characters holds generally in the old tales from which Shakespeare borrowed his plots; while in his workmanship the connection becomes inherent and essential; there being indeed no difference in this respect, whether he first conceives the characters, and then draws out their actions, or whether he first plans a course of action, and then shapes the characters from which it is to proceed.

   Much Ado has a large variety of interest, now running into grotesque drollery, now bordering upon the sphere of tragic elevation, now revelling in the most sparkling brilliancy. The play indeed is rightly named: we have several nothings, each in its turn occasioning a deal of stir and perturbation: yet there is so much of real flavour and spirit stirred out into effect, that the littleness of the occasions is scarcely felt or observed; the thoughts being far more drawn to the persons who make the much ado than to the nothing about which the much ado is made. The excellencies, however, both of plot and character, are rather of the striking sort, involving little of the hidden or retiring beauty which shows just enough on the surface to invite a diligent search, and then enriches the seeker with generous returns. Accordingly the play has always been very effective on the stage; the points and situations being so shaped and ordered that, with fair acting, they tell at once upon an average audience; while at the same time there is enough of solid substance beneath to justify and support the first impression; so that the stage-effect is withal legitimate and sound as well as quick and taking.

   The characters of Hero and Claudio, though reasonably engaging in their simplicity and uprightness, offer no very salient points, and are indeed nowise extraordinary. It cannot quite be said that one "sees no more in them than in the ordinary of Nature's sale-work"; nevertheless they derive their interest mainly from the events that befall them; the reverse of which is generally true in Shakespeare's delineations. Perhaps we may justly say that, had the course of love run smooth with them, its voice, even if audible, had been hardly worth the hearing.

Hero is indeed kind, amiable, and discreet in her behaviour and temper: she has just that air, nay, rather just that soul of bland and modest quietness which makes the unobtrusive but enduring charm of home, such as I have seen in many a priestess of the domestic shrine; and this fitly marks her out as the centre of silent or unemphatic interest in her father's household. She is always thoughtful, never voluble; and when she speaks, there is no sting or sharpness in her tongue: she is even proud of her brilliant cousin, yet not at all emulous of her brilliancy; keenly relishes her popping and sometimes caustic wit, but covets no such gift for herself, and even shrinks from the laughing attention it wins. As Hero is altogether gentle and womanly in her ways, so she offers a sweet and inviting nestling-place for the fireside affections. The soft down of her disposition makes an admirable contrast to the bristling and emphatic yet genuine plumage of Beatrice; and there is something very pathetic and touching in her situation when she is stricken down in mute agony by the tongue of slander; while the "blushing apparitions" in her face, and the lightning in her eyes, tell us that her stillness of tongue proceeds from any thing but weakness of nature, or want of spirit. Her well-governed intelligence is aptly displayed in the part she bears in the stratagem for taming Beatrice to the gentler pace of love, and in the considerate forbearance which abstains from teasing words after the stratagem has done its work.

Claudio is both a lighter-timbered and a looser-built vessel than Hero; rather credulous, unstable, inconstant, and very much the sport of slight and trivial occasions. A very small matter suffices to upset him, though, to be sure, he is apt enough to be set right again. All this, no doubt, is partly owing to his youth and inexperience; but in truth his character is mainly that of a brave and clever upstart, somewhat intoxicated with sudden success, and not a little puffed with vanity of the Prince's favour. Notwithstanding John's ingrained, habitual, and well-known malice, he is ready to go it blind whenever John sees fit to try his art upon him; and even after he has been duped into one strain of petulant folly by his trick, and has found out the falsehood of it, he is still just as open to a second and worse duping. All this may indeed pass as indicating no more in his case than the levity of a rather pampered and over-sensitive self-love. In his unreflective and headlong techiness, he fires up at the least hint that but seems to touch his honour, without pausing, or deigning to observe the plainest conditions of a fair and prudent judgment.

But, after all the allowance that can be made on this score, it is still no little impeachment of his temper, or his understanding, that he should lend his ear to the poisonous breathings of one whose spirits are so well known to "toil in frame of villainies." As to his rash and overwrought scheme of revenge for Hero's imputed sin, his best excuse therein is, that the light-minded Prince, who is indeed such another, goes along with him; while it is somewhat doubtful whether the patron or the favourite is more at fault in thus suffering artful malice to "pull the wool over his eyes." Claudio's finical and foppish attention to dress, so amusingly ridiculed by Benedick, is a well-conceived trait of his character; as it naturally hints that his quest of the lady grows more from his seeing the advantage of the match than from any deep heart-interest in her person. And his being sprung into such an unreasonable fit of jealousy towards the Prince at the masquerade is another good instance of the Poet's skill and care in small matters. It makes an apt preparation for the far more serious blunder upon which the main part of the action turns. A piece of conduct which the circumstances do not explain is at once explained by thus disclosing a certain irritable levity in the subject. On much the same ground we can also account very well for his sudden running into a match which at the best looks more like a freak of fancy than a resolution of love, while the same suddenness on the side of the more calm, discreet, and patient Hero is accounted for by the strong solicitation of the Prince and the prompt concurrence of her father. But even if Claudio's faults and blunders were greater than they are, still his behaviour at the last were enough to prove a real and sound basis of manhood in him. The clean taking-down of his vanity and self-love, by the exposure of the poor cheats which had so easily caught him, brings out the true staple of his character. When he is made to feel that on himself alone falls the blame and the guilt which he had been so eager to revenge on others, then his sense of honour acts in a right noble style, prompting him to avenge sternly on himself the wrong and the injury he has done to the gentle Hero and her kindred.

Critics have unnecessarily found fault with the Poet for the character of John, as if it lay without the proper circumference of truth and nature. They would prefer, apparently, the more commonplace character of a disappointed rival in love, whose guilt might be explained away into a pressure of violent motives. But Shakespeare saw deeper into human nature. And perhaps his wisest departure from the old story is in making John a morose, sullen, ill-conditioned rascal, whose innate malice renders the joy of others a pain, and the pain of others a joy, to him. The wanton and unprovoked doing of mischief is the natural luxury and pastime of such envious spirits as he is. To be sure, he assigns as his reason for plotting to blast Claudio's happiness, that the "young start-up hath all the glory of my overthrow"; but then he also adds, "If I can cross him any way, I bless myself every way"; which shows his true motive-spring to be a kind of envy-sickness. For this cause, any thing that will serve as a platform "to build mischief on" is grateful to him. He thus exemplifies in a small figure the same spontaneous malice which towers to such a stupendous height of wickedness in Iago. We may well reluct to believe in the reality of such characters; but, unhappily, human life discovers too many plots and doings that cannot be otherwise accounted for; nor need we go far to learn that men may "spin motives out of their own bowels." In pursuance of this idea, the Poet takes care to let us know that, in John's account, the having his sour and spiteful temper tied up under a pledge of fair and kindly behaviour is to be "trusted with a muzzle, and enfranchised with a clog"; that is, he thinks himself robbed of freedom when he is not allowed to bite.

Ulrici, regarding the play as setting forth the contrast between life as it is in itself and as it seems to those engaged in its struggles, looks upon Dogberry as embodying the whole idea of the piece. And, sure enough, the impressive insignificance of this man's action to the lookers-on is only equalled by its stuffed importance to himself: when he is really most absurd and ridiculous, then it is precisely that he feels most confident and grand; the irony that is rarefied into wit and poetry in others being thus condensed into broad humour and drollery in him. The German critic is not quite right however in thinking that his blundering garrulity brings to light the infernal plot; as it rather operates to keep that plot in the dark: he is too fond of hearing himself talk to make known what he has to say, in time to prevent the evil; and amidst his tumblings of conceit the truth leaks out at last rather in spite of him than in consequence of any thing he does. Dogberry and his "neighbour Verges" are caricatures; but such as Shakespeare alone of English writers has had a heart to conceive and a hand to delineate; though perhaps Sir Walter comes near enough to him in that line to be named in the same sentence. And how bland, how benignant, how genial, how human-hearted, these caricatures are! as if the Poet felt the persons, with all their grotesque oddities, to be his own veritable flesh-and-blood kindred. There is no contempt, no mockery here; nothing that ministers an atom of food to any unbenevolent emotion: the subjects are made delicious as well as laughable; and delicious withal through the best and kindliest feelings of our nature. The Poet's sporting with them is the free, loving, whole-hearted play of a truly great, generous, simple, child-like soul. Compared to these genuine offspring of undeflowered genius, the ill-natured and cynical caricatures in which Dickens, for example, so often and so tediously indulges, seem the workmanship of quite another species of being. The part of Dogberry was often attempted to be imitated by other dramatists of Shakespeare's time; which shows it to have a decided hit on the stage. And indeed there is no resisting the delectable humour of it: but then the thing is utterly inimitable; Shakespeare being no less unapproachable in this vein than in such delineations as Shylock and Lear and Cleopatra.

Benedick and Beatrice are much the most telling feature of the play. They have been justly ranked among the stronger and deeper of Shakespeare's minor characters. They are just about the right staple for the higher order of comic delineation; whereas several of the leading persons in what are called the Poet's comedies draw decidedly into the region of the Tragic. The delineation, however, of Benedick and Beatrice stays at all points within the proper sphere of Comedy. Both are gifted with a very piercing, pungent, and voluble wit; and pride of wit is with both a specially-prominent trait; in fact, it appears to be on all ordinary occasions their main actuating principle. The rare entertainment which others have from their displays in this kind has naturally made them quite conscious of their gift; and this consciousness has not less naturally led them to make it a matter of some pride. They study it and rely on it a good deal as their title or passport to approval and favour. Hence a habit of flouting and raillery has somewhat usurped the outside of their characters, insomuch as to keep their better qualities rather in the background, and even to obstruct seriously the outcome of what is best in them.

Whether for force of understanding or for solid worth of character, Benedick is vastly superior both to Claudio and to the Prince. He is really a very wise and noble fellow; of a healthy and penetrating intelligence, and with a sound underpinning of earnest and true feeling; as appears when the course of the action surprises or inspires him out of his pride of brilliancy. When a grave occasion comes, his superficial habit of jesting is at once postponed, and the choicer parts of manhood promptly assert themselves in clear and handsome action. We are thus given to know that, however the witty and waggish companion or make-sport may have got the ascendancy in him, still he is of an inward composition to forget it as soon as the cause of wronged and suffering virtue or innocence gives him a manly and generous part to perform. And when the blameless and gentle Hero is smitten down with cruel falsehood, and even her father is convinced of her guilt, he is the first to suspect that "the practice of it lies in John the bastard." With his just faith in the honour of the Prince and of Claudio, his quick judgment and native sagacity forthwith hit upon the right clew to the mystery. Much the same, all through, is to be said of Beatrice; who approves herself a thoroughly brave and generous character. The swiftness and brilliancy of wit upon which she so much prides herself are at once forgotten in resentment and vindication of her injured kinswoman. She becomes somewhat furious indeed, but it is a noble and righteous fury,—the fury of kindled strength too, and not of mere irritability, or of a passionate temper.

As pride of wit bears a main part in shaping the ordinary conduct of these persons; so the Poet aptly represents them as being specially piqued at what pinches or touches them in that point. Thus, in their wit-skirmish at the masquerade, what sticks most in Benedick is the being described as "the Prince's jester," and the hearing it said that, if his jests are "not marked, or not laughed at," it "strikes him into melancholy"; while, on the other side, Beatrice is equally stung at being told that "she had her good wit out of *The Hundred Merry Tales*." Their keen sensitiveness to whatever implies any depreciation or contempt of their faculty in this kind is exceedingly well conceived. Withal it shows, I think, that jesting, after all, is more a matter of art with them than of character.

As might be expected, the good repute of Benedick and Beatrice has been not a little perilled, not to say damaged, by their redundancy of wit. But it is the ordinary lot of persons so witty as they to suffer under the misconstructions of prejudice or partial acquaintance. Their very sparkling seems to augment the difficulty of coming to a true knowledge of them. How dangerous it is to be so gifted that way, may be seen by the impression these persons have had the ill luck to make on one whose good opinion is so desirable as Campbell's. "During one half of the play," says he, "we have a disagreeable female character in Beatrice. Her portrait, I may be told, is deeply drawn and minutely finished. It is; and so is that of Benedick, who is entirely her counterpart, except that he is less disagreeable." And again he speaks of Beatrice as an "odious woman." I am right sorry that so tasteful and genial a critic should have such hard thoughts of the lady. In support of his opinion he quotes Hero's speech, "Disdain and scorn ride sparkling in her eyes," &c.; but he seems to forget that these words are spoken with the intent that Beatrice shall hear them, and at the same time think she overhears them; that is, not as being true, but as being suited to a certain end, and as having just enough of truth to be effective for that end. And the effect which the speech has on Beatrice proves that it is not true as regards her character, however good it may be for the speaker's purpose. To the same end, the Prince, Claudio, and Leonato speak as much the other way, when they know Benedick is overhearing them; and what is there said in her favour is just a fair offset to what was before said against her. But indeed it is plain enough that any thing thus spoken really for the ear of the subject, yet seemingly in confidence to another person, ought not to be received in evidence against her.

But the critic's disparaging thoughts in this case are well accounted for in what himself had unhappily witnessed. "I once knew such a pair," says he; "the lady was a perfect Beatrice: she railed hypocritically at wedlock before her marriage, and with bitter sincerity after it. She and her Benedick now live apart, but with entire reciprocity of sentiments; each devoutly wishing that the other may soon pass into a better world." So that the writer's strong dislike of Beatrice is a most pregnant testimony to the Poet's truth of delineation; inasmuch as it shows how our views of his characters, as of those in real life, depend less perhaps on what they are in themselves than on our own peculiar associations. Nature's and Shakespeare's men and women seem very different to different persons, and even to the same persons at different times. Regarded, therefore, in this light, the censure of the lady infers such a tribute to the Poet, that I half suspect the author meant it as such. In reference to the subject, however, my judgment goes much rather with that of other critics: That in the unamiable passages of their deportment Benedick and Beatrice are playing a part; that their playing is rather to conceal than to disclose their real feelings; that it is the very strength of their feelings which puts them upon this mode of disguise; and that the pointing of their raillery so much against each other is itself proof of a deep and growing mutual interest: though it must be confessed that the ability to play so well, and in that kind, is a great temptation to carry it to excess, or to use it where it may cause something else than mirth. This it is that justifies the repetition of the stratagem for drawing on a match between them; the same process being needed in both cases in order "to get rid of their reciprocal disguises, and make them straightforward and in earnest." And so the effect of the stratagem is to begin the unmasking which is so thoroughly completed by the wrongs and sufferings of Hero: they are thus disciplined out of their playing, and made to show themselves as they are: before we saw their art; now we see their virtue,—the real backbone of their characters; and it becomes manifest enough that, with all their superficial levity and caustic sportiveness, they yet have hearts rightly framed for the serious duties and interests of life.

It is very considerable, also, how their peculiar cast of self-love and their pride of wit are adroitly worked upon in the execution of the scheme for bringing them together. Both are deeply mortified at overhearing how they are blamed for their addiction to flouting, and at the same time both are highly flattered in being made each to believe that the other is secretly dying of love, and that the other is kept from showing the truth by dread of mocks and gibes. As they are both professed heretics on the score of love and marriage, so both are tamed out of their heresy in the glad persuasion that they have each proved too much for the other's pride of wit, and have each converted the other to the true faith. But indeed that heresy was all along feigned as a refuge from merry persecutions; and the virtue of the thing is, that in the belief that they have each conquered the other's assumed fastidiousness, they each lay aside their own. The case involves a highly curious interplay of various motives on either side; and it is not easy to say whether vanity or generosity, the self-regarding or the self-forgetting emotions, are uppermost in the process.

The wit of these two persons, though seeming at first view much the same, is very nicely discriminated. Beatrice, intelligent as she is, has little of reflection in her wit; but throws it off in rapid flashes whenever any object ministers a spark to her fancy. Though of the most piercing keenness and the most exquisite aptness, there is no ill-nature about it; it stings indeed, but does not poison. The offspring merely of the moment and the occasion, it catches the apprehension, but quickly slides from the memory. Its agility is infinite; wherever it may be, the instant one goes to put his hand upon it, he is sure to find it or feel it somewhere else. The wit of Benedick, on the other hand, springs more from reflection, and grows with the growth of thought. With all the pungency, and nearly all the pleasantry of hers, it has less of spontaneous volubility. Hence in their skirmishes she always gets the better of him; hitting him so swiftly, and in so many spots, as to bewilder his aim. But he makes ample amends when out of her presence, trundling off jests in whole paragraphs. In short, if his wit be slower, it is also stronger than hers: not so agile of movement, more weighty in matter, it shines less, but burns more; and as it springs much less out of the occasion, so it bears repeating much better. The effect of the serious events in bringing these persons to an armistice of wit is a happy stroke of art; and perhaps some such thing was necessary, to prevent the impression of their being jesters by trade. It proves at least that Beatrice is a witty woman, and not a mere female wit. To be sure, she is rather spicy than sweet; but then there is a kind of sweetness in spice,—especially such spice as hers.

I have already referred to the apt naming of this play. The general view of life which it presents answers well to the title. The persons do indeed make or have *much ado*; but all the while to us who are in the secret, and ultimately to them also, all this much ado is plainly *about nothing*. Which is but a common difference in the aspect of things as they appear to the spectators and the partakers; it needs but an average experience to discover that real life is full of just such passages: what troubled and worried us yesterday made others laugh then, and makes us laugh to-day: what we fret or grieve at in the progress, we still smile and make merry over in the result.

1873—Roderich Benedix. From *Die Shakespearomanie*

Julius Roderich Benedix (1811–73) was a prominent German playwright and musical librettist best known for his lighthearted farces. His work *Die Shakespearomanie*, which criticizes the fawning adoration Shakespeare often received in the Victorian era, was published shortly after Benedix's death. In the following selection, Benedix begins by arguing that "here is no stuff for a comedy," suggesting that the plight of Hero in *Much Ado about Nothing* is too tragic to be taken lightly. Benedix even laments that Hero is forced, in the end, to marry Claudio, noting that most of the characters are lacking in substantial ways: Claudio is a "vain coxcomb, with no will of his own"; Don Pedro is a gossip who "neither attempts nor achieves anything." Benedix argues the same for Leonato and suggests that his brother, Antonio, is an old bore. The villains Benedix likewise finds "insipid" and "uninteresting" and calls the entire lot "poetically worthless." The plot, too, Benedix finds fault with, suggesting that its swift resolution is ridiculous and unbelievable. It is only Beatrice and Benedick that Benedix praises; like many critics of his day, Benedix believes that Beatrice and Benedick are the saving graces of the work and one of Shakespeare's more worthy pairings.

Here is no stuff for a comedy. A girl slandered and ill-treated to an unutterable extent is not an object to awaken merriment. And it is degrading that she should finally, without hesitation, marry her slanderer.

Consider the persons concerned. Here is Claudio, a vain coxcomb, with no will of his own. What can poor Hero expect from a marriage with such a wretch? Here is the prince, pervading the entire play, gossipping interminably, and never arousing in us the faintest sympathy. He neither attempts nor achieves anything. Here is the governor, of whom the same may be said. To swell the crowd of bores he has a brother, Antonio, so old that he 'waggles his head' and has 'dry hands.' Here is the rascally slanderer, a rascal only because the poet chooses him to be one; he himself has no reason for it. Here are his two accomplices, rascals also, but who, when they are caught and questioned, confess everything with amiable frankness. And there are several waiting maids running about through the play. All these persons are poetically worthless, for they are uninteresting, nay, well-nigh tiresome. We cannot characterize them, unless their having no character at all will serve our turn. They are all insipid.

Essentially different are the two leading characters; they alone, Benedick and Beatrice, make it possible to sit through the play; they alone excite interest and give pleasure. Beatrice is Hero's cousin, a rather strong, audacious, girlish creature, who delights in inveighing against matrimony. Thus she pleases us intellectually, and she appeals to our hearts because she is the only person who takes her cousin's part, and enters the lists in her defence. Therefore she ranks far above all the other personages of the play; she is an admirable creation. Benedick is her companion part. He too abuses love and matrimony, but is, nevertheless, a fine, honest fellow. . . . Undeniably the perpetual pyrotechnic display of sneering and jeering wit that goes on between these two is somewhat spun out; puns, quibbles, plays upon words are very richly profuse, nevertheless some of the conceits are good, and the whole is fresh and vivid. This play upon words, be it noted, is characteristic of all the personages in the play, and at times becomes insufferable. The piece could never be put upon our stage unabbreviated. There is a third group in the play formed by the foolish Watch, whose stupidity unmasks the slander. Those belonging to this group are caricatures, and, like all caricatures, are really amusing. But there is rather too much of them, for they appear in four scenes. The Poet has, perhaps, provided too much for even the tough nerves of the English public. As regards the structure of the play, the combination of incidents does not lead to any fitting result. The principal event is, if not tragic, at least grave, and agitating. It should have a natural result. There should have been serious atonement for the malicious and wanton insult offered to Hero by Don Pedro and Claudio. But the play must be a comedy, and consequently there is universal reconciliation in the twinkling of an eye. It is inexcusable that a deep-laid dramatic plot should come to nothing; that a dramatic cause should produce no dramatic effect. The scandalous interruption of the marriage in the fourth Act results only in its postponement to the fifth Act.

1877—F. J. Furnivall. From the introduction to *The Leopold Shakespeare*

A well-known man of letters, Frederick James Furnivall (1825–1910) was one of the co-founders and co-creators of the *Oxford English Dictionary*. Furnivall was also a well-regarded literary scholar, famous for his critical editions of medieval and Renaissance texts. Noting that *Much Ado about Nothing* falls directly in the middle of seven significant Shakespearean comedies, Furnivall here examines what the play borrows from, redacts, or owes its earlier predecessors (*Merchant of Venice, Taming of the Shrew,* and *Merry Wives of Windsor*) and how it informs those works yet to come (*As You Like It, Twelfth Night,* and *All's Well That Ends Well.*)

This central comedy of Shakspere's middle happiest time (the *Merchant, Shrew, Merry Wives* went before, *As You Like It, Twelfth Night, All's Well* followed after) is full of interest, as, on the one side, gathering into itself and developing so much of his work lying near it, and, on the other side, stretching one hand to his earliest genuine work, another to his latest complete one. *First.* Of the links with the other plays near it, we may note Benedick's and Beatrice's loving one another 'no more than reason,' with Slender's so loving Anne Page, I will do as it shall become one that would do 'reason.' *Second.* Dogberry, Verges, and the Watch, miscalling names, with Slender's 'decrease' and 'dissolutely,' etc., in *The Merry Wives. Third.* As to *The Shrew,* isn't *Much Ado* in a certain sense a double taming of the shrew, only here each tames himself and herself by the answer of his and her richer, nobler nature, to an overheard appeal to its better feelings, an unseen showing of where its poor, narrow, shrewishness was leading it? Dogberry's conceit, and Verges's belief in him, are like Bottom's in the *Midsummer Night's Dream,* and his companions' belief in him; while *The Merchant's* scene between Launcelot Gobbo and his father and Bassanio is developed in that of Dogberry and Verges with Leonato in *Much Ado.* Leonato's lament over Hero here, 'grieved I, I had but one,' etc., must be compared with Capulet's complaint about Juliet. Benedick's dress in *Much Ado,* III, ii, is to be compared with the young English baron's in *The Merchant.* Friar Francis's advice that Hero shall be supposed dead for awhile, is like Friar Laurence's advising that Juliet should counterfeit death for forty-two hours. Leonato's refusing to be comforted by any who hadn't suffered equal loss with him is to be compared, on the one hand, with Constance's 'He talks to me that never had a son,' in *King John,* and, on the other, with Macduff's 'He has no children' in *Macbeth.* Hero's caving in under the unjust accusation brought against her is like Ophelia's silence in her interviews with Hamlet, and to be compared with

Desdemona's ill-starred speeches that brought about her death, and the pathetic appeal of Innogen that she was true, and the noble indignation of Hermione against her accusers. Such comparisons as these bring out with irresistible force the growth of Shakspere in spirit and temper as well as words.

Of the reach backward and forward of this play, remember that Benedick and Beatrice are but the development of Berowne and Rosalind in Shakspere's first genuine play, *Love's Labour's Lost*, while Hero is the prototype of Hermione in *Winter's Tale*, Shakspere's last complete drama. Hermione,—'queen, matron, mother,' who, like Hero, unjustly suspected and accused, is declared innocent, and yet for sixteen years suffers seclusion as one dead, with that noble magnanimity and fortitude that distinguish her, and then without a word of reproach to her base and cruel husband, throws herself,—but late a statue of stone, now warm and living,—into his arms. Look at the 'solemn and profound' pathos of that situation, and contrast it with the Hero and Claudio one here, and see how Shakspere has grown from manhood to fuller age, just as when you set the atonement of Aegeon and his family in *The Comedy of Errors* beside the reunion of Pericles, his daughter, and wife, in *Pericles*, you'll see the difference between youth and age, between the First and Fourth Periods of Shakspere's work and art. The many likenesses between Benedick and Beatrice and Berowne and Rosalind in *Love's Labour's Lost* are caught at once. We need only dwell on the moral of the earlier play, as Rosalind preaches it at Berowne, the utter worthlessness of wit, the mocking spirit, and the need that the gibing spirit should be choked, thrown away, and remember that the moral is repeated here, in Beatrice's wise and generous words (she, woman-like, instinctively goes to the heart of the matter):—'Stand I condemn'd for pride and scorn so much,' etc.

1880—Algernon Swinburne. From *A Study of Shakespeare*

Algernon Charles Swinburne (1837-1909) was a noted Victorian poet and prose author. Swinburne considered *Much Ado about Nothing* Shakespeare's "most perfect comic masterpiece," emphasizing the work's composition and characters as evidence for such lofty praise.

If it is proverbially impossible to determine by selection the greatest work of Shakespeare, it is easy enough to decide on the date and name of his most perfect comic masterpiece. For absolute power of composition, for faultless balance and blameless rectitude of design, there is unquestionably no creation of his hand that will bear comparison with *Much Ado about Nothing*. The ultimate marriage of Hero and Claudio, on which I have already remarked as in itself a doubtfully desirable consummation, makes no flaw in the dramatic perfection of a piece which could not otherwise have been wound up at all. This was its one inevitable conclusion, if the action were not to come to a tragic end; and a tragic end would here have been as painfully and grossly out of place as is any but a tragic end to the action of *Measure for Measure*. As for Beatrice, she is as perfect a lady, though of a far different age and breeding, as Célimène or Millamant; and a decidedly more perfect woman than could properly or permissibly have trod the stage of Congreve or Molière. She would have disarranged all the dramatic proprieties and harmonies of the one great school of pure comedy. The good fierce outbreak of her high true heart in two swift words,—"kill Claudio,"—would have fluttered the dove-cotes of fashionable drama to some purpose. But Alceste would have taken her to his own.

1884—Heinrich Bulthaupt. From *Dramaturgie der Classiker*

German poet and playwright Heinrich Bulthaupt (1849-1905) trained as a lawyer and worked as a librarian before producing adaptations of Shakespeare's plays in Germany. As Wilhelm Wetz points out in a subsequent excerpt in this section, Bulthaupt is the critic most associated with rebuking Shakespeare for the character of Claudio and his treatment of the defenseless Hero. In a famous essay, excerpted here, Bulthaupt harshly condemns both Claudio and his actions, neither excusing the young man his behavior nor the playwright for ultimately allowing him to marry the woman he so heartlessly slanders. The entire main plot of *Much Ado about Nothing*, involving Hero and Claudio, infuriates Bulthaupt, who only finds redemption for the play in the sunny affair between Beatrice and Benedick. Still, the "grave" action between Hero and Claudio discomfits Bulthaupt greatly, and he laments that Hero ultimately excuses Claudio and that, in act 5, she is still busy defending her honor when her innocence—and Claudio's wrongdoing—have already been firmly established. Bulthaupt relishes Beatrice's description of Claudio's actions and intentions as being full of "unmitigated rancour" and believes that the ending is ultimately too pat and too perfunctory to reach any satisfying conclusion.

Bulthaupt also thoroughly castigates the character of Don John, whom he calls an "ill-natured, bitter, revengeful scoundrel." Though Don John is the obvious villain in the play, many critics have overlooked this figure in favor of discussing more developed characters, partly because, up until the late nineteenth century, Don John's motivations and characterization have been viewed as perfunctory and shallow. Here, Bulthaupt gives Don John the critical attention he deserves, though partly to show how foolish Claudio must have been to be taken in by such an obvious cad. Ultimately, for Bulthaupt, despite the joy he finds in Beatrice and Benedick and the more worthy aspects of the other characters in the play, it is Claudio who most defines and defiles Shakespeare's work in *Much Ado about Nothing*.

Among those of Shakespeare's comedies, which are enacted solely upon earthly soil, *Much Ado about Nothing* would have been one of the finest, the richest, the most charged with colour, had the plot of the play centred only round the two persons from whom it took its original title, *Benedick and Beatrice*. Unfortunately, the gloomy shadow of the grave events that form the secondary action of the play falls upon these two incomparable figures and well-nigh obliterates them. Shakespeare has never more thoroughly dimmed the fresh, sunny impression of a comedy, than in this specimen of his persistent method of blending, in a romantic whole, two plots, one cheerful, and one sad. A worse selection from his fund of old Italian tales he has hardly ever made. If Ariosto's story of *Ariodante and Ginevra* produces a painful impression, enacted as it is in a fanciful world, swarming with monster fish, winged steeds, ogres, fairies, and sorcerers, how much more distressing is the effect of the slander, and its positively flippant, poetic treatment, in the drama, where we see before us the people of whom Ariosto only tells, and with every fanciful accessory lacking.

If we can conceive that Claudio should give credence to the slander against his love,—if we can think possible the conversation between Borachio and the guileless Margaret, which, wisely enough, is not carried on upon the stage, it is inconceivable, and altogether too base for belief that the ardent lover should defame his betrothed in public, at the very altar, thereby producing a most harrowing scene. Had he really loved Hero he would have charged her with her infidelity alone or perhaps in presence of her father only, and would have shown himself overwhelmed with grief, not thirsting for revenge. Instead of which his vile conduct is such as no girl, not even one as gentle as Hero, could forgive. And how she forgives! She herself and her old father, but just now fire and flame, come to the front, and drag again into publicity what, were it even possible, should not be discussed save in the quiet seclusion of home. Silly Claudio, after a little talk, is persuaded to marry Leonato's niece, and in his new bride discovers the rejected Hero. It all begins flippantly; it all ends flippantly. If we were only not required to sympathize with this Claudio, and with this Hero, who was so charming and attractive in the first part of the play! Here we have the vulnerable Achilles-heel of the piece; its other half is pure grace and delicacy. Benedick and Beatrice ensure it an immortality, to which the admirable Watch contributes its share. Never has Shakespeare's art achieved a greater triumph in repartee than in the skirmish of words between the two converted misogamists. And not only Benedick and Beatrice, the others also, the governor, the elegant and easy-going prince, the gloomy bastard, are all portrayed with the clearest distinctness. We take the keenest satisfaction in the charming dialogue, which is never halting, in the fine tone of earnestness which the character of each of the glib-tongued lovers assumes after the scene in the church, the result of which, as revealed afterward in Beatrice and Benedick, goes far to reconcile us to that scene. But alas! this feeling is false.

Of course, so much has been done in the way of explanation and extenuation of the evident neglect and carelessness of Shakespeare's treatment of this part of the play, that our judgement may well be warped, even to the mistrusting of our first distinct and true impression. But no Critic has ventured to defend the outrage before the altar. And although it may be maintained that the whole play leaves us in a merry mood, and that we, 'Philistines,' laugh with the lovers and their friends at such an *Ado about Nothing*,—I, for my part, declare that the enumeration of Claudio's heroic deeds always arouses my deep disgust, and that I should have left the theatre, but for the presence of Benedick, Beatrice, and the Watch, whom I always regard distinctly apart from the Count. What Shakespeare does for Claudio barely suffices to allow Claudio to impose himself for an hour or two upon respectable society; no one could endure the empty braggart any longer, and had he dared to appear in aesthetic circles in a sixth act he would have been sent to Coventry. Without his military laurels, the prince's favour, and the recommendation of good looks, and an amiable disposition, he would be absolutely insufferable. He is not without noble traits, else how could he appear as a gentleman? When, in an interview with Hero's father, he thoughtlessly lays his hand upon his sword-hilt, and the old man in his excitement suspects him of meditating a personal attack, he repels the suspicion with dignity. Possibly he is not a bad man, certainly his hot-headed outbursts, his rashness in both love and hate do not indicate the worn-out worldling with his knowledge of mankind, and of womankind in particular. His youthful impetuosity, the spoiling he has had at the hands of fortune, may suffice, perhaps, to explain the frivolous credulity with which he accepts Don John's calumnies, but not the malicious revenge which he takes upon his betrothed, and, indirectly, upon her father, who is the Governor of Messina, and his host. This makes Claudio aesthetically impossible; only a deeply tragic turn to the drama could rehabilitate him. Instead of which, Shakespeare makes him cap the climax of his insolence by the heartless way in which he jeers at Benedick and his challenge, thus revealing the utter degradation of his character. It is not worth the test of psychological criticism. Its moral impossibility is patent. The pity is that such a man as this Claudio should drag down with him into aesthetic ruin Hero, Leonato, Antonio, and even Benedick and Beatrice. A man who thinks he can expiate a piece of villainy,—*his villainy*,—by hiring some musicians to sing an elegy, who complacently shifts a crime from himself to 'slanderous tongues': 'Done to death by slanderous tongues Was the Hero that here lies,' who, in place of his dead bride,—the bride whom he has killed,—takes up with her cousin, and yet, in the end, declares to the former his previous love for her,—such a man must be classed among aesthetic and psychological abortions, and so must the injured girl, who, in spite of her bitter experience of him, accepts such a husband, and the father, who is weak enough to consent to the device of a 'cousin,' and afterwards to his daughter's marriage. And could a Beatrice, a Benedick be friends with such a man? It has been maintained that what shocks us in Claudio's conduct is softened, excused by the tone of frank gayety, of easy living that pervades the entire play, and I should be the last to deny that Shakespeare, with this intangible something in tone, has done all that is possible. The whole play, as Kreyssig expresses it, fairly reeks with roast meat and pastry. But if the love of pleasure, the easy morality of the Prince of Arragon and his train, as well as of the dwellers in Messina, both low and lofty, really illustrates and palliates in some degree the relation of these persons to the plot, it is none the more excusable. I cannot estimate highly any means by which our judgement is muddled, not clarified. Besides it all does not avail much, for Shakespeare allows no lack of antidotes. Beatrice herself brands Claudio's conduct as *unmitigated rancour.* She wishes that she were a man that she 'might eat his heart in the market-place.' Thus Shakespeare himself points out to us the view which he unfortunately relinquishes so soon, but which ought to be taken of the young Count and his fellows.

A still more powerful antidote for the joy, which we would so fain allow to conquer all distressing scruples, is to be found in the slanderers themselves. I should like to see the man who could take any satisfaction in a creature like Don John. It is the dismal veracity with which this character is drawn that makes it so impressive. A thoroughly ill-natured, bitter, revengeful scoundrel, whose passions are too sordid for any heroic crime,—a gloomy, isolated egotist. His schemes are concocted in the darkest secrecy. He is afraid to carry them out, and escapes responsibility for them by flight. The mere sight of him is gall and wormwood. Even the merry Beatrice cannot look at him without suffering from heartburn for an hour. One single paradoxical stroke of the pen would have overdrawn him, and have made him ridiculous. But Shakespeare, with his easy command of such a means, scorns it here. He draws upon his vast knowledge of human nature to create this figure; he employs all his art in modelling it, that it may intensify the gravity of the situation; and to this scoundrel, stamped by nature as such, this fellow who deceives no one, to this Don John who is at variance with the Prince, Claudio surrenders the honour and welfare of Leonato and his daughter! Without hesitation he credits the calumny, and with what inconceivable clumsiness is the slander devised! The vulgar Borachio Hero's favoured lover! Verily our indignation against Claudio grows with every circumstance that shows the absurdity of his suspicion. The pure delicate Hero, just before her marriage, prefers Borachio to Claudio! as is made to appear by a notorious back-biter! and a simpleton falls into the trap thus set! Although, even *before* the scene in the church, Claudio, vacillating and effeminate, does not capture our hearts, he may perhaps please as a poetic creation, upon whom we are not yet called upon to pass moral judgement; upon whom, indeed, the poet himself has as yet passed no judgement. Thus it is with the other characters of the play, who are implicated in the catastrophe. Before this tragic turn spoils them, they are drawn with the greatest poetic truth and delicacy. The young travelled idler of a prince is a classic model of an elegant trifler, polished, amiable, but lacking in mind and character, a genuine *universally popular* heir to the throne, quite ready to be affable and 'hail-fellow-well-met' with all, and who, when he comes into his inheritance, will waver for a while between kindly condescension and great dignity, until he developes into the full-blown despot. The budding loveliness of Hero gains an added charm from the merry readiness which she shows to join in the plot to entrap Benedick and Beatrice. Margaret and Ursula are the sauciest and most winning of waiting maids. All are gay, happy people. Even old Leonato, in spite of his high rank, does not think it beneath him to share in their merry schemes. He loves a joke, and the mildness of his sway reveals itself in his cordial treatment of his neighbours, the Watch. Under his rule one can easily understand the lax performance of duty on the part of the Watch, how the evil-doer who will not 'stand' is to be 'let go,' because 'they that touch pitch will be defiled.' He who could invest with office a Dogberry, *and* a Verges, who could listen so composedly to their arrant nonsense, and have nothing to say in reply save: 'Neighbours, you are tedious,' must indeed be a kindly soul. All these pleasant, innocent people, who are sometimes angered, but ever ready to wink at the faults of others, would have been an admirable foil for Don John and his dark designs,—were it not for the catastrophe! One hesitates to remonstrate with such a poet as Shakespeare, but we may be permitted to ask if it would not have been possible to make Claudio's love so noble and profound, that his miserable revenge would have been impossible? He might have credited the slander, might have even repudiated Hero, could we but have been made to feel the pain it cost him. Then Hero's love might well have endured. The truth might have come to light, either by mere accident, which would have been perfectly admissible in a comedy, or through the agency of the stupid Watch, to whom Shakespeare's magnanimity has dealt the best cards for the purpose. The silly device of Leonato's 'niece' would, of course, have been omitted. The circle of good fellowship, concord, and love would have been again complete. The clouds, veiling the clear Italian skies would disperse; jest and merriment would once more reign in the sunlit gardens. And the characters of the two principal personages, who carry on their warfare with such witty weapons, such gay arrogance, until the treaty of peace ends it so brilliantly, would scarce have suffered under such or similar modifications. They are amusing from first to last. The course that their skirmishing takes is the most natural in the world. In Beatrice's quarrelsome wit, in Benedick's exaggerated repudiation of the idea that he could ever bend his neck beneath the matrimonial yoke we plainly see the interest each takes in the other. Beneath the thorns slumbers the rose of love. What the poet lost in Catharine and Petruchio, because of coarseness of material, and still coarser workmanship, is brought forward here with the noblest effect. We have the frank, maidenly girl, with her scorn of all sentimentality, we have the frank, manly man hiding his merits beneath a blunt exterior; they must quarrel, but they are made for each other. The cunning of the matchmaker succeeds instantly. It needed but to strike the spark to produce a clear flame. Beatrice learns to sigh, and Benedick to trim his beard, and to study the fashion of his dress. The sterling quality of each nature is always evident. When Claudio's revenge bewilders the others, they alone find the right words in which to stigmatize the slanderers. Then first the genuine moral essence of their natures is revealed; it is the salt that preserves them from the insipidity resulting from the honeyed life led by the others. Hitherto they have merely amused us and made us laugh; now we take them to our hearts. In this part of the play the truest genius is shown in that the two characters are never false to their natures. When Beatrice bursts out indignantly at the Count's contemptible conduct, when Benedick, grave and manly, challenges Claudio, shaming him and his fellows, it needs but a word from the poet to reveal to us that behind the clouds the sun of their gay dispositions is always shining. But could not the pure gold in the heart of each have been brought to light without the odious scene in the church? This must always remain a question with us. For Benedick and Beatrice would surely gain by Claudio's being made more possible as a friend. But this is all that mars the perfection of the incomparable pair.

1885—Helena Faucit, Lady Martin. From
On Some of Shakespeare's Female Characters: By One Who Has Impersonated Them

Helena Faucit, Lady Martin (1817–98), was a leading English stage actress in the mid-nineteenth century, particularly known for her portrayals of Desdemona, Juliet, and Cordelia. In 1885, she published *On Some of Shakespeare's Female Characters: By One Who Has Impersonated Them*, which began as a series of letters to some of Martin's personal friends on the women in Shakespeare. These letters were eventually serialized in *Blackwood's Edinburgh Magazine* before being published in a popular collection. The following letter is written about Beatrice, whom Martin admires but of whom "I cannot write with the same full heart, or with the same glow of sympathy, with which I wrote of Rosalind."

To Martin, Beatrice reflects ably her own line in which she says she was born to "speak all mirth and no matter." Martin criticizes the perpetual good fortune that has seemingly been Beatrice's lot in life: "Sorrow and wrong have not softened her nature, nor taken off the keen edge of her wit." Martin also admires Beatrice's wit, but she views the function of it as merely sport. More interesting to Martin is Beatrice's own interest in Benedick; it is clear from her opening lines that Benedick has been on her mind, even in his absence, suggesting that she views in him qualities that may be worthy of a mate, even before her cousin and attendants convince her of Benedick's love for her.

Martin goes on to recount her first experience playing Beatrice on the stage, opposite the great actor Charles Kemble. Martin's experience acting the part and her subsequent encounter with Kemble take up much of the middle part of her letter and provide fascinating glimpses into the life of a working actress in the mid-nineteenth century. Martin writes that the part of Beatrice "grew" on her the more she played it. This unique perspective gave her insight into the part itself. Martin concludes that prior to the play's beginning Beatrice and Benedick must be relatively well-acquainted, long before the military action that is concluded at the play's open had been initiated. This prior interaction wholly informs Beatrice's current actions, and Martin suggests that understanding them is key to understanding the character of Beatrice herself.

Of Beatrice I cannot write with the same full heart, or with the same glow of sympathy, with which I wrote of Rosalind. Her character is not to me so engaging. We might hope to meet in life something to remind us of Beatrice; but in our dreams of fair women Rosalind stands out alone.

Neither are the circumstances under which Beatrice comes before us of a kind to draw us so closely to her. Unlike Rosalind, her life has been and is, while we see her, one of pure sunshine. Sorrow and wrong have not softened her nature, nor taken off the keen edge of her wit. When we are introduced to her, she is the great lady, bright, brilliant, beautiful, enforcing admiration as she moves 'in maiden meditation fancy free,' among the fine ladies and accomplished gallants of her circle. Up to this time there has been no call upon the deeper and finer qualities of her nature. The sacred fountain of tears has never been stirred within her. To pain of heart she has been a stranger. She has not learned tenderness or toleration under the discipline of suffering or disappointment, of unsatisfied yearning or failure. Her life has been

  'A summer mood,
'To which all pleasant things have come unsought,'

and across which the shadows of care or sorrow have never passed. She has a quick eye to see what is weak or ludicrous in man or woman. The impulse to speak out the smart and poignant things, that rise readily and swiftly to her lips, is irresistible. She does not mean to inflict pain, though others besides Benedick must at times have felt that 'every word stabs.' She simply rejoices in the keen sword-play of her wit, as she would in any other exercise of her intellect, or sport of her fancy. In very gaiety of heart she flashes around her the playful lightning of sarcasm and repartee, thinking of them only as something to make the time pass brightly by. 'I was born,' she says of herself, 'to speak all mirth and no matter.' . . .

Wooers she has had, of course, not a few; but she has 'mocked them all out of suit.' Very dear to her is the independence of her maidenhood,—for the moment has not come when to surrender that independence into a lover's hand is more delightful than to maintain it. But though in the early scenes of the play she makes a mock of wooers and of marriage, with obvious zest and with a brilliancy of fancy and pungency of sarcasm that might well appal any ordinary wooer, it is my conviction that, although her heart has not yet been touched, she has at any rate begun to see in 'Signor Benedick of Padua,' qualities which have caught her fancy. She has noted him closely, and his image recurs unbidden to her mind with a frequency which suggests that he is at least more to her than any other man. The train is laid, and only requires a spark to kindle it into flame. How this is done, and with what exquisite skill, will be more and more felt the more closely the structure of the play and the distinctive qualities of the actors in it are studied.

Indeed, I think this play should rank, in point of dramatic construction and development of character, with the best of Shakespeare's works. It has the further distinction, that whatever is most valuable in the plot is due solely to his own invention. . . . How happy was the introduction of such men as Dogberry,—dear, delightful Dogberry!—and his band, 'the shallow fools who brought to light' the flimsy villainy by which Don Pedro and Claudio had allowed themselves to be egregiously befooled! How true to the irony of life was the accident, due also to Shakespeare's invention, that Leonato was so much bored by their tedious prate, and so busy with the thought of his daughter's approaching marriage, that he did not listen to them, and thus did not hear what would have prevented the all but tragic scene in which that marriage is broken off! And how much happier than all is the way in which the wrong done to Hero is the means of bringing into view the fine and generous elements of Beatrice's nature, of showing Benedick how much more there was in her than he had imagined, and at the same time proving to her, what she was previously prepared to 'believe better than reportingly,' that he was of a truly 'noble strain,' and that she might safely trust her happiness in his hands! Viewed in this light the play seems to me to be a masterpiece of construction, developed with consummate skill, and held together by the unflagging interest which we feel in Beatrice and Benedick, and in the progress of the amusing plot by which they arrive at a knowledge of their own hearts.

I was called upon very early in my career to impersonate Beatrice; but I must frankly admit that, while, as I have said, I could not but admire her, she had not taken hold of my heart as my other heroines had done. Indeed, there is nothing of the heroine about her, nothing of romance or poetic suggestion in the circumstances of her life,—nothing, in short, to captivate the imagination of a very young girl, such as I then was. It caused me great disquietude, when Mr Charles Kemble, who was playing a series of farewell performances at Covent Garden, where I had made my *début* on the stage but a few months before, singled me out to play Beatrice to his Benedick on the night when he bade adieu to his profession. That I who had hitherto acted only the young tragic heroines was to be thus transported out of my natural sphere into the strange world of high comedy, was a surprise indeed. To consent seemed to me nothing short of presumption. I urged upon Mr Kemble how utterly unqualified I was for such a venture. His answer was, 'I have watched you in the second act of Julia in *The Hunchback*, and I know that you will by-and-by be able to act Shakespeare's comedy. I do not mean now, because more years, a greater practice, greater confidence in yourself, must come before you will have sufficient ease. But do not be afraid. I am too much your friend to ask you to do anything that would be likely to prove a failure.' This he followed up by offering to teach me the 'business' of the scene. What could I do? He had, from my earliest rehearsals, been uniformly kind, helpful, and encouraging,—how could I say him 'Nay'? My friends, too, who of course acted for me, as I was under age, considered that I must consent. I was amazed at some of the odd things I had to say,—not at all from knowing their meaning, but simply because I did not even surmise it. My dear home instructor, of whom I have often spoken in these letters, said, 'My child, have no fear, you will do this very well. Only give way to natural joyousness. Let yourself go free; you cannot be vulgar, if you tried ever so hard.'

And so the performance came, and went off more easily than I had imagined, as so many events of our lives do pass away without any of the terrible consequences which we have tormented ourselves by anticipating. The night was one not readily to be forgotten. The excitement of having to act a character so different from any I had hitherto attempted, and the anxiety natural to the effort, filled my mind entirely. I had no idea of the scene which was to follow the close of the comedy, so that it came upon me quite unexpectedly.

The 'farewell' of a great actor to his admiring friends in the arena of his triumphs was something my imagination had never pictured, and all at once it was brought most impressively before me, touching a deep sad minor chord in my young life. It moved me deeply. As I write, the exciting scene comes vividly before me,—the crowded stage, the pressing forward of all who had been Mr Kemble's comrades and contemporaries,—the good wishes, the farewells given, the tearful voices, the wet eyes, the curtain raised again and again. Ah, how can any one support such a trial! I determined in that moment that, when my time came to leave the stage, I would not leave it in this way. My heart could never have borne such a strain. I need not say that this resolve has remained unchanged. I could not have expected such a demonstrative farewell; but, whatever it might have been, I think it is well the knowledge that we are doing anything for the last time is kept from us. I see now those who had acted in the play asking for a memento of the night,—ornaments, gloves, handkerchiefs, feathers one by one taken from the hat, then the hat itself,—all, in short, that could be detached from the dress. I, whose claim was as nothing compared with that of others, stood aside, greatly moved and sorrowful, weeping on my mother's shoulder, when, as the exciting scene was at last drawing to a close, Mr Kemble saw me, and exclaimed, 'What! My Lady baby[1] Beatrice all in tears! What shall I do to comfort her? What can I give her in remembrance of her first Benedick?' I sobbed out, 'Give me the book from which you studied Benedick.' He answered, 'You shall have it, my dear, and many others!' He kept his word, and I have still two small volumes in which are collected some of the plays in which he acted, and also some in which his daughter, Fanny Kemble, who was then married and living in America, had acted. These came, with a charming letter, on the title-page addressed to his 'dear little friend.'[2]

He also told my mother to bring me to him, if at any time she thought his advice might be valuable; and on several occasions afterwards he took the trouble of reading over new parts with me, and giving me his advice and help. One thing which he impressed upon me I never forgot. It was, on no account to give prominence to the merely physical aspect of any painful emotion. Let the expression be genuine, earnest, but not ugly. He pointed out to me how easy it was to simulate distortions,—for example, to writhe from the supposed effect of poison, to gasp, to roll the eyes, etc. These were melodramatic effects. But if pain or death had to be represented, or any sudden or violent shock, let them be shown in their mental rather than in their physical signs. The picture presented might be as sombre as the darkest Rembrandt, but it must be noble in its outlines; truthful, picturesque, but never repulsive, mean, or commonplace. It must suggest the heroic, the divine, in human nature, and not the mere everyday struggles or tortures of this life, whether in joy or sorrow, despair or hopeless grief. Under every circumstance the ideal, the noble, the beautiful should be given side by side with the real. . . .

(P. 297). Mr Kemble was before everything pre-eminently a gentleman; and this told, as it always must tell, when he enacted ideal characters. There was a natural grace and dignity in his bearing, a courtesy and unstudied deference of manner in approaching and addressing women, whether in private society or on the stage, which I have scarcely seen equalled. Perhaps it was not quite so rare in his day as it is now. What a lover he must have made! What a Romeo! What an

Orlando! I got glimpses of what these must have been in the readings which Mr Kemble gave after he left the stage, and which I attended diligently, with heart and brain awake to profit by what I heard. How fine was his Mercutio! What brilliancy, what ease, what spontaneous flow of fancy in the Queen Mab speech! The very start of it was suggestive,—'O, then, I see Queen Mab' (with a slight emphasis on 'Mab') 'hath been with you!' How exquisite the play of it all, image rising up after image, one crowding upon another, each new one more fanciful than the last! 'Thou talk'st of nothing,' says Romeo; but oh, what nothings! As picture after picture was brought before you by Mr Kemble's skill, with the just emphasis thrown on every word, yet all spoken 'trippingly on the tongue,' what objects that one might see or touch could be more real? I was disappointed in his reading of Juliet, Desdemona, etc. His heroines were spiritless, tearful,—creatures too merely tender, without distinction or individuality, all except Lady Macbeth, into whom I could not help thinking some of the spirit of his great sister, Mrs Siddons, was transfused. But, in truth, I cannot think it possible for any man's nature to simulate a woman's, or *vice versa*. Therefore it is that I have never cared very much to listen to 'readings' of entire plays by any single person. I have sometimes given parts of them myself; but very rarely, and only, like Beatrice, 'upon great persuasion.'

Pardon this digression. It was so much my way to live with the characters I represented, that, when I sit down to write, my mind naturally wanders off into things which happened to me in connection with the representation of them. It was some little while before I again performed Beatrice, and then I had for my Benedick, Mr James Wallack. He was by that time past the meridian of his life; but he threw a spirit and grace into the part, which, added to his fine figure and gallant bearing, made him, next to Mr Charles Kemble, although far beneath him, the best Benedick whom I have ever seen. Oh, for something of the fervency, the fire, the undying youthfulness of spirit, the fine courtesy of bearing, now so rare, which made the acting with actors of this type so delightful!

By this time, I had made a greater study of the play; moved more freely in my art, and was therefore more able to throw myself into the character of Beatrice than in the days of my novitiate. The oftener I played the character, the more it grew upon me. The view I had taken of it seemed also to find favour with my audiences. I well remember the pleasure I felt, when some chance critic of my Beatrice wrote that she was 'a creature, overflowing with joyousness,—raillery itself being in her nothing more than an excess of animal spirits, tempered by passing through a soul of goodness.' That she had a soul, brave and generous as well as good, it was always my aim to show. All this was easy work to me on the stage. To do it with my pen is a far harder task; but I must try.

It may be mere fancy, yet I cannot help thinking that Shakespeare found peculiar pleasure in the delineation of Beatrice, and more especially in devising the encounters between her and Benedick. You remember what old Fuller says of the wit-combats between Ben Jonson and Shakespeare, in which he likens Jonson to a Spanish galleon, 'built high, solid, but slow;' and Shakespeare to an English man-of-war, 'lesser in bulk, but lighter in sailing, tacking about and taking advantage of all winds by the quickness of his wit and invention.' It is just this quickness of wit and invention which is the special characteristic of both Benedick and Beatrice. In their skirmishes, each vies with each in trying to outflank the other by jest and repartee; and, as is fitting, the victory is generally with the lady, whose adroitness in 'tacking about, and taking advantage of all winds,' gives her the advantage even against an adversary as formidable as Benedick.

That Beatrice is beautiful, Shakespeare is at pains to indicate. If what Wordsworth says was ever true of any one, assuredly it was true of her, that

'Vital feelings of delight
Had reared her form to stately height.'

Accordingly, we picture her as tall, and with the lithe elastic grace of motion which should come of a fine figure and high health. We are made to see very early that she is the sunshine of her uncle Leonato's house. He delights in her quaint, daring way of looking at things; he is proud of her, too, for with all her sportive and somewhat domineering ways, she is every inch the noble lady, bearing herself in a manner worthy of her high blood and courtly breeding. He knows how good and sound she is in heart no less than in head,—one of those strong natures which can be counted on to rise up in answer to a call upon their courage and fertility of resource in any time of difficulty or trouble. Her shrewd sharp sayings have only a pleasant piquancy for him. Indeed, however much weak colourless natures might stand in awe of eyes so quick to detect a flaw, and a wit so prompt to cover it with ridicule, there must have been a charm for him and for all manly natures in the very peril of coming under the fire of her raillery. A young, beautiful, graceful woman, flashing out brilliant sayings, charged with no real malice, but with just enough of a sting in them to pique the self-esteem of those at whom they are aimed, must always, I fancy, have a pecu-liar fascination for men of spirit. And so we see, at the very outset, it was with Beatrice. Not only her uncle, but Don Pedro and the Count Claudio also, have the highest admiration of her. That she was either a vixen or a shrew was the last idea that could have entered their minds. 'By my troth, a pleasant-spirited lady!' says Don Pedro; and the words express what was obviously the general impression of all who knew her best.

How long Benedick and Beatrice have known each other before the play begins is not indicated. I think we may fairly infer that their acquaintance is of some standing. It certainly did not begin when Don Pedro, in passing through Messina, . . . picked Benedick up, and attached him to his suite. They were obviously intimate before this. At all events there had been time for an antagonism to spring up between them, which was natural, where both were witty, and both accustomed to lord it somewhat, as witty people are apt to do, over their respective circles. Benedick could hardly have failed to draw the fire of Beatrice by his avowed and contemptuous indifference to her sex, if by nothing else. To be evermore proclaiming, as we may be sure he did, just as much before he went to the wars as he did after his return, that he rated all women cheaply, was an offence which Beatrice, ready enough although she might be herself to make epigrams on the failings of her sex, was certain to resent. Was it to be borne, that he should set himself up as 'a professed tyrant to her whole sex,' and boast his freedom from the vassalage to 'love, the lord of all?' And this, too, when he had the effrontery to tell herself, 'It is certain I am loved of all ladies, only you excepted.'

It is true that Beatrice, when she is pressed upon the point, has much the same pronounced notions about the male sex, and the bondage of marriage. But she does not, like Benedick, go about proclaiming them to all comers; neither does she denounce the whole male sex for the faults or vices of the few. Besides, there has clearly been about Benedick, in these early days, an air of confident self-assertion, a tendency to talk people down, which has irritated Beatrice. The name, 'Signior Montanto,' borrowed from the language of the fencing school, by which she asks after him in the first sentence she utters, and the announcement that she had 'promised to eat all of his killing,' seem to point to the first of these faults. And may we not take, as an indication of the other, her first remark to himself 'I wonder you will still be talking, Signor Benedick; nobody marks you;' and also the sarcasm in her description of him to her uncle, as 'too like my lady's eldest son, evermore tattling'?

What piques Beatrice, also, is the undeniable fact that this contemptuous Benedick is a handsome, gallant young soldier, a general favourite, who makes his points with trenchant effect in the give and take of their wit-combats, and, in short, has more of the qualities to win the heart of a woman of spirit than any of the gallants who have come about her. She, on the other hand, has the attraction for him of being as clever as she is handsome, the person of all his circle who puts him most upon his mettle, and who pays him the compliment of replying upon his sharp sayings with repartees, the brilliancy of which he cannot but acknowledge, even while he smarts under them. We can tell he is far from insensible to her beauty by what he says of her to Claudio when contrasting her with Hero. 'There is her cousin, an she were not possessed with a fury, exceeds her as much in beauty as the first of May doth the last of December.' No wonder, therefore, that, as we see, they have often come into conflict, creating no small amusement to their friends, and to none more than to Leonato. When Beatrice, in the opening scene of the play, says so many biting things about Benedick, Leonato, anxious that the Messenger shall not carry away a false notion of their opinion of him, says, 'You must not, sir, mistake my niece; there is a kind of merry war between Signor Benedick and her; they never meet but there's a skirmish of wit between them.' Life, perhaps, has not been so amusing to Leonato since Signor Benedick went away. It is conceivable that Beatrice herself may have missed him, if for nothing else than for the gibes and sarcasm which had called her own exuberance of wit into play.

I believe we shall not do Beatrice justice unless we form some idea, such as I have suggested, of the relations that have subsisted between her and Benedick before the play opens. It would be impossible otherwise to understand why he should be uppermost in her thoughts, when she hears of the successful issue of Don Pedro's expedition, so that her first question to the Messenger who brings the tidings is whether Benedick has come back with the rest. . . .

(P. 327). I have told you of my first performance of Beatrice. Before I conclude, let me say a word as to my last. It was at Stratford-upon-Avon, on the opening, on the 23d of April, 1879 (Shakespeare's birthday), of The Shakespeare Memorial Theatre. I had watched with much interest the completion of this most appropriate tribute to the memory of our supreme poet. The local enthusiasm, which would not rest until it had placed upon the banks of his native stream a building in which his best plays might be from time to time presented, commanded my warm sympathy. It is a beautiful building; and when, standing beside it, I looked upon the church wherein all that was mortal of the poet is laid, and, on the other hand, my eyes rested on the site of New Place, where he died, a feeling more earnest, more reverential, came over me than I have experienced even in Westminster Abbey, in Santa Croce, or in any other resting-place of the mighty dead. It was a deep delight to me to be the first to interpret on that spot one of my great master's brightest creations. Everything conspired to make the occasion happy. From every side of Shakespeare's county, from London, from remote provinces, came people to witness that performance. The characters were well supported, and the fact that we were acting in Shakespeare's birthplace, and to inaugurate his Memorial Theatre, seemed to inspire us all. I found my own delight doubled by the sensitive sympathy of my audience. Every turn of playful humour, every flash of wit, every burst of strong feeling told; and it is a great pleasure to me to think that on that spot and on that occasion I made my last essay to present a living portraiture of the Lady Beatrice.

The success of this performance was aided by the very judicious care which had been bestowed upon all the accessories of the scene. The stage, being of moderate size, admitted of no elaborate display. But the scenes were appropriate and well painted, the dresses were well chosen, and the general effect was harmonious,—satisfying the eye, without distracting the spectator's mind from the dialogue and the play of character. It was thus possible for the actors to engage the close attention of the audience, and keep it. This consideration seems to me now to be too frequently overlooked.

The moment the bounds of what is sufficient for scenic illustration are overleaped, a serious wrong is, in my opinion, done to the actor, and, as a necessary consequence, to the spectator also. With all good plays this must, in some measure, be the case; but where Shakespeare is concerned, it is so in a far greater degree. How can actor or actress hope to gain that hold upon the attention of an audience by which it shall be led to watch, step by step, from the first scene to the last, the developement of a complex yet harmonious character, or the links of a finely adjusted plot, if the eye and ear are being overfed with gorgeous scenery, with dresses extravagant in cost, and not unfrequently quaint even to grotesqueness in style, or by the bustle and din of crowds of people, whose movements unsettle the mind and disturb that mood of continuous observation of dialogue and expression, without which the poet's purpose can neither be developed by the performer nor appreciated by his audience?

For myself, I can truly say I would rather the *mise-en-scène* should fall short of being sufficient, than that it should be overloaded. However great the strain,—and I have too often felt it,—of so engaging the minds of my audience, as to make them forget the poverty of the scenic illustration, I would rather at all times have encountered it, than have had to contend against the influences which withdraw the spectator's mind from the essentials of a great drama to dwell upon its mere adjuncts. When Juliet is on the balcony, it is on her the eye should be riveted. It should not be wandering away to the moonlight, or to the pomegranate trees of Capulet's garden, however skilfully counterfeited by the scene-painter's and machinist's skill. The actress who is worthy to interpret that scene requires the undivided attention of her audience. I cite this merely as one of a host of illustrations that have occurred to my mind in seeing the lavish waste of merely material accessories upon the stage in recent years.

NOTES

1. I must explain that 'baby' was the pet name by which Mr Kemble always called me. I cannot tell why, unless it were because of the contrast he found between his own wide knowledge of the world and of art, and my innocent ignorance and youth. Delicate health had kept me in a quiet home, which I left only at intervals for a quieter life by the seaside, so that I knew, perhaps, far less of the world and its ways than even most girls of my age.

2. The letter was in these terms:—

'MY DEAR LITTLE FRIEND,—To you alone do these parts, which were once Fanny Kemble's, of right belong; for from you alone can we now expect the most efficient representation of them. Pray oblige me by giving them a place in your study; and believe me ever your true friend and servant,

C. Kemble'

1885—W. Oechelhäuser. From
Einführungen in Shakespeare's Bühnen-Dramen

Wilhelm Oechelhäuser (1820–1902) was a member of the Prussian House of Deputies (1852–53) and the German Reichstag (1878–93). He authored more than a dozen books in his lifetime, including several on Shakespeare. In *Einführungen in Shakespeare's Bühnen-Dramen*, Oechelhäuser is critical of *Much Ado about Nothing*, suggesting that it is the only one of Shakespeare's plays that does not improve on its source material. Though Oechelhäuser faintly praises a couple of the alterations Shakespeare made to the source, he sharply criticizes numerous others, including the transformation in the character of Claudio, from a lofty-minded fellow named Timbreo into the "insignificant, superficial, uncertain" Claudio; the swap of the villain Don John for the previous villain, a rival suitor for Hero; and, most damningly, the hasty ending of the text. In the original, Timbreo had to wait a year before being allowed to marry his Hero; in the play, his wait is only a day, a pause that Oechelhäuser suggests is hardly adequate, rendering the conclusion of the play "unsatisfactory" and "the inevitable consequence of the faulty method of construction" behind Shakespeare's adaptation of the earlier work.

The changes which Shakespeare has made in the material of Bandello's novel have rendered the attempted performance of an impossible task absolutely repulsive. I perfectly agree with A. Schmidt, when he points to *Much Ado about Nothing* as the only one of Shakespeare's plays in which 'he has not' elevated and ennobled the material he has chosen to use; it is even a question 'whether in this instance the contrary be not the case.'

Twice only do we recognise the ennobling of the material furnished by the novel, due to the usual delicate tact of the Poet. The first is with regard to the social rank of Claudio. In the novel it is far superior to that of Leonato, Timbreo must condescend to Leonato's family; in Shakespeare the contrary is the case, so that Claudio's rejection of the wealthy heiress is more to the advantage of his sense of honour. The other case is where the grievous tension of the scene in the church is greatly mitigated by the *previous* capture of Borachio, which assures the audience that Hero's innocence *must* soon be established, that the struggle *cannot* have a tragic ending. But these two improvements, unfortunately, go side by side with other, more important, changes for the worse; as, for example, the transformation of the lofty-minded Timbreo of the novel into the rather insignificant, superficial, uncertain Claudio, whose determination to shame Hero publicly, in the very church, framed before he has the confirmation of her infidelity, is unworthy, to say the least; in the novel the rejection is made through a third person. On the other hand, the stage effect gains indirectly, since the interrupted marriage scene forms the most effective theatric climax to the tragic part of the play, an effect which closer adherence to the plan of the novel would make impossible. Shakespeare has also been most unfortunate in the substitution of his improvised villain, Don John, for the jealous suitor of the novel. Jealousy is psychologically a thoroughly legitimate motive for slandering Hero that Claudio may be frightened into rejecting the alliance. Don John's unadulterated malice lacks all motive, and his personality brings into far more irreconcilable contrast the colouring of the crisis with the humourous tendency of the play, than appears in the novel. The psychological portrayal of the *plain-dealing villain* is quite as unsatisfactory, and so is Borachio's sudden and unaccountable fit of remorse, leading him to a voluntary and thorough confession of his guilt. But perhaps the most unfortunate departure aesthetically from the scheme of the novel is found in Claudio's consent to another marriage upon the very day after Hero's public disgrace, when her innocence is made plain. In the novel an entire year elapses, while in the play, without even a decent pause, Leonato throws his niece, and double heiress, into the arms of the faithless bridegroom. It really would seem as if our poet in several of his dramas and comedies, notably in *Measure for Measure, Two Gentlemen of Verona*, and *All's Well that Ends Well*, had lost, for the time being, that ethical sensitiveness which is so peculiarly his own. The unsatisfactory final scene in *Much Ado about Nothing* is the inevitable consequence of the faulty method of construction which attempts, not only to reconcile what is irreconcilable, but to weld it together.

This criticism makes it impossible for me to agree with the favourable judgement of some critics. The entire play is a slight piece of work, reminding us in some respects, of the equally slight *Merry Wives of Windsor*, which was, according to tradition, composed by the Poet in fourteen days. In both plays the preponderance of prose over blank verse is characteristic. In the *Merry Wives* nine-tenths, and in *Much Ado* three-fourths of the Play are written in prose.

1890—W. Wetz. From *Shakespeare von Standpunkte der vergleeichenden Literatur*

Wilhelm Wetz (1858-1910) was a well-known German scholar and author. In this selection, Wetz defends the actions of Claudio and Don Pedro in the play, labeling their behavior understandable given the circumstances of the deception placed before them and the threat of damage to their own honor had their beliefs proved correct. Responding to critics such as Bulthaupt and Gervinus, who are quick to condemn the pair, Wetz argues that Claudio's action stems from his deep hurt, and thus his swift remorse upon learning of his mistake is just as heartfelt as his condemnation of Hero earlier. Wetz suggests that both Claudio and Don Pedro believe that Leonato is part of the

deception, attempting to marry off a daughter he knows to be a strum-
pet to an honorable and well-positioned youth. Wetz describes their
laughter after the confrontation with Leonato and Antonio as nervous
laughter, arising from their discomfort and their continued belief in the
veracity of their claims.

Wetz also suggests that critics have been too harsh in judging
Hero's father for his famous assault on his daughter after she stands
accused. Though characters such as the Friar and Benedick are more
patient observers of the scene, and Beatrice is quick to defend her
cousin, Wetz argues that it is understandable that Leonato would
become enraged at such a moment, especially when Hero has done
little to vigorously defend herself against such an accusation. Wetz
concludes that such harsh critical response stems from the desire
to pass judgment on Shakespeare's characters, when, rather, critics
should strive to understand their motivations and Shakespeare's in
fashioning his characters as he did.

No greater mistake can be made than to judge Shakespeare's lovers by our
modern standard. Their love, as well as their jealousy, is infinitely more ardent
and glowing than that which we see now-a-days, whether in life or in literature. Therefore, it ought not to surprise us that the expression of their feelings
is much more vigorous and intense, or that the Poet should make free use of
this expression without attaching to it, as our public is often tempted to do, the
reproach of harshness and brutality. Moreover, as concerns Claudio, we cannot
believe that any one save Bulthaupt has utterly condemned him. The majority
of readers and spectators may blame his conduct, but they judge him much more
leniently. The pain that quivers in Claudio's every word in the church, as well as
the intensity of his remorse afterwards, shown in his readiness to undergo any
penance that may be imposed upon him to atone for his misconduct, prove that
he was no low scoundrel, but a man of noble mind whose temperament, vehement and prone to suspicion, leads him astray. Moreover, from their own words
we can perfectly understand how Don Pedro and Claudio are driven to slander
Hero publicly, thereby insulting her father also. They believe that Leonato
was aware of his daughter's vile character, and had meant to take advantage of
their ignorant confidence. They credit him with betrayal of friendship. Claudio
says to the father: 'Give not this rotten orange to your friend '; and the Prince
feels himself dishonoured in his part of advocate:—'I stand dishonoured that
have gone about To link my dear friend to a common stale.' If the two friends
thought themselves thus falsely betrayed, was the revenge that they took in
publicly branding a low woman and her accomplices, morally wrong or merely
unbecoming? It seems certainly surprising that, while Hero, even if guilty, is
to be treated with distinguished courtesy, so harsh a sentence should be passed

upon two men who, if they erred, did so from a noble motive,—an outraged sense of honour. As for the jesting at Benedick, for which Claudio is so blamed, at such a time, we must remember that characters as impulsive, as those of Shakespeare, need but the smallest occasion, in the midst of the gravest circumstances, to be converted to extreme gayety. In *2 Hen. IV*: II, ii and iv, Prince Hal feels profound grief at hearing of his father's illness, and yet cannot help jesting with Poins over Falstaff's letter, and on that very evening, disguised as a Drawer, he looks on at the gluttonous, wanton Sir John, passing the last hours before joining the army, in the company of Doll Tearsheet and Mrs Quickly.

And after all, Claudio is not so merry as his detractors would have it appear. Neither he nor Don Pedro is easy in mind when he sees the consequences of his conduct, and the sufferings of the two old men. Yet, since they believe themselves to have acted rightly, they do not yield to their uneasiness, but try to laugh it off. Their jests do not come from their hearts, as is hinted in the words with which Claudio greets Benedick: 'We have been up and down to seek thee; for we are high-proof melancholy and would fain have it beaten away. Wilt thou not use thy wit?' . . .

(P. 160). Equal readiness has been shown in giving an unfavourable character to Don Pedro; and with just as little reason, as far as the Poet is concerned, as in the case of Claudio. Bulthaupt says: 'The young travelled idler [why travelled idler? Spanish princes had often visited Sicily for serious purposes—Don Pedro himself came hither first upon some military business.] is a classic model of the elegant triller, polished, amiable, but lacking in mind and character, a genuine universally popular heir to the throne, quite ready to be affable and hail-fellow-well-met with all; and when he comes into his inheritance he will waver for a while between kindly condescension and great dignity, until he developes into the full-blown despot.' Now there is no reason to suppose that Shakespeare intended Don Pedro to be anything more than an amiable, good, young fellow. It is improper to draw any conclusions as to his future political career, since the Poet wishes us to see in him, as in the Duke of Illyria in *Twelfth Night*, in spite of his lofty rank, only the private gentleman upon a perfect equality with his friends.

To complete the adverse criticism,—the two old men, Leonato and Antonio, are accused, because of their indignant impetuosity, of most unseemly behaviour. Of much that Gervinus has to say of their intemperance, we give but one sample: Leonato, 'when misfortune assails him is utterly helpless, and unhinged. He wishes Hero were dead, he wishes to stab her, to tear her to pieces, and this without making any investigation, without even, like Father Francis, observing. He rejects all consolation, and all exhortation to be patient.' It does seem verily a great deal,—to require of a father such cold-blooded self-control at such a moment. We should like to see a father capable of calmly investigating, not to mention observing, like an unconcerned priest, the signs of guilt or innocence in his daughter's face, just when he was agonized with grief and shame, and beside himself with the affront to his pride, and to the honour of his family; the testimony of two honourable gentlemen, one of them the bridegroom who accused his betrothed with tears, having left no doubt as to the girl's criminality. And we need not remind our readers how violent and passionate Shakespeare's fathers[1] are, when they are angry with their daughters. According to Gervinus, to bear his trials should have been easy for Leonato; according to Leonato, Gervinus is one of those who speak patience to 'those that wring under the load of sorrow.'

We have expatiated upon all this, because it seems to us that the frequent misconceptions of the Poet are due to the fact that the critics hasten to *pass judgement* upon Shakespeare's characters, when they should first make it their aim to *understand* them. Instead of being sure beforehand of the Poet's point of view, and making it a criterion, each critic has used his own view as such. The consequence is that there is often the greatest diversity of opinion as to the same point, although we surely ought to expect that with a Poet whose work is so distinguished for unity, it should be possible to agree as to facts, in regard to what he himself meant. Our greatest mistake seems to have been that we suspect some deep moral significance in every subordinate character, and have thus considered ourselves justified in inflicting either moral praise or censure. And it must be also confessed that our German critics have not been sufficiently careful to steer clear of this rock, and that Gervinus in especial has not shown sufficient caution and circumspection in the solution of problems thus presenting themselves.

NOTE
1. See Old Capulet, Lear, Cymbeline.

1891—Andrew Lang. From *Harper's Magazine*

Andrew Lang (1844–1912) was a famous Scottish author and critic who is best known today for his work on fairy tales and folklore. In this piece from *Harper's Magazine*, Lang takes some minor offense at the quality of Beatrice's wit, labeling it strictly "Elizabethan" and suggesting it lacks polish and intellect. Many critics of the later Victorian era admired the wit of Shakespeare's play, but Lang found it lacking and clumsy. He finds other qualities in Beatrice to admire, including her gallantry and her steadfastness, but concludes that her wit is dated and "blunt."

Beatrice's wit, let it be frankly avowed, is uncommonly Elizabethan. It would have been called 'chaff' if our rude forefathers had known the word in that sense. She utters 'large jests,' ponderable *persiflage*. If she did not steal it from the *Hundred Merry Tales*, as was said, she had been a scholar in that school of coquettes. We cannot be angry with the French for failing to see the point or edge of this lady's wit. It has occasionally no more point or edge than a bludgeon. For example:—

> '*Benedick*. God keep your ladyship still in that mind I so some gentleman or other shall 'scape a predestinate scratched face.
> *Beatrice*. Scratching could not make it worse, an 'twere such a face as yours.'

This kind of merry combat would be thought blunt by a groom and a scullion. There is no possibility of avoiding this distressing truth. Beatrice, while she has not yet acknowledged her love to herself, nor been stirred by the wrong done to Hero, is not a mistress of polished and glittering repartee; but it were absurd, indeed idiotic, to call her 'odious.' Other times, other manners. Wit is a very volatile affair. Look, for example, at Mr Paley's collection of rudenesses and ineptitudes called *The Wit of the Greeks*. It is *humor* that lives,—the humor of Falstaff, of Benedick when he is not engaged in a wit-combat. . . .

Though Hero forgave Claudio, we may be happily certain that Beatrice never did. Our friends' wrongs are infinitely more difficult to pardon than our own, and Beatrice was not a lady of general and feeble good-nature. It is difficult not to regret that Benedick let Claudio off so easily, with contempt and a challenge, but so the fortune of the play must needs determine it. Claudio throughout behaves like the most hateful young cub. He is, perhaps, more absolutely intolerable when he fleers and jests at the anger of Leonato than even when he denounces Hero, making her a sacrifice to the vanity of his jealousy. It is his self-love, not his love, that suffers from the alleged conduct of Hero. . . .

Perhaps nobody will carry heresy so far as to say that this piece is better to read than to see on the stage; on the other hand, it lives for the stage, and on the stage. It is a master-work for the theatre, glittering with points and changes, merry or hushed with laughter and surprises. It is said that Benedick was Garrick's favorite Shakespearian part; it requires such humor, dignity, and gallantry as will try the greatest actor's powers to the highest. A Benedick who makes faces and 'clowns' the part, for example, where he listens to the whispered discourse on Beatrice's love, leaves a distinct and horrible stain on the memory. And she who acts Beatrice, again, like her who acts Rosalind, must above all things be a lady, and act like a lady. . . .

The wit combats must be judged historically. The two-handed sword of Signior Montanto was just going out in the duel; the delicate sword was just coming in. Even court wit was clumsy in Shakespeare's time, and trammelled by euphuistic flourishes, as fencing was encumbered by a ponderous weapon, and perplexing secret *bottes*, and needless, laborious manoeuvres. The wit of Beatrice is of her own time; her gallant and loyal nature is of all times. The drama in which she lives is 'a mellow glory of the British stage,' rather than, like the *Midsummer Night's Dream* or *As You Like It*, the poetic charm for solitary hours in the life contemplative. Played first, probably, in 1599 or 1600, the comedy is of Shakespeare's happiest age and kindliest humor. Nobody is melancholy here; not one of the poet's favorite melancholies holds the stage; for we cannot number the morose and envious Don John with Jaques or with Hamlet. He is not a deeply studied character, like Iago, and is a villain only because a villain is needed by the play. In fact, Claudio is the real villain as well as the *jeune premier* of the piece. It is pretty plain that Shakespeare loved not the gay rufflers of his age, though, after all, in opposition to the sullen and suspicious vanity, the heartless raillery, of Claudio, he has given us the immortal Mercutio as a representative of the gallants of his time.

⟶⟶ ⟶⟶ ⟶⟶

1891—Grace Latham. From "Julia, Silvia, Hero and Viola"

Grace Latham was a frequent contributor to the publications of the New Shakspere Society (active 1883–1893). She was known for frequently criticizing Shakespeare's depiction of women in his plays, whom she felt often worked from a "subordinate position." In her examination of Hero, Latham calls the character a "slave," suggesting, as Carol Cook and others will do nearly a century later, that Hero is a product of a patriarchal society that created her in the image they most desire, leaving her impotent to defend herself at the most crucial moment of the play.

Discipline is one of Shakspere's favourite subjects, whether it be of life or of education; and we find it especially associated, particularly in certain phases, with his female characters, women being more often subject to it than men, from their subordinate position, far more marked in his day than it is in ours. . . .

In *Much Ado About Nothing* we find [Shakespeare] has recognized the fact, that to be perfectly successful, discipline must consist of a planting and fostering as well as a weeding out of qualities, and must be carried on with the active co-operation of the will of the subject on which it is exercised. If it be merely, or even chiefly, the work of an external force, more powerful than the nature of the pupil, it acts like iron chains, cramping and weakening, instead of strengthening; just as a scholar may be reduced to a mere machine, with all originality crushed out by him, by an education which is too deep or extensive for his mind to digest.

It is among certain of Shakspere's women that we must look for this aspect of discipline, not among his men; for the reason that it is much more rare to find a boy who has been crushed in this way, their frames and nervous systems being tougher, and their early life and education freer and less monotonous than their sister's [*sic*].

With Hero, in *Much Ado About Nothing*, discipline has been an exterior tyranny, not the lesson of self-government. Father and uncle have busily led their darling in the way in which she should go, forgetting that she must one day shape her course alone; and that to do this with safety, the weak points in her character should have been strengthened. The superior energy of Beatrice, joined to her sarcastic tongue, have thrust her dearly-loved cousin still farther into the background. Hero is too sweet-natured to resent this, and she never tries to gain her ends by unworthy means. Obedience and submission are duties to her, and have been instilled into her until they have become an instinctive habit. Gentle, modest, and unassuming, she plays her part in society, with a quietness which is only saved from insipidity by its grace and good-breeding. This short, brown, pretty creature is the ideal young lady of parents and teachers, and in truth she is perfect as her education will allow her to be; kind, loving, humble without servility, and bearing grave wrong without personal resentment or desire for vengeance. . . .

But, alas! Hero has lost any small power of self-assertion, or of independent action that she may ever have had. She can only open her lips when there is no fear of contradiction; a slave does not tell her desire lest they should be thwarted.

1896—Frederick S. Boas. From *Shakespeare and His Predecessors*

Frederick Samuel Boas (1862-1957) was a prominent English scholar of Elizabethan drama. Here, Boas embraces the title of the play as the theme of his criticism, suggesting that the drama reads like the misadventures of a group on holiday, adding to the comic overtone of the text. He compares Beatrice to Katharina in *The Taming of the Shrew*, though Beatrice is viewed more favorably by Boas than Shakespeare's infamous "shrew." To him, Beatrice evolves past her shrewish connotations and becomes a more fully developed character; her scene with Benedick after Hero's humiliation, when she famously wishes she could challenge

Claudio and "eat his heart in the market-place" demonstrates the limitations and frustrations Beatrice has with her ascribed gender role.

According to Boas, this may perhaps be the only moment in the text that is not "much ado about nothing." Boas considers the scene of Hero's castigation at the wedding the "crowning instance" of the theme, despite the horror with which the scene was perceived by the critics of his day. Dogberry and Verges are also examples of "much ado about nothing," both in the simple manner in which they capture the villains and in the manner in which they behave throughout the play. Boas even suggests that the theme of "much ado about nothing" hearkens happy tidings for Beatrice and Benedick. Responding to several nineteenth-century critics who believed that the union between the two would not prove a happy one, Boas suggests that Shakespeare's title indicates that all the bluster we have seen pass between them is "nothing," and that they, too, will live happily ever after.

The comedy may be aptly termed a fugue upon the theme of *Much Ado About Nothing*. The title is admirably suggestive of the character of the piece, which introduces us to a society whose atmosphere is one of perpetual holiday; where everybody, from high to low, having time enough on hand and to spare, indulges in leisurely, circuitous fashions of speech and action, productive of mistakes and misapprehensions—in short, of much ado which, in the long run, always proves to be about nothing . . . before Benedick appears on the scene, we see clearly that Beatrice has an interest in him, to which she gives expression by making 'much ado' about his non-existent faults. . . .

Benedick, a favourite of nature and of fortune, 'of noble strain, of approved valour and confirmed honesty,' with a piercing wit and a ready tongue, has adopted an attitude of hostility to women, and of cynical contempt for love and marriage. By an irresistible impulse he pours his views chiefly into the ear of Beatrice, who is his feminine counterpart in character and intellect, and whom he singles out as certain above all others to resent the outrage to her sex. In some aspects Beatrice cannot but recall Katharine in *The Taming of the Shrew*, though the comparison illustrates the great advance that Shakspere had made in his art. Here, as there, a motherless girl, in a luxurious household, with an indulgent guardian, and a single pliant relative of her own sex, develops an exaggerated self-will and self-love that go far to obscure a radically sound nature. Beatrice is indeed quite free from Katharine's worst faults of jealousy and acrid ill-humour. She is on the most affectionate terms alike with her uncle and her cousin, and her heart keeps on the windy side of care, so that she is 'never sad but when she sleeps, and not ever sad then.' But she is too proud to acknowledge that there is any lack in her nature which marriage would fill, and she cannot endure to hear tell of a husband. This instinct has been strengthened by her encounter with Benedick, who poses as 'an obstinate heretic in the despite of beauty.' She is piqued into the resolution to outdo him with his own weapons, to answer scorn with yet greater scorn. Hence, as Leonato declares, they never meet but there is a skirmish of wit between them. But yet deeper, and unacknowledged even to herself, lies a resolution of another kind: to bring to her feet this sworn foe of her sex, whose brilliant qualities she cannot but recognize, and whose powerful personality has a magnetic influence upon her own. . . . when Benedick, pressed by Claudio for his opinion of Hero, draws a distinction between his 'simple true judgement' and his customary verdicts in the capacity of a 'professed tyrant to their sex.' He cannot discuss Hero without dragging in the name of Beatrice (as she had done with his, when the talk ran on Claudio), and proving that he is by no means insensible to her charms: 'There's her cousin, an she were not possessed with a fury, exceeds her as much in beauty as the first of May doth the last of December.' Such a hint discounts beforehand all his railings against marriage, . . . the exaggerated vehemence with which the pair are constantly repudiating the idea of matrimony proves that it is always uppermost in their thoughts, and gives more than an inkling that this much ado will prove to be about nothing. . . . Claudio . . . brave, honourable, and pure in heart, . . . is so far fitted to be the wooer of the gentle and modest Hero. But his sudden elevation has dazzled his somewhat superficial nature, and even in speaking of his love to Don Pedro and Benedick he lets fall the ominous conditional clause, 'If my passion change not shortly.' Moreover, the rise in his own fortunes has made him keenly alive to the outward advantages of wealth and position. So before taking any steps to secure Hero as his bride, he is careful to satisfy himself that Leonato has no son, and that his daughter is the only heir. His devotion is thus not so intense but that it can find utterance through other lips than his own, and he readily falls in with Don Pedro's proposal . . . Such a roundabout proceeding is a minor case of much ado about nothing, which brings others in its train. For this conversation is partially overheard by a servant of Leonato's brother Antonio, who reports that Don Pedro is in love with Hero and means to woo her for himself; whereupon Leonato hurries off with the news to his daughter, that she may be the better prepared with an answer. A more correct version is retailed by another eavesdropper, Borachio, the servant of Don John, and from this more serious consequences spring. . . .

Amongst Shakspere's malefactors he (Don Juan) is distinguished by his complete lack of humor, and of the kindred power to dissemble his real nature. As he says himself, 'I cannot hide what I am . . . it better fits my blood to be disdained of all than to fashion a carriage to rob love from any.' It would seem as if the dramatist in this most radiant of comedies had not wished to focus our attention upon the villain by investing him with the fascination which underlies evil-doing masquerading under the guise of good-humoured honesty. Moreover, we are not inclined to augur very disastrous results from the schemes of a mischief-maker who wears his heart upon his sleeve in so transparent a fashion, and who seems so ill-fitted for an intriguer's part. . . . while . . . by a roundabout process the hero and heroine of the main story are being brought together, the gulf between Benedick and Beatrice is widening till it seems impassable. . . . The very extremity to which the pair have pushed their hostilities provides a piquant suggestion for the onlookers, who have to while away a week between Hero's betrothal and her marriage. . . . the train is already fired for his overthrow, or rather the overthrow of the disguise with which he has cloaked his true nature, in part even from himself. Yet with delicate tact the poet takes care that the transition shall not be too abrupt. A pause is made in the action of the story while Balthazar, who contributes his quota of much ado about nothing by his preliminary flourishes of pleas for indulgence, sings his ditty, 'Sigh no more, ladies.' Our spirits are thus attuned to changes of sentiment and situation, while the burden of the ballad strikes the keynote of the dialogue that follows. Don Pedro and his friends, in the hearing of Benedick, discourse upon 'the enraged affection passing the infinite of thought' with which Beatrice loves him, and agree that it were better for her to sigh no more, but to seek to suppress her passion. Benedick is thus attacked through his weakest point—his excessive self-appreciation, which has hitherto prompted his rebellious attitude towards love. He now pays the full penalty, for it is this very failing that delivers him into the hands of the conspirators. . . . He foresees . . . the world's ridicule, but he parries its shafts in advance with an ingenuity worthy of Falstaff: 'When I said I would die a bachelor, I did not think I should live till I were married.'

Beatrice in her turn is easily trapped by Hero and Ursula, . . . the more so that her self-love is mortified by hearing herself censured for scorn and pride of wit. Less self-conscious, however, than Benedick, and with a deeper emotional nature, she surrenders at discretion, without any quibbling pleas on her own behalf. We realize what a change has come over her, when she ceases to speak poniards and actually declares her feelings in verse. Thus the two birds are limed; the net has not been spread in sight of them in vain. Of the pair, Benedick, who has been the more stalwart rebel against love, goes through the more open and humiliating transformation. He dresses in outlandish fashions, studies the niceties of his toilet, is sad and silent in company, and puts it down to the tooth-ache. Beatrice too sighs and speaks in the sick tune, and lets herself be outmatched in repartee by Hero's waiting-women. The jesters *par excellence* have to submit to a brief period of not unmerited chastisement, till the turn of events shows that they are sounder of heart and keener of penetration than those who for the moment have the laugh of them.

Don Pedro's merry device for filling up the interval before the marriage has had a criminal counterpart in an infamous scheme of his brother, who, foiled in his first effort at mischief-making, has sought the ruin of Claudio's happiness by more desperate means. . . . far from reproaching Shakspere for an extravagant violation of probability in representing the lover and his patron as convinced of so heinous an offence on such slender evidence, we should recognize that this is in strict accord with the genius of the play, where, throughout, the most momentous inferences are built upon overheard scraps of dialogue, and much ado thus results about nothing.

A similar answer may be made to Kreyssig's criticism that Shakspere has neglected the necessary dramatic sequence of cause and effect in his account of the discovery of the plot. This, it is maintained, should have resulted from some false step on the part of Don John, and not, as is the case, from a casually overheard dialogue between his subordinates. But this roundabout method in which the conspiracy comes to light is entirely in harmony with the tortuous direction that events take throughout the play, while it serves as the source of further complications, and introduces new actors on the scene in the shape of the city watch, headed by master-constable Dogberry and his colleague Verges. The long-winded charge in which Dogberry instructs his subordinates in their duties is a fresh instance of much ado about nothing, for it amounts to an elaborate exhortation to leave everything undone that they are appointed to do. . . . with a characteristic misconstruction of a whispered phrase, they believe that they are on the track of 'one Deformed,' a fictitious personage about whom they make much ado. Thus the conspiracy is unmasked apparently in time to frustrate its evil aim—but this is to reckon without Dogberry and Verges. It is strange that Coleridge should have spoken of them 'as forced into the service of the plot when any other less ingeniously absurd watchmen would have answered the mere necessities of the action.' On the contrary, the necessities of the action absolutely demand these twin specimens of blundering officialdom, for had they been less given to illogical and perverse circumlocution of speech, the exposure of Hero would have been avoided, and, with it, the occasion that finally unites Beatrice and Benedick. . . .

The reader however, more fortunate than Leonato, knows that Don John's agents are already in custody, and is thus less pained than he would otherwise be by the well-nigh tragic situation in the church, when Claudio with foul calumny casts back the innocent Hero into her father's arms. This is the crowning instance of much ado about nothing, which finds yet another illustration in Leonato's hysterical lamentation over his daughter's supposed shame. . . . at this crisis the deeper nature of each (Beatrice and Benedick) leaps into sudden, unashamed light, and through the very catastrophe that has overwhelmed Hero the way is made easy for a mutual confession of love. Beatrice weeping! At such a sight must not Benedick's lips shape themselves into the avowal, 'I do love nothing in the world as well as you'? And there is only one answer that can come back through the tears, 'You have stayed me in a happy hour: I was about to protest I loved you.' But with characteristic vehemence she at once tests her wooer's devotion to the uttermost by the command to kill Claudio. When he refuses, she mounts through ever-rising stages of passionate indignation at the Count's misconduct to the final outburst, 'O God, that I were a man. I would eat his heart in the market-place.' Mrs. Jameson shows little of her usual insight in setting down this speech to temper. It springs rather from 'a noble and righteous fury, the fury of kindled strength'; but in the very measure of her strength the woman is made, with the finest truth, to find the measure of her weakness, and Beatrice, in this hour of her self-revelation, cries aloud for the powers of the sex that has hitherto been the butt of her scorn. Benedick can supply what she lacks, and, the triumph of the thought sweeping away his scruples, he goes forth to challenge Claudio. . . .

But a change is at hand . . . while Dogberry is making much ado about nothing by bewailing that . . . he has not been written down an ass, the Sexton hurries off with proofs of the plot to Leonato. . . . the Count is struck with remorse, but his is not a nature to be agonized even by the consciousness that he has done his affianced bride a fatal wrong. With frivolous disloyalty to her memory he accepts at once Leonato's offer of a niece, 'almost the copy of his child that's dead.' He hangs with elaborate funeral pomp the prescribed elegy upon Hero's cenotaph, only to find it a case of much ado about nothing. For when, on the morrow, his new-made bride unmasks, she is seen to be no other than Hero—dead only as long as her slander lived . . . Beatrice and Benedick next step forth to claim the friar's good offices, . . . And the critics who, with singular lack of penetration, seek to mar our satisfaction at the union of this delightful couple by dismal predictions of a stormy matrimonial career, may be confidently assured that they have caught the infection of the play, and are supplying an additional instance of much ado about nothing.

<hr />

1899—Horace Howard (H. H.) Furness.
From the preface to the New Variorum
edition of *Much Ado About Nothing*

Horace Howard Furness (1833-1912) has often been considered the most important American Shakespearean scholar of the nineteenth century. He is given this title because of his scholarly edition of Shakespeare's collected works—the New Variorum editions of the playwright's oeuvre, often called the Furness Variorum—that thoroughly annotated, catalogued, and collected relevant commentary from the preceding three hundred years for each of the Bard's works. Furness worked on the series for forty years, and the task was ultimately finished by his son after Furness's death. In the following excerpt, Furness addresses the character of Dogberry, a source of frequent criticism in the late nineteenth century. Furness argues that Shakespeare's inclusion of Dogberry—and the affectations of Dogberry's character—are integral to the function of the play. Furness suggests that the appearance of these "infinitely stupid watchmen . . . is by no means merely to make us laugh, but to give us assurance that the play is still a comedy."

The Text, here reprinted, is that of the First Folio; which is not, however, the earliest. *Much Ado About Nothing* had already appeared, in a Quarto form, in the year 1600, twenty-three years before it was printed in the First Folio. Nevertheless, there is in reality but one text, inasmuch as it is from this Quarto that the Folio itself was printed, a fact which any one can discern for himself by an examination of the *Textual Notes* in the following pages. Wherever the Folio differs from the Quarto, it is 'mostly,' DYCE says, 'for the worse;' this 'worse,' however, consists chiefly of trivial typographical errors. Occasionally, the variations in the Folio are improvements, as, for instance, where, in the Quarto, Dogberry says 'any man that knowes the statutes,' the Folio, with a nearer approach to Dogberry's language, has 'anie man that knowes the Statues;' again, where the Quarto regardless of rhyme says:—

'Hang thou there vpon the toomb
'Praising hir when I am dead,'

the Folio has:—

'Hang thou there vpon the tombe
'Praising her when I am dombe.'

Where Leonato, full of amazed horror at the sight of Borachio, recoils and asks (according to the Quarto):

'Art thou the slaue that with thy breath hast killd
'Mine innocent child?'

the Folio, with heightened dramatic effect, repeats the 'thou', 'Art thou thou the slaue that with thy breath hast kild mine innocent childe?'

Furthermore, the stage directions are rather more exact, even to the specifying of names of actors, in the Folio than in the Quarto; where the Quarto has 'Enter prince, Leonato, Claudio, Musicke,' the Folio has 'Enter Prince, Leonato, Claudio, and Jacke Wilson.'

The most noteworthy difference between the two texts is the omission in several places in the Folio of lines and portions of lines which are in the Quarto. This of itself proves that the Folio was not printed from an independent text. Were it otherwise, there would be lines in the text of the Folio not to be found in the Quarto, and of such there is not a single one. All the noteworthy changes lie in words, in omissions, and in stage directions. The inference, therefore, may be fairly drawn not only that HEMINGE and CONDELL used a copy of the Quarto as the text for their Folio, but that it was a copy which had been used on the stage as a prompt-book, wherein for the benefit of the prompter, fuller stage-directions had been inserted, even, as we have seen, to the very names of the actors, such as Jack Wilson, who were to be summoned, and wherein, possibly, some passages had been stricken out. We all know that these two friends of SHAKESPEARE assert in their *Preface* to the Folio that they had used the author's manuscripts, and in the same breath denounce the Quartos as stolen and surreptitious. When we now find them using as 'copy' one of these very Quartos, we need not impute to them a wilful falsehood if we suppose that, in using what they knew had been printed from the original text, howsoever obtained, they held it to be the same as the manuscript itself,—most especially if the copy had been a prompter's book during the very years when SHAKESPEARE himself was on the stage, and, *possibly*, used by the great Master himself at some of the many performances of a play, whereof the extreme popularity we learn from LEONARD DIGGES, who says:—

'let but Beatrice
'And Benedicke be scene, loe in a trice
'The Cockpit, Galleries, Boxes all are full.'

To set forth in detail, or to tabulate, all the variations of the Folio, its additions of words or syllables, its omissions of lines or phrases, its reproduction of unusual spellings, or of misspellings, in the Quarto, its prose where the Quarto has verse, etc., etc., is superfluous in a volume, like the present, where all the material for such a summary is presented in the *Textual Notes* on every page. If the student be so happily, or unhappily, constituted as to find refreshment or intellectual growth in such work, it is better for him to make the tables for himself. If he find no interest therein, (and in a stage *aside*, let me whisper that he has my cordial sympathy,) it would be a sheer waste of time to make it for him; let him, therefore, tranquilly accept the assurance drawn from a laborious collation, which I gladly spare him, that the Text of the Folio, as I started with saying, is taken from a copy of the Quarto, which probably contained some manuscript changes, and that variations between it and the Folio are mainly accidental; where they are noteworthy, and apparently not accidental, they will be discussed, in due course, as they occur in the following pages.

As I have had occasion, more than once, to say, if this printed text of the Folio, over which we pore so earnestly, had been ever scanned by SHAKESPEARE's eyes, then we might accept it as a legacy where every comma becomes respectable; but since we know that, when the Folio was printed, SHAKESPEARE had been in his grave seven years, we discover that we are herein dealing merely with the skill, intelligent or otherwise, of an ordinary compositor; and that in our minute collation we are devoting our closest scrutiny to the vagaries of a printer.

Thus we have the source of the Text of the Folio, but when we seek to discover that of the Quarto, we are met by the mystery which seems inseparable from all things connected with SHAKESPEARE's outward life (I marvel that in the four thousand ways, devised by Mr WISE, of spelling SHAKESPEARE's name no place is found for spelling it '*m–y–s–t–e–r–y*'), and yet, in the present instance, I doubt that mystery is the exactest term. It is merely our ignorance which creates the mystery. To SHAKESPEARE's friends and daily companions there was nothing mysterious in his life; on the contrary, it possibly appeared to them as unusually dull and commonplace. It certainly had no incidents so far out of the common that they thought it worth while to record them. SHAKESPEARE never killed a man as JONSON did; his voice was never heard, like MARLOW's, in tavern brawls; nor was he ever, like MARSTON and CHAPMAN, threatened with the penalty of having his ears lopped and his nose slit; but his life was so gentle and so clear in the sight of man and of Heaven that no record of it has come down to us; for which failure, I am fervently grateful, and as fervently hope that no future year will ever reveal even the faintest peep through the divinity which doth hedge this king.

We are quite ignorant of the way in which any of the Shakespearian Quartos came to be published. Were it not that HEMINGE and CONDELL pronounced them all to be 'stolne and surreptitious' we might have possibly supposed that SHAKESPEARE yielded to temptation and sold his Plays to the press,—a dishonest practice indulged in by some dramatists, as we learn from HEYWOOD's *Preface* to his *Rape of Lucrece* where he says: 'some have used a double sale of their labours, first to the Stage, and after to the Presse.' But not thus dishonestly would the sturdy English soul of SHAKESPEARE act,—a trait not sufficiently considered by those who impute to him an indifference to the offsprings of his brain. His Plays once sold to the Theatre passed for ever from his possession, and to all allurements of subsequent money-getting from them he gave an honest kersey no.

This vexed question of origin, the Quarto of *Much Ado about Nothing* shares in common with all the other Quartos, and, in addition, has a tidy little mystery of its own, which it shares with only three or four other Plays. The earliest mention of it appears in the *Stationers' Registers* as follows:—[1]

> 4 Augusti
> *As you like yt* / a booke
> *Henry the Ffift* / a booke
> *Euery man in his humour* / a booke to be staied.
> *The commedie of muche Adoo about*
>   *nothing* a booke /

This item does not stand in the body of the volume of the *Stationers' Registers*, but is on one of a couple of fly-leaves at the beginning, whereon are thirteen or fourteen other entries, all of which contain a caveat, such as: 'This to be entred to hym yf he can gett Aucthority for yt' or 'yf he can get yt aucthorised.' The year is not given. With one exception, all the other entries on this and the opposite page, nine in number, are dated 1603. The exception, immediately preceding the *Much Ado* entry, is dated in the margin: '27 May 1600.' It is quite possible to suppose, with MALONE, that the clerk seeing this date, 1600, in the preceding item, did not think it worth while to repeat it in the present. It is also quite possible to suppose, that the date being of less importance than the fact that the plays were 'to be staied,' the clerk believed that his memory would be sufficiently jogged by the heading, at the top of the page: 'my lord chamberlens menns plaies Entred.' But after all, here the date is of small importance; a subsequent entry gives us a date beyond gainsaying. The real mystery lies in the three words: 'to be staied.' Why they should be stayed, or at whose instigation, must for ever remain a problem. It is reasonable to suppose that, inasmuch as the plays were the property of 'my lord chamberlens menn,' the remonstrance against their printing, came from these proprietors. And yet if this remonstrance was effective in the first week in August, why did its efficacy fail in the last week of August, when the Quarto actually appeared? It never did fail in the case of *As You Like It*, whereof the appearance was stayed until it was issued in the Folio, in 1623. Dr WILLIAM ALDIS WRIGHT, our highest living Shakespearian authority, suggests, in regard to this latter play, *As You Like It*, that the staying was due to the fact that the announcement was 'premature and that the play may not have been ready,' and he adduces certain signs of haste in the naming of the *Dramatis Persona*, such as two Jaques, etc.[2] But the staying in the case of *Much Ado about Nothing* was not permanent, as it was in the case of *As You Like It*, and yet we have in it a possible sign of haste rather more emphatic than any in *As You Like It*, in the introduction of a character, Innogen, who never speaks throughout the entire play. Moreover, to 'stay' the play because it was not ready, implies, I am afraid a certain complicity on the part of SHAKESPEARE in the publication of the Quartos which I, for one, should be loath to accept.

Mr FLEAY suggested at one time[3] that all these four plays were ordered to be staied, because 'they were probably suspected of being libellous,' and were therefore 'reserved for further examination.' Since the "war of the theatres" was at its height, they may have been restrained as not having obtained the consent of the Chamberlain, on behalf of the company, to their publication.' Inasmuch as *Henry the Fifth, Every Man in his Humour*, and *Much Ado about Nothing*, when they finally did appear, were issued by different publishers, Mr FLEAY afterward[4] said: 'it seems clear that the delay, of which so many hypothetical interpretations have been offered, was simply to enable Millington and Busby, who *probably* [Italics mine] had the copyrights of all four plays, to complete the sales thereof to the other publishers.' It seems equally clear, it must be acknowledged, that an explanation which rests on a *probability* is not far removed from all others of a hypothetical nature; and when once hypothesis has sway, what is to hinder us from supposing that in this, as in other cases, the cause of the 'staying' was JAMES ROBERTS? It has been assumed by all editors, I think without exception, since the days of MALONE, that the entry in the *Stationers' Registers* of August the fourth belongs to the year 1600, because the entry immediately preceding bears that date, and the clerk thought it needless to repeat it. But the preceding entry couples, with the date 1600, the name 'JAMES ROBERTS,' as the stationer who wished to enter two plays. Now, if the clerk thought it needless to repeat the 1600, why is it not equally likely that he thought it needless to repeat the name, JAMES ROBERTS, if to him both entries belonged? What may be assumed of a date, surely may be assumed of a name, especially since all six plays belonged to the Chamberlain's company. Thus stand the entries on the page of the *Register*:—

my lord chamberlens menns plaies Entred

viz

27 May 1600   *A moral of clothe breches and velvet hose*
To master Robertes
27 May   *Allarum to London* /
To hym

       4. Augusti
As you lihe yt / a booke
Henry the Ffift / a booke
Euery man in his humour / a booke to be staied
The commedie of muche Adoo about
nothing a booke /

Is it straining the plain facts before us too far, to assume that all these plays were entered by JAMES ROBERTS, and that the caveat was due to his shifty character? It will be merely *crambe repetita* to rehearse what I have heretofore assumed[5] as to the character of JAMES ROBERTS, and his influence in connection with SHAKESPEARE's company,—an influence, whereof the origin and extent must remain to us unknown, merely because we do not know and never shall know what was once the common gossip of the day. Nor, in reality, is the 'staying' of these Shakespearian Quartos of any real importance; it is worth mentioning only as another happy instance of our utter ignorance of SHAKESPEARE's mortal life.

But little more remains to be said about the Quarto. In the *Stationers' Registers*[6] under the running title: '42 *Regin[a]e*,' that is, 1600, we find as follows:—

23 Augusti
Andrewe Wyse
William Aspley

Entred for their copies vnder the handes of the wardens Two bookes. the one called *Muche a Doo about nothinge*. Thother *the second parte of the history of hinge Henry the iiif*[th] *with the humours of Sir John Ffallstaff*: Wrytten by master Shakespere xij[d]

Here, then, we have the exact, final date of the publication of the Quarto.

ARBER remarks, in parenthesis, after the foregoing entry, that this is 'the first time our great poet's name appears in these Registers.' It is perhaps worth while to remark in reference to the spelling of the name, as there given, that both COLLIER and DYCE in reproducing the entry spell it *Shakespeare*, so uncertain is the reading of old chirography,—especially if it be Court-hand or Chancery-hand, which SHAKESPEARE used when he subscribed to his Will, and to the Blackfriars Deed and in which, like other laymen, he was but little skilled. HALLIWELL-PHILLIPPS[7] reproduces the same entry from the *Stationers' Registers*, and yet his copy varies from Arber's in ten or twelve minute particulars, such as *twoo* where the latter has 'Two,' *adoo* for 'a Doo,' *Kinge* for 'kinge,' *humors* for 'humours,' *Mr.* for 'master', &c.—quite insignificant all of them, it may be readily acknowledged, but, nevertheless, they are variations, and full of sad warning when we approach the awful problem of the spelling of the Poet's name as deduced from his written signature. For myself, I at once acknowledge that I prefer to accept the spelling, SHAKESPEARE, adopted by the Poet himself, and so printed by his fellow-townsman, RICHARD FIELD, in both *Venus and Adonis* and in *Lucrece*. This alone is for me quite sufficient, and evidently his contemporaries shared the same opinion. Out of all the twenty-eight editions of the Quartos bearing the author's name on the title-page, and published during the Poet's lifetime, fifteen spell the name SHAKESPEARE, twelve spell it SHAKE-SPEARE, and one spells it SHAK-SPEARE. To this unanimity (the hyphen is merely a guide to the pronunciation) we may add the Poet's personal friends, HEMINGE and CONDELL, who thus print it, SHAKESPEARE, in the First Folio.

There is one other item, in reference to the Text, which I think worthy of note. When it is asserted that the Folio follows the text of the Quarto, we assume that the compositors of the Folio had before them, as 'copy,' the pages of the Quarto, either printed or in manuscript. If this assumption be correct, there will remain an unexplained problem. At the present day, when compositors set up from printed copy, they follow that copy slavishly, almost mechanically. Surely, the same must have been true of the less intelligent compositors of SHAKESPEARE'S time, and we might justly expect that the printed page of the Quarto which had served as copy would be exactly reproduced in the Folio, in spelling, in punctuation, in the use of capitals, and of Italics. Yet, this is far, very far from being the case; 'don Peter of Arragon' in the Quarto of the present play, becomes *'Don Peter of Arragon'* in the Folio, in Italics, and with a capital *D*; with 'happy' before him in print, it is almost unaccountable that the compositor of the Folio should take the trouble of adding another type and spell the word 'happie;' or that he should change '4 of his fiue wits' into 'foure of his fiue wits' or change 'lamb' into 'Lambe' with a needless capital and a needless *e*; and so we might go on in almost every line throughout the play. And yet it is incontestable that the Folio was printed from the Quarto,—the very errors of the Quarto are repeated in the Folio, such as giving the names of the actors, Kemp and Cowley, instead of the names of the characters they impersonated.

The solution of the problem is to be found, I think, in the practice of the old printing offices, where compositors set up the types not from copy before them, which they themselves read, but by hearing the copy read aloud to them. We now know that in the printing offices of aforetime, it was customary to have a reader whose duty it was to read aloud the copy to the compositors.[8] This will explain not only all these trivial differences of spelling, punctuation, and of Italics, which I have just mentioned, but also the cause of that more important class of errors which Shakespearian Editors have hitherto attributed either to the hearing of the text delivered by actors, in public, on the stage, or to the mental ear of the compositor while carrying a sentence in his memory. The voice believed to be that of the actor is in reality the voice of the compositors' reader. Be it understood that I here refer mainly to the instances where the Folio was printed from a Quarto. That plays were sometimes stolen by taking them down from the actors' lips on the stage, we know,—HEYWOOD denounces the practice in that same address 'To the Reader' prefixed to his *Rape of Lucrece*.

The happy days, the Golden Age, when *Much Ado about Nothing* was seen, enjoyed, and read by men, unvexed by questions of its Date of Composition, came to an end with MALONE, of whom, in this regard, I am afraid GRATTAN'S description is true, when he spoke of that worthy commentator as 'going about looking through strongly magnifying spectacles for pieces of straw and bits of broken glass.' Since the days of MALONE the study of the *Chronology* of SHAKESPEARE'S plays has been deemed of prime importance, and it is become needful that our accumulated evidence in that regard should be duly marshalled; we must have External Evidence, which is indisputable, and, forsooth, Internal

Evidence, which is of imagination all compact; and, owing to the voluminous detection of this internal evidence, the heap of bits of broken glass assumes portentous proportions, under which the plays themselves are like to be hid; reminding us of the venerable cemetery at Prague, where the records of departed worth are hidden under the pious pebbles deposited by admiring friends.

Happily for us, in the present play the External Evidence of the *Date of Composition* is concise, and the Internal Evidence meagre. To the former belong merely two facts: the entry in the *Stationers' Registers* (which has been given above) and the title-page itself of the Quarto, which is as follows:—

> 'Much adoe about | Nothing. | *As it hath been sundrie times publickly* | acted by the right honourable, the Lord | Chatnberlaine his seruants. | *Written by William Shakespeare.* | [Vignette] | LONDON | Printed by V. S. for Andrew Wise, and | William Aspley. | 1600.'

This title-page, (where, by the way, 'V. S.' stands for Valentine Simmes,) and the entries in the *Stationers' Registers* are all that we know of the *Date of Composition.* How long before August, 1600, SHAKESPEARE wrote the play, we can merely guess. The title-page says that the play had been sundry times acted; even without this assertion we might have been reasonably certain of the fact. Unless a play were many times acted, it is not likely to have been popular; unless it were popular, no stationer would care to publish it, as a Quarto, especially if, in addition, there would have to be some trouble in procuring the Manuscript.

It has been assumed by a majority of editors that an early limit has been found in the fact that MERES, in 1598, does not mention this play, by name, among the other plays of SHAKESPEARE which he enumerates. MERES nowhere professes to give complete lists of all the works of the authors whom he mentions. Mr FLEAY, however, believes that, in the case of SHAKESPEARE, MERES's list of twelve, includes every one of SHAKESPEARE's plays which had been 'either newly written or revived between June 1594 and June 1598.'[9] Nay, as a fact, MERES does more; he gives the title of one play: *Love labours wonne* whereof no trace is known elsewhere. The late Mr A. E. BRAE maintained, and Mr FLEAY agrees with him, that under this title the present play is designated. When MERES wrote: 'so *Shakespeare* among the English is the most excellent in both kinds for the stage; for Comedy, witnesse his *Gentlemen of Verona*, his *Errors*, his *Loue labors lost*, his *Loue labours wonne*, his *Midsummer's night dreame*, and his *Merchant of Venice*: for Tragedy his *Richard the second*, *Richard the third*, *Henry the fourth*, *King John*, *Titus Andronicus* and his *Romeo and Juliet*,'[10] he must have written from memory, and, under *Love labours wonne*, I suppose he may have had in mind any one of several Comedies, wherein the labours of love were successful, as they generally are in all Comedies.

But BRAE is not of this opinion, and the whole question is germane to the present subject only in so far as that, if BRAE be correct, the Date of Composition may be placed at any indefinite time before 1598. His argument, that the present play is *Love's Labours Won* will be found in full in the *Appendix*; in brief, it is that because *Much Ado about Nothing* was printed in 1600, it does not follow that it was not known several years before that date, especially since the title-page says that 'it hath been sundrie times publickly acted.' BRAE further contends that in its plot *Much Ado about Nothing* affords the needed contrast to *Love's Labour's Lost*, he quotes certain passages which show an assumed similitude or parallelism between the two plays. Lastly, he maintains that in *Love's Labours* it is the labours of the little god of love that are intended and not the love manifested by the characters in the play.

BRAE's strong point is that *Much Ado about Nothing* actually appeared in Quarto form in 1600, within only two years of MERES's enumeration in 1598; he might have made it stronger, had he noticed that in this respect *Much Ado about Nothing* stands in the same relation, to MERES, as far as the date is concerned, as stand *A Midsummer Night's Dream* and *The Merchant of Venice*, both of which are in MERES's list, and both appeared in 1600. The appearance of these two Comedies proves unquestionably that there were plays which, although written before 1598, were not printed till 1600; and what is true of these two might be easily true of a third.

BRAE's weak point is in claiming for *Much Ado about Nothing* a date of composition several years before publication, and at the same time denying it to other Comedies. Neither *The Two Gentlemen of Verona* nor *The Comedy of Errors* appeared in print until 1623, and yet both were written twenty-five years before this date; MERES mentions them. Mr FLEAY believes[11] that MERES enumerates all of SHAKESPEARE's Comedies, which had appeared; but until this can be conclusively proved, it is possible that there were others, already then written, which had to wait, like *The Two Gentlemen of Verona* and *The Comedy of Errors*, for the publication of the Folio; it is, therefore, uncritical, I think, to exclude wholly from a competition for the place of *Love's Labour's Won* all the Comedies which appeared only in the Folio.

BRAE's weakest point lies in the 'similitude and contrast,' of which he endeavours to prove the existence, between *Much Ado about Nothing* and *Love's Labour's Lost*. If a companion to *Love's Labour's Lost* is to be sought for, which in 'similitude and contrast' shall prove *Love's Labour's Won*, it would not be hard to find it in *As You Like It*, or in *Twelfth Night*. Dr FARMER and a majority of editors believe that *All's Well that Ends Well* is the missing Comedy. HUNTER thought that he had found it in *The Tempest*; and CRAIK and HERTZBERG urge the claims of *The Taming of the Shrew*. But it is all guess-work, from which the guessers alone retire with intellectual benefit. However, 'the fox is worth nothing when caught,' says SYDNEY SMITH, 'it is the catching alone that is the sport.'

In conclusion, all that to us simple folk is given, and we must get from it what comfort we can, is the fact that *Love's Labours Won* is not come down to us, and to *know* that *Much Ado about Nothing* was published in the year 1600. "'I hope," cried the Squire, "that you'll not deny that whatever is, is."—"Why," returned Moses, "I think I may grant that, and make the best of it."'

Thus far External Evidence.

It is a subject of congratulation that the severe scrutiny, to which all of these plays have been subjected, has been able to discover in the present play only four items of Internal Evidence of the Date of Composition; three of them harmonize, within a year, with the External Evidence.

The first item, which is thought to indicate the Date of Composition, was detected by CHALMERS, who, in the wars from which Don Pedro is returned, where, as Beatrice says, there were 'musty victuals,' finds an undoubted reference to the Irish campaign of 1599. 'The fact is,' says CHALMERS,[12] 'as we may learn from Camden, and from Moryson, that there were complaints of the badness of the provisions, which the contractors furnished the English army in Ireland. And such a sarcasm, from a woman of rank, and fashion, and smartness, must have cut to the quick; and must have been loudly applauded by the audience; who, being disappointed by the events of the campaign, would be apt enough to listen to a lampoon on the Contractor, rather than on the General; who, by his great pretensions and small performances, had disappointed the expectations of the Queen and the hopes of the nation. From all those intimations, it appears to be more than probable, that *Much Ado about Nothing* was originally written in the autumn of 1599.'

First, as for the wars, which CHALMERS thinks refer to the Irish campaign, they are in Bandello's *Novel*, from which SHAKESPEARE is supposed to have drawn his plot, whereof the scene is laid in Messina, whither Don Pedro of Arragon repaired after defeating in battle Charles the Second of Naples.

Secondly, CHALMERS cites Camden and Moryson for his authorities in regard to 'musty victuals,' but does not name chapter or page; he evidently trusted to his memory. A careful reading of the account of Essex's expedition to Ireland given by Fynes Moryson fails to reveal a single complaint as to the provisions. The soldiers were disheartened by the defeats inflicted on them by the Earl of Tyrone, but I can find no word against either the sufficiency or the quality of their food. An equally careful reading of Camden has been alike fruitless. To be sure, Camden wrote several volumes, but I examined that one where, if anywhere, the complaints referred to by CHALMERS would be most likely to be found. I do not say that these special complaints about musty victuals in Essex's campaigns are not mentioned by Camden. All I am sure of is that there is no word about them in his *Annales Rerum Anglicarvm et Hibernicarvm, Regnante Elizabetha*, etc., ed. 1625. The soldiers in the year 1599 are mentioned only twice, as far as I can find. Once their numbers are given, and again (p. 736), in speaking of Essex, Camden says, 'Nee ante mensem Iulium jam divergentem rediit, militibus lassatis afflictis, numerisque supra fidem accisis.' I am thus urgent about a trifle, because CHALMERS's assertion has been accepted without questioning, down to this day.

The second item, which is supposed to have a bearing on the Date of Composition, lies in the reference by the Watch to 'one Deformed, a vile thief this seven year.' This is said to be an allusion to 'Amorphus, or the Deformed,' a character in BEN JONSON's *Cynthia's Revels*. Apart from the somewhat refractory fact that *Cynthia's Revels* and *Much Ado about Nothing* both appeared in the same year (according to GIFFORD *Much Ado about Nothing* preceded *Cynthia's Revels*) there is no intimation that JONSON's 'Amorphus' had been a thief within or without seven years. In reality, there is not the smallest trait soever in common, in the two men; and, if GIFFORD be right, an allusion by SHAKESPEARE to JONSON's 'Amorphus' is an absolute impossibility. That there may be a topical allusion in 'Deformed' is not impossible; but it is not needed, and, if it exist, is probably now for ever lost.

This 'Deformed,' however, is not to be whistled down the wind thus easily; his yield of allusions is not exhausted. Mr FLEAY thrills us with a solution of the mystery which makes the bedded hair start up and stand on end. The Deformed in *Much Ado about Nothing* is of 'course,' he says,[13] 'an allusion to SHAKESPEARE himself. "A vile thief these seven year," indicates the time that he had been stealing instead of inventing his plots.' We pause in doubt with which emotion to dilate: the effrontery of the thief, or the magnanimous, and uncalled for, confession of the Poet. Had this remark been made about SHAKESPEARE by a luckless foreigner, it is painful to imagine the character of the chorus, led, I fear, by Mr FLEAY, with which it would have been received.

Dr FURNIVALL[14] discovered a contemporary, political allusion, (the third item) in the following lines:—

'—like fauourites
'Made proud by Princes, that aduance their pride,
'Against that power that bred it.'—III, i, 11–13.

Here, we are supposed to have a reference to the petted and insolent favourite, Essex, who, disgraced by his fatal campaign in Ireland, had been put in confinement, only to issue therefrom on the twenty-sixth of August, 1600, and plot against the Queen, who had so bred his advancement. To be sure, the date is unlucky; it is later than either the fourth or the twenty-third of August, the dates when *Much Ado about Nothing*, already written, was presented for registration at Stationers' Hall. This obstruction, however, Dr FURNIVALL smoothes away by 'noticing that the evident "political allusion" is in just two lines, removable from the text, and that it may, therefore, have been inserted after the play was first written, and after the outbreak of Essex's conspiracy.' Dr FURNIVALL accepts 'favourite' in the special sense of *minion*.

This acceptation, Mr RICHARD SIMPSON[15] denies, and asserts that 'favourite' means merely 'the confidential agent or minister of a prince.' Thus interpreted, the allusion is to 'Cecil, or the Lord Admiral, or to Raleigh, who were accused of monopolising all her [the Queen's] favours.' A difficulty here, not undetected in the discussion by Dr FURNIVALL, is that nowhere do we find the Cecils or Raleigh advancing their pride against Elizabeth.

The fourth and last item which furnishes Internal Evidence of the Date of Composition, has been detected by Mr FLEAY; it induces him to place this date far earlier than any other critic has placed it, whereby the striking and unusual unanimity of editors and critics in this regard is broken. Mr FLEAY puts the date at 1597–98, and he would have, probably, put it much earlier were it not that he draws a distinction between the original play and the play as we have it. The Almanacs are invoked to help us to the date of *A Midsummer Night's Dream*, and Mr FLEAY invokes them here. 'It is very frequent,' says this author,[16] 'in old plays, to find days of the week and month mentioned; and when this is the case, they nearly always correspond to the almanac of the year in which the play was written.' [Qu. performed? It is to be regretted that examples are not furnished.] 'Now, in this play alone in SHAKESPEARE is there such a mark of time; comparing I, i, 274 "The sixth of July, your loving friend, Benedick" and II, i, 341: "Not till Monday, my dear son, which is hence a just "seven night," we find that the sixth of July came on a Monday; this suits the years 1590 and 1601, but none between; an indication that the original play was written in 1590. Unlike *Love's Labour's Lost*, it was almost recomposed at its reproduction, and this day-of-the-week mention is, I think, a relic of the original plot, and probably due, not to SHAKESPEARE, but to some coadjutor.'

It is so very satisfactory to know not merely the year of composition, but the exact day, that we are filled with regret that the resources of knowledge, in this drama, are, possibly, still unexplored and unexhausted. One fact, hitherto unnoticed, may yet cheer and elevate us. From what Beatrice says, in the first Scene of the Second Act, that a 'Partridge wing will be saved' at supper in consequence of Benedick's melancholy, it is reasonable to suppose that SHAKESPEARE was particularly fond of 'partridge wings' and contemplated with keen zest that one would be saved for his luncheon on Tuesday noon, the seventh of July, on the day after the supper on Monday evening, the sixth of July.

Finally, Mr FLEAY, in corroboration of his date of 1597–8, for this play, observes[17] that 'Cowley and Kempe play the Constables; but Kempe had left the company by the summer of 1599.' This is, I think, a mere inference on Mr FLEAY's part. Kempe acted in *Romeo and Juliet* in 1599, and is introduced in *The Return from Parnassus*, 1601, IV, iii, where he speaks of SHAKESPEARE as his fellow-actor. That the name of an actor of a part should be entered on the prompter's book in place of the name of the character he impersonated is likely enough, but that his name should be there retained after he had left the company and when another actor was supplying his place, is not so easy of belief. The fact that Kempe's name appears in the Qto of 1600 is a proof so decided that he had not then left the company that it would compel Mr FLEAY, I should think, to be extremely cautious, and certainly to lay before the reader all proofs, within his power, of his assertion. A temporary trip to the Continent does not prove a retirement from a company.

To SHAKESPEARE the plots of his dramas were of trifling importance, be it that they are as involved as the plot of the *Comedy of Errors*, or be it that the imaginary characters are as few as they are in his *Sonnets*; he took plots wherever he found them made to his hand. Any situation that would evoke characteristic traits in any *Dramatis Persona* was all that was needed. Dr JOHNSON, as we all know, went so far as to say that SHAKESPEARE 'has not only shown human nature as it acts in real exigencies, but as it would be found in trials, to which it cannot be exposed.' What need then had SHAKESPEARE to invent plots? Under his hand all stories were available, but, apparently, those especially with which his audience was familiar, who, *possibly*, found a certain pleasure in recognizing old friends under new faces, and who could, assuredly, bestow on the characters themselves an attention, which need not be distracted by the need of unravelling an unfamiliar plot. Has a comedy ever been written which gives more pleasure than *As You Like It*? Well may it be called flawless. And yet it contains absurdities in its construction so gross, that their readiest explanation is the supposition that the original commonplace thing, on which the play is founded, has been allowed, by SHAKESPEARE's careless indifference, here and there to obtrude: there are two characters bearing the same name,—it is unthinkable that a dramatist in devising a new play should have committed such an oversight; in one scene Celia is taller than Rosalind, and in another Rosalind is taller than Celia; the Touchstone of the First Act is not the same Touchstone as in succeeding Acts, and, though he has been the clownish Fool about the old court all his days, neither Jaques, nor the Exiled Duke, has ever before seen him when they meet in the Forest where the Duke has been in exile only a few months. And can there be any device to end a story, more preposterous than that a headstrong, violent tyrant at the head of 'a mighty power' should, merely after 'some question with an old religious man,' be 'converted' and instantly relinquish his campaign and retire from the world? But what did SHAKESPEARE, or what do we, care for all such things? They are no part of the play. It is Rosalind who enthralls our hearts, and love is blind. Were there oversights ten times as gross the play would still have power to charm. They are worth mentioning solely as indications that SHAKESPEARE's play is a superstructure. And thus it is, also, with this present *Much Ado about Nothing*. We may read, as I have tried to gather them in the *Appendix*, every story in literature, wherein parallels to this play may be traced, and yet the *fons et origo* will not be there. The old insignificant play (had it been other than insignificant, it would have survived), whereof the dramatic possibilities SHAKESPEARE detected, and moulded into living forms,—this old, insubstantial play, discarded as soon as its brighter offspring appeared, has long since faded and left not a wrack behind, except where here and there its cloth of frieze may be detected beneath SHAKESPEARE's seams of the cloth of gold. At the very first entrance of the players on the stage, for instance, there is what I regard as an unmistakable trace of the original play: 'Innogen,' the wife of Leonato and the mother of Hero, is set down as entering with the others, and yet she utters no single word throughout the play, not even at that supreme moment when her daughter is belied before the altar, and when every fibre of a mother's heart would have been stirred. That her name is here no chance misprint is clear; she reappears in the stage direction at the beginning of the Second Act. Her recorded presence merely shows that for one of the characters with which the original play started, SHAKESPEARE found no use, and through carelessness the name was allowed to remain in the MS promptbook where nobody was likely to see it but the prompter, who knew well enough that no such character was to be summoned to the stage. Then again, it is likely, or, rather, *possible*, that in the old play the paternity of Beatrice was distinctly given. In the present play, there is no hint of it; indeed, it is not unreasonable to ask of a dramatist that in developing his action he should give some account of his heroine, a line will be sufficient, and perhaps save some confusion, which in the present play has really arisen. An eminent critic speaks of Beatrice as the 'worthy daughter of the gallant old Antonio;'[18] undoubtedly Brother Anthony was both gallant and old, but in neither attribute so advanced, as to be obliged to commit his daughter to the care of a 'guardian.' We see clearly why, dramatically, Beatrice must be not a daughter, but a niece, and an orphan; a father or a mother would have checked that brave and saucy tongue. All I urge is that a dramatist in writing a new play, and not rewriting an old one, would hardly have failed to refer to the parents of his heroine. Furthermore, many a critic has somewhat plumed himself on what he considers his singular shrewdness in detecting that Beatrice and Benedick are in love with each other at the opening of the play. But the assertion of Beatrice, in the First Scene of the Second Act, is always overlooked that 'once before' she had possessed Benedick's heart and he had won hers; which is only one of many unexplained allusions to events which occurred before the opening of the play; when, for instance, Beatrice had promised to eat all the victims of Benedick's sword; and when Benedick had set up his bills in Messina and challenged Cupid at the flight. In all these allusions, I think we may discover traces of the original groundwork of SHAKESPEARE's plot. It is *possible* that in the old play of *Benedicte and Betteris* we have this original, and in it the hero and heroine are acknowledged lovers, but become separated by a lover's quarrel, in the course of which Beatrice earns the name of 'Lady Disdain,' and the quarrel is smoothed away by the device which SHAKESPEARE afterward adopted. This, of course, is pure conjecture,—but does it herein differ from the majority of Shakespearian assertions?

This same play of *Benedicte and Betteris* demands a word of reference, I wish I could say, of explanation. In the Lord-Treasurer Stanhope's Accounts[19] 'for all such Somes of money as hath beine receaved and paied by him within his office from the feaste of St. Michael Tharchangell, Anno *Regni* Regis Jacobi Decimo [1612], vntill the feaste of St. Michaell, Anno *Regni* Regis Jacobi vndecimo [1613], conteyning one whole yeare,' there occur the following two items:—

'Item paid to John Heminges vppon the cowncells war*rant* dated att Whitehall XX° die Maij 1613, for presentinge before the Princes Highnes the *Lady* Elizabeth and the Prince Pallatyne Elector fowerteene severall playes, viz: one playe called ffilaster, one other called the knott of ffooles, One other Much adoe abowte nothinge;' etc. (The titles of the remaining eleven do not concern us here.)

Again: 'Item paid to the said John Heminges vppon the lyke warrant, dated att Whitehall XX° die Maij, 1613, for presentynge sixe severall playes, viz: one playe called a badd beginininge [*sic*] makes a good endinge, . . . And one other called Benedicte and Betteris.'

It is extremely easy to assume, with INGLEBY and *The New Shakspere Society*, that these two titles refer to the same play; but the fact that no other of the plays was acted twice, and after the title, as it has come down to us, had been distinctly given in one warrant, that a different title should be given, in a second warrant, issued on the same day, to the same play, must give us pause. It seems to me that where two titles are given the logical assumption is that two plays are referred to. At the same time, it is possible that *Much Ado about Nothing* may have had, originally, a second alternative title, like *Twelfth Night; or, What you Will*, and that this alternative title bore the names of the two principal characters. HALLIWELL[20] says that Charles the First, in his copy of the Second Folio, preserved in Windsor Castle, has added the names 'Benedick and Beatrice,' as a second title. Could it be proved conclusively that *Benedicte and Betteris* is not *Much Ado about Nothing* but an entirely distinct play, it would much simplify the question of the Source of a portion of the Plot.

In the present play, as in others of SHAKESPEARE, there are two separate actions: here, there is the false personation of Hero, and the deceit practised on Beatrice and Benedick. Unless we suppose that there existed a preceding play combining both actions, SHAKESPEARE must have drawn from two separate sources. For the dual deception of Beatrice and Benedick, no parallel has been found; we may therefore concede thus much to SHAKESPEARE's originality, but we must do so on tiptoe lest we waken the commentators, who will not listen to SHAKESPEARE's originality in any direction; but for the former action, the false personation of Hero, it is said that he had but to go to ARIOSTO, or to ARIOSTO's translator HARINGTON, where he might find this false personation of a heroine by one of her ladies-in-waiting. He would find this there, it is true, but he would find nothing more; there is no feigned death and burial to bring repentance to the lover, but instead a grand tournament whereat the false contriver of the harm is slain by the renowned Rinaldo. When, therefore, POPE repeated that the plot of the present play was taken from ARIOSTO, he was only partially correct, which is, after all, about as exact as POPE is generally in his notes on SHAKESPEARE, so that really no great harm is done. And when we come to look still further into details, we find the discrepancy between ARIOSTO and SHAKESPEARE becomes still greater. The scene in ARIOSTO is laid in Scotland; in SHAKESPEARE the scene is in Messina; *Genevra* in ARIOSTO becomes Hero in SHAKESPEARE; *Ariodante*, Claudio; *Dalinda*, Margaret; *Polynesso*, Don John; *Polynesso* is prompted to his wicked stratagem by love of Genevra, Don John by innate depravity; *Polynesso* attempts to kill Dalinda, his mistress and the decoy, Don John has no acquaintance with Margaret, who is supposed to have been an unwitting and innocent accomplice; when Ariodante becomes convinced of Genevra's falseness, he attempts to drown himself, but, changes his mind in the water, unromantically though not unnaturally, and swims ashore; how very far Claudio's thoughts were from suicide, we all know, together with his treatment of Hero. Without continuing this comparison further, it is evident, I think, that ARIOSTO could not have been among the direct sources whence SHAKESPEARE drew this portion of his plot. The sole incident common to both ARIOSTO and *Much Ado about Nothing* is a woman dressed in her mistress's garments, at a midnight window, and for this incident SHAKESPEARE might have been indebted to common gossip concerning an actual occurrence,—an explanation which I do not remember to have seen noted. HARINGTON, in a note at the end of his translation of the Fifth Book of the *Orlando*, wherein is set forth the story of *Ariodante and Genevra*, remarks: 'Some others affirme, that this very matter, though set downe here by other names, happened in Ferrara to a kinsewoman of the Dukes, which is here figured vnder the name of *Geneura*, and that indeed such a practise was used against her by a great Lord, and discovered by a damsell as is here set downe. Howsoever it was,' he goes on to say, 'sure the tale is a prettie comicall matter, and hath beene written in English verse some few yeares past (learnedly and with good grace) though in verse of another kind, by *M. George Turberuil.*'

Here we have the story stated as a fact, and mention of a translation of ARIOSTO into English; the commentators can now resume their secure nap, which we had like to have disturbed by suggesting that SHAKESPEARE could have originated anything. Turbervil's version, however, is not come down to us, according to COLLIER, who, therefore, casts some doubt on its existence, and suggests that HARINGTON's memory played him false. But this need not daunt us; in the same breath COLLIER tells us of a version whereof the title is given by WARTON[21] as '*The tragecall and pleasaunte history of Ariodanto and Jeneura daughter vnto the kynge of Scots,*' by Peter Beverley. This evidently points to ARIOSTO; which is really more than can be affirmed of the title as it appears in the *Stationers Registers'*, under date of 22 July, 1565: 'Recevyd of henry Wekes for his lycense for pryntinge of a boke intituled tragegall and pleasaunte history Ariounder Jeneuor the Dougther vnto the kynge of [?] by Peter Beverlay.'[22]

This 'history,' written in verse by Beverley, maybe the foundation of the play to which we find a reference in the *Extracts from the Accounts of the Revels at Court*, edited by PETER CUNNINGHAM for *The Shakespeare Society*, 1842, where (p. 177), under date of 1582, is the following entry:—'A Historie of Ariodante and Geneuora shewed before her Matie on Shrovetuesdaie at night enacted by Mr Mulcasters children. For wch was newe prepared and Imployed, one Citty, one battlem^t of Canvas vij Ells of sarcenet and ij dozen gloves. The whole furniture for the reste was of the store of this office, whereof sundrey garments for fytting of the Children were altered and translated.' *Possibly*, this play, founded on ARIOSTO, may have given SHAKESPEARE the idea of having Hero personated by Margaret; but it is not probable, inasmuch as there are many circumstances, such as the feigned death, the burial, the epitaph and the second marriage, whereof there is no trace in ARIOSTO; the one solitary incident of a maid's appearance in her mistress's robes does not form an adequate connection, when that incident might have been well known as a fact within the common knowledge of Italians, or of Italian actors, then in London.

It is to CAPELL, the learned, intelligent, and infinitely uninteresting editor, that we are indebted for the discovery that a story, similar in many respects to that of Hero, is to be found in a novel by BANDELLO, the same source to which we owe a version of the story of *Romeo and Juliet* and of *Twelfth Night*. We have not, it is true, in this novel by BANDELLO, a maid personating her mistress, but to offset this we have several springs of action common to both novel and play, and springs of action are more potent in revealing paternity than identity of the names or even the repetition of certain words or phrases; these may have occurred by hap-hazard, but those are of the very fibre of the plot. BANDELLO and ARIOSTO were contemporaries and it is extremely unlikely that the *Orlando Furioso* was unknown to the Bishop of Agen, and as the latter was fond in his stories of imparting to them an air of truth by fixing dates, and giving well-known scenes and names, he may have changed this personation of a lady by her maid, for the very purpose of taking it out of that domain of allegory in which the *Orlando* is written. Be this as it may, we have in BANDELLO the ascent of a man at night by means of a ladder to the chamber of the heroine, the despair and fury of the lover, his rejection of his mistress, her death, her secret revival, her seclusion, her pretended funeral, with an epitaph on her tomb. At this point, there is a divergence in the two stories; in BANDELLO the repentance and confession of the villain, whose motive had been jealousy, are brought about by remorse, and, at the tomb of his victim, he proffers his sword to the heart-broken lover, and entreats the lover to kill him, but the lover forgives, and the two disconsolate men mingle their tears over the past,—a situation of such dramatic power and pathos, that I cannot but believe that had SHAKESPEARE ever read it, we should have received *Much Ado about Nothing*, from his hands, in a shape different from that it now bears. There is one character who figures prominently in BANDELLO, to wit: the heroine's mother; she appears by mistake, as I have just noted, in the stage directions of SHAKESPEARE's play, under the name 'Innogen.' As far as any inference is to be drawn from the similarity of names BANDELLO is only very slightly better than ARIOSTO. The scene, however, is laid in Messina, both with BANDELLO and SHAKESPEARE; we have *Don Pedro* and *Leonato* common to both, and there an end. Hero is *Fenecia*; Claudio is *Don Timbreo di Cardona*; Don John, *Signor Girondo Olerio Valentiano*; and Brother Anthony is *Messer Girolamo*. The conclusions of the story and the play run parallel, and the end in BANDELLO is reached amid the gayest of festivities, wherein, *perhaps*, we may see the Dance at the end of *Much Ado about Nothing*, a jocund ending used nowhere else by SHAKESPEARE.

Here, then, we have what is unquestionably *a* source of *a Much Ado about Nothing*, whether or not it be SHAKESPEARE's source, and SHAKESPEARE's *Much Ado about Nothing*, who can tell? BANDELLO's novels have never been translated into English until within recent years.

For those, however, who would deny SHAKESPEARE any knowledge of Italian, there is a version of BANDELLO, it cannot be called a translation, by BELLE-FOREST. But this version is in French, and, therefore, to those who would deny any learning whatsoever to SHAKESPEARE, almost as unpalatable as the Italian of the original. But there is no help for it. SHAKESPEARE read it either in French or not at all. I incline to the latter belief, not by any means because I think SHAKESPEARE could not read French, but because he needed to read nothing save the old play which he remodelled. BELLE-FOREST I would eliminate entirely from consideration. I do not believe SHAKESPEARE made use of him, nor do I believe that the elder dramatist made use of him. There are dramatic elements in the French version, such as the dishonourable wooing of the heroine, accompanied by languishing love-songs, and high moral sentiments expressed in return, of which a dramatist with the story before him would be likely to retain some trace. Minor details common to both story and play I leave to the reader to discover for himself in the *Appendix* to the present volume.

In brief, the remote Source of the Plot of *Much Ado about Nothing* is, I think, BANDELLO's novel. The immediate source, I believe to be some feeble play modelled on Bandello and containing Dalinda's personation of Generva, which vanished from sight and sound on the English stage, the day that SHAKESPEARE's play, with its added plot of Benedick and Beatrice, was first seen and heard.

There still remains another question which deserves consideration in any investigation of the Source of the Plot. We meet with it in dealing with *The Tempest*, *The Merchant of Venice*, *The Two Gentlemen of Verona*, and of others of SHAKESPEARE's plays. To enter into all the details of this question, which concern the history of the German stage more deeply than that of the English, would exceed the limits of this present volume. It must be sufficient to give general conclusions merely, and, for authorities, refer the reader to the *Appendix*.

In 1811, TIECK[23] called attention to the remarkable fact that, at the beginning of the seventeenth century, there was travelling through Germany a troupe of English comedians, who performed plays, mainly at court, in their own language, before German audiences.

From that day to the present, German scholars have been busy ransacking *Archives* and *Court Journals* until now, thanks to HAGEN, KOBERSTEIN, COHN, GENÉE, TRAUTMANN, MEISSNER, TITTMANN, and many others, we know not only the routes travelled by these strolling English players, and the companies into which they were divided, but even their names, and, occasionally, the titles and subjects of their performances. It is these last two: who the actors were, and what were their plays, which mainly concern us here.

That the visits of English actors to Germany were well known in England and that they were actors of repute, although some of them were mere clowns and posturemasters, we learn from an unexpected English source. HEYWOOD,[24] SHAKESPEARE's fellow-actor and dramatist, informs us that: 'At the entertainement of the Cardinall Alphonsus and the infant of Spaine in the Low-Countreyes, they were presented at Antwerpe with sundry pageants and playes: the King of Denmarke, father to him that now reigneth, entertained into his service a company of English comedians, commended unto him by the honourable the Earle of Leicester: the Duke of Brunswicke and the Landgrave of Hessen retaine in their courts certaine of ours of the same quality.' Elsewhere (p. 58) HEYWOOD refers incidentally to these, his strolling countrymen, and to their fair reputation:—'A company of our English comedians (*well knowne*) [Italics mine] travelling those countryes [Holland], as they were before the burghers and other chiefe inhabitants, acting the last part of the Four Sons of Aymon,' etc. The company commended to the King of Denmark by the Earl of Leicester touches us more nearly than would be at first supposed. It is not unlikely (this unfortunate refrain, which is fated to accompany, as a ground tone, every assertion connected with SHAKESPEARE) it is not unlikely, that, at one time, Will Kempe was a member of this same troupe, which Leicester took with him on his ill-fated expedition to the Netherlands. Sir PHILIP SYDNEY accompanied Leicester and a few months before his own honourable and pathetic death wrote, under date of 24 March, 1586, to his father-in-law, Mr Secretary Walsingham: 'I wrote yow a letter by Will, my lord of Lester's jesting plaier, enclosed in a letter to my wife,' etc. Mr BRUCE[25] shows, by a process of exclusion, that this 'Will' can be none other than William Kempe named, in the First Folio, as the actor of Dogberry.

The list of names which the records in Germany reveal is scanty; naturally, the names, not of every individual in a troupe, but only of the leaders are recorded.

Among these we find GEORGE BRYAN and THOMAS POPE, all-sufficient to bring us close to SHAKESPEARE; these two are familiar to us in the list of twenty-six actors given in the First Folio. Thus we learn, that actors from SHAKESPEARE'S own troupe travelled in Germany, and went even further south into Italy (we know that Kempe, for instance, went to Venice), just as Italian companies came to London, where in 1577–8 there was an Italian *Commediante*, named Drousiano with his players,—a fact, by the way, disclosing an intimate relationship at that early day between the English and the Italian stage of which too little account is made by those who wish to explain SHAKESPEARE'S knowledge of Italian manners and names. That these foreign trips of English actors to Germany were profitable, may be inferred from the comfortable fortune of which Thomas Pope died possessed, as shown by his Will.[26]

With his fellow-actors thus combining pleasure and profit on the Continent, can it be that SHAKESPEARE remained at home? Of course, there are not wanting those who maintain that SHAKESPEARE actually did travel professionally. Mr FLEAY,[27] for instance, says that inasmuch as SHAKESPEARE'S company, Lord Strange's, 'visited Denmark and Saxony, he [SHAKESPEARE] in all probability accompanied them; we are not told which way they came home, but if Kempe took the same route as he did in 1601, he came through Italy. This would account for such local knowledge of Italy as SHAKESPEARE shows.' This 'probable' transportation of SHAKESPEARE into Germany and Italy incites me to say that profound as are my veneration and gratitude to SHAKESPEARE as a poet, they are deeper to him as a man. With that prophetic glance, vouchsafed only to the heaven-descended, he foresaw the inexhaustible flood of imaginings which would be set abroach to account for any prolonged obscurity enveloping his life. Clearly, with this end in view, he evaded all public notice for seven long years. From 1585, when his twin children were baptised (common decency must assume that he was present at that ceremony,) until 1592, we know absolutely nothing of him. For one momentary flash, in 1587 when the terms of a mortgage given by his father, had to be adjusted, we may possibly catch a glimpse of him; but for all the rest a Cimmerian midnight holds him. And what a priceless boon! What an unobstructed field wherein to prove that he so devoted himself to the study of every trade, profession, pursuit, and accomplishment that he became that master of them all, which his plays clearly show him to have been. It was during these seven silent years, while holding horses at the doors of theatres for his daily bread, that he became, if we are to believe each critic and commentator, a thorough master of law and practice down to the minutest quillet; a thorough master of medicine, with the most searching knowledge of the virtue of every herb, mineral, or medicament, including treatment of the insane and an anticipation of Harvey's circulation of the blood; he became skilled in veterinary medicine and was familiar with every disease that can afflict a horse; he learned the art of war, and served a campaign in the field; he became such an adept in music that long afterward he indicated prodigies and eclipses by solmisation; he went to sea and acquired an absolute mastery of a ship in a furious tempest, and made only one slight mistake, long years afterward, in the number of a ship's glasses; he studied botany and knew every flower by name; horticulture, and knew every fruit; arboriculture, and knew the quality and value of all timber; that he practised archery daily, who can doubt? and when not hawking, or fishing, he was fencing; he became familiar with astronomy and at home in astrology; he learned ornithology through and through, from young scamels on the rock to the wren of little quill; a passionate huntsman, he was also a pigeon-fancier, and from long observation discovered that doves would defend their nest, and that pigeons lacked gall; he was a printer and not only set up books, but bound them afterward; as we have just seen he was a strolling actor in Germany, and travelled in Italy, noting the tide at Venice and the evening mass at Verona; he got his Bible by heart, including the Apocrypha; he read every translation of every classic author then published, and every original in Greek, Latin, Italian, and French (of course he learned German while strolling) and, finally, he read through the whole of English literature, from Chaucer down to every play or poem written by his contemporaries, and as he read he took voluminous notes (sly dog!) of every unusual word, phrase, or idea to palm it off afterward as his own!

My own private conviction is that he mastered cuneiform; visited America; and remained some time in Boston,—greatly to his intellectual advantage.

Having discovered who some of these English comedians are, it behooves us next to learn something of the plays they acted. Here a curious fact is revealed. Although nowhere are the plays of these English comedians professedly printed, there yet exist certain German plays, written during the years that these English players were strolling in Germany, whereof the titles and the plots impressively remind us, not only of plays then on the English stage, but even of certain plays by SHAKESPEARE himself. Among the earliest of these German plays are those written by a certain Duke HEINRICH JULIUS of Wolfenbüttel, who, in 1590, went to Denmark to marry the sister of that King to whom, four years before, LEICESTER had handed over his company of actors. It is highly probable (pardon the stereotyped phrase!) that the Duke brought away with him some of these former players of LEICESTER. Be this as it may, certain it is, that from this date Duke HEINRICH JULIUS, during eleven years, wrote about as many Comedies, Tragedies, and Tragi-comedies, which remained for a long time, unrivalled, I think, in the German drama, such as it was; they bear unmistakable signs of English influence. The only one which concerns us here is the *Comoedia von Vincentio Ladiszlao* wherein HERMAN GRIMM, whose opinions are worthy of all respect, finds the prototype of Benedick. The subject will be found more fully treated in the *Appendix*.

As certain critics, mostly German, detected the plot of *The Tempest* in JACOB AYRER's *Die schoene Sidea*, so here in the same old ponderous folio of AYRER, printed at 'Nürmberg Anno M DC XVIII.,' it is suggested that the plot of *Much Ado about Nothing* is to be found, that is, as much of the plot as relates to Hero and Claudio. It is hardly worth while to enter into a discussion of the date when AYRER wrote his comedies. He died in 1605, and COHN[28] thinks that it is 'beyond a shadow of doubt that he wrote nearly all his pieces after 1593.'

Keeping in mind that SHAKESPEARE's indirect source was BANDELLO, it is only requisite to show that AYRER's source was not BANDELLO, but BELLE-FOREST, in order to prove that no connection exists between SHAKESPEARE and AYRER.

The full title of AYRER's play from which SHAKESPEARE is supposed to have drawn his inspiration is: *'A Mirror of Womanly Virtue and Honour. The Comedy of the Fair Phoenicia and Count Tymbri of Golison from Arragon, How it fared with them in their honourable love until they were united in marriage.'* In this title alone there is almost sufficient evidence of the source of AYRER's plot. It can hardly be BANDELLO. In BANDELLO Don Timbreo is never once styled a 'Count' and far less 'Count of Colisano;' that he had received the 'County of Colisano' is mentioned only once at the beginning of BANDELLO's story. It is BELLE-FOREST, who speaks habitually of the 'Comte de Colisan.'

Moreover, BELLE-FOREST, within the first few lines of his story, speaks of the conspiracy of Giovanni di Procida, which led to the 'Sicilian Vespers,' and styles the conspirator *'Jean Prochite.'* BANDELLO refers to the 'Sicilian Vespers,' but never mentions Procida. In AYRER, at the very beginning when Venus enters and complains of the coldness in love affairs of 'Tymborus Graf von Golison,' she acknowledges that he fought most bravely 'When, in Sicily, that great slaughter was made by *Prochyte.*' The presence alone of this name and in its French form, is sufficient, I think, to show that AYRER's source was BELLE-FOREST. For many other similar parallelisms, such as love-letters and love-songs, etc., the reader is referred to the *Appendix.* Were it not for these parallelisms, there might be a faint possibility that AYRER was indebted to a play of which we find a notice in the *Revels Accounts*, for the '18th of Decembre,' 1574, as follows:[29]—'The expence and charge wheare my L. of Leicesters men showed theier matter of panecia.' If under this disguise 'panecia' we detect *Fenicia*, then the date which is too early for BELLE-FOREST indicates BANDELLO, whose Novels were issued in 1554. In view, however, of the many proofs that it was BELLE-FOREST and not BANDELLO to whom AYRER was indebted, 'my L. of Leicesters' 'panecia' need not disturb our conclusions.

My present purpose is attained in the statement that while AYRER's direct source was BELLE-FOREST, SHAKESPEARE's indirect source was BANDELLO; and that SHAKESPEARE was not indebted to AYRER; a conclusion not without its gain if it set at rest the supposition that in AYRER we have the original plays which SHAKESPEARE afterward remodelled. I think it was shown in the *New Variorum Tempest*, that there is no connection whatever between that play and AYRER's *Schoene Sidea*. Nevertheless, Mr FLEAY[30] in speaking of these plays of AYRER, together with those contained in another collection first printed in 1620, four years after SHAKESPEARE's death, says: 'A close examination of these German versions convinces me that they were rough drafts by juvenile hands in which great license was left to the actors to fill up, or alter extemporaneously at their option. [There is no indication of this option in Ayrer that I can detect.] Successive changes made in this way have greatly defaced them; but enough of the originals remains to show that they were certainly in some cases, probably in others, the earliest forms of our great dramatist's plays. I have no doubt he drew up the plots for them while in Germany.'

If this last assertion be correct, it is pleasing to reflect how thoroughly and utterly in after years SHAKESPEARE discarded these juvenile drafts. That these first feeble bantlings of the German drama were, on the contrary, the offspring of the plays acted by English comedians I have no doubt; at times we feel the very whiff and wind of the early London stage; than this, there is, I think, nothing more substantial. Nay, does not the very Preface of AYRER's folio (p. iii) acknowledge that his plays were written after the new English fashion—'*auff di neue Englische manier vnnd art*'? and are not four of his *Operettas*, so to call his *Singets Spil*, sung 'to the tune of the English Roland'? These early German dramas will always remain a curious and interesting field to English and German students. It would be pleasant to think that we might turn to Germany to find the plays, lost to England, which SHAKESPEARE remodelled, but, I fear, it is not to be. Possibly, the connection between the present play, *Much Ado about Nothing* and *The Fair Phoenicia* is as close as any we shall ever find between the English and the German plays.

In a note on the first line of the present play COLERIDGE is quoted as saying that 'Dogberry and his comrades are forced into the service, when any other less ingeniously absurd watchmen and night-constables would have answered the mere necessities of the action.' *Aliquando bonus Homerus*, etc. This remark by him who is, perhaps, our greatest critic on SHAKESPEARE, has been, it is to be feared, the cause of much misunderstanding not only of SHAKESPEARE's plays in general, but of this present play in particular. An idea is thereby conveyed that SHAKESPEARE worked, to a certain extent, at hap-hazard, or, at least, that at times he lost sight of the requirements of his story and was willing to vary the characters of his creation at the suggestion of caprice, to introduce a blundering constable here or a drunken porter there just to lighten his play or to raise a horse-laugh in the groundlings. It would be difficult to imagine a falser imputation on SHAKESPEARE's consummate art. Never did SHAKESPEARE lose sight of the trending of his story; not a scene, I had almost said not a phrase, did he write that does not reveal the true hard-working artist labouring, with undeviating gaze, to produce a certain effect. The opinion is abroad that SHAKESPEARE produced his Dogberry and Verges out of the mere exuberance of his love of fun and that in this 'starry-pointed' comedy, they are the star of comicality, merely to give the audience a scene to laugh at. This inference is utterly wrong. They do, indeed, supply endless mirth, but SHAKESPEARE *had* to have them just as they are. He was *forced* to have characters like these and none other. The play hinges on them. Had they been sufficiently quick-witted to have recognised the villainy of the plot betrayed by Borachio to Conrade, the play would have ended at once. Therefore, they had to be stupid, most ingeniously stupid, and show 'matter and impertinency' so mixed that we can understand how they came to be invested with even such small authority as their office implies. Men less stupid would never have had their suspicions aroused by what they supposed to be an allusion to 'Deformed, a vile thief;' even this allusion is not hap-hazard; stupid by nature as these watchmen are, no chance must be given them to discern the importance of their prisoners, their attention must be diverted from the right direction to something utterly irrelevant, which shall loom up as important in their muddled brains. Hence, this 'Deformed' is not a mere joke, but a stroke of art; and does not, of necessity, involve a contemporary allusion, as is maintained. At no previous point in the play could Dogberry and Verges have been introduced; where they first appear is the exact point at which they are needed. Through the villainy of Don John and the weakness of Claudio the sunshine of this sparkling comedy is threatened with eclipse, and the atmosphere becomes charged with tragedy. Just at this point appear these infinitely stupid watchmen, all whose talk, preliminary to the arrest of Borachio and Conrade, is by no means merely to make us laugh, but to give us assurance that the play is still a comedy and that however ludicrous may be the entanglement in which these blundering fools will involve the story, the resolution, the denouement, will be brought about by their means and that the plot against Hero, which we see is hatching, will by them be brought to nought. Had Dogberry been one whit less conceited, one whit less pompous, one whit less tedious, he could not have failed to have dropped at least one syllable that would have arrested Leonato's attention just before the tragic treatment of Hero in the marriage scene, which would not have taken place and the whole story would have ended then and there. Dogberry *had* to be introduced just then to give us assurance that Don John's villainy would come to light eventually, and enable us to bear Hero's sad fate with such equanimity that we can listen, immediately after, with delighted hearts to the wooing of Benedick and Beatrice.

I do by no means say that SHAKESPEARE could have dramatised this story in no other way, his resources were infinite, but I do say that, having started as he did start, he was *forced*, by the necessities of the action, to have stupidity rule supreme at those points where he has given us the immortal Dogberry.

KNIGHT among editors, and BOAS among critics, are the only ones that I can recall, who have had even an inkling of the true position which Dogberry holds.

One pleasure yet remains to me whereby to enliven the dulness of a *Preface*: to thank my sister, MRS ANNIS LEE WISTER, for translating the extracts, in the *Appendix*, from German Critics. In regard to one portion, therefore, of this volume I can be shut up in measureless content.

H. H. F.
November, 1899.

NOTES

1. Arber's *Transcript,* vol. iii, p. 37.
2. See *As You Like It,* p. 295, of this edition.
3. *Life and Work,* 1886, p. 40.
4. *Chronicle of the English Drama,* 1891, vol. ii, p. 184.
5. *At You Like It,* p. 296, *Merchant of Venice,* p. 271, *Midsummer Night's Dream,* p. xvi, of this edition.
6. Arber's *Reprint* iii, 170.
7. *Outlines of the Life of Shakespeare,* 1882, p. 528.
8. *The Invention of Printing,* &c., by T. L. De Vinne, New York, 1876, p. 524.
9. *Life and Work of Shakespeare,* 1886, p. 135.
10. *Wits Common Wealth, The Second Part,* by F. M. 1598, p. 623.
11. *Life and Work,* p. 135.
12. *Supplemental Apology,* 1799, p. 380.
13. *Introduction to Shakespearian Study,* 1877, p. 23.
14. *The Academy,* 18 Sept. 1875.
15. Ibid., 25 Sept. 1875.
16. *Life and Work of Shakespeare,* p. 204.
17. *Op. Cit.,* p. 205.
18. *Introduction* to 'The Leopold Shakspere,' p. lvi.
19. Rawl. MS. A. 239. leaf 47 (*in the Bodleian*). Reprinted in *Shakespeare Soc.* Papers, ii, 123; *New Shakspere Soc.* Trans., 1875–6, p. 419; Ingleby's *Centurie of Prayse,* p. 103.
20. *Outlines,* etc. p. 262.
21. *History of English Poetry,* iii, 479, ed. 1781.
22. Arber's *Transcript,* i, 312.
23. *Alt-Englisches Theater,* p. xii.
24. *Apology for Actors,* p. 40, ed. Shakespeare Society.
25. *Shakespeare Society's Papers,* 1844, i, 88.
26. Collier's *Memoirs of Actors,* etc., 1846, p. 125.
27. *Trans. of the Royal Hist. Soc.* 1881, vol. ix.
28. *Shakespeare in Germany,* 1865, p. lxiii.
29. *Revels at Court in the Reign of Queen Elizabeth,* etc., Shakespeare Society, 1842, p. 87.
30. *Op. cit.* p. 4.

MUCH ADO ABOUT NOTHING IN THE TWENTIETH AND TWENTY-FIRST CENTURIES

✌

Critical reception of *Much Ado about Nothing* in the nineteenth century helped pave the way for further exploration in the twentieth and twenty-first centuries. Much of the criticism done on the work in the last one hundred years is dominated by two distinct reactions to earlier nineteenth-century criticism—examining further the concepts of "noting" and "nothing" derived by Elizabeth Inchbald, H. N. Hudson, Frederick S. Boas, and others and scrutinizing those characters often overlooked by earlier critics, especially Hero.

W. H. Auden (1946) was one of the first modern critics to take up the mantle of the "noting" discussion started by Inchbald when he argued that *Much Ado about Nothing* is very much a play of deception and pretense. Auden's work actually bridges older forms of critical inquiry with new. He begins by examining the dualistic nature of the plot, suggesting that the Hero/Claudio storyline is as conventional as the Beatrice/Benedick storyline is not. Auden then uses these contrasting notions of conventional/unconventional to partition the rest of the play's characteristics, including characters, scenes, and responses, as conventional or unconventional, manufactured or realistic, pretense or true emotion. The result demonstrates those aspects through which, Auden suggests, Shakespeare intended to provide a more realistic sense of catharsis for the audience (from the love of Beatrice and Benedick to Antonio's reaction to his niece's public repudiation to Don John's villainy) and those that reflect the larger pretense of the play (much of the Hero/Claudio storyline, Leonato's challenge of Don Pedro and Claudio after the wedding scene, the contrived "punishment" for Claudio at the end of the play). This reflects the singular concept of pretense that dominates the play, as those characters and moments more wallowing in subterfuge or deception tend to suffer more at each others' hands and also lack an overall artistic connection to the audience or the text.

Graham Storey (1959) further develops this notion by suggesting that there are no fully realized characters in *Much Ado about Nothing*; rather, he argues, everyone is a "mask," a caricature of sort. Ultimately, it is the characters themselves who are the deceptions. Only Beatrice and Benedick are more fully fashioned figures—they are, for lack of a better term, more "real"—and thus they escape the punishment and agony that Hero and Claudio must endure. Marvin Felheim (1964) likewise advances this notion by remarking that every character in the play is involved in the act of deception, whether as a deceiver, as the deceived, or (as in most cases) both. Character, Felheim suggests, is not key to understanding *Much Ado about Nothing*; plot is, or rather, plotting, since the act of plotting dominates the play. While most of Shakespeare's comedies rely on misunderstandings and deceptions that structure the plot of the text (think of Viola's gender deception in *Twelfth Night* or Bianca's deception of her father in *The Taming of the Shrew*), no play relies on deceptions more than *Much Ado about Nothing*. Carl Dennis (1973) argues that the real key to understanding *Much Ado About Nothing* is in letting go of commonly held perceptions, misperceptions, misapprehensions, and misunderstandings. The act of deception is vital to the action here, but perhaps more important is the construct of holding on to notions that, while deeply believed, are flat-out wrong. These include Beatrice and Benedick's professed dislike of marriage, Claudio's fears of Hero's faithlessness and lack of trust in his affianced wife, and Don Pedro's belief in his brother's rehabilitation and capitulation. These variously held and usually erroneous perceptions are the true "much ado about nothing" that hallmark the play; by the end of the work, these notions are eradicated, and thus a happy ending is finally possible for all.

As is evident, this examination of "noting" in its many guises throughout the play dominated critical interest in *Much Ado about Nothing* throughout much of the twentieth century. It culminates in the work of Nova Myhill (1999), who argues that the act of witnessing—as she calls it, "spectatorship"—is just as important as the act of noting, or hearing, as much of what is misperceived is often seen as well as heard. Myhill's work brings Inchbald's original concept back full circle, suggesting the route of deception in one's mind and the "much ado" that can be made over it. The consistency of critical thought and its continual buildup of these notions, one upon the other, creates a continuum of scholarship extending over the entire century that is not commonly witnessed; breathtaking in its scope, it demonstrates a real critical trajectory that ultimately has formed and shaped scholarly and dramatic reading of the text.

Character, the popular bastion of nineteenth-century thought, is not ignored in the twentieth century, though the perspective on character has been influenced by those figures within the world of the play who have been perceived as receiving less attention than others in the nineteenth century and by adapting applications of critical theory to the text. Charlotte Porter (1906) demonstrates the roots of this mode of thought in her work; like many critics in the previous century, she focuses on the dynamics of Beatrice and Benedick, but her critical eye is turned largely toward the male member of the duo, suggesting that Benedick ultimately alters his own self-fashioning in his desire to woo Beatrice. The changes she notes are numerous and evident, but until her work, many critics had passed over

Benedick in favor of either Beatrice alone or looking at Beatrice and Benedick together. Much later, Carol Cook (1986) produced what many consider to be the seminal work on Hero. In her evaluation, Cook, utilizing a feminist perspective that nineteenth-century scholars often assumed in examining Beatrice, describes Hero as the product of her environment, a perfectly dutiful example of Elizabethan womanhood. Cook notes the terror with which the men of the play seem to perceive such a creature. For all her bluster, Beatrice speaks her mind and reproduces speech patterns that are often considered male in application, and this invokes little of the same male fear, despite the fact that her outspoken nature would seem to make her more anathematic to the male perspective. However, Cook demonstrates that it is the silent Hero whom men truly fear, her unknowableness proving to be the reason behind the reactions Claudio, Don Pedro, and even her own father espouse in the wedding scene.

Both works closely examine the language (or, in Hero's case, the lack of said language) of each character within their analysis; previous character-driven assessment of the play also focused on the language of some individual characters, especially Dogberry and Beatrice. More generalized linguistic study has proved a new area of scholarly application for the play in recent years. Alexander Leggatt (1974), for example, completed an analysis of the two main storylines from a linguistic perspective, concluding that the language found within the Hero/Claudio plot is largely conceived of in a conventional style, and that the language found within the Beatrice/Benedick plot is often as innovative and unconventional as its main characters. This demonstrates further divide between these two sections of the play, continuing and expanding on research begun in the seventeenth and eighteenth centuries. Maurice Hunt's (2000) more recent work on the play unifies and codifies these three seemingly disparate ideas that dominated twentieth-century thought on the play. His essay suggests that the act of speaking is as important as the act of listening, and that the speaker is perhaps in many cases even more important than the listener. This is certainly a response to the "noting" scholarship begun by Inchbald and continued by Auden, Storey, Felheim, and Dennis in the twentieth century. Thus he emphasizes character (building off the work of Cook and others) in regard to the auspices of language and ultimately suggests that the deceptions that contaminate the play matter less than the fact that these deceptions work so capably well because they bring to the surface feelings and ideas that are already present within the speaker or receiver. Thus Claudio's repudiation of Hero is not so much the result of Don John's lies but comes about because of the insecurities inherent within Claudio himself. This builds on the three prevailing threads of twentieth-century criticism: the emphasis on "noting," the concept of "nothing," and its significance within the play; the examination of largely overlooked figures within the play; and the examination of the language of the text itself. Hunt thus perhaps demonstrates the culmination of twentieth-century criticism on *Much Ado about Nothing*, as well as proffers a way forward for the next century in examining this rich, ripe Shakespearean classic.

1906—Charlotte Porter. Introduction
to *Much Adoe About Nothing*

A well-regarded American scholar and editor of Robert Browning, Elizabeth Barrett Browning, and Shakespeare, Charlotte Porter (1859-1942) was also the editor of the journal *Shakespeariana* from 1883-87. The following text, the introduction to Porter's edition of *Much Ado About Nothing*, begins by labeling the play a comedy with a "heart"—and that "heart," Porter contends, is key to the play's success. Unsurprisingly, the heart of the play is most in evidence in the characters of Beatrice and Benedick, and by focusing her discussion on the famous "Kill Claudio" scene of act 4, scene 1, Porter demonstrates that the most emotionally satisfying moments in *Much Ado about Nothing* occur not when Beatrice and Benedick spar with wit or declare their love but rather at the moment Beatrice, in her intense desperation to right the wrong that has befallen her cousin, turns to Benedick for the only remedy she can conceive. Benedick initially refuses, but as Porter points out, this response was "born of all that was the Benedicke of old." After a moment's reflection, Benedick realizes that his love for Beatrice has fashioned a new personage for himself—has literally made a new man out of him—and he agrees to the challenge. Though some critics have considered the intensity of this scene at odds with the jocular nature of the duo's scenes in the rest of the play, Porter contends that "such an enhancement as this of an unreal and therefore comic situation by a sub-tragic intensity and a profoundly true psychology of love is—Shakespearian."

Porter then argues that the Shakespearean play most closely aligned to *Much Ado about Nothing* is *Love's Labour's Lost*. Both plays enjoin a unique approach to the genre of comedy, one that Porter believes distinguishes the genre over the baser forms Shakespeare presents in other plays. Both also criticize "post and artifice," even among those characters within them (such as Don John) who reflect those precepts. Among the numerous qualities that unite the two works, however, is one that distinguishes them and through which, Porter suggests, *Much Ado about Nothing* surpasses all other Shakespearean comedies. In the play, Shakespeare creates a "feminine opposition to masculine ideas" (as evidenced in the above mentioned scene between Beatrice and Benedick.) This is a construct only found in *Much Ado about Nothing* and

The Taming of the Shrew, and, by Porter's standards, the former play is much more skillfully rendered in plot, characterization, and genre than the latter farce. The end result, Porter suggests, is that *Much Ado about Nothing* is the most sublime of Shakespeare's comedies and the pinnacle of the genre in his work.

MUCH ADOE ABOUT NOTHING stands apart from the other plays of Shakespeare strikingly on several counts. It is related, also, more closely to one other play than to any one of the rest.

Out of the muster-roll of the thirty-seven dramas how many are there that treat wholly of the situations, types, and poses of the unextraordinary worldly world? How many show that cool and clever, light and level touch which never breaks through or breaks down, and is the somewhat prosaic yet sparkling characteristic of pure Comedy?

As if to bear witness that he could easily, when he chose, command this realm of art, too, 'Much Adoe' glistens out in the list of the plays of Shakespeare.

But the greater part of the list may be called to bear witness to the fact that his instinctive sovereignty was exercised less over the governable civil domain of the witty, sensible, and purely intellectual, as over the tumultuously passionate, unruly, though decidedly not lawless universe of the adventurous, the tragic, and the ardent. The bent of his creative taste seems toward both the ideally and the crudely human; and they are each alike removed from the middle region of the worldly world of sophisticated Comedy.

Or else,—and it amounts really to the same thing,—after a few artistic experiments made during the first decade of his career, when he was finding himself, 'Much Adoe' being the consummate one of these experiments, he must have instinctively grown to rate this middle region of pure Comedy as less potential in life than the peaks and roots of human nature, and, therefore, also, less potential in Art. And so he gave it place without prominence, without separation from the scenic presentation of the totality of living summed up more usually thereafter by his peculiar art in every play.

In 'Much Adoe about Nothing' Comedy bears rule as the supreme interest. Even there, however, it is not altogether detached from the deeper rooted activities of heart and will. There is only one thrust through the social crust to the quivering tissues of the tragic in this play; and that one thrust, in the church-scene of Claudio's repudiation of Hero, amid all the fencing over the surface of life during the rest of the action, draws the red blood of emotion, then, so as to make the steel of wit and sense sparkle brighter.

Here comes the real climax of interest. It is the instant actually testing the internal worth of the 'noting' out of which the external action is built. What interior action lies back of it is here brought out and questioned. In the conflict between the tragic element fleetingly introduced here, and the elsewhere even tenor of Comedy, the lightning of Beatrice's fierce 'Kill Claudio!' is the culmination

Benedicke's instinctive recoil,—'Ha, not for the wide world,'—is his first response. It is born of all that was the Benedicke of old, before he thought he should live to be married. Beatrice then aims her arrow of speech straight to the heart of the new Benedicke. The choice her words put before him, the admission as to the new Beatrice which they contain shuts up the whole situation between them, with an inexorable click: 'You kill *me* to denie, farewell.' He begins to understand, of course, wants a minute to think, but beside, he half tries to slip out without quite relinquishing what he wants, either. Man-like he woos; 'Tarrie sweet Beatrice,' with his arms about her, forcibly containing her.

But physical emotion and physical control in themselves are nothing to Shakespeare's Beatrice, and she will not be commanded. Till the whole man is dominated by the new relation, neither is her will dominated by it. It is no use to hold her, till he holds her good will. 'I am gone though I am here, there is no love in you.' So unerringly she forces the new Benedicke to show himself true steel. So unerringly she shows and sheathes her own passion, and matches this climax of the play and Shakespeare's handling of his consummate comedy by embodying them.

For the desperate intensity she feels and excites is a mere foil enhancing the situation marvelously on the Comedy side. As the audience knows, Benedicke is really committed by it to nothing more deadly than if the situation were *opera bouffe*. Dogberry cannot possibly be so tedious as to obscure much longer Borachio's trick, Don John's malice, and Claudio's good fortune in being retrievably victimized.

The tragic reality of the emotion comes perilously near the edge of the limits of Comedy for the lovers, but since it never goes over them for the author and the audience, therefore the situation is held, as unerringly as Beatrice's good wit and passion blended in one are held, within the control of the Comedy-idea. Intense feeling is everywhere curbed by a spirited adroitness as apt and amusing as it is judicious and vital.

The fact remains, however, that such an enhancement as this of an unreal and therefore comic situation by a sub-tragic intensity and a profoundly true psychology of love is—Shakespearian. No standards outside of those drawn from Shakespeare himself are big enough to approach the breadth and depth of his grasp here.

It is significant that in this the most unmitigatedly brilliant of his comedies the tears of Beatrice outsparkle her laughter and yet are most genuine tears. Actresses rarely let their audiences enjoy to the full the perilous edge of the contrast here between the unreality of situation and the intense truth of character. They forget that their coy banter is not needed to explain what the dramatist has so skillfully explained and prepared, in order to mirror the whole more sharply in these genuine tears of Beatrice.

There are times when even the sea seems superficial so gay and glancing is its mood. Yet even at such times its brightness seems the brighter through some furtive contrast with its hidden strength. There are plays when Shakespeare seems merely brilliant so quiescent lie the depths below a shimmering surface. Yet even in such a play the brightness of surface is heightened by the subconsciousness of underlying tides of power. But are there more than four such plays in which brilliancy and merriment predominate unbrokenly? Or are there really but two?—for of the four that recur to mind—'The Comedie of Errors,' 'The Merry Wives of Windsor,' 'Loves Labour's Lost,' and 'Much Adoe About Nothing,' the 'Errors' like the 'Shrew' is boisterous with a sort of foregone intenton. It is another man's idea of Farce which is being worked out on lines already laid down. Although he was unhampered in it by prior work, as it can well nigh be proven he was not in the 'Shrew'; still he merely made of it so dextrous a piece of workmanship in the farce line, so out-Plautus-ing Plautus, that he never needed to recur to that Latin kind of fun, henceforth. What there was of native English Farce in 'the Shrew' he seems to have taken up experimentally and worked out in a new guise in the 'Merry Wives.' Farce, pure and simple, however, appears to have been a somewhat perfunctory, although masterly occupation of alien territory, like the ocean running up a narrow river-bed.

In the two comedies remaining we seem alone to recognize the genius proper to Shakespeare indulging itself in being merely brilliant in the worldly world of real life. 'As You Like It' is not an exception, for there, as in the whimsical 'Midsommer Nights Dreame,' it is as poet and idealist that he refuges life from itself, and in order to reconcile it with its actualities places it apart from the world in the wildwood of Arden, as in an imaginative golden age. So also in the 'Dreame' he redeemed his lovers' difficulties by placing them in the world of faërie.

The charm of his only other comedy that revels protractedly in high animal spirits without a tragic plunge, 'Twelfe Night,' relegates the flow of hilarity to the minor half of the play, and for its main interest carries an ardor of poetry and love and most sensitive idealism. It can scarcely be maintained, therefore, for a moment, that it is merely brilliant, dextrous, intellectually alert and keen as 'Loves Labour's Lost' and 'Much Adoe' are. These qualities place these plays in a class by themselves. In these two only out of the thirty-seven does Shakespeare's genius seem to display itself in the comedy of social life as distinguished from the farcical, on the one side, or the imaginative, on the other. Here he holds in check both the poetic fire and the human profundity that run together under a free rein in the great tragedies, and in the great romances are infinitely suggestive both of the tears and laughter of all of human life.

That sounding eighteenth century phrase of Dr. Johnson's is quoted now by children of the just past and the present centuries as generally applicable to Shakespeare's supremacy as a dramatist. But this is to quote it with a remarkable difference from its original strictly special application.

When Johnson wrote, in 1765, in the Preface to his Edition of Shakespeare, these famous words: 'The stream of time, which is continually washing the dissoluble fabricks of other poets, passes without injury by the adamant of Shakespeare,'—he narrowed its application to the 'comick scenes.' These special portions of his work—due subtraction for his quibbling exuberances being made—were recognized by Johnson as having 'suffered little diminution from the changes made by a century and a half.' Because these 'comick scenes' were not 'adventitious' they were, therefore 'durable'; while in his 'tragick scenes,' as Johnson declared, 'there was always something wanting . . . his performance seems constantly to be worse as his labour is more. The effusions of passion which exigence forces out, are for the most part striking and energetick; but whenever he solicits his invention and strains his faculties, the offspring of his throes is tumour, meanness, tediousness, and obscurity.' While in his 'comick scenes'—thus Johnson draws the distinction,—'he seems to produce without labour what no labour can improve,' in his tragic scenes 'he often writes with great appearance of toil and study, what is written at last with little felicity.' He concludes: 'His tragedy seems to be skill, his comedy instinct.'

Johnson assented, thus, to Rymer's judgment of the limitation of Shakespeare's excellence as an artist, that his natural disposition . . . led him to 'comedy.' And this corroboration by Johnson of Rymer which Joseph Warton, the critic, brother of Thomas Warton, Poet-Laureate of England, accepted as tending 'to lessen the unrivalled excellence of our divine bard,' he says he is 'sorry to perceive gains ground.'

It must, of course, be urged in Johnson's behalf, when he is quoted to this effect, that he was no clearer-sighted than his age. He accepted prevalent standards of Tragedy and Comedy by which he measured Shakespeare, while he apologized for the Poet's supposed ignorance of these standards. That the Poet chose his realm could not occur to him. And note the curious assumption, questionable now, that criticism has any vitality of its own apart from genius. It had scarcely dawned upon the mind, then, that the tests of the criticism of that age were 'adventitious,' therefore not 'durable,' and that the exhaustless flood of Shakespeare's genius must be continually 'washing away the dissoluble fabricks' of narrowing criticism.

It is enough, now, to forbear judgment, and adduce merely as an observation, to be drawn from data Shakespeare himself supplies, the counter-statement that his natural disposition led him away from unmixed comedy, since, aside from the more or less farcical pieces mentioned, 'Much Adoe' and 'Loves Labour's

Lost' stand apart and comparatively unchequered by the ardors and profundities of the other plays.

There is also to be seen alike in 'Much Adoe' and 'Loves Labour's Lost' an implicit criticism of pose and artifice in the interest of genuine feeling. The comprehension of the foibles of mankind shown in the plays generally is in these plays a shade less genial and non-commital.

Despite the good-nature and wisdom behind the thrusts of merriment, the manner is hard and mocking. It may be that this is not altogether due to the artistic method adopted for the sake of attaining the satiric effects sought in light and pure Comedy; but, rather, that the skeptical point of view of the artist toward certain intellectual assumptions led him here and at this period of his genius to Comedy.

The academic, anti-feminine, anti-secular—in a word, the cloistral conception of life, whose inherent foolishness is so gayly exhibited in 'Loves Labour' may have gone against such a poet's grain. Enough so to make him just a little of an advocate,—as little of an avowed advocate, naturally, as a dramatic artist can betray himself to be—of unrestricted life, and the larger experience genuine emotion evokes, whether crude and rude as in Costard and Jaquenetta, or as socially fruitful in its leading as it promised to become in Berowne and Rosaline.

In 'Much Adoe' there also appears a kindred animus against the exclusiveness of the ultra masculine view of life and of love embodied in Benedicke, as in 'Love Labour's Lost' it was embodied in the Academicians. And the position taken against love in the one play by the scholar, in the other by the soldier, is made doubly effective by the introduction of an opposite and ultra feminine view similarly bent on excluding love.

For this reason—*i.e.*, the introduction of feminine opposition to masculine ideas, 'Much Adoe' and 'The Shrew' have a link of association. But 'Much Adoe' is, by its plan, primarily and more essentially linked with the comedy that brings to confusion the vows of the celibate scholars, as it brings to confusion those of Benedicke—Benedicke, the bachelor, who when he said he should die a bachelor, did not think he should live till he was married. The 'Shrew,' on the other hand, is through 'Much Adoe,'—which it more closely resembles, its central idea being related to Beatrice,—only secondarily allied to 'Loves Labour.'

In 'Much Adoe,' again, as in 'Loves Labour,' the poet seems to betray just enough more relish of his work than is necessary to bring the predestined plot our right artistically, to suggest that he has guided the issue from the first as an advocate of love against restriction. The plot is devised,—directly, by the author, in 'Loves Labour,' indirectly, in 'Much Adoe,' through the instrumentality of Don John's plan,—in order to reveal the supremacy of love as an emotional motive-power in life to those who have decried, depreciated, and opposed it. In all the other plays, important as the part is which love plays in each of them, its supremacy does not depend upon the defeat of opposition in the will of the lovers to Love, considered impersonally, as a necessary emotional power in life to which they have intellectually refused allegiance.

The instrumentality of Don John laboring to this end is, also, seconded by the creator of Don John in a very striking manner. Shakespeare goes so far as almost to throw the other half of the plot in the service of this half of it—by turning the Claudio and Hero half into a means to solve the Benedicke and Beatrice half. He subordinates everything, and he introduces besides a special factor—the Dogberry and Verges element, mainly in order to give himself a tool, enabling him so to subordinate the whole to this half that it becomes, if it were not so intended from the first, the dominant issue. The increasing interest of the play is the confusion of Benedicke and the chastening of his heart and will so as to elicit and deserve Beatrice's. Why is the plot so centered upon him, and Beatrice as its subtlest instrument, when she bids him 'Kill Claudio!' save to reveal the value to his good wit, yes, and to his manly prowess, his honor, and his good blade besides, of that same love which 'first learned in a Ladie's eye,' as Berowne discovered, 'Lives not alone emured in the braine, But with the motion of all elements courses as swift thought in every power, And gives to every power a double power, Above their functions and their offices?'

'Measure for Measure' is the only other play whose art can similarly be suspected of ministering toward a criticism of the imposition upon Life of over rigid restrictions past human nature to sustain. There seem to be no other whose art is not too veiled to permit the temper of the artist to be guessed. But if the inference be fair as to that play, then the criticism of restriction it also enfolds, as there applied in another direction, is in general accord with the criticism similarly expressed in 'Loves Labour's Lost' and 'Much Adoe.'

The art of comedy in 'Loves Labour' is young and slight compared with the finished skill and mastery of 'Much Adoe;' but they are alike young in their spiritedness of onset, and the sprightly warmth of their wit against these clever persons who so little know life and their own human nature that they forswear what their own character is bound to evoke and their own place in life to require.

That these are twin plays, the outcome of a special point of view discoverable from them, and that they are distinguishable, also, in their manner of pure comedy from the rest of the plays is the more notable because the plot of 'Loves Labour' is Shakespeare's own, built up fancifully out of current incidents and interests . . . and the plot of the better half of 'Much Adoe,' that is, the Benedicke and Beatrice half, is also Shakespeare's own or else 'Loves Labour' itself is its source.

Benedicke is a supplementary but contrasting figure to Berowne. He is conceived from a distinctly new standpoint. He is a less poetic, equally brainy Berowne who does not, from the academic side, but from the prosaic, worldly side, as a man of intellect and action, consider Woman and Love unnecessary to him. Berowne, moreover, was intuitive, and suspected from the first that they were necessary.

The labor of Love spent in winning Berowne as a lover against his vow, and as an advocate of the emotion of love as doubling the powers of the personality; and that labor lost to him in another sense, so far as any fruition with Rosaline, inside the limits of the play, was concerned, is spent, within the limits of 'Much Adoe,' upon winning Benedicke as a lover of Beatrice, and as a man who purposes to marry and thinks 'nothing to any purpose that the world can say against it.'

The vow of the celibate scholars in their cloistered 'Achademe' over which love prevails, becomes in 'Much Adoe' the vow of Benedicke, the man of action to 'live a batcheller,' and wreak out his vigor in every experience except love, or else—Pick out his eyes 'with a Ballet makers penne,' and hang him up 'for the signe of blinde Cupid.' And just this Shakespeare does for him.

This mention of the ballad-maker is a reminder of a number of other links between the two plays wherein the conquest of Cupid is signalized by the kindled desire of the lover to discourse with the subtle tongue of the poet. Benedicke objects to this sign of heightened emotion in Claudio. There was once no music for Claudio, he says, but the drum and fife of war. He who was blunt of speech, like 'an honest man and a soldier,' is now 'turn'd orthography,' and his words are so many 'fantasticall' dishes.

So Armando in 'Loves Labour' cries 'Adue Valour, rust Rapier, bee still Drum, for your manager is in love; yea, hee loveth. Assist me some extemporal god of Rime, for, I am sure I shall turne Sonnet.' And so, when, as Berowne says, Cupid imposes his plague for 'neglect of his Almighty dreadfull little might' upon the sworn Academicians, they all 'turne Sonnet.'

The inimitable scene follows where they all overhear and 'note' one another; but from their 'forheads wipe away' the 'perjured note,' finding that 'none offend where all alike doe dote.' The overhearing and noting, so amusing in this scene, and being overheard by Boyet, so productive of fresh amusement in the following scene, is improved upon to the last degree of dramatic ingenuity in 'Much Adoe.' Mr. F. S. Boas has shown conclusively and admirably how the whole plot of 'Much Adoe' is based upon overhearing and noting. . . . He has done this so entirely as the present writer would have been disposed to show it had he not made it unnecessary, that reference here to his exposition of it alone is needed, with this addition, that the 'noting' idea employed successfully in 'Loves Labour's Lost' is transferred with elaboration and consummate success to 'Much Adoe.'

The fact that this complete net-work of 'noting' and overhearing which knits in and unifies this play is not traceable to any source, but seems to be due, like the Benedicke and Beatrice half of the plot and the Dogberry episode, to Shakespeare alone, again brings into significant relation these two plays of Love's conquest of persons forswearing his power.

Further agreement of plan with relation to that heightening of emotion and subtilizing of tongue which prompts the lover to 'turn Sonnet' is evidenced in Benedicke after the manner he so scorned in Claudio, when he confesses he has tried hard to express his love to Beatrice in rime. Despite his good will he cannot woo in 'festival terms,' since he was 'not born under a riming plannet.'

Finally, also, when the beneficent trick of Don Pedro which betrayed Beatrice and Benedicke to each other is made clear to them and they again take to hedging and hiding, their secret hearts are revealed by a 'noting' of their own, past gainsaying. The Sonnets each had written to the other are the crowning evidence neither can resist (V. iv. 91–7).

The other half of 'Much Adoe,' the Claudio and Hero half, diverged in motive from that presented by Love's labor to bring Benedicke and Beatrice 'into a mountaine of affection, th' one with th' other.' But it is interesting to notice that the parallel element of the double plot—the intervention of Don Pedro for Love's sake—is made dominant by Shakespeare's device. It has no prototype in the sources whence he derived the Claudio half of the plot. Claudio has been unjustly censured for wooing by proxy, when that he should do so was one of the requirements of the plot from the artistic point of view. This is like finding fault with Romeo that he was not a less desperate lover when he believed Juliet was dead, and so slower about taking his poison. Just as Shakespeare's Romeo must love to desperation, so Shakespeare's Claudio must depend upon his powerful and devoted friend, even in his wooing. Plot and character strike together the chord desired in the musician's harmony. It is for us who hear to 'consider and bow the head.'

How closely blended with Claudio's repudiation of Hero is the critical moment of the vital revelation of Benedicke and Beatrice to each other in the Church scene has been noticed as the climax toward which the plot was built. This tests for each of them the inner value of the mere hearsay that has smitten them. This makes Beatrice unflinchingly lay bare her heroic beauty of heart. This tries the loyal mettle of Benedicke's sword.

The two halves of the plot are so necessary to each other and the Beatrice and Benedicke half so surmounts it in interest throughout the play, and so dominates it at the climax, when the two streams flow together, that the present writer doubts either that the plot of Benedicke and Beatrice could be separated and exist apart from the Claudio and Hero half, or that the latter was sought and developed less on its own account than in order to further and illumine the main idea of the author—namely, to effect the conquest for Love, of the two sterling hearts that disowned the power of the god. To throw the other plot into relief and light is the similar office of the double love plots so often employed by Shakespeare, as notably in 'As You Like It' and 'Twelfe Night.'

Do these inner ties of idea and structure in the two plays that stand so apart from the others as examples of pure and brilliant Comedy suffice to designate

'Much Adoe,' as the twin piece mentioned by Meres, in 1598, along with Shakespeare's *'Love labors lost'* as his *'Love labours wonne'*? In the absence of external proof . . . who is so omniscient that he may affirm that Meres or others once so titled or sub-titled it in order to pair the two plays?

Too much has been sworn to before now upon Shakespearian questions which would better have been forborne lest it be forsworn. That among the possibilities the question admits this is the most probable seems demonstrable to the present writer.

It is worth noting, too, that there is no external fact yet discovered to forbid as early a date as 1598. The 'Midsommer Night's Dreame' Quarto is dated, like the 'Much Adoe' Quarto, in 1600, and that play is mentioned by Meres two years earlier. The accomplished artistry of 'Much Adoe' as Shakespeare's consummate output in pure Comedy must be attributed to his ability before 1600, under any circumstances. Who shall say that he must have done in 1599 what he could not do in 1598?

Difficult as it is to limit exclusively to one time these miracles of all time, they themselves lie freely open to our scrutiny and wonder. And that such internal cousinship of plan and artistic temper as is here indicated belongs to two of them, any reader may happily see for himself.

<hr />

1946—W. H. Auden. *"Much Ado About Nothing"* from *Lectures on Shakespeare*

Wystan Hugh Auden (1907-73) was an Anglo-American author and is often considered one of the chief poets of the twentieth century. In addition to producing myriad books of poetry, Auden lectured on numerous topics, including a series on individual Shakespeare plays. Auden begins by noting that the main plot of *Much Ado about Nothing* is, to use Auden's word, "boring." The story of Hero and Claudio exists only as a parallel to the subplot of Beatrice and Benedick, largely to contrast the "comic, light duel of wits in the foreground and the dark malice of Don John in the background." Auden suggests these two contrasting plots also work to parallel a relationship between "pretense and reality." One key to understanding this is found in Balthazar's song "Sigh no more, ladies" in act 2, scene 3. The song's references to inconstant, deceptive men reference not only the fickle affections of Claudio and Benedick's changing view of love but also Don John's machinations, bridging the world between both main plot and subplot effectively. Another key to understanding the play's construct of pretense and reality occurs in the manner in which characters express grief. Auden argues that some characters, such as Leonato, express grief more out of concern for the self than the other. Auden writes that for Leonato grief "is an expression of social embarrassment," irrespective of whether his grief is supposed real or false (such as he exhibits to Don Pedro and Claudio after the watch has uncovered proof of Hero's innocence). A character like Antonio, on the other hand, always expresses true grief for others; in the scene in which he and Leonato confront the men who have wronged Hero, Antonio expresses honest rage for Hero's humiliation despite the fact that Hero has yet to be vindicated. Auden argues that Antonio's grief is real because the character feels wronged that neither Claudio nor Don Pedro kept faith with Hero and Leonato, and thus Antonio expresses this betrayal on the part of his family.

According to Auden, pretense and deception are at the core of *Much Ado about Nothing*. Beatrice and Benedick are fooled into loving each other and, at the end, lie about their feelings; Don John attempts multiple deceptions aimed at disrupting the relationship between Claudio and Hero; the Friar convinces the wedding party to say Hero is dead when she is not, which enables the investigation into Claudio's claims; Leonato and the members of the Messina household must continue deceiving Don Pedro and Claudio after Hero's innocence is established to punish the two for their actions and allow Hero's innocence to be more wholly declared. At the heart of much of the deception is the character of Don John, whom Auden labels "the defiant rebel . . . a destructive misfit." It is Don John's flaw of character that causes him to act as he does; any motivation based on material greed or jealousy does not apply to his crimes. He is an unconventional character, as are Beatrice, Benedick, and Dogberry, creations Auden celebrates. (Conversely, a character such as Claudio is highly conventional in Auden's mind.) All ultimately add to the contrast between light and dark that Auden suggests is at the heart of most Shakespearean plays.

The first thing to notice about *Much Ado About Nothing* is that the subplot overwhelms and overshadows the main plot. The main plot consists of the story of Hero and Claudio and the conspiracy of Don John. Its sources are Bandello, Ariosto, and a Greek romance. Shakespeare treats the story perfunctorily, and except for Don John, it's boring. And Shakespeare shows some carelessness in putting it together: for example, Margaret—didn't she know what she was doing? And Borachio's plans to be called Claudio from the window don't come off—anyhow, Claudio is listening. The whole story is a foil to the duel of wits between Beatrice and Benedick.

How have we seen Shakespeare use the subplot? First, as a parallel. In *Love's Labour's Lost* Armado parallels the gentry—his affected language is a comment on Berowne's poetic affectations, and he has to accept Jacqueline, an inferior wife, as Berowne has to "jest a twelvemonth in an hospital" (V.ii.880). In *A Midsummer Night's Dream* Bottom suffers from the same kinds of illusion as the lovers, and, like the lovers, he is eventually delivered from them. Shakespeare also uses the subplot as a contrast: Shylock is juxtaposed against Venetian life in *The Merchant of Venice,* and Falstaff is elaborately developed as a contrast to the heroic life of Hal and the nobles in *Henry IV.* There is also a very sketchy contrasting subplot in the *Comedy of Errors*—the tragic background of the father doomed to death unless he can raise the money to pay a large fine.

Much Ado provides another case of contrast, with the comic, light duel of wits in the foreground and the dark malice of Don John in the background. How does Shakespeare keep the tragic plot from getting too serious? He treats it perfunctorily as a background. This draws attention to an artistic point—the importance of boredom. In any first-class work of art, you can find passages that in themselves are extremely boring, but try to cut them out, as they are in an abridged edition, and you lose the life of the work. Don't think that art that is alive can remain on the same level of interest throughout—and the same is true of life.

The relation of pretense and reality is a major concern of the play, and the keys to understanding it can be found in two passages. One is Balthazar's song, "Sigh no more, ladies, sigh no more" (II.iii.64–76). Where and how songs are placed in Shakespeare is revealing. Let's look first at two or three other examples. In *The Two Gentlemen of Verona*, we have the song, "Who is Silvia? What is she, / That all our swains commend her?" (IV.ii.39–53). The song, which is sung to Silvia, has standard Petrarchan rhetoric—cruel fair, faithful lover—but the music is being used with conscious evil intent. Proteus, who has been false to his friend, has forsworn his vows to Julia, and is cheating Thurio, serenades Silvia while his forsaken Julia, disguised as a boy, listens:

Host. How now? Are you sadder than you were before? How do you, man? The music likes you not.
Jul. You mistake, the musician likes me not.
Host. Why, my pretty youth?
Jul. He plays false, father.
Host. How? Out of tune on the strings?
Jul. Not so; but yet so false that he grieves my very heartstrings.
Host. You have a quick ear.
Jul. Ay, I would I were deaf! It makes me have a slow heart.
Host. I perceive you delight not in music.

Jul. Not a whit, when it jars so.
Host. Hark, what fine change is in the music!
Jul. Ay, that change is the spite.
Host. You would have them always play but one thing?
Jul. I would always have one play but one thing.

    (IV.ii.54–72)

"O mistress mine, where are you roaming?" in *Twelfth Night* (II.iii.40–53), which is sung to Sir Toby Belch and Sir Andrew Aguecheek, is in the "Gather ye rosebuds" tradition, but taken seriously the lines suggest the voice of elderly lust, not youth, and Shakespeare makes us conscious of this by making the audience for the song a pair of aging drunks. In *Measure for Measure*, the betrayed Mariana is serenaded by a boy in a song that does not help her forget her unhappiness but indulges it. Being the deserted lady has become a role. The words of the song "Take, O, take those lips away" (IV.i.1–6) mirrors her situation exactly, and her apology to the Duke when he surprises her gives her away:

I cry you mercy, sir, and well could wish
You had not found me here so musical.
Let me excuse me, and believe me so,
My mirth it much displeas'd, but pleas'd my woe.

    (IV.i.10–13)

In each of these three cases, the setting criticizes the song's convention. The same is true in *Much Ado About Nothing*. The serenade convention is turned upside down in Balthazar's song, and its effect is to suggest that we shouldn't take sad lovers too seriously. The song is sung to Claudio and Don Pedro for the benefit of Benedick, who is overhearing it, as they plot to make him receptive to loving Beatrice. In the background, also, is the plot of Borachio and Don John against Claudio.

Sigh no more, ladies, sigh no more!
  Men were deceivers ever,
One foot in sea, and one on shore;
  To one thing constant never.
    Then sigh not so,
    But let them go,
  And be you blithe and bonny,
Converting all your sounds of woe
  Into Hey nonny, nonny.

Sing no more ditties, sing no moe,
  Of dumps so dull and heavy!

> The fraud of men was ever so,
>   Since summer first was leavy.
>   Then sigh not so, &c.
>
>   (II.iii.64–76)

Claudio, in his dreamy love-sick state, is shortly to prove such a lover as the song describes, and Benedick, who thinks himself immune to love, is shortly to acknowledge his love for Beatrice. If one imagines the sentiments of the song being an expression of character, the only character they suit is Beatrice, and I do not think it is too far-fetched to imagine that the song arouses in Benedick's mind an image of Beatrice, the tenderness of which alarms him. The violence of his comment when the song is over is suspicious: "An he had been a dog that should have howl'd thus, they would have hang'd him; and I pray God, his bad voice bode no mischief. I had as live have heard the night raven, come what plague could have come after it" (II.iii.81–85).

Historically and individually there are new discoveries, like courtly love, which create novelty and give new honesty to new feelings. As time goes on, the discovery succeeds because of its truth. Then the convention petrifies and is employed by people whose feelings are quite different. Petrarchan rhetoric had its origin in a search for personal fidelity versus arranged marriage, and was then used to make love to a girl for an evening. To dissolve the over-petrified sentiments and unreality of a convention, one must apply intelligence. "Sigh no more, ladies, sigh no more" is Petrarchan convention seen comically through the lens of a critical intelligence.

Man must be an actor, and one always has to play with ideas before one can make them real. But one must not forget one is playing and mix up play with reality. When Antonio tries to comfort his brother Leonato about Hero, Leonato resists his counsel:

> My griefs cry louder than advertisement.
>   *Ant.* Therein do men from children nothing differ.
>   *Leon.* I pray thee peace. I will be flesh and blood;
> For there was never yet philosopher
> That could endure the toothache patiently,
> However they have writ the style of gods
> And made a push at chance and sufferance.
>
>   (V.i.32–38)

This is the other key to the issue of pretense and reality in *Much Ado*: just as feeling can petrify, there can be a false rhetoric of reason that genuine grief can detect. Too much concern for play widens the gap between convention and reality, resulting in either a brutal return to reality or a flight to a rival convention.

Leonato's grief is not real—it is an expression of social embarrassment. Antonio, though he tries to console Leonato, is the one who really grieves, as his curses against Claudio and Don Pedro for their lack of faith show:

> God knows I lov'd my niece,
> And she is dead, slander'd to death by villains,
> That dare as well answer a man indeed
> As I dare take a serpent by the tongue.
> Boys, apes, braggarts, Jacks, milksops!. . . .
> Scambling, outfacing, fashion-monging boys,
> That lie and cog and flout, deprave and slander.

(V.i.87–91, 94–95)

So it is Antonio who really feels, Leonato who puts on an act.

Beatrice and Benedick are essentially people of good will—their good will and honesty are what create their mockery and duels of wit. Don John is honest and cynical, but behind that is ill will. All three characters are intelligent, able, and honest. *Much Ado About Nothing* is not one of Shakespeare's best plays, but Benedick and Beatrice are the most lovable, amusing, and good people—the best of combinations—he ever created. They are the characters of Shakespeare we'd most like to sit next to at dinner. The great verbal dexterity of Beatrice and Benedick is paralleled by the great verbal ineptitude of Dogberry, an ineptitude which itself becomes art. All three love words and have good will—they are divided in verbal skill and intelligence. The honest, original people in the play use prose, the conventional people use verse. A general criticism of an Elizabethan sonneteer is that he is too "poetic." Every poet has to struggle against "poetry"— in quotes. The real question for the poet is what poetic language will show the true sensibility of the time.

Much Ado About Nothing is full of deception and pretense. Benedick and Beatrice fool themselves into believing they don't love each other—they mistake their reactions against the conventions of love for lovelessness. Claudio, Hero, and Don Pedro pretend to Benedick and Beatrice that the two love each other, and—with good will—they use Benedick and Beatrice to bolster their own conventions of love. Don John, Borachio, and Margaret's pretense, on the other hand, is animated by pure malice and ill will. Their deception succeeds because those who are deceived are conventionally-minded. They are stupid and don't recognize malice, unlike Benedick, who at once suspects Don John (IV.i.189–90), and Beatrice, who at once believes that Hero is innocent (IV.i.147).

Claudio turns away from Hero, Hero faints instead of standing up for herself, and Leonato is taken in by Don John's pretense because he doesn't want to believe that princes lie—he's a snob. When Beatrice says that she was not Hero's bedfellow on the night in question, though she has been so for a twelvemonth, Leonato declares:

Confirm'd, confirm'd! O, that is stronger made
Which was before barr'd up with ribs of iron!
Would the two princes lie? And Claudio lie,
Who lov'd her so that, speaking of her foulness,
Wash'd it with tears? Hence from her! Let her die.

    (IV.i.151–55)

Leonato and Hero subsequently follow the Friar's advice to pretend that Hero is dead and to disguise her as a cousin—yet more pretense. And, finally, Dogberry pretends to know language and to be wiser than he is.

The individual versus the universal. Among animals there is no universal like marriage or justice—only man can be false by following his nature. A human being is composed of a combination of nature and spirit and individual will. Laws are established to help defend his will against nature and to get the individual meaningfully related to the universal. When the individual has only an abstract relation with the universal, there is a hollow rhetoric and falsity on both sides. There are three possibilities in relating to law. First is the defiant rebel, who is a destructive misfit. Second is the conformist, whose relation to law remains abstract. And third is the creative, original person, where the individual relation to law is vivifying and good on both sides. Don John the bastard is in the first, temperamentally melancholic, group. Don John uses that temperament to take a negative position outside the group, like Shylock, as opposed to a character like Faulconbridge, who is an outsider with a positive attitude. "I thank you," Don John says sullenly to Leonato at the start of the play, "I am not of many words, but I thank you." (I.i.158–59). To Conrade, who advises him to behave more ingratiatingly to his brother Don Pedro, he says,

> I had rather be a canker in a hedge than a rose in his grace, and it better fits my blood to be disdain'd of all than to fashion a carriage to rob love from any. In this, though I cannot be said to be a flattering honest man, it must not be denied that I am a plain-dealing villain. I am trusted with a muzzle and enfranchis'd with a clog; therefore I have decreed not to sing in my cage. If I had my mouth, I would bite; if I had my liberty, I would do my liking. In the meantime let me be that I am, and seek not to alter me.
>
> *Con.* Can you make no use of your discontent?
>
> *John.* I make all use of it, for I use it only.
>
>   Enter *Borachio*
>
> Who comes here? What news, Borachio?
>
> *Bora.* I came yonder from a great supper. The Prince your brother is royally entertain'd by Leonato, and I can give you intelligence of an intended marriage.

John. Will it serve for any model to build mischief on? What is he for a fool that betroths himself to unquietness?

    (I.iii.28–50)

Don John's discontent is infinite. His view of marriage is superficially like Benedick and Beatrice's, but his motive is the hatred of happiness. Like the Devil, he wants to be unique. He has little feeling, great intelligence, and great will.

Claudio is chief among the conventional characters—characters who are either functions of the universal or are destroyed by it. Claudio has some intelligence, some feeling, and very little will. Don Pedro has to coax him to declare his love for Hero. When Claudio asks whether Leonato has a son, he's indirectly saying he wants to marry for money, an attitude that Benedick's honesty has already detected: "Would you buy her, that you enquire after her?" (I.i.181–82). There's some conventional stuff about his having been at war and having had no time for love. He really wants to get married—no matter to whom, and he turns to entirely conventional forms of love-making. Benedick says of him,

> I have known when there was no music with him but the drum and fife; and now had he rather hear the tabor and the pipe. I have known when he would have walk'd ten mile afoot to see a good armour; and now will he lie ten nights awake carving the fashion of a new doublet. He was wont to speak plain and to the purpose, like an honest man and a soldier; and now is he turn'd orthography; his words are a very fantastical banquet—just so many strange dishes.
>
>   (II.iii.13–23)

Claudio is a conventional tough soldier, a conventional Petrarchan lover—and his jealousy is conventional, expressed in conventional puns: "fare thee well, most foul, most fair! Farewell, / Thou pure impiety and impious purity!" (IV. i.104–5). The remedy for the conventional is the exceptional: Hero's supposed death makes him a killer, and he is punished by being forced to marry her "cousin," which proves that he's not an individual. The song Claudio sings for Hero in the churchyard, "Pardon, goddess of the night" (V.iii.12–21) is a suitably bad song that keeps the tragedy cursory. Don Pedro and Claudio skip off to the final reconciliation nonchalantly.

Now to the people who are both critical and creative. The conventions of love-making are criticized in the courtship of Berowne and Rosaline in *Love's Labour's Lost*, in which Rosaline is superior, and in the courtship and marriage of Petruchio and Katherina in *The Taming of the Shrew*, in which Petruchio is superior. Benedick and Beatrice mark the first time that both sides are equally matched. Both are critics of Petrarchan convention, and both hate sentimentality because they value feeling. When they really love, they speak directly:

> *Bene.* I do love nothing in the world so well as you. Is not that strange?
> *Beat.* As strange as the thing I know not. It were as possible for me to
> say I loved nothing so well you. But believe me not; and yet I lie not.
> I confess nothing, nor I deny nothing. I am sorry for my cousin.
> *Bene.* By my sword, Beatrice, thou lovest me.
> *Beat.* Do not swear, and eat it.
> *Bene.* I will swear by it that you love me, and I will make him eat it
> that says I love not you.
> *Beat.* Will you not eat your word?
> *Bene.* With no sauce that can be devised to it. I protest I love thee.
> *Beat.* Why then, God forgive me!
> *Bene.* What offence, sweet Beatrice?
> *Beat.* You have stayed me in a happy hour. I was about to protest I
> loved you.
> *Bene.* And do it with all thy heart.
> *Beat.* I love you with so much of my heart that none is left to protest.
> *Bene.* Come, bid me do anything for thee.
> *Beat.* Kill Claudio.
>
>   (IV.i.269–91)

Beatrice wants action here, though Benedick is right in thinking Claudio is not entirely responsible.

Beatrice and Benedick have a high ideal of marriage. Before the dance, Beatrice kids Hero:

> For, hear me Hero: wooing, wedding, and repenting is as a Scotch jig, a
> measure, and a cinque-pace: the first suit is hot and hasty like a Scotch
> jig—and full as fantastical; the wedding, mannerly modest, as a measure,
> full of state and ancientry; and then comes Repentance and with his bad
> legs falls into the cinque-pace faster and faster, till he sink into his grave.
> *Leon.* Cousin, you apprehend passing shrewdly.
> *Beat.* I have a good eye, uncle; I can see a church by daylight.
>
>   (II.i.75–86)

Beatrice and Benedick demand a combination of reason and will, a combination Benedick displays in the soliloquy in which he resolves to love Beatrice after hearing how she loves him:

> This can be no trick. The conference was sadly borne; they have the
> truth of this from Hero; they seem to pity the lady. It seems her
> affections have their full bent. Love me? Why, it must be requited. I
> hear how I am censur'd. They say I will bear myself proudly if I perceive

the love come from her. They say too that she will rather die than give any sign of affection. I did never think to marry. I must not seem proud. Happy are they that hear their detractions and can put them to mending. They say the lady is fair—'tis a truth, I can bear them witness; and virtuous—'tis so, I cannot reprove it; and wise, but for loving me— by my troth, it is no addition to her wit, nor no great argument of her folly, for I will be horribly in love with her. I may chance have some odd quirks and remnants of wit broken on me because I have railed so long against marriage. But doth not the appetite alter? A man loves the meat in his youth that he cannot endure in his age. Shall quips and sentences and these paper bullets of the brain awe a man from the career of his humour? No, the world must be peopled. When I said I would die a bachelor, I did not think I should live till I were married.

    (II.iii.228–53)

Benedick's reasons are not those of feelings. Conventional people protest in a rhetoric of feeling.

    There is a gay conclusion for Benedick and Beatrice. At the end one feels absolutely confident of the success of their marriage, more than of other marriages in Shakespeare. They have creative intelligence, good will, a lack of sentimentality, and an ability to be open and direct with each other in a society in which such directness is uncommon. For us, the modern convention of "honesty" is now the danger. People must learn to hide things from each other a little more. We need a post-Freudian-analytic rhetoric.

    The play presents law in a comic setting. Dogberry is an imperfect human representation of the law, and he's conceited. He and the Watch don't understand what's happening, and they succeed more by luck than ability. Dogberry's "line" is like Falstaff's, but he's not against law. He says to the Watch and Verges,

If you meet a thief, you may suspect him, by virtue of your office, to be no true man; and for such kind of men, the less you meddle or make with them, why, the more is for your honesty.
    2. Watch. If we know him to be a thief, shall we not lay hands on him?
    Dog. Truly, by your office you may; but I think they that touch pitch will be defil'd. The most peaceable way for you, if you do take a thief, is to let him show himself what he is, and steal out of your company.
    Verg. You have been always called a merciful man, partner.

    (III.iii.52–65)

Dogberry and his company do indeed raise the problem of mercy versus justice. They are successful against probability, and that they are suggests (1) that police are dangerous because they become like crooks in dealing with crooks, and (2)

that good nature pays off better than efficiency. Efficiency at the expense of kindness must be checked, which is more a British than an American attitude.

A contrast between light and dark is always present in Shakespeare. It is made explicit in *Much Ado About Nothing* in the contrast Don Pedro draws, after visiting Hero's tomb, between kindness and the possibilities of malice and tragedy, between the gentle day and the wolves of prey:

> Good morrow, masters. Put your torches out.
>   The wolves have prey'd, and look, the gentle day,
> Before the wheels of Phoebus, round about
>   Dapples the drowsy east with spots of grey.
> Thanks to you all, and leave us. Fare you well.
>
>   (V.iii.24–27)

With this passage in mind, let me conclude by reading from Rimbaud's "Génie":

> He is affection and the present since he has made the house open to foamy winter and to the murmur of summer—he who has purified food and drink—he who is the charm of fleeing places and the super-human delight of stations.—He is affection and the future, love and force whom we, standing among our rages and our boredoms, see passing in the stormy sky and banners of ecstasy.
> . . . . .
>   And we remember him and he has gone on a journey . . . And if Adoration goes, rings, his promise rings: "Away! superstitions, away! those ancient bodies, those couples, and those ages. It is this present epoch that has foundered!"
>   He will not go away, he will not come down again from any heaven, he will not accomplish the redemption of the angers of women and the gaieties of men and all this Sin: for it is done, he being and being loved.
>   He has known us all and all of us has loved; take heed this winter night, from cape to cape, from the tumultuous pole to the castle, from the crowd to the shore, from look to look, force and feelings weary, to hail him, to see him and to send him away, and under the tides and high in the deserts of snow, to follow his views,—his breaths,—his body,—his day.

1959—Graham Storey. "The Success of *Much Ado About Nothing*" from *More Talking of Shakespeare*

The English scholar and university professor Graham Storey (1920–
2005) is best known for his editions of the letters of Charles Dickens
and the journals of Gerard Manley Hopkins. According to Storey,
the success of *Much Ado about Nothing* is based on understanding the
work as a comedy and the work's relationship to genre itself. Storey
notes that the work follows established patterns for comedy in the
Elizabethan era (though, Shakespeare being Shakespeare, these patterns are sublimely followed). Storey challenges conventional critical
thought from the nineteenth century through his time period that the
main plot of *Much Ado about Nothing* is too serious and too dramatic
for a comedy, and that what befalls Hero is no laughing matter. Storey
argues that the characters of the main plot are not fully realized figures
but caricatures, or as he calls them, "masks." Our reaction to the wedding scene is mitigated because we do not feel for Hero and Claudio
as we do for Beatrice and Benedick. It is the latter pair who remain the
emotional center of the play, the pair the audience most unabashedly
roots for. The plot line involving Beatrice and Benedick is often considered a comic parallel to the more serious story of Hero and Claudio;
yet Storey argues that this perspective is inverted, and that ultimately
the audience views Beatrice and Benedick as the true center of the play.
Thus Benedick's conclusion to the text—"for man is a giddy thing, and
this is my conclusion" (5.4.107–08)—is most apt in understanding the
true, comic nature of the play itself.

May I confess that I only added the first words of my title when I was well into
preparing this lecture? Do not mistake me: the riches of the play—the sheer
exhilaration of the encounters between Benedick and Beatrice and their arabesques of wit; the superb stupidity of Dogberry and Verges and *their* arabesques
of misunderstanding; the skilful weaving and disentanglement of the comic
imbroglio—all these are a joy to see and hear, and belong to Shakespeare's most
assured writing. But it is a commonplace of criticism that a successful play, like
any other work of art, must be a unity: what Coleridge called the Imagination's
'esemplastic power' must shape into one its individual forces and beauties.
Whether *Much Ado* has this unity was the question that worried me.

It did not worry Shakespeare's contemporaries. The play offered an exciting
Italianate melodrama, enlivened by two variegated sets of 'humours': the wit-
combats and properly-rewarded over-reachings of Benedick and Beatrice,
and the low-life comedy of Dogberry and Verges; and remember that George
Chapman and Ben Jonson had just started a run of fashionable 'humour' plays.
As in all proper comedies, the story came out all right in the end. 'Strike up,
pipers! *Dance.*' The formula ends that other comedy with a similarly riddling
title, *As You Like It*; and whatever the differences of tone, the effect does not vary

so much from that of the conclusion of *Twelfth Night*, the third of this group of plays written at the turn of the century:

A great while ago the world begun,
With hey, ho, the wind and the rain;
But that's all one, our play is done,
And we'll strive to please you every day.

The humours were what the contemporary audience remembered the play by. '*Benedicte and Betteris*,' say the Lord Treasurer's accounts for 1613: and *Much Ado* was almost certainly meant. 'Benedick and Beatrice', wrote Charles I in his second Folio, as a second title to the play—exercising a similar Stuart prerogative in renaming *Twelfth Night* 'The Tragedy of Malvolio'. The 'main plot' is clearly being regarded as a kind of serious relief to the much more absorbing comedy. When, with the Restoration, Shakespeare had to face the formidable canons of the neo-Classic critics, this central plot came in for some hard questioning. The criticism was, as we should expect, formal: the *decorum* was at fault. 'The fable is absurd,' writes Charles Gildon, in 1710, in an essay[1] often reprinted during the eighteenth century; 'the charge against Hero is too shocking for tragedy or comedy, and Claudio's conduct is against the nature of love'. He is almost equally concerned that the people of Messina do not act and talk, he says, like natives of a warm country.

But, at the turn of this century, one or two critics began to show a quite new uneasiness about the play. They found, not unity, not the almost unblemished gaiety that they found in *As You Like It* or *Twelfth Night*; but jarring tones, a gratuitous suffering and heartlessness in crisis—the Church Scene—that the rest of the play could not wipe out, and a distressing inconsistency in the characters of Claudio, the Prince and Leonato. The critical approaches were different: but the resultant *uncomfortableness* they generated was much the same. And it has undoubtedly left its mark upon many performances since.

The most frequent cause of uneasiness has been to respond to the play as though the protagonists were psychologically real. It is indeed the most expected response, as the dominant mode of the theatre is still naturalism. But it plays havoc with *Much Ado* as *comedy*. Stopford Brooke, writing in 1913[2] as a Bradleyan, shows what happens. He clearly wants to like the play; yet its very centre, the exposure in church, is, he writes, 'a repulsive scene'. 'In it all the characters will be tried in the fire'; and, as a Victorian clergyman of strong, if sensitive views, he tries them. They emerge—Claudio, Don Pedro and Leonato—shallow, wilfill, cruel, inconsistent with what they were before; and the play, its centre contaminated, is virtually handed over to Benedick and Beatrice. That, I am convinced, is not how Shakespeare wrote the play. But the figures of the main plot are bound to appear in this light, if we see them as fully-rounded characters and subject them to the tests of psychological consistency. I see them as something much nearer 'masks': as not quite so far removed from the formalized figures of *Love's Labour's Lost*, where most of the play's life resides in the plot-pattern and the dance of verbal wit, as many critics have suggested. I will return to this suggestion later. Meanwhile, I only want to insist that the opposite approach—that of naturalistic realism—stretches the play much further than a comedy can go, and makes almost impossible demands of the actors for the last two Acts. It can also lead to a quite ludicrous literalism, as where Stopford Brooke, quoting the magnificent, absurd *finale* of Beatrice's outburst against Claudio after the Church Scene—'O God, that I were a man! I would eat his heart in the market-place'—solemnly comments, 'of course, she would not have done it.'[3]

Others though, besides the 'naturalist' critics, have found *Much Ado* disturbing: and disturbing because they do not discover in it the unity that I have made my main question. Sir Edmund Chambers,[4] writing fifty years ago, was probably the first to note what he called its 'clashing of dramatic planes'. 'Elements,' he wrote, 'of tragedy, comedy, tragi-comedy, and farce are thrust together;' and the result is not unity, but 'an unco-ordinated welter', a dramatic impressionism that sacrifices the whole to the brilliance of individual scenes or passages of dialogue or even individual lines. Other writers have more recently said much the same: the play's elements are incompatible; the plot too harsh for the characters; it is the wrong kind of romantic story to blend with comedy. 'This happy play,' as 'Q.' called it in his Introduction to the *New Cambridge Shakespeare*, 1923, seems, in fact, to be in danger of losing its central place in the canon of Shakespeare's comedies (or it would be, if critics were taken too seriously).

I think that all these critics have seriously underrated the comic capacity of both Shakespeare and his audience: the capacity to create, and to respond to, varying and often contradictory experiences simultaneously; to create a pattern of human behaviour from their blendings and juxtapositions; and to obtain a keen enjoyment from seeing that pattern equally true at all levels. I will try to apply this claim to *Much Ado*.

'For man is a giddy thing, and this is my conclusion,' says Benedick in the last scene; and this is surely the play's 'cause' or ruling theme. 'Giddy', a favourite Elizabethan word: 'light-headed, frivolous, flighty, inconstant', it meant by 1547; 'whirling or circling round with bewildering rapidity' (1593); mentally intoxicated, 'elated to thoughtlessness' (in Dr. Johnson's *Dictionary*). *Much Ado* has all these meanings in abundance. And Benedick's dictum, placed where it is, followed by the dance (reminiscent perhaps of the *La Ronde*-like Masked Ball of Act II), suggests eternal recurrence: 'Man is a giddy thing'—and ever more will be so. The impetus to two of the play's three plots is the impetus to all the comedies, the propensity to love-making: one plot begins and ends with it; the other ends with it. And the impetus to the third plot, the antics of the Watch ('the vulgar humours of the play,' said Gildon,[5] 'are remarkably varied and distinguished'), is self-love: the innocent, thoughtless, outrageous love of Dogberry for himself and his position.

Inconstancy, mental intoxication, elation to thoughtlessness: the accompaniment of all these states is deception, self-deception, miscomprehension. And deception, the prelude to 'giddiness', operates at every level of *Much Ado*. It is the common denominator of the three plots, and its mechanisms—eavesdroppings, mistakes of identity, disguises and maskings, exploited hearsay—are the major stuff of the play.

In the main plot—the Italian melodrama that Shakespeare took from Matteo Bandello, Bishop of Agen—the deception-theme is, of course, the most harshly obvious. Don John's instrument, Borachio, deceives 'even the very eyes' of Claudio and the Prince; Claudio, the Prince and Leonato are all convinced that Hero has deceived them; Hero is violently deceived in her expectations of marriage, stunned by the slander; the Friar's plan to give her out as dead deceives everyone it is meant to.

The deceptions of Benedick and Beatrice in Leonato's garden-bower serve a function as a comic echo of all this. They are also beautifully-managed examples of a favourite Elizabethan device: the over-reacher over reached, the 'engineer hoist with his own petar', the marriage-mocker and husband-scorner taken in by—to us—a transparently obvious trick. (It is a major part of the play's delight that the audience always knows more than the actors: hints are dropped throughout; a Sophoclean comic irony pervades every incident.) Here, the metaphors of stalking and fishing are both deliberately overdone; and the effect is to emphasize that each of these eavesdroppings is a piece of play-acting, a mock-ceremonious game:

> DON PEDRO: Come hither, Leonato: what was it you told me of to-day,
> that your niece Beatrice was in love with Signior Benedick?
> CLAUDIO: O! ay: (Stalk on, stalk on; the fowl sits.) I did never think
> that lady would have loved any man.[6]

And in the next scene:

> URSULA: The pleasant'st angling is to see the fish
> Cut with her golden oars the silver stream,
> And greedily devour the treacherous bait:
> So angle we for Beatrice. . . .
> HERO: No, truly, Ursula, she is too disdainful;
> I know her spirits are as coy and wild
> As haggards of the rock.[7]

The contrast between prose and a delicate, artful blank verse makes sharper the difference of the fantasy each of them is offered. Benedick is given a superbly ludicrous caricature of a love-sick Beatrice, which only his own vanity could believe:

> CLAUDIO: Then down upon her knees she falls, weeps, sobs, beats her heart, tears her hair, prays, curses: 'O sweet Benedick! God give me patience! ...' Hero thinks surely she will die.[8]

And his own response, a mixture of comically solemn resolutions and illogical reasoning, is equally exaggerated:

> I must not seem proud: happy are they that hear their detractions, and can put them to mending.... No; the world must be peopled.[9]

Beatrice has her feminine vanity played on more delicately, but just as directly: she is given a not-too-exaggerated picture of herself as Lady Disdain, spiced with the praises of the man she is missing. And her response, in formal verse, clinches the success of the manoeuvre:

> What fire is in mine ears? Can this be true?
> Stand I condemn'd for pride and scorn so much?
> Contempt, farewell! and maiden pride, adieu!
> No glory lives behind the back of such....[10]

'Elated to thoughtlessness' indeed (and particularly after all their earlier wit): but not only by a trick. Benedick and Beatrice are both, of course, perfect examples of self-deception: about their own natures, about the vanity their railing hides (and none the less vanity for its charm and wit), about the affection they are capable of—in need of—when the aggression is dropped, about their real relations to each other. This gives the theme of deception in their plot the higher, more permanent status of revelation. Hence much of its delight.

But no one in the play is more mentally intoxicated than Dogberry. He is king of all he surveys: of Verges, his perfect foil; of the Watch; of the peace of Messina at night. Only words—engines of deception—constantly trip him up; though, like Mrs. Malaprop, he sails on magnificently unaware:

> Dost thou not suspect my place? Dost thou not suspect my years? O that he were here to write me down an ass! ... I am a wise fellow; and, which is more, an officer; and, which is more, a householder; and, which is more, as pretty a piece of flesh as any in Messina....[11]

With Dogberry, the theme of giddiness, of self-deception, of revelling in the appearances that limitless vanity has made true for him, reaches miraculous proportions.

There is, though, the further meaning of 'giddy', also, I suggested, warranted by Benedick's conclusion: 'whirling or circling round'. The structure of *Much Ado*—the melodramatic Italian love-story, enlivened by two humour-plots of Shakespeare's own invention—follows an established Elizabethan comedy-pattern: Chapman was to use it in *The Gentleman Usher* and *Monsieur d'Olive*; *Twelfth Night*—allowing for obvious differences in the tone of the central plot—is the obvious successor. Musically, we could call it a theme and variations. But you have merely to consider the Chapman comedies, where the two plots only arbitrarily meet—or Thomas Middleton, who brought in a collaborator to help him with the 'echoing sub-plot' of his tragedy, *The Changeling*—to see Shakespeare's extraordinary structural skill here. 'Faultless balance, blameless rectitude of design,' said Swinburne: he is right, and it was not what most of his contemporaries recognized in *Much Ado*. But it still does not strongly enough suggest the grasp, the intellectual energy, that holds the play together and makes the kind of suggestions about reality in which the Elizabethan audience delighted. Here, again, Benedick's conclusion says more. Not only the play's wit—a microcosm of its total life—whirls and circles, with often deadly effect ('Thou hast frighted the word out of his right sense, so forcible is thy wit,' cries Benedick to Beatrice in the last Act: it suggests that wit—and wit's author—can destroy or create at will) one of man's main instruments of living; but, in their vibrations and juxtapositions, the three plots do much the same.

Twice the plots fuse—once to advance the story, once to deepen it—and the achievement gives a peculiar exhilaration. Each time it is something of a shock; and then we see that, within the rules of probability laid down by Aristotle for writers of tragedy (we can validly apply them to comedy too), it is wonderfully right that it should have happened like that.

The first occasion is the discovery by the Watch of the plot against Hero. When they line up to receive their instructions from Dogberry and Verges—on the principle of peace at all costs—it seems incredible that they should ever discover anything. But they do: though, admittedly, Shakespeare has to make Borachio drunk to make it possible. The Watch and their Officers are now locked firmly into the main plot, with all their ripples of absurdity; and the final dénouement is theirs. The innocent saved by the innocent, we may say; or, more likely (and certainly more Elizabethanly), the knaves caught out by the fools. 'Is our whole dissembly appeared?' asks Dogberry, as he looks round for the rest of the Court. 'Which be the malefactors?' asks the Sexton. 'Marry, that am I and my partner,' answers Dogberry, with pride.

However we look at it, the impact has clearly changed the status of the villains. 'Ducdame, ducdame, ducdame,' sings Jaques (it is his own verse) to his banished companions in the Forest of Arden. 'What's that "*ducdame*"?' asks Amiens. ''Tis a Greek invocation to call fools into a circle.' Here in *Much*

Ado, the knaves have been thrust in with the fools: if it makes the fools feel much more important than they are, it makes the villains much less villainous; or villainous in a way that disturbs us less. This is one device by which the interlocking of plots establishes the play's unity, and, in doing so, creates a new, more inclusive tone.

The entry of the Watch into the centre of the play advances the story. The entry of Benedick and Beatrice, in that short packed dialogue after the Church Scene, where they declare their belief in Hero and their love for each other, seems as though it must do so too; but in fact it does not. Rather, it does not if we see the heart of the play now as Hero's vindication. That is brought about without help from Benedick; and, indeed, Benedick's challenge to Claudio, vehemently undertaken and dramatically presented, is, by the end of the play, treated very casually: only perfunctorily recalled, and easily brushed aside in the general mirth and reconciliation of the ending. Perhaps, then, this scene *removes* the play's centre, puts it squarely in the Benedick and Beatrice plot? That is how many critics have taken it; and what, for example, was in 'Q's' mind when he wrote of the scene's climax: '"Kill Claudio!" These two words nail the play'; and again, '. . . at this point undoubtedly Shakespeare transfers [the play] from *novella* to drama—to a real spiritual conflict'.[12] It is certainly how many producers and actors—with understandable temptation—have interpreted the scene.

Much Ado demands, of course, a continual switching of interest. We focus it in turn on Benedick and Beatrice, on Hero and Claudio, on Don John and Borachio, on Dogberry and Verges, back to Hero and Claudio, and so on. This gives something of the controlled whirl and circling motion I have commented on. It is also true that this scene between Benedick and Beatrice has a new seriousness; that their shared, intuitive belief in Hero's innocence has deepened their relations with each other, and our attitude towards them. But that is not the same as saying that the play has become something different, or that its centre has shifted. That would seriously jeopardize its design; and, although there *are* flaws in the play, I am sure that its design is what Shakespeare intended it to be.

The play's true centre is in fact neither a plot nor a group of characters, but a theme: Benedick's conclusion about man's giddiness, his irresistible propensity to be taken in by appearances. It is a theme that must embody an *attitude*; and it is the attitude here that provides *Much Ado*'s complexity: its disturbingness (where it does disturb; its ambiguities, where the expected response seems far from certain; but its inclusiveness too, where it is assured. For Shakespeare's approach to this theme at the turn of the century (one could call it the major theme of his whole writing-life, probed at endlessly varying levels) was far from simple. The riddling titles of the group of comedies written within these two years, 1598–1600, are deceptive, or at any rate ambiguous. *Much Ado About Nothing, As You Like It, Twelfth Night; or, What You Will*: these can all, as titles, be interpreted lightly, all but cynically, as leaving it to the audience how to take them with a disarming, amused casualness. Or, equally, they can leave room for manoeuvre, include several attitudes, without committing themselves to any. This blending or jostling of sympathies is sufficiently evident in these comedies to have won for itself the status of a convention. Dr. M. C. Bradbrook, who has lovingly pursued all the conventions of the Elizabethan theatre, has called it 'polyphonic music',[13] Mr. S. L. Bethell, more directly concerned with the Elizabethan audience, calls their capacity to respond to difficult aspects of the same situation, simultaneously, but in often contradictory ways, 'multi-consciousness'.[14] *Much Ado* exhibits the one and demands the other in the highest degree.

We must, I think, respond in much the same way as the Elizabethan audience did, if we are to appreciate to the full the scene between Benedick and Beatrice in the church; and that oddly-tempered, but still powerful scene of Leonato's outbursts to Antonio at the beginning of Act V. For both these scenes, however different—the first is set in a half-comic key, the second employs a rhetoric that is nearer the formally 'tragic'—employ deliberate ambiguities of tone and demand a double response.

I will examine the Benedick and Beatrice scene first. Here, Shakespeare clearly means us to sympathize with Beatrice's vehement attacks on Claudio on Hero's behalf, and with the mounting strength of Benedick's allegiance to her. At the same time, he overdoes the vehemence, exposes it to the comedy of his wry appraisal, brings both characters to the edge of delicate caricature. The scene's climax (I have quoted 'Q.'s' remarks on it) has been taken to show the maximum deployment of Shakespeare's sympathy. It also exhibits perfectly his comedy. Benedick and Beatrice have just protested they love each other with all their heart:

> BENEDICK: Come, bid me do anything for thee.
> BEATRICE: Kill Claudio.
> BENEDICK: Ha! not for the wide world.
> BEATRICE: You kill me to deny it. Farewell.[15]

Superbly dramatic: three fresh shocks in three lines, and, with each, a new insight into human nature; but also highly ironical. To demand the killing of Claudio, in the world established by the play, is ridiculous. To refuse it at once, after the avowal to do anything, equally so, however right Benedick may be ethically (and the irony demands that he refuse at once: I am sure Dr. Bradbrook[16] is wrong in saying that he hesitates). And for Beatrice, upon this refusal, to take back her heart, having given it a moment before, completes the picture: passionately generous to her wronged cousin, if we isolate the exchange and treat it as a piece of magnificent impressionism; heroic, absurd and a victim to passion's deception, if we see it—as we surely must—within the context of the whole play.

Mr. T. W. Craik, in an admirably close analysis of *Much Ado in Scrutiny*,[17] makes this scene between Benedick and Beatrice a pivot of the play's values. It is, he says, "'placed'" by the scene's beginning [i.e. the earlier events in the church]. Putting the point crudely, it represents the triumph of emotion over reason; the reasonableness of Friar Francis's plan for Claudio and Hero. . . . '[18] I agree with him when he goes on to say that 'emotion's triumph' is laughable in Benedick (though I think he exaggerates its extent). But surely it is an oversimplification to identify Shakespeare's attitude—as he seems to do more explicitly later in his essay[19]—with the Friar's common sense. The Friar is essential to the plot (and much more competent in guiding it than his brother of *Romeo and Juliet*); and his calm sanity admirably 'places' Leonato's hysteria in the Church Scene. But the whole spirit of the play seems to me antagonistic to any *one* attitude's dominating it. And the second scene I want to examine—Leonato and Antonio in V. i.—appears to bear this out.

For here Antonio begins as the repository of the Friar's wisdom, as the Stoic, calming Leonato down. Yet, as experience floods in on him—the memory of wrong in the shape of Don Pedro and Claudio—he too becomes 'flesh and blood', and ends up by out-doing Leonato:

> What, man! I know them, yea,
> And what they weigh, even to the utmost scruple,
> Scrambling, out-facing, fashion-monging boys,
> That lie and cog and flout, deprave and slander,
> Go antickly, show outward hideousness,
> And speak off half a dozen dangerous words,
> How they might hurt their enemies, if they durst;
> And this is all!
> LEONATO: But, brother Antony,—[20]

The roles are neatly reversed. But the invective is too exuberantly Shakespearian to be merely—or even mainly—caricature. Can we say the same of Leonato's outburst that begins the scene?

> I pray thee, cease thy counsel,
> which falls into mine ears as profitless
> As water in a sieve: Give nor me counsel;[21]

Considered realistically, it must make us uneasy. Leonato knows (Antonio does not) that Hero is in fact alive: to that extent, most of his emotion is counterfeit. Again, we remember his hysterical self-pity of the Act before, when his attitude to his daughter was very different:

Do not live, Hero; do not ope thine eyes;
... Griev'd I, I had but one?
Chid I for that at frugal nature's frame?
O! one too much by thee. Why had I one?
Why ever wast thou lovely in mine eyes?[22]

To some extent, he is still dramatizing himself in this scene, still enjoying his grief. But his language is no longer grotesque or self-convicting, as that was. He echoes a theme—'experience against auctoritee', the Middle Ages called it—which in *Romeo and Juliet* had been nearer a set piece:

FRIAR LAURENCE: Let me dispute with thee of thy estate.
ROMEO: Thou canst not speak of that thou dust not feel ...[23]

but here it has a new authenticity in movement and image:

for, brother, men
Can counsel and speak comfort to that grief
Which they themselves not feel; but, tasting it,
Their counsel turns to passion, which before
Would give preceptial medicine to rage,
Fetter strong madness in a silken thread,
Charm ache with air and agony with words.[24]

Again, as with Benedick and Beatrice, the whole scene, ending with the challenge of Claudio and the Prince to a duel, presents a mixture of tones: appeal to our sympathy, exaggeration which is on or over the edge of comedy.

Both these scenes, peripheral to the main plot, but of the essence of the play's art, demand, if they are to be fully appreciated, a complex response. What, then, of the crux of *Much Ado*, the shaming of Hero in church? On any realistic view it must, as has been said, be a repulsive scene: an innocent girl slandered and shamed by her betrothed, with apparently deliberate calculation, during her marriage-service, and in front of her father—the city's Governor—and the whole congregation. However we see it, Shakespeare's writing here is sufficiently powerful to give us some wincing moments. No interpretation can take away the shock of Claudio's brutal

There, Leonato, take her back again:
Give not this rotten orange to your friend;[25]

or of the Prince's heartless echo:

What should I speak?
I stand dishonour'd, that have gone about
To link my dear friend to a common stale.

The clipped exchange between Leonato and Don John that follows seems to
give the lie the ring of finality, to make false true in front of our eyes:

LEONATO: Are these things spoken, or do I but dream?
DON JOHN: Sir, they are spoken, and these things are true.

The generalizing assent, helped by the closed-circle form of question and
answer, has a claustrophobic effect on both Hero and us (I think of the nightmare world of 'double-think' closing in in Orwell's *Nineteen Eighty-Four*: this
is a verbal nightmare too). Momentarily, we have left Messina and might well
be in the meaner, darker world of that later play of similarly quibbling title, but
much less pleasant implications, *All's Well That Ends Well*. There 'these things'
are commented on by a Second French Lord, who knows human nature; knows
Parolles and his hollowness: 'Is it possible he should know what he is, and be
that he is?'; and Bertram and his meanness: 'As we are ourselves, what things are
we!' ('Merely our own traitors,' adds the First Lord, almost redundantly.)

Then, with a jolt, we remember that 'these things' are not true. They are not
true in the play, which is the first thing to remind ourselves of, if we wish to
preserve the play's balance as comedy. For in the later and so-called 'Problem
Comedies' (tragi-comedies, I prefer to follow A. P. Rossiter in calling them)—
All's Well, Troilus and Cressida, Measure for Measure—such accusations *are* true,
or would be true if those accused of them had had their way—had not been
tricked into doing something quite different from what they thought they were
doing (Cressida comes into the first category; Bertram and Angelo into the
second). But here the characters are playing out an act of deception, each of
them (except Don John) unaware in fact of what the truth is. To that extent,
they are all innocent, Claudio and the Prince as well as Hero: played on by the
plot, not (as we sense wherever tragic feeling enters) playing it, willing it. The
situation is in control.

Secondly, they are not true *outside* the play. To state that at all probably sounds
absurd. But genuine tragic feeling in Shakespeare forces its extra-theatrical truth
on us: continuously in the tragedies, spasmodically—but still disturbingly—in
the tragi-comedies. We know only too well how permanently true are *Hamlet,
Othello, Macbeth*. But the exposures of the tragi-comedies (Hero's shaming by
no means exhausts the *genre*) inflict on us truths about human nature—we may
prefer to call them half-truths. 'But man, proud man,' cries out Isabella (and she
has every justification),

Drest in a little brief authority,
Most ignorant of what he's most assur'd,
His glassy essence, like an angry ape,
Plays such fantastic tricks before high heaven
As make the angels weep; who, with our spleens,
Would all themselves laugh mortal.[26]

Here, all the possibilities of human nature are on the stage. We are *involved with* the people who are hurt or betrayed or even exposed (Angelo, as he cries out on the 'blood' that has betrayed him, is potentially a tragic figure); we are involved too in the language and its scaring comments on human frailty or baseness.

But go back to the scene in *Much Ado*, and, after the first shock, we are no longer fully involved. First, because the identities of Hero and Claudio have been kept to all irreducible minimum. That is why I earlier called them 'masks'. They have a part to play in a situation that is the climax to the whole play's theme; but they have not the core of being—or of dramatic being—which suffers or deliberately causes suffering. It would be quite different—ghastly and impossible—to imagine Beatrice in Hero's position.

And, secondly, the whole scene's deliberate *theatricality* lessens our involvement and distances our emotions. It emphasizes that it is, after all, only a play and intended for our entertainment;[27] we know that the accusation of Hero is false and—as this is a comedy—is bound to be put right by the end. First Claudio, then Leonato, takes the centre of the stage: the effect is to diminish any exclusively tragic concern for Hero, as we appraise the responses of the other two. There can be no doubt about Leonato's: it is highly exaggerated and hovers on the edge of caricature. We recognize the tones from *Romeo and Juliet*. There, vindictive, absurd old Capulet hustles Juliet on to a marriage she abhors; and then, in a stylized, cruelly comic scene, is shown (with his wife and the Nurse) over-lamenting her when she feigns death to avoid it. Shakespeare has little pity for this kind of selfishness. Here, as Leonato inveighs against his daughter—now in a swoon—we have self-pity masking itself as righteous indignation: the repetitions show where his real interest lies:

But mine, and mine I lov'd, and mine I prais'd,
And mine that I was proud on, mine so much
That I myself was to myself not mine,
Valuing of her . . . [28]

Yet, as he goes on, the tone alters, as so often in this volatile, quick-changing play:

> . . . why, she—O! she is fallen
> Into a pit of ink, that the wide sea
> Hath drops too few to wash her clean again,
> And salt too little which may season give
> To her foul tainted flesh.[29]

That is still over-violent, but the images of Hero's stain and of the sea failing to make her clean introduce a different note. We have heard it in Claudio's accusation:

> Behold! how like a maid she blushes here.
> O! what authority and show of truth
> Can cunning sin cover itself withal. . . . [30]

and in his outburst against seeming: 'Out on thee! Seeming! I will write against it. . . . '

Again, there is more here than his earlier, calculated stage-management of the scene. It is as though the situation has suddenly taken charge, become horribly true for a moment; and as if Shakespeare has injected into it some of the disgust at sexual betrayal we know from the dark Sonnets and from the crises of a host of later plays: *Measure for Measure, Troilus and Cressida, Hamlet, Othello, Cymbeline.*

This apparent intrusion of something alien—seemingly personal—into the very centre of the play was what had led me to doubt its success. I was wrong, I think (and it follows that I think other doubters are wrong), for three reasons. First, the intrusion, the cold music, is only a touch; one of several themes that make up the scene. Its language is harsh, but chimes in with nothing else in the play: no deadly vibrations or echoes are set up. Compare Claudio and Leonato with Troilus or Isabella, or, even more, with Hamlet or Othello, in whose words we feel a wrenching, an almost physical dislocation of set attitudes and beliefs: and the outbursts here have something of the isolated, artificial effect of set speeches.

Secondly, the play's central theme—of deception, miscomprehension, man's 'giddiness' at every level—is dominant enough to claim much of our response in *every* scene: including this climax in the church that embodies it most harshly, but most fully. And, in its many-sidedness and 'many-tonedness', this theme is, as I have tried to show, one well within the tradition of Elizabethan comedy.

Thirdly, and lastly, the *tone* of *Much Ado*—animated, brittle, observant, delighting in the ado men make—does not have to stretch itself much to accommodate the moments of questioning in the church. And this tone is ultimately, I think, what we most remember of the play: what gives it its genuine difference from *As You Like It* and *Twelfth Night*. Although two of its most loved figures are Warwickshire yokels (and nothing could change them), the aura of

Bandello's Italian plot pervades the rest. The love of sharp wit and the love of melodrama belong there; so do the sophisticated, unsentimental tone, and the ubiquitous, passed-off classical references: to Cupid and Hercules, Leander and Troilus. Gildon was wrong: in essentials, the people of Messina *do* act and talk like natives of a warm country.

The tone I mean is most apparent—most exhilarating and most exacting—in the wit-flytings between Benedick and Beatrice; but it dominates the word-play throughout: and this is one of the most word-conscious and wittiest of all Shakespeare's comedies. If I have said little about the words and the wit, this is because no one was more at home there, and could better communicate his enjoyment of them, than the late A. P. Rossiter: and you can read his lecture[31] on the play from one of the last of his memorable Shakespeare courses at Cambridge. My own debt to him will be very clear to all of you who heard his many lectures here at Stratford.

NOTES

1. *Remarks on the Plays of Shakespeare*: included in *Shakespeare's Poems*, 1710 (supplementary vol. to Rowe's *Works of Shakespeare*).

2. *Ten More Plays of Shakespeare*, 1913, p. 21.

3. Op. cit., p. 27: quoted by T. W. Craik in *Much Ado About Nothing* (*Scrutiny*, October 1953).

4. Introduction to *Much Ado* (Red Letter Shakespeare, 1904–8). Reprinted in *Shakespeare: A Survey*, 1925.

5. Op. cit.

6. II. iii. 98–103.

7. III. i. 26 ff.

8. II. iii. 162–5 and 191.

9. Ibid., 248 ff.

10. III. I. 107 ff.

11. IV. 2. 79 ff.

12. Op. cit., pp. xiii and xv.

13. In *Shakespeare and Elizabethan Poetry*, 1951: the title of Chapter X.

14. In *Shakespeare and the Popular Dramatic Tradition*, 1948, *passim*.

15. IV. i. 293–296.

16. Op. cit., p. 183.

17. October 1953, op. cit.

18. p. 308.

19. p. 314.

20. V. i. 92–9.

21. V. i. 3–5.

22. IV. i. 125, 129–32.

23. III. iii. 62–3.

24. V. i. 20–6.

25. IV. i. 31–2.

26. *Measure for Measure*, II. ii. 117–23.

27. S. L. Bethell makes the same point about the ill-treatment of Malvolio: op. cit., pp. 33–4.

28. IV. i. 138–41.

29. Ibid., 141–5.

30. IV. i. 34–6.

31. One of twelve lectures given at Stratford and Cambridge, to be published in 1959 by Longmans.

⸺⸺ ⸺⸺ ⸺⸺

1964—Marvin Felheim. "Comic Realism in *Much Ado About Nothing*"

The American educator and scholar Marvin Felheim (1914–1979) taught at the University of Michigan for more thirty years and published numerous books and articles on a wide variety of subjects. Here, Felheim argues that the characters in *Much Ado about Nothing* are, as compared to Shakespeare's other comedies, of a rather ordinary sort; contradicting what earlier critics like Ulrici have written, Felheim sees no fools, no unusual characterizations in their midst (as opposed to a play like *Twelfth Night*, for example, which not only contains Feste the Fool but such characters as Malvolio, Andrew Aguecheek, Sir Toby, and Maria). To Felheim, *Much Ado about Nothing* is not a play of characters but a play of plots and of plotting. Felheim points out that nearly every character in *Much Ado about Nothing* is deceived or duped at one point in the text, and that the play rests on each individual's desire to deceive or culpability in being deceived. Throughout the play, the audience continually knows more than any of the characters: They know of the deception against Beatrice and Benedick; they know of Hero's innocence; they know of Don John's varying plots. Tension derives from the audience's knowing, both comic tension (such as at Benedick's pompous bombast in his speech in act 2, scene 3) and dramatic tension (such as at the wedding scene). Comedy, and the tension created by it, thus has the important role in showing the flaws inherent in most of the characters, from Beatrice and Benedick's humorous derision of love to Leonato's selfishness at the affront to his honor when his daughter stands accused during the wedding scene. Thus, this comedy of plots and plotting reveals character to the audience, which finds humor in the situation and both the best and worst instincts in each character brought to light because of it.

I

As in the case of *As You Like It* and *Twelfth Night*, Shakespeare, in *Much Ado about Nothing*, combined a popular romance with some comic characters and situations of his own inventing, the result of which is a charming but sometimes difficult play. I do not subscribe to the critical notion that the two plots (one, the Hero-Claudio story, the other that of Beatrice and Benedict) do not cohere. For one thing, they are a comment on each other; they are the two sides of the coin, for both deal with love and wooing. For another thing, the characters in both plots are firmly linked, by ties of friendship or kinship, together. Finally, the two plots interweave; there would be no play if either were omitted and to ignore or reduce one throws the play out of balance.

For *Much Ado about Nothing* is a play of balance, of structure, of plot. Here no Viola or Rosalind dominates and determines the action, nor here are there such characters as Malvolio and Feste, Jacques and Touchstone to give the play extra dimension by means of their vivid personalities or through the nature of the philosophic position they take or represent. The closest we come to an eccentric or humor character here is Don John; "he is," we are told by Hero, "of a very melancholy disposition" and the sight of him makes Beatrice "heart-burn'd an hour after"; "sadness without limit" seems to be his dominant characteristic; like a minor Iago, he tells us, "I cannot hide what I am" and, also like Iago, he is somewhat cynical about marriage (anyone is a "fool" he states who "betroths himself to unquietness"). He seeks revenge upon Claudio, the "young start-up" who has "all the glory of my overthrow." Like Edmund, he is a bastard brother. And like all villains, he takes advantage of a situation which "may prove food to my displeasure," trusting to the weakness and gullibility of others to achieve his ends. But beyond these details, he is a shadowy individual; unlike other villains, he lets another invent the evil plot he uses and once his villainy starts to work he flees like a coward. Indeed, in this last respect, he is life-like in a different way than, say, Edmund is, but we must remember that he functions in a comedy; his flight, like the capture of Borachio and Conrade, is definitely absurd. He literally disappears (as do Shylock and Malvolio). And at the end, Benedict cautions, like Scarlett O'Hara to "think not on him till tomorrow" (and even then, we remember, Benedict will be on his honeymoon, hardly the time to "devise . . . brave punishments . . .").

In the absence of the kind of characters we are talking about, *Much Ado about Nothing* more than the other major comedies (including *The Merchant of Venice* and *The Taming of the Shrew*) is a play of plot. True, Beatrice and Benedict are fascinating character studies, but they are, in one sense, types—the wrangling lovers—and secondly they are dupes, tricked and "acted upon"; they do not instigate action; they do not provoke situations (their love affair is clearly foreseen by the audience; they have been designed for marriage and for each other); even Beatrice's "Kill Claudio" is made somewhat ridiculous by the fact that we know he is innocent and that the remedy is, in fact, at hand. Indeed, every major character in *Much Ado about Nothing* except, miraculously, the Friar, is, at one time or another, duped or deceived. Every character is the victim of some kind of plot, either secretly hatched or misconstrued as the result of eavesdropping. The play is one grand charade, one continual masked-ball, one double-cross after another. Only the wit of the language, the presence of Dogberry, Verges and the Watch, and the faith of Friar Francis—only these factors keep *Much Ado about Nothing* from being tragic; these are truly the comic elements, these things make up here the comic vision.

It is curious that in a play of plot or intrigue, such as *Much Ado about Nothing*, there are so many loose ends. These inconsistencies, minor though they may be, pervade the whole play. The clearest method of dealing with them is simply by means of an enumeration:

(1) In both the Quarto and the Folio, the opening, stage direction indicates "Enter Leonato Governour of Messina, Innogen his wife, Hero his daughter, and Beatrice his Neece, with a messenger"; again, in the direction for Act II, scene i, there is a reference to Leonato's "Wife". Now, this worthy woman never speaks a word and in most productions she is omitted, on the presumably commendable principle that her silent presence would be embarrassing. What would be her response, for instance, to the following questions and speeches?

Don Pedro: I think this is your daughter.

Leonato: Her mother hath many times told me so.

Benedict: Were you in doubt, sir, that you ask'd her? Further, in none of the major comedies (*The Merchant of Venice*, *As Yon Like It*, *Twelfth Night*) is there an adult woman relative; these are plays about young ladies who are motherless, but whose relationships with their fathers, dead or alive, are significant; hence the presence of a mother for Hero and an aunt for Beatrice would be an exception to the general practice and would raise issues of behavior and loyalties which do not concern the dramatist here:

(2) There are two characters in the play who are referred to quite early in the action but who never appear although they might reasonably be expected in terms of subsequent events. The first of these is Claudio's uncle, who is mentioned in I, i, 14. Leonato tells the Messenger who brings good news of Claudio's valor that the young man "hath an uncle here in Messina will be very much glad" to hear of him and his "feats." The Messenger replies, "I have already delivered him letters," after which the Messenger and Leonato speak of the Uncle's tearful response to the *good* news. "How much better it is," exclaims Leonato, "to weep at joy than to joy at weeping!" But with this pious and somewhat pompous pronouncement, all reference to Claudio's uncle ceases; the mentioning of him occupies some ten lines of prose, involves two speakers and occurs at a strategic spot dramatically, in the very opening scene. But the uncle is not included among the named wedding guests, nor is he on hand to share in either the griefs or the joys which surround his young nephew in Messina.

A similar character is Antonio's son. Leonato, in the first line of scene ii of Act I asks his brother, "Where is my cousin, your son?" Antonio answers that "He is very busy" providing music for the entertainment (dinner and dancing) which Leonato is offering to his guests. The matter of these speeches is flatly contradicted in Act V, when Leonato suggests that Claudio, since he cannot be "my son-in-law," should "be yet my nephew . . . My brother hath a daughter," he continues, "And she alone is heir to both of us." One wonders what has become of the son and especially what has happened to his inheritance rights. (Of course, we realize that there is no such daughter, as the one Leonato is to produce, but that still does not explain away the son.)

(3) A third inconsistency raises questions about staging. The stage directions indicate that Act I scene i occurs "Before Leonato's house." After the initial meetings and greetings, all the characters "exeunt" except Benedict and Claudio who "manent" to talk of Claudio's love for Hero. Then Don Pedro returns and, after Benedict's departure, he agrees to help Claudio by wooing Hero for him and by making the necessary arrangements for the marriage with Leonato. Presumably they do not move, during this discussion, from the front of Leonato's house; at least nothing in either the stage direction or in their conversation itself indicates any change of scene.

Yet, this incident is later reported by two characters, each of whom sets it in a different locality. Antonio's report to his brother Leonato not only contains mistaken information (he thinks the Prince not Claudio is in love with Hero) but falsifies the locale as well. Antonio says his information comes from "a man of mine" who "overheard" the Prince and Claudio as they were "walking in a thick-pleached ally in mine orchard." At whose house were they?

Borachio, reporting the same conversation to Don John, gives it yet another setting. "Being entertain'd for a perfumer," he states (why should a follower of a guest be so employed we wonder) "as I was smoking out a musty room, comes me the Prince and Claudio hand in hand, in sad conference. I whipt me behind the arras." Then, according to Borachio, he overheard their conversation.

Are we to account for these discrepancies by saying that Shakespeare was careless? Or should we assume that there is evidence here of another, now missing play? Or are we confronted with an absurdly bad text? Finally, may it not be that these reports were deliberately designed in this manner so that we, knowing the truth, can make some estimate of the characters of Antonio and Borachio and draw some conclusions about the practice of eavesdropping?

(4) The villainy which results from Borachio's eavesdropping has important consequences for the plot. But it is curious that the villainy is really of Borachio's invention and ingenuity rather than of the established villain, Don John.

In Act II, scene ii, Don John tells us, simply, that "Claudio shall marry the daughter of Leonato"; he seems resigned to this state of affairs, until Borachio tells him, "I can cross it." Then Don John admits that "any cross, any impediment, will be med'cinable to me" and asks Borachio "How canst thou cross this marriage." Borachio then recounts his intimacy with Margaret, but still Don John sees no opportunity. "What life is in that . . . ?" he asks. Borachio spells out the plan: Don John shall "poison" the Prince and Claudio. Don John still hedges: "What proof shall I make . . . ?" he wants to know. Borachio elaborates; Don John finally agrees and offers a "fee."

But not only is this plot unusual in being suggested to rather than by the villain; it is further curious that, according to its instigator, Borachio, it will provide "proof enough to misuse the Prince, to vex Claudio, to undo Hero, and kill Leonato," a series of events which proves almost true, but a series which is directed not so much against the Prince and Claudio as Hero and Leonato, who, it is true, do hear the brunt of the villainy.

The problem, then, is that the evil hurts chiefly the wrong people, and only indirectly upsets the ones Don John hates. This results in a kind of nastiness in *Much Ado about Nothing*: innocent people are made to suffer presumably without cause except, of course, for the existence of evil people in their world; all of which is very close to the tragic situation in such a play as *Othello*; all of which gives an extra and certainly an un-romantic tinge to this comedy. On the other hand, the "innocence" of Leonato could certainly be questioned, for his refusal to hear out Dogberry undoubtedly results in the near tragic consequences of Act IV; indeed, one could presume that his indifference to the Watch (as Governor he must not be unconcerned for the welfare of Messina) results in immediate punishment, that, curiously enough, his own pretentiousness (possibly as contrasted with the monstrous proclivity in Dogberry), is singled out for retribution.

(5) Finally, if one looks at the play in terms of character, one might ask questions of this sort: (a) Why doesn't the usually quick-to-speak Beatrice speak up in Church and say that "until last night, I have this twelve month been her [Hero's] bedfellow" so that at least one part of Don Pedro's accusation (that these "vile encounters" have taken place "a thousand times") will be discredited? (b) Isn't it curious that Margaret, who seems more a friend than a servant of Hero's, should engage at all in such deception and that she should never be shown as sharing any responsibility other than having, in Leonato's words, "some fault . . . although against her will"?

All of these inconsistencies, it will be noted, are related more to questions of character than to plot. They are, also, as presented, all connected with one kind of realism—the realism of life, of psychology, of cause and effect—rather then to the realism of the theatre, where, as a matter of fact, they would probably not, in a first-class production, be noted. In other words, we are dealing in this play, as in the others, with two kinds of realism: to life and to art. The latter kind is what is significant, for true-to-life realism is, ordinarily, not necessarily dramatic, nor is it integral to the poet's vision, which is true to a realism larger and more meaningful than that of mere events or mere characterization; the poet's realism is true to the truth behind life, to what Aristotle calls the truth of poetry as contrasted with the truth of history. So, these inconsistencies and questions are relevant not because they expose loose ends or indicate Shakespeare's faulty or rapid craftsmanship or the existence of an old play which he may have used (any or all of which may be correct) but because they help us to distinguish one kind of truth or reality from another. It is in the larger sense (as well as frequently in the other, too) that Shakespeare's plays are realistic.

II

Much Ado about Nothing is, par excellence, a play of plot and plots. Practically every character engages in plotting of some kind, and at no point in the action is there not some plot afoot. What makes all this acceptable, even delightful, is that the audience always knows all; from the very opening lines, we are invariably informed about what's coming next; there are no secrets from us; indeed, most of our pleasure comes from the fact that we simply watch the revelations as they come; there is hardly any suspense, but there is plenty of excitement in the continual unfolding of events which have been so carefully prearranged.

The very first scene of the play sets the pattern. A messenger comes in with a letter which tells of the impending arrival of Don Pedro, fresh from "a victory." Eighty lines later the Prince enters, as forecast. The Messenger merely enabled the scene to be set, provided the occasion for a word or two to be spoken about Claudio's uncle, and served as the foil for Beatrice's first "skirmish of wit" on the subject of Signior Mountanto (Benedict). But his presence and his letter prepare us for the ensuing action and thus from the very first moment the basic pattern of *Much Ado about Nothing* is established.

Almost at once we learn, first in the conversation between Claudio and Benedict, next in the talk between Claudio and Don Pedro, that the young Count has fallen in love with Hero. This repetition, with variation, is also characteristic of events in this play; everything seems to happen twice (or even three times). The conversation between Claudio and Don Pedro is overheard by two others (Antonio's man and Borachio) who report it in two further scenes. Benedict is fooled, then Beatrice by the same device (and then the Watch, as a kind of counterpoint, overhears Borachio and Conrade). There is a masked dance, and a final scene when Hero and the other ladies all enter "masked." The Prince engages in two plots: one to woo Hero for Claudio, the other "to bring Signior Benedict and the Lady Beatrice into a mountain of affection th' one with th' other." Claudio is twice deceived by Don John and Borachio: once into thinking that Don Pedro has wooed Hero for himself, and again when he is convinced that Hero is dishonest. And to match Don John and Borachio's villainy (and evil plot), there is Friar Francis's goodness (and helpful plan). There are two dances, two sets of lovers, two old men, two "gentlewomen attending on Hero," two "followers of Don John," two named clowns, Dogberry and Verges, and the play ends, just as it began, with the appearance of a messenger. (There are even two songs, Balthasar's "Sigh no more" and "Pardon, goddess of the night," which is sung in the churchyard.) All this repetition and duplication lend the play its balance (there are, we remember, two plots) and reinforce its basic nature: a neatly manipulated comedy of plot or intrigue.

Claudio's falling in love brings about two conflicting plots (Don Pedro's and Don John's) and in the ensuing action he is, temporarily, taken in by both plans, even though he has been party to one of them. Most critics find him, as a consequence, a weak character. He is also, we must remember, young and suspicious. (Earlier, when Don Pedro is first informed of Claudio's love by Benedict, the Prince says graciously that "the lady is very well worthy"; but Claudio, ever suspicious and touchy, turns on his protector: "You speak this to fetch me in, my lord?") But, more importantly, he is a character (like Hero and Leonato, too) who is in a sense the victim of the balanced and carefully organized plotting. So, although the Prince had clearly indicated that he would woo Hero for Claudio, the young Count nevertheless is easily deceived, by Don John and Borachio, into crediting their falsehood that the Prince woos for himself. This early, and certainly somewhat silly, instance of Claudio's gullibility will be repeated later with seemingly more serious consequences, and will be engineered by the same two villains, of course.

One of the best insights into Claudio's character can be gained by inspecting his language. He speaks a great amount of verse, actually more than any other character in the play. Ordinarily, this could be considered an indication of his extreme youthfulness and romantic nature. And so, certainly, on the obvious level we must treat his predilection for poetry. But when we look more closely at the kind of verse he uses, we gain a further insight into his personality. Claudio first speaks in verse to Don Pedro; the subject of their conversation, which begins with Claudio's revealing statement,

My liege, your Highness may do me good,

is Claudio's love for Hero, a subject he has also just raised with Benedict—in prose. Now, he asks for favors, for help, and he is appropriately polite, appropriately rhetorical. Furthermore, Don Pedro's plot to help

I will assume thy part in some disguise,
And tell fair Hero I am Claudio;
And in her bosom I'll unclasp my heart
And take her hearing prisoner with the force
And strong encounter of my amorous tale

is a silly plot anyhow. Why shouldn't Claudio do his own wooing? There are no obstacles to this match. The only reason is that the plot must be served, by a conniving Prince, to allow for the counterplot and to prove, perhaps, that

The course of true love never did run smooth.

But the key to our understanding lies in the fact that, in a predominantly prose play, this plan is undertaken in verse. It is, in other words, something exceptional, somewhat flamboyant; perhaps the rhetoric suggests somehow the pretentiousness and absurdity. At any event, the next time Claudio speaks in verse, an eleven line soliloquy shows us the consequences: he believes himself deceived. He is sad; he pretends to philosophy

> Friendship is constant in all other things
> Save in the office and affairs of love

and, too late, he has learned to "trust no agent." But, of course, we know all this is wrong. As we always know more than the characters. To keep Claudio, from being too absurd, Shakespeare allows him to speak in poetry, the language of emotion; we recognize thereby that he is overwrought, and we indulge him; Shakespeare must establish Claudio's gullibility: what better way than this?

Once his nature has thus been set forth, Claudio continues to use poetry, particularly in the big scenes which follow: the church scene, at Hero's presumed grave, and in the final scene of reconciliation. Throughout, Claudio's use of verse reinforces our impressions of him; as such it is, perhaps ironically, as aspect of realistic characterization. But in addition, inasmuch as Claudio is a type of the young, sentimental lover and since he must accept love or defeat or a new love all with good grace, then Shakespeare has him do it in poetry—rhetorically and dramatically. And I submit that Shakespeare is here not only presenting youthful, somewhat sentimentalized love, but he is also, by means of the formality of verse, making fun of it. This love affair has more than a tinge of absurdity to it; it lacks reason and reasonableness, however socially acceptable it may be. To build up the sentiment and, at the same time, skillfully to mock it Shakespeare has the principal sentimentalist, Claudio, deliver himself in language that serves both the character's and the author's purpose.

Whereas Claudio's falling in love results in plots, the reverse is true in the case of Beatrice and Benedict. As a result of plots, they fall in love. And one of the neat dramatic ironies of *Much Ado about Nothing* is that Claudio and Hero are instrumental in carrying out the deception of Beatrice and Benedict who are thus deceived into love exactly as their deceivers become the victims of deception. Here, too, then, the requirements of a balanced plot help explain the seeming cruelty of the denunciation of Hero; in a sense, perhaps, this smacks somewhat of cynicism: love seems to be at the mercy of intrigue. Only a well-contrived "labour of Hercules" can bring Beatrice and Benedict together (although, as it turns out, they are willing enough) and another equally carefully devised plan easily separates Hero and Claudio. True, love can be said to conquer in the end, particularly if we accept Hero's rejoinder to Ursula's "we have caught her [Beatrice]":

> If it proves so, then loving goes by haps
> Some Cupid kills with arrows, some with traps.

But, certainly, it is part of the complexity of this comedy that we should see in the situation of the two pairs of lovers both the triumph of love and the recognition that there is something else as well, some awareness that love is not simply the result of Cupid's work with bow and arrow; other factors, even human ones, are also at work. As a matter of fact, each of these couples is particularly well matched, not only in appropriate terms of wit (Beatrice and Benedict) and sentiment (Hero and Claudio) but also in more worldly terms of position and possessions. Claudio is a young Count of Florence, who has recently distinguished himself in battle and won the favor of Don Pedro, Prince of Arragon; Hero is also young, appropriately aristocratic (daughter of the Governor of Messina) and, more importantly (in spite of Benedict's "she's too low for a high praise, too brown for a fair praise, and too little for a great praise"), "his only heir." As a matter of fact, her financial status is emphasized twice, first by Don Pedro who tells Claudio that Leonato has "no child but Hero," evidently a necessary prelude to their discussion of love and marriage, and secondly by Leonato himself, when, after all the trouble has been cleared up, he recommends his brother's "daughter" on two counts to Claudio: she is

> Almost the copy of my child that's dead;
> And she alone is heir to both of us.

An appropriate marriage, indeed. Since financial and class considerations are satisfactory, let love enter in, or, to put the order in terms of the play: Claudio came and saw, investigated, then conquered, a very realistic procedure.

A footnote might be added here to reinforce the realistic air which surrounds this match. Claudio rejects Hero on a very realistic basis: she is a "rotten orange," an image which echoes Beatrice's earlier statement about him: "The Count is neither sad, nor sick, nor merry, nor well: but civil count—civil as an orange and something of that jealous complexion." (Shakespeare's use of this particular fruit is most appropriate; the orange was a luxury food, a delicacy fit for aristocratic palates.) Claudio's rejection of Hero

> She knows the heat of a luxurious bed
> Her blush is guiltiness, not modesty

leads Leonato at first to suspect that Claudio has "vanquish'd the resistance of her youth, and made defeat of her virginity—," a situation which however deplorable would not be unsurmountable. Claudio understands this clearly

> I know what you would say. If I have known her
> You will say she did embrace me as a husband
> And so extenuate the 'forehand sin.

This brief discussion, which takes place, one must remember, in "A church," presumably at the altar, and which involves technicalities of the most intimate sort, is certainly evidence enough of one of the realistic strands which pervade this comedy. To treat *Much Ado about Nothing* as merely a romantic charade is to ignore such searing lines in favor of superficiality.

No less realistic, in another sense, is the love affair of Beatrice and Benedict. Obviously they have been destined for one another. Leonato tells us that "they never meet but there's a skirmish of wit between them"; this remark characterizes them as belonging to that same genre as Katherine and Petruchio, wrangling lovers. Then, they both protest, publicly and privately, against matrimony, against, indeed, the opposite sex, although Beatrice relents a bit, graciously, in favor of Don Pedro.

Benedict's protestations, if they are not those of a very young man (and presumably he is not for he asks, "Shall I never see a bachelor of three-score again?"), sound real enough: he is, he freely admits, "a professed tyrant" to the female sex who "will live a bachelor" and who has some rather unpleasant things to say about love and women (he trusts none). Further, his standards are high: his ideal must be "rich . . . that's certain; wise, or I'll none; virtuous, or I'll never cheapen her; fair, or I'll never look on her; mild, or come not near me; noble, or not I for an angel; of good discourse, an excellent musician, and her hair shall be of what colour it please God." His cynicism is best illustrated by his answer to Claudio's question, "Can the world buy such a jewel?" *i. e.* Hero; Benedict replies, "Yes, and a case to put it into."

Beatrice is equally convinced of her own good sense: "I have a good eye uncle," she says; and, although she suspects that when she was born "a star danc'd," yet she admits that "my mother cried." In this same realistic tone she rejects all men both as sexual partners (they are either too young or too old) and as husbands ("Adam's sons are my brethren; and, truly, I hold it a sin to match in my kindred").

Both reject love good naturedly—but firmly. The problem is how to get them together. The method is to use a trick, a trick which will expose to each his own sentimental nature and yet allow him to surrender without a loss of self-esteem. The trick, labeled by Don Pedro as veritably "one of Hercules' labours" is to evoke the pity of one for the other; justification is never even mentioned. This is a very realistic society in which young people get married; here is the underlying, realistic assumption—despite the reservations of both Beatrice and Benedict, there is no other way to live: the married state is the human state; only in heaven, under the watchful eye of St. Peter do bachelors and maids "live as merry as the day is long." On earth, they marry, for better or for worse.

Presumably Beatrice has all the qualities Benedict has enumerated as essential; he, in turn, is described as "of a noble strain, of approved valour, and confirm'd honesty." They are well-matched in wit, honor and social status. Enter "the only love-gods": their friends. And so this is a match made on earth, very much before our eyes. The victims deserve no better; we, and their friends, will be amused, and nature will be served.

But the most realistic aspect of the Beatrice and Benedict match is the way in which each accepts the faked evidence. Benedict believes "this can be no trick." (And not for a moment, except at the very end, does Benedict relinquish this opinion. Even when Don Pedro and Claudio, themselves disillusioned by Hero's presumed dishonesty, try to bait him with the truth [Don Pedro's statement, "The old man's daughter told us all," is followed by Claudio's more open "'God saw him when he was hid in the garden'"], he ignores their words as "jests . . . which, God be thanked, hurt not.") He then enumerates her qualities: she is "fair . . . and virtuous . . . and wise"; so much for the personal side. In addition, there is the social argument: "the world must be peopled." Beatrice's reaction is somewhat more selfish (more feminine?); she wants to disprove Hero's suggestion that she is proud and scornful. And she accepts Benedict's worthiness on the word of "others." So much for romantic attitudes. These lovers can indeed "see a church by daylight."

Shakespeare juxtaposes the two very similar scenes in which Benedict and Beatrice are in practically identical fashions fooled. But he makes one significant variation: the first, the tricking of Benedict, is in prose; the second, the fooling of Beatrice, is in verse. There is nothing particularly unusual in the use of prose for the first of these actions; seventy-five per cent of the lines of *Much Ado about Nothing* are prose. But in a Shakespearean play which has only twenty-five per cent of its lines in verse (only *The Merry Wives of Windsor*, in the whole canon, has a greater percentage of prose and it has a staggering eighty-eight per cent, but *The Merry Wives* is a most unusual play), it is consequently of some significance when and where verse is used. Since the whole of this scene—the fooling of Beatrice—is in verse, we must stop for comment and speculation.

First of all, the verse is used to mark the scene as being different from its predecessor, the fooling of Benedict, which is in prose. There is a further refinement: verse is (appropriately?) reserved for the ladies; perhaps it softens somewhat or makes palatable the catty things which Hero and Ursula are forced to say about Beatrice. Secondly, there is a definite technical build-up in the verse as Hero concludes their conversation with a couplet, one of only two so used—that is, to mark a dramatic moment, in this case an exit—in the whole play (and, appropriately, the couplet is a kind of wise saw):

> If it proves so, then loving goes by haps
> Some Cupid kills with arrows, some with traps.

After Hero and Ursula depart, Beatrice has a ten-line soliloquy, in which she decides to "requite" Benedict for his love. This speech is in rhyme, not couplets but two quatrains (abab, cdcd) followed by a couplet (cc) which concludes the scene. (Beatrice's soliloquy is one of three times in the play when rhyme is used; the other two: first, the last speech of the Friar in the church, when he sums up the plans and also gives the exit cue; and, second, the speeches of Claudio and Don Pedro—a total of twelve lines—in the tomb scene; of course, there are also the play's two songs.) The only two dramatic couplets in *Much Ado about Nothing*, then, both occur in this scene. So the verse is used not only as an aspect of characterization, but it gives the scene a definite lift at the end, partly, perhaps, to compensate for the fact that Beatrice (as befits a girl of her era, we must remember) gives in a bit too easily; at least, we can say that by virtue of the poetry she gives in more elegantly; or, to put it another way, since her capitulation lacks logic (at least as compared with Benedict's) it is granted rhetoric; he rationalizes in prose; she emotes in verse.

Together with six lines in the church scene (IV, i) and four in the final scene (V, iv), this ten-line soliloquy makes a total of twenty lines of verse spoken by Beatrice in the whole play. Benedict has thirteen and a half lines in the church scene and seventeen in the final scene for a total of thirty lines of verse. He has three soliloquies, one before and one after he is hoodwinked (II, iii) and a very brief one in V, ii, but all three are in prose, although the subject of all three is his attitude toward women, love and marriage. When they are alone, Beatrice and Benedict invariably speak in prose; indeed, except for Beatrice's soliloquy (in a scene all in verse), these lovers use verse only in the two big poetic scenes of the play. Wit, their dominant linguistic characteristic, is for them, unlike their predecessors, Katherine and Petruchio, a prose game. This fact, then, supports our impression that there is a serious non- or antiromantic side to these Shakespearean comic lovers.

These witty lovers are not the only prose-bound group in *Much Ado about Nothing*. Dogberry, Verges and the Watch are even more prosaic. They appear in four scenes; they all use prose exclusively; the comedy they provide results from the pretentiousness of Dogberry, the ineptitude of Verges and the general absurdity, mostly implied, in the behavior of the others. Dogberry and Verges are humor characters rather than clowns; they lack both the penetrating wit and philosophical aloofness of Touchstone or Feste; they are not clever men; they are fools, wonderfully funny but limited by their creator to certain very specific roles: low comedy which results from Dogberry's misuse of words, and a very important role in the plot.

The Watch appears late in the action: not until Act III, scene iii, almost at the climax, classically considered, of the action. The reason for their delayed entrance is quite simple—they were not needed earlier; until the end of Act II and the beginning of Act III, the comic element in the play was most skillfully supplied by the witty skirmishes between Beatrice and Benedict; after the two scenes involving their deception, their function is altered: they, as well as the actors in the main plot, become more serious. So the task of supplying the comedy devolves upon Dogberry, Verges and the Watch, a function they fulfill magnificently. But it is significant that the nature of the comedy changes from high comedy to low, from brilliant repartee to the broadly funny linguistic errors of Dogberry; the type of comedy doesn't alter: it is still largely a matter of language but its level noticeably falls. This shift, dramatically, is most exciting. For after scene iii of Act III, Beatrice and Benedict engage in no further battles of wit; when they meet now, they have more serious business to talk about: their own new-found love and the situation of Hero. Each has a typically witty scene of the earlier kind, but, significantly, each has it with, of all people, Margaret (III, iv and V, ii); and, in each case, the joking consists mainly of lewd puns (perhaps a way of subtly denigrating Margaret?). So it falls to Dogberry, Verges and the Watch to continue the earlier linguistic game. The lowering of the level (and here I imply no loss of humor; on the contrary, I find Dogberry funnier than Beatrice) coincides with the shift in the main plot: from the pursuit of love to deceit and slander; in both instances, this represents a coarsening.

But the requirements of the plot provide the main reason for the introduction of the Watch in the third act. At this point they are needed to apprehend the villains. And the irony is that they do. Why Conrade and Borachio agree to "obey" the Watch can be conjectured: Borachio's change of heart, so noticeable in Act V, may prompt him to surrender once he has committed his foul deed; or, of course, there is the irony involved: that such bumpkins as the Watch should be the means of capturing these crafty villains tends to mitigate the seriousness of the crime and to allow the comic view of life to dominate the apparently (and potentially) tragic one. The important factor is that Borachio and Conrade are apprehended prior to Claudio's accusation of Hero and, as a matter of fact, if Leonato were not in such a hurry to get to the church on time (III, v) he might have averted the sadness which his haste makes inevitable; this is stunning comic plotting: that fools should apprehend conniving villains and that pompous haste makes waste. It is important that we should not forget these points as we witness the unpleasant church scene which follows immediately. Comedy here is not only an end in itself but is most significantly a means of maintaining itself. This is artistry.

Although indications are strong that plot interests determine the actions of both Dogberry and Leonato, nevertheless, both behave in terms of basic character traits as well. Both are motivated by self-interest. One of Dogberry's chief concerns is to reverse the slander Conrade heaps upon him. The labels "coxcomb" and "ass" stick unhappily upon this "wise fellow," this "pretty . . . piece of flesh." He is determined to rid himself of the abuse; "this plaintiff here, the offender, did call me an ass," he complains. Further, "I beseech you let it be remembered in his punishment." Leonato is no less self-satisfied. He cannot take time to listen to the tedious Dogberry. He gives instructions to and interrupts Friar Francis at the Church. After Claudio and Don Pedro have slandered Hero, Leonato's first concern is for himself:

Hath no man's dagger here a point for me?

Next, he wishes his daughter dead rather than disgraced (a provocative echo of Shylock). All his concern is for the family name, not at all for Hero who lies in a swoon. He pontificates:

Death is the fairest cover for her shame.

Finally, in a long harangue, he chides the barely conscious Hero for her sins, chiefly against himself. Even Benedict bids him "Sir, sir, be patient." But he can only rage, "Let her die." Even when the Friar interposes to suggest that Hero may be innocent, Leonato will have no part of it:

Why seek'st thou then to cover with excuse
That which appears in proper nakedness?

He relents not because of love for or faith in his daughter but simply because of his "honour"; only after the Friar has made his proposal to "change slander to remorse" does Leonato grieve, but even now he has nothing to say to or for Hero; his grief, like Dogberry's concern, is all for himself. Thus Shakespeare's magnificent comic portraits of the governor and constable of Messina.

III

A great deal has been made of the noting–nothing relationship in *Much Ado about Nothing*; this combination is most clearly set forth in the lines in which Don Pedro persuades the reluctant Balthasar to sing

Don Pedro: Nay, pray thee, come;
Or if thou wilt hold longer argument,
Do it in notes.

Balthasar: Note this before my notes:
There's not a note of mine that's worth the noting.
   Don Pedro: Why, these are very crotchets that he speaks;
Notes, notes, forsooth, and nothing!

The end of all this speculation is to the effect that the "nothing" in the title
of *Much Ado about Nothing* contains an implied word-play on "noting"; indeed,
noting, in the expanded sense of eavesdropping, seems a most meaningful way
to describe a great deal of the action in the play. This speculation seems to me
entirely acceptable. However, I would add another aspect. For if noting is significant, there is an equally important symbol: letters.

The play opens with a Messenger who has just delivered two letters: one to
Claudio's mysterious uncle, the other to Leonato. Both letters are superfluous,
in that we never see anything more of the uncle and the subject matter of the
letter to Leonato is the basis of the opening conversation in the play. If letters,
though, are the symbols of human relationships mentioned in the opening
scene, they serve as a concluding device as well. For the play ends on a most
peculiar note: at the last minute, Beatrice and Benedict revert to their former
selves, announce that they do not love each other, and say, in fact, that they
themselves as well as the others have been deceived. Some means must be
found for a quick and satisfying resolution. A plot device suffices, one which
balance the opening: letters are "found," a "halting sonnet" from Benedict, and
"another" from Beatrice, "written" in their own "hands." Then, it is Benedict
who exclaims "A miracle! here's our own hands against our hearts." (And,
of course, it will be remembered that Leonato and Claudio in their original
deceiving of Benedict referred to the fact that Beatrice gets up "twenty times a
night" to write to Benedict.) Thus letters serve both as dramatic devices and as
dramatic symbols effecting human relationships.

There are other references to letters and writing as well. Claudio and Don
Pedro in the latter part of the opening scene "mock" Benedict by making up a
letter of departure for him. Later, when Claudio denounces Hero in the church
he reinforces his argument against "seeming" by shouting "I will write against
it," a somewhat curious threat until one remembers that letters in this play have
a symbolic function. Actually, all the writing Claudio does is to compose an
"epitaph" which he hangs upon Hero's tomb with the promise "Yearly will I do
this rite." So that instead of writing against Hero, he finds himself lamenting his
cruelty to her—and thus the act of writing for him symbolizes the climax of his
relationship with Hero, first the attack, then the repentance.

There are, as one would expect, two instances where writing is exploited for
comic effect. One occurs in the late scene between Margaret and Benedict when
she asks him to "write . . . a sonnet" in praise of her beauty, a facetious comment,
of course, upon his subsequent confession, in soliloquy, that he is having trouble

in finding rhymes and a foreshadowing of the final scene when his "halting sonnet" to Beatrice is actually produced (although not read). The other comic use of writing is connected, naturally, with the low comedians. In answer to Dogberry's query, "Who think you the most desartless man to be constable?" two candidates are recommended: Hugh Oatcake and George Seacole; their qualifications: "they can write and read." Dogberry is not to be intimidated by such accomplishments; well he knows, or pretends to, that "To be a well-favoured man is the gift of fortune; but to write and read comes by nature." Well-favoured Dogberry may assume himself to be, but he later has great cause to mourn his lack of gifts at nature's hands: three times (the magic number) he is made to moan: "O that I had been writ down an ass!"

All this writing, of letters and sonnets, is accomplished both in prose and verse. And with the interrelationship of these two modes it is appropriate to conclude this discussion. A notable feature of *Much Ado about Nothing* is that it begins and ends in prose; further, the conclusion is a dance, not a wedding. Even Benedict's concluding piece of advice to Don Pedro—"get thee a wife"—is followed by his cynical "There is no staff more reverend than one tipp'd with horn.") Aware that "man is a giddy thing," Benedict overrides Leonato's objection and insists that "music" comes "first"; so the play ends with his command to "Strike up, pipers."

Prose is thus the characteristic medium of this play; it serves admirably and exactly the non-sentimental tone and becomes easily the medium both of high and low comedy. Poetry, on the other hand, is used to suggest sentimentality. The most consistent speaker of verse is Claudio. Verse turns up, as we would expect, to be the medium of the church scene, where it fits the mood and the heroics, but where it more than a little suggests the bombast. In this connection one place in particular must be noted: the conclusion of Act III, scene ii. Here, in prose, Don John has been about his business of warning Claudio and the Prince of Hero's "disloyalty"; he proposes the midnight rendezvous beneath her window to "let the issue show itself." The scene then concludes with four lines of poetry:

> Don Pedro: O day untowardly turned!
> Claudio: O mischief strangely thwarting!
> Don John: O plague right well prevented!
> So will you say when you have seen the sequel.

Since we already know well that his plan is dishonest, these lines strike us with all their rhetoric exposed. They represent Shakespeare's way of capping absurdity in an appropriately fantastic way, a flourish of self-conscious exclamations which can succeed only in rendering the characters somewhat ridiculous. The intent is humor, for we must remember that we are in the midst of comedy. As a matter of fact, with the departure of the above characters from the platform, their grandiose remarks still echoing in the air, the stage is prepared for the only possible sequel: "Enter Dogberry and his compartner Verges, with the Watch."

1973—Carl Dennis. "Wit and Wisdom in *Much Ado About Nothing*"

The American poet Carl Dennis (b. 1939) won the Pulitzer Prize in poetry in 2002 for his collection *Practical Gods*. Dennis has been on the teaching faculty of the State University of New York at Buffalo since 1966 and is currently artist-in-residence there. In the following article, Dennis examines the roles of wit and belief in the play, suggesting that these two modes of experiential perception continually oppose each other throughout the text. Wit is the intellect relying on evidence and reason gained by the senses, while belief is related more to intuition, to those constructs that are more often "felt" rather than explicitly understood. Dennis argues that for the characters to successfully navigate the world of the play, they must learn to let go of their perceptions and misconceptions of the world and take what is ultimately a blind leap of faith. Beatrice and Benedick are the best example of this in the text; their early bantering skirmishes reflect their own fears of intimacy and dependency. Later, once they have been led to believe in the other's love, they willingly accept without evidence the truth of what they have overheard. Claudio, on the other hand, lacks this faith in Hero, which suggests why he is so ready to turn on her in act 4.

Recent critics of *Much Ado About Nothing* have tended to agree with Mr. Graham Storey's convincing suggestion that the play is about "man's irresible propensity to be taken in by appearances."[1] "Deception," Mr. Storey writes, "operates at every level of *Much Ado*: it is the common denominator of the three plots, and its mechanism—eavesdroppings, mistakes of identity, disguises and maskings, exploited heresay—are the stuff of the play."[2] What causes the characters to be so often deceived is one of the central critical questions that the play raises. Mr. Storey attributes all the confusion to man's innate "giddiness," following Benedick's concluding assertion that "man is a giddy thing" (V.iv.107); but the term is perhaps too imprecise to clarify the particular limitations of the protagonists.[3] Perhaps a more helpful suggestion is made by Mr. A. P. Rossiter, who considers almost all the characters to be "self-willed, self-centered, and self-admiring creatures, whose comedy is at bottom that of imperfect self-knowledge which leads them on to fool themselves."[4] Surely Beatrice and

Benedick are betrayed by their overreaching cleverness when they spy on their friends; Claudio is led astray when he proudly assumes that his eavesdropping gives him the knowledge and the right to vilify Hero; and Dogberry hopelessly distorts facts because of his infatuation with his own imagined excellences. But self-centeredness and self-deception are such generally pervasive flaws in Shakespearean comedy that without being further discriminated they are not very useful in defining the distinctive attributes of any particular group of characters. In this essay I want to try to sharpen the meaning of the various mistakings and discoveries of *Much Ado*, of the many changes from blindness to insight and from insight to blindness, by relating them to an opposition which the play develops between two ways of perceiving the world. One mode of perception presented here, which may be called "wit," relies on prudential reason and practical evaluation of sensory evidence; the other, the opposite of wit, rejects practical reason for intuitive modes of understanding. The drama of the play resides in the protagonists' moving from one way of seeing to the other; and their practical and moral success is determined by their willingness to lay down their wits and approach the world through faith, through irrational belief.[5]

The characters whom the reader associates most immediately with wit are Beatrice and Benedick, though in their cases wit seems to be not so much rational calculation as a simple delight in verbal ingeniousness, in wittiness, which the reader admires for the sharpness of mind and the playfulness of spirits which it betokens. But this wittiness also implies a certain view of life. Taking the form of playful insults between a man and woman, it expresses indirectly a detached attitude to love, a sophisticated amusement at conventional romantic attitudes. It thus is not simply evidence of a quick mind but an indirect affirmation of rational self-control as opposed to emotional self-indulgence that carries man away from reality on the tide of feeling. For both Beatrice and Benedick, perhaps especially for Benedick, a lover like Claudio is a pathetic lunatic. From a plain-speaking, battle-loving soldier he becomes a lover whose "words are a very fantastical banquet—just so many strange dishes" and whose "soul is ravished [with] sheep's guts" (II.iii.21–22, 60–61). The witty man, on the other hand, keeping his wits about him, is able to avoid anything as irrational as love.

The desire of Benedick and Beatrice to keep their practical reasons dominant is perfectly understandable; for they are experts in the exercise of their cleverness and rank amateurs in the exercise of their emotions. But problems arise when their bias towards reason deludes them into believing that they have no emotional selves that require expression. When this happens their verbal wittiness is used not so much to expose foolishness in others but to disguise to themselves the state of their own feelings. To insult playfully a person to whom one feels attracted is a way of proving to oneself that the attraction does not exist. In Benedick's case this self-deception is also dramatized by his vexation at Claudio's immediately falling in love with Hero. To Benedick his impulsive friend is an image of his own emotional self which he is unconsciously trying to suppress; and his laments about Claudio's giving up manly soldiership for effeminate love express his unacknowledged war against his own latent desire for love. The war is doomed to failure, not only because feelings cannot be ignored indefinitely, but also because a refusal to acknowledge them weakens one's ability to cope with them when they finally surface. Much of the humor of the eavesdropping scenes where Beatrice and Benedick decide to take pity on each other results from the speed in which their defenses are broken down.

Along with this distrust and denial of the emotions, a bias toward wit is associated with a hard-headed, skeptical attitude to human worth. Beatrice and Benedick mock lovers as being not only impulsive and fantastical but also prone to see value where none exists. Their battles of wit take the form of insults because they want to show themselves as being under no idealistic delusions about the worth of the opposite sex. Benedick's skepticism about women calls particular attention to itself because it involves a complete reversal of the conventional view of man as woman's pursuer. Doubtless his abuse of women is done in part for sport. He himself distinguishes his "custom" of speaking as "a professed tyrant to their sex" from "the simple true judgment" of his more serious moods (I.i.169–170). But he would hardly adopt the role of woman-hater if it did not correspond, however indirectly, to some real aspect of his own beliefs. And when he doffs his guise of the "tyrant" to speak "truly" about Hero, he still refuses to acknowledge any of her obvious merits. He is still, as Don Pedro says, "an obstinate heretic in the despite of beauty" (I.i.236–237). If he does not actually believe that all women make their husbands cuckolds and prisoners, as he asserts he does, he at least has serious doubts about the value of their society. The shrewd man of wit knows that to idealize a woman is to play the fool.

But all this shrewdness of practical reason turns out to be blindness, not insight. Benedick's prudential skepticism is not based on any actual experience of human nature, on any specific knowledge of particular women, but on foolish pride. His distrust of love and marriage results in good part from an overestimation of his own worth, from his seeing himself as superior in kind to women in general. He gives himself away most obviously in his soliloquy in Leonato's orchard, in which he defines the woman who will be worthy of his love: "One woman is fair, yet I am well; another is wise, yet I am well; another virtuous, yet I am well. But till all graces be in one woman, one woman shall not come in my grace" (II.iii.28–31). To be "well," to be prudently rational, is identified here with being impervious to love, with complete self-sufficiency. But since the rationale for this resistance is Benedick's ridiculous assurance of his own perfection, the wisdom of wit turns out to be foolishness. To identify giving "grace," giving unmerited favor, with finding "all graces," all perfections, in the object, is to willfully ignore the necessity of unearned trust, of irrational, unprovable faith, in every bond that holds people together. If strictly followed prudential wit, with its proud demand for positive proof of perfection, leads logically to a state of complete isolation, to a repudiation of the social communion that Shakespeare's comedies invariably celebrate.

Although Benedick avoids this kind of isolation by falling in love with Beatrice, we are given a grotesque example of what can happen to the man of skepticism and pride in the figure of Don John. The melancholy that Don John admits suffering from, which prevents him from liking anyone and impels him to stir up mischief, is finally not the result of particular injuries but the fruit of a morbid pride that makes him consider all society with others a diminishment of his self-sufficiency. What seems to aggravate him most when he is first presented to us is not so much his failure to defeat his brother in their recent quarrel but his being forgiven for starting it, since the forgiveness places him in the role of an inferior: "I had rather be a canker in a hedge than a rose in his grace, and it better fits my blood to be disdained of all than to fashion a carriage to rob love from any. In this, though I cannot be said to be a flattering honest man, it must not be denied but I am a plain-dealing villain" (I.iii.27–33). His claims to self-sufficiency, to "smile at no man's jests" and "tend to no man's business," are of course specious (I.iii.15, 17). Just as in a lighter vein Benedick seeks out the company of the woman he overtly spurns, because of his suppressed attraction to her, so in a sinister vein Don John spends his time thinking of ways to hurt the people whom he overtly pretends to ignore, feeling a suppressed admiration for them which his pride refuses to acknowledge.

The great moral difference between Benedick and Don John is rooted in the fact that Benedick is merry and Don John melancholy. Beatrice herself points out this contrast: "He were an excellent man that were made just in the midway between him [Don John] and Benedick. The one is too like an image and says nothing, and the other too like my lady's eldest son, evermore tatling" (II.i.7–11). The overflow of good spirits that underlies at least some part of Benedick's wit-play is a safeguard against dangerous pride because it expresses a general delight in human relations, a delight that makes isolation from society impossible. The world pleases Benedick too much for him to reject it. The same kind of delight in life is associated with the sportive aspects of Beatrice's wittiness. She is, as Don Pedro comments, "a pleasant-spirited lady"; and her uncle, Leonato, drives the point home: "There's little of the melancholy element in her; she is never sad but when she sleeps, and not ever sad then" (II.i.356, 357–359). Wittiness, then, can have positive meaning as well as negative. If, on the one hand, it can be used as a tool of practical reason in the service of emotional repression, distrust, and pride, it can also express a light-hearted playfulness, a love of life, that undermines the vices of proud reason and brings man into communion with his fellows. Thus the playful side of Beatrice's and Benedick's wit-cracking prepares us for their transformation into lovers and their abandonment of bad wit.

Because Beatrice and Benedick are duped into loving each other, we may at first not be inclined to see their love as an indication of an important shift of internal perspective. After all, the trick played on them seems to appeal basically to their vanity. Each decides to love the other partly because he is flattered by the other's supposed adoration. But to move from a pride that rejects all potential lovers as unworthy to a vanity that is willing to reciprocate another's admiration is to make a crucial moral adjustment. Vanity, unlike pride, is social; it requires the good will of others in order to thrive. And the good will that Beatrice and Benedick seek is not only that of each other but the good opinion of their friends. They are duped successfully by their friends because neither wants to be thought hard-hearted and disdainful by the people they most respect. They want to fulfill the values of their community.

In accepting the criticism of their friends Beatrice and Benedick show not only a desire for approval and communion but a willingness to lay aside a reliance on their own wits and rely instead on the perceptions of others. They believe on trust that their friends can see them more clearly than they can see themselves. Thus Beatrice's acceptance of the criticism she overhears is immediate:

What fire is in mine ears? Can this be true?
Stand I condemned for pride and scorn so much?
Contempt, farewell, and maiden pride, adieu:
No glory lives behind the back of such.
And Benedick, love on, I will requite thee,
Taming my wild heart to thy loving hand.

    (III.i.107–112)

In submitting here without question to the censure of her friends, Beatrice seems to be rejecting the authority of autonomous reason. This willingness of both Beatrice and Benedick to use other eyes than their own applies of course to their views of each other as well as of themselves. When at the close of the play Leonato says that the lovers were "lent" their eyes by their friends (V.i.23–26), he means primarily that each was encouraged to love the other by overhearing reports of the lovelorn state of the other. Though in this regard they are completely mistaken, their being deceived is perhaps a step in the right direction. By rejecting objective appearances of disdain in the other by a subjective belief in the other's devotion, they indirectly repudiate the skeptical reason that supported their disdain. To be sure, they are supporting their faith here on hearsay, on circumstantial evidence. But they are willing to believe this evidence so quickly only because it agrees with their own hidden desire for love. And if they are in one sense fools, their foolishness is finally vindicated; for their very acts of irrational belief in each other's love help to bring their real love for each other into being.

That genuine love entails giving up the outer eye of reason for the inner eye of faith becomes clear later in the play when Beatrice and Benedick are tested by the crisis of Hero's vilification. Beatrice here proves her powers of commitment by believing without question in her friend's innocence. She is the only one, along with the holy Friar Francis, to give no credence whatever to the accusations of Don Pedro and Claudio. She requires no factual evidence for her conviction, relying rather on an act of subjective trust. Benedick's powers of commitment are tested during this crisis when he places himself completely at Beatrice's disposal, agreeing even to obey her command to challenge his friend Claudio to a duel. He agrees not simply because he wants to keep Beatrice's love, but because his love for her enables him to trust in the rightness of her commands:

> *Benedick*: Tarry, good Beatrice, By this hand, I love thee.
> *Beatrice*: Use it for my love some other way than swearing by it.
> *Benedick*: Think you in your soul the Count Claudio hath wronged Hero?
> *Beatrice*: Yea, as sure as I have a thought or a soul.
> *Benedick*: Enough, I am engaged, I will challenge him.
>
>   (IV.i.327–331)

In accepting without external evidence the absolute wisdom of his beloved Benedick proves that he has abandoned the external perception of wit for the inner vision of faith.

It has been argued by some critics that Beatrice and Benedick are comically emotional in their defense of Hero, that we are meant to laugh at Beatrice's command, "Kill Claudio," and at Benedick's zealous obedience. If before the pair were too witty, it is contended, now they have become too romantic. This argument is true in the literal sense that the lovers are over-hasty in their revenge against Claudio, in the sense that they are ignorant of how he was deceived. But in the larger moral context of the play this emotional impetuosity is a proof of the sincerity of their trust, and hence of their moral maturity. Only through their emotions are they led to the unprovable insight that Hero is innocent. Calm self-control and rational sifting of evidence cannot lead them to this all-important truth.

As has already been suggested, to say that Beatrice and Benedick abandon bad wit is not to say that they abandon wittiness. Humorous joking can express a playfulness founded on a love of life; and at the end of the play the pair are as playfully witty as ever. Now, however, the negative side of their wit is repudiated. Instead of concealing their feelings, their joking actually expresses them. Thus after brief and humorless assertions that they love each other "no more than reason," they submit to the evidence of their love-letters and acknowledge their emotions by the use of witty irony:

Benedick: A miracle! Here's our own hands against our hearts. Come, I will have thee, but by this light, I take thee for pity.

Beatrice: I would not deny you, but by this good day, I yield upon great persuasion, and partly to save your life, for I was told you were in a consumption.

(V.iv.91–96)

Wittiness here takes the form not of an insult ingeniously clever, but an insult transparently a lie. Their new wit is finally directed towards themselves rather than towards others. It gently mocks the fundamental irrationality of love, though it accepts that irrationality as an essential part of life.

While Beatrice and Benedick develop morally by abandoning the perception of skeptical reason for that of intuitive faith, by leaving wit for a higher wisdom, Claudio degenerates in the course of the play by rejecting subjective faith for prudential doubt. He compromises his initial emotional involvement with Hero by relying on his wits to understand her character. The fatal flaw in his love for Hero is not its impetuosity; for though it begins rather suddenly, it is based on some prior acquaintance and attraction and is directed toward a woman who is intrinsically admirable. The flaw, rather, is its lack of depth. Underneath Claudio's impetuous ardor is a latent uncertainty about the rightness of his own emotions and the value of love. This uncertainty shows itself first in the cautiousness with which Claudio tells Benedick of his feelings for Hero. Instead of boldly declaring his love at once, he begins by asking Benedick for his opinion, and when he later does acknowledge his feelings, he hedges his acknowledgement in a series of gentle qualifications. "In mine eye she is the sweetest lady that ever I looked on," he tells Benedick (I.i.189–190), guarding his praise by admitting indirectly the possible bias of his emotions. And when he later asserts, "If my passion change not shortly, God forbid it should be otherwise" (I.i.221–222), he seems to admit a lack of complete confidence in the strength and stability of his emotions.

This lack of confidence may perhaps result partly from mere inexperience; for Claudio appears to be a young man who is more practiced as a soldier than as a courtier. He does not know the subtle workings of love, and for this reason is happy to have his friend Don Pedro woo Hero as his substitute. But when he believes Don John's lie that Don Pedro has wooed and won Hero for himself, he shows a lack of generosity as well as a lack of experience. He is too ready to distrust not only his own feelings but the intentions of others. He sees man as an easy prey to irresponsible infatuations that betray all other commitments:

'Tis certain so. The Prince woos for himself.
Friendship is constant in all other things
Save in the office and affairs of love;
Therefore all hearts in love use their own tongues.

> Let every eye negotiate for itself,
> And trust no agent, for beauty is a witch
> Against whose charms faith melteth into blood.
>
> (II.i.181–187)

This explanation of Don Pedro's supposed inconstancy in friendship, it should be noticed, not only degrades man by viewing him as a passive victim of his feelings, but also degrades women by viewing her attractions as Circean enchantments that make men act with the amorality of animals. In opposing blood to faith, love to constancy, Claudio is actually stripping love of its greatest virtue. He is blind to the fact that faith lies at the very center of love's power of perception; and this blindness prepares the way for his great blunder, his mistrust of Hero.

Some critics have tried to mitigate the guilt of Claudio's condemnation of Hero by reminding us that he is duped into his false belief not only by the slanders of Don John but by the seemingly conclusive proof of his own observation. Claudio in fact uses this argument to defend himself. "Yet sinned I not but in mistaking," he assures Leonato when he finally discovers the truth (V.i.284–285). But this defense overlooks the crucial fact that real love abandons the external perception of the eye and ear for internal subjective perception. It rejects circumstantial appeals to practical wit, to skeptical prudence, for unconditional trust. Claudio is disposed to accept flimsy appeals to his senses because he has never fully committed himself to Hero, never rejected his suppressed doubts about the value of love. It has been argued that Don Pedro's acceptance of the false evidence is a proof of its power, that we must excuse Claudio's credulity if the good-hearted and sensible Don Pedro is duped as well. But there is obviously one all-important difference between the two men: Claudio is in love with Hero, or thinks he is, and Don Pedro is not. If love means anything here it should mean a special will to believe in the goodness of the beloved. Because Claudio's love is superficial, that special will does not exist. At the crucial moment he relies on wit, not faith.

Abetting Claudio's lack of trust in Hero is the kind of pride that we have seen supporting Benedick's initial commitment to wit. One of the reasons behind Claudio's decision to expose Hero in public is a desire to punish her for daring to dishonor him. He seems to be moved as much by the need of personal revenge as by the claims of moral justice. His dignity is offended that someone would be brazen enough to try to trick so noble a man as himself. By deciding to "bear her in hand until they come to take hands" (the phrase is Beatrice's, IV.ii.305–306), by feigning ignorance until the last moment, he intends to prove that he can overmatch her craft with his own. The hurt to his pride accounts for the viciousness of his attack, for his willingness to hurt cruelly the feelings of Hero's father and uncle in order to make her suffer, for the preponderance of anger over pity as he says to Leonato, "take her back again, / Give not this rotten orange to your friend" (IV.i.32–33). To the extent that Claudio's sense of justice is tainted by proud vengefulness he becomes like Don John, the man who is angry at the world and who is the prime agent in causing Claudio's distrust of Hero.

After his condemnation of Hero, Claudio holds a position in relation to Benedick that exactly reverses their original relations. While Benedick has rejected the perceptions of the skeptic for those of the lover, Claudio has moved from love to skepticism. Where the old Benedick who trusts no woman is left behind for the new Benedick who trusts one woman completely, the old love-seeking Claudio is abandoned for a new Claudio who decides "to lock up all the gates of love" and "turn all beauty into thoughts of harm" (IV.i.106, 108). Because Benedick has abandoned wit for the will to believe, he can see the goodness of Hero that is hidden from her apparent lover, Claudio, who has abandoned the will to believe for wit. The extent to which they have developed in opposite direction is shown most emphatically in the scene in which Benedick challenges Claudio to a duel. Benedick here is now in deadly earnest, attacking his former friend with honest indignation; Claudio is now the flippant man of wit, hiding under his wittiness whatever qualms he may feel about Hero's death. He expects Benedick to provide some witty entertainment, unaware that the old Benedick no longer exists:

> *Claudio*: We have been up and down to seek thee, for we are high-proof melancholy and would fain have it beaten away. Wilt thou use thy wit?
> *Benedick*: It is in my scabbard. Shall I draw it?
> *Don Pedro*: Dost thou wear thy wit by thy side?
> *Claudio*: Never any did so, though very many have been beside their wit. I will bid thee draw as we do the minstrels, draw to pleasure us.
>
>   (V.i.122–129)

Though Claudio and Don Pedro amuse themselves by joking about Benedick's loss of wit and his falling in love, Benedick is now wit-proof, as he says in his parting speech to Claudio: "Fare you well, boy. You know my mind. I will leave you now to your gossip-like humor. You break jests as braggarts do their blades, which, God be thanked, hurt not" (V.i.187–190). The laugh that Claudio and Don Pedro have at Benedick's new seriousness, at the love-striken man who "goes in his doublet and hose and leaves off his wit" (V.i.202–203), is cut short when they learn from Borachio just how much their own wits have been deceived. "I have deceived," affirms Borachio, "even your very eyes" (V.i.238).

In order for Claudio to deserve Hero's love at the end of the play, he must repudiate the prudential reason and reliance on sensory evidence that comprises bad wit. At first it may be a little difficult to see him accomplishing this; for when he tells Leonato that he sinned "But in mistaking," he seems to overlook, as we have mentioned, the lack of trust which made this mistaking possible. Yet when he mourns Hero at her tomb he not only shows real grief at what his mistaking has done, but makes no effort to mitigate his guilt. The epitaph he writes for her affirms that she was "Done to death by slanderous tongues" and identifies her murderers with her mourners:

> Pardon, goddess of the night,
> Those that slew thy virgin knight,
> For the which, with songs of woe,
> Round about her tomb they go.
>
> (V.iii.12–15)

Moreover, in yielding himself up completely to the will of Leonato, in agreeing even to marry any woman that Leonato chooses, Claudio seems to be renouncing his reliance on self-sufficient intelligence. Just as Benedick finally relies on Beatrice's perception, so Claudio is finally willing to let someone else see for him and "dispose / For henceforth of poor Claudio" (V.i.305). And his not being allowed even to see the face of his wife before the marriage suggests symbolically the need to abandon external perception of the outer eye. The apparent miracle of Hero's resurrection comes about only by repudiating the kind of skeptical wit that caused her apparent death.[6]

The crowning blow to the claims of wit in *Much Ado* is given in farcical terms by the antics of Dogberry and Verges. For these blundering clowns, who are completely witless, manage to stumble into the truth that is denied Claudio and Don Pedro. As Borachio tells the deceived noblemen, "What your wisdoms could not discover, these shallow fools have brought to light" (V.i.238–240). In the task of discovering clever criminals, crafty wit must yield to well-intentioned stupidity. Instead of cautioning prudent vigilance, Dogberry and Verges tell the watches to avoid getting into trouble; but the culprit gives himself away. They completely misconduct the trial, but they seem to know somehow that Borachio is a villain; and when they finally bring Conrad and Borachio before Leonato, Dogberry is able to give the crime its right name, although he is too ignorant to count to six: "Marry, sir, they have committed false report; moreover, they have spoken untruths; secondarily, they are slanders; sixth and lastly, they have belied a lady; thirdly, they have verified unjust things; and, to conclude, they are lying knaves" (V.i.220–224). What seems to lie behind the success of their witlessness is their good will. They are simple-minded, but their hearts are in the right place. Their respect for Leonato's good name, for example, is ridiculously expressed, but is finally commendable:

> *Leonato*: Neighbors, you are tedious.
> *Dogberry*: It pleases your Worship to say so, but we are the poor Duke's officers. But truly, for mine own part, if I were as tedious as a King, I could find in my heart to bestow it all of your Worship.
> *Leonato*: All thy tediousness on me, ah?

Dogberry: Yea, an 'twere a thousand pound more than 'tis, for I hear as good exclamation on your Worship as of any man in the city, and though I be but a poor man, I am glad to hear it.
Verges: And so am I.

(V.i.20–31)

In the world of the play such good feelings seem to be enough to enable one to stagger into truth.

While Dogberry and Verges, when taken together, represent the triumph of witlessness, Dogberry taken by himself can be seen to expose wit in even a more direct way. For with all his stupidity Dogberry believes that he is a clever man; and by his fatuous pride in his wit he parodies unconsciously the pride of Benedick and Claudio. Thus his malapropisms, which result partly from his desire to display his vocabulary, are related in motive to the word-play of his betters, which expresses, at least in its debased form, a kind of intellectual vanity.[7] And Dogberry's patronizing lament that old Verges's "wits are not so blunt" as they should be, that "when the age is in, the wit is out," recalls Benedick's initial patronizing of love-lorn Claudio, and looks forward to Claudio's laughing lament over Benedick's foolishness as a lover. The relation of Dogberry to Claudio is especially close. Dogberry's examination of Borachio and Conrade follows immediately after Claudio's public examination of Hero; and the absurd mishandling of the villains' hearing (though Dogberry has promised to "spare no wit" in the matter (III.v.66)) is a commentary on the injustice of Hero's hearing. Even Dogberry's horror that he should have "been writ down an ass" (IV.ii.90) may perhaps echo Claudio's angry indignation at the affront to his dignity which might be caused by Hero's supposed deception. The men of wit in the play, then, are not only less successful than the fools in seeing truth, but are mocked by one fool's aping of their witty pretensions.

The inadequacy of wit as a mode of perception is perhaps suggested by the very title of *Much Ado About Nothing*. It has been often pointed out that "noting" and "nothing" were pronounced alike in Elizabethan England, and one recent critic, Miss Dorothy Hockey, has suggested in a very useful article that *Much Ado* is really a "dramatization of mis-noting," pointing out the many specific references to hearing and seeing in the play that underscore the mistakes of observation.[8] We can enlarge the meaning of this point if we keep in mind the relation of noting to wit; for wit in *Much Ado*, as we have seen, entails a skeptical prudence that relies on sensory facts rather than on intuitive belief. The pun in the title, which suggests that to depend on noting is to depend on nothing, thus vindicates indirectly the intuitive mode of perception to which wit is opposed.

NOTES

1. Graham Storey, "The Success of *Much Ado About Nothing*," in *Discussions of Shakespeare's Romantic Comedy*, ed. Herbert Weil, Jr. (Boston, 1966), p. 44.

2. Storey, p. 40.

3. Citations from Shakespeare in this essay are to *The Complete Works*, ed. G. B. Harrison (New York, 1968).

4. A. P. Rossiter, *"Much Ado About Nothing,"* in Weil, p. 26. This essay appeared originally in *Angel with Horns* by A. P. Rossiter, ed. Graham Storey (London, 1961).

5. The importance of the notion of wit in *Much Ado* has been particularly emphasized by two critics, Mr. Walter N. King and Mr. William G. McCollom. Mr. King, in his interesting article, *"Much Ado About Something,"* SQ, XV (1964), limits the meaning of wit to the use of word-play, contending that the expressive practice of this kind of joking buries "natural instinct" under a layer of conventionality. Mr. McCollom, on the other hand, contending that wit is a positive force in *Much Ado*, argues that the play is "about the triumphing of true wit (or wise folly) . . . over false or pretentious wisdom," with Beatrice and Benedick being the truly wise and "Don John, Borachio, Don Pedro, Claudio, and even Leonato . . . present[ing] in very different ways the false wisdom which deceives others or itself" ("The Role of Wit in *Much Ado About Nothing,"* SQ, XIX (1968), pp. 166, 173). The problem with this formulation is that it fails to notice that the wit-play of Benedick and Beatrice has potentially negative qualities that lead to self-deception, and that a reliance on wit, in the general sense of practical reason, leads to error more often than to insight. The opposition between pride and humility is doubtless a crucial distinction in the play; but Mr. McCollom does not make clear enough how the mistakes of Claudio and Don Pedro are attributable to pride, or how Beatrice's and Benedick's belief in Hero is the result of their humility.

6. I must admit that I agree with the many critics who are disturbed by Claudio's joviality during his wedding. His punning jokes at Benedick, his rather crude question, "Which is the lady I must seize upon?" (V.i.53), and his playful request to look under the bride's veil before the ceremony suggest that his remorse over Hero's death is somewhat superficial. A more somber bearing here would make us more willing to believe that he deserves Hero, that he has reached the moral plane of Beatrice and Benedick.

7. Mr. Rossiter makes a similar point, contending that "wit and nitwit share a common obsessive delight in the wonder of words" (p. 28).

8. Dorothy C. Hockey, "notes notes, Forsooth. . . . ," SQ, VIII (1957), p. 354.

1986—Carol Cook. "'The Sign and Semblance of Her Honour': Reading Gender Difference in *Much Ado about Nothing*"

In addition to the following selection, Carol Cook (b. 1953) has also published on *Antony and Cleopatra* and self-fashioning in Shakespeare. In her seminal text included here, Cook suggests that the essential conflict in the text is male versus female. The plotting, the dialogue, the themes, all reflect male fears of female sexuality. Cook demonstrates this by noting the numerous references to cuckoldry in the text, as well as the numerous jokes and puns centered on phallic references and other sexual innuendo—often suggesting sexual inadequacy or the fears of such. Cook also notes that Beatrice's aggressive speech reflects more masculine patterns, and that "Beatrice tacitly accepts her culture's devaluation of 'feminine' characteristics—of weakness, dependence, vulnerability—and sees conventionally masculine behavior as the only defense against them." This is why Beatrice can speak so boldly and forthrightly and not be punished for her assertions. To the males in the play, Beatrice is acting almost like she is "one of the guys." Hero's more silent, more acquiescent, more traditionally feminine character becomes threatening because it is difficult for the men around her to know what she is thinking (unlike Beatrice, who seems to vocalize many of her thoughts), and, consequently, what she is doing. To Claudio, Hero "is less a character than a cipher," and this is why he so readily believes the lies Don John and Borachio invent about her. As Cook notes, "Hero's nothing invites nothing, her blankness produces marking." Thus, as the title of Cook's article suggests, Hero becomes "the sign and semblance of her honour," because her lack of vocalization and the distinctly Elizabethan feminine values she espouses (silence, obedience, chastity) render her unknown to her fiancé, her father, and the other men of the play.

Much Ado about Nothing begins with news of an ending; a rebellious brother has been defeated in battle, and the victorious prince and his retinue are approaching Messina. Don Pedro, Claudio, and Benedick return from one kind of conflict to enter another: before they set foot in Messina we hear of a "merry war," the ongoing "skirmish of wit," between Benedick and Beatrice (1.1.62–63). Responding to the centrality of sexual conflict in *Much Ado*, critics have sometimes read the play as a struggle in which humane feminine qualities ultimately supersede inadequate masculine values. Barbara Everett has written that

> the play concerns itself with what can only be called the most mundane or "local" fact in that world of love, in all its forms, that the comedies create: that is, that men and women have a notably different character, different mode of thinking, different system of loyalties, and, particularly, different social place and function. Not only this: but this is the first play, I think, in which the clash of these two worlds is treated with a degree of seriousness, and in which the woman's world dominates. (320)

John Crick, after describing the limitations of Messina's "predominately masculine ethos," suggests that Beatrice's "feminine charity triumphs. . . . Benedick becomes acceptable to her when he symbolically joins his masculine qualities to her feminine principles by taking up, however reluctantly, her attitude to Claudio . . ." (37). Janice Hayes borrows the psychological terms *instrumental* and *expressive* to characterize masculine and feminine modes of behavior and experience in the play. Contrasting "the traditionally male sphere of war, honors, and triumph" and "the private and potentially expressive world of Messina, a world whose functioning is communal and cyclical and whose heirs are women," Hayes sees the Claudio-Hero plot as a ritual action in which Claudio's "narcissistic instrumentality" is overcome in his symbolic penance at Hero's tomb and his acceptance of an unknown bride (79).

These readings find a resolution to sexual conflict in the play in a thematic movement that privileges the feminine and provides moral closure. In my view, however, whatever conversion or movement the play offers is notably incomplete, for while the sexual conflict points in an illuminating way to the question of gender differences and what is at stake in them, their relation to subjectivity and authority, the play cannot resolve its contradictions from within its own structures of meaning. My reading of *Much Ado* begins by tracing the signifying differences that produce or represent gender in the play, differences especially evident in the cuckold jokes of the opening scene, and suggests that what is at stake in these differences is a masculine prerogative in language, which the play itself sustains. I argue that the play masks, as well as exposes, the mechanisms of masculine power and that insofar as it avoids what is crucial to its conflicts, the explicitly offered comic resolution is something of an artful dodge.

The pervasive masculine anxiety that characterizes the play's Messina might be read psychoanalytically as castration anxiety; the imagery of horns and wounds in the cuckold jokes points rather insistently in this direction. But "castration anxiety" is not so much an answer to the play's questions about gender difference as another formulation of them that requires some further explanation, for the phallus and its loss only signify within a larger structure of meanings. *Much Ado* sets up a complex chain of association among the word, the sword, and the phallus, marking off language as the domain of masculine privilege and masculine aggression. The masculine, in the world of the play, is the place of speaking and reading subjects, of manipulators and interpreters of signs. The characters are much concerned with self-concealment and the exposure of others, with avoiding objectification by others, the abjection of which the cuckold's horn becomes the fearful sign. To read others in this play is always an act of aggression; to be read is to be emasculated, to be a woman. Masculine privilege is contingent on the legibility of women, and the ambiguous signifying power of women's "seeming" is the greatest threat to the men of Messina, who engage various defensive strategies against it, from the exchange of tendentious jokes to the symbolic sacrifice of Hero. The play itself is implicated in these strategies, insofar as the characters' plot to recuperate Claudio through the fiction of Hero's death is also the plot of the play: the stability necessary for comic closure requires the exorcism of a disturbingly polysemous image of woman. The strategy is only partially successful, however, for though the "false knaves," Don John and his henchmen, are ultimately revealed as the manipulators of misreadings, they function as scapegoats, deflecting attention from the unresolved anxieties about language and gender that have been responsible for the play's catastrophe.

I

We can learn a good deal about the place of gender difference in the life and language of *Much Ado*'s Messina by looking at the most persistent theme in the witty discourse of the play's male characters—that of cuckoldry. The cuckold jokes begin when Leonato, asked whether Hero is his daughter, replies, "Her mother hath many times told me so" (1.1.105), and end with Benedick's closing advice to Don Pedro: "get thee a wife, get thee a wife! There is no staff more reverent than one tipp'd with horn" (5.4.122–24)—an absolute equation of marriage with cuckoldry. The tirelessness with which these men return to such jokes suggests an underlying anxiety that is present when the play opens and that has not been dispelled by the resolution of the plot's various complications.

The imagery of the play's cuckold jokes reveals much about the anxiety that motivates them. Leonato's casual remark about Hero's mother is a witty circumlocution of the sort that dominates the sophisticated small talk of Messina. In itself it is a trifle, a hackneyed joke that comes automatically to mind and rolls easily off the tongue. We are not to infer that Leonato is harboring serious doubts about the fidelity of his wife. The very conventionality of the comment, though, points to a larger cultural picture in which men share a sense of vulnerability because they have only a woman's word for the paternity of their children. A man may be a cuckold, it is suggested, and not be aware of his horns.

This anxiety about women's potential power over men is particularly apparent in Benedick's self-consciously misogynistic banter in the first scene, where he airs some of his antiromantic doctrine for the benefit of Claudio and Don Pedro:

> That a woman conceiv'd me, I thank her; that she brought me up, I likewise give her most humble thanks; but that I will have a rechate winded in my forehead, or hang my bugle in an invisible baldrick, all women shall pardon me. Because I will not do them the wrong to mistrust any, I will do myself the right to trust none; and the fine is (for which I may go the finer), I will live a bachelor. (238–46)

To submit oneself to a woman by loving and marrying her is to "have a rechate winded" in one's forehead—a trumpet blast blowing from one's forehead, announcing one's humiliation to the world. Marriage forces a man to "hang his bugle in an invisible baldrick." This somewhat obscure metaphor seems to be a concentrated expression of the masculine fears about feminine power in the play. The gloss given for this line in the Riverside edition runs as follows: "carry my horn not in the usual place on the usual strap (baldrick) but where no strap is seen (because none is present)—on my forehead" (335). As a symbol of man's betrayal and humiliation, the horn displaced from its rightful place to a wrong one must be read, it seems to me, in the light of the play's two metaphoric uses of the word *horn*, for horns are not only signs of cuckoldry but also phallic symbols.[1] What Benedick's metaphor of the invisible baldrick suggests is that marriage emasculates a man and flaunts the evidence of his emasculation by displaying the displaced phallus in his forehead. This theme is sustained in the lines that follow:

> *Bene.* . . . Prove that ever I lose more blood with love than I will get again with drinking, pick out mine eyes with a ballad-maker's pen and hang me up at the door of a brothel-house for the sign of blind Cupid.
> *D. Pedro.* Well, if ever thou dost fall from this faith, thou wilt prove a notable argument.
> *Bene.* If I do, hang me in a bottle like a cat and shoot at me; and he that hits me, let him be clapp'd on the shoulder and call'd Adam.
> *D. Pedro.* Well, as time shall try: "In time the savage bull doth bear the yoke."
> *Bene.* The savage bull may, but if ever the sensible Benedick bear it, pluck off the bull's horns and set them in my forehead, and let me be wildly painted, and in such great letters as they write "Here is good horse to hire," let them signify under my sign, "Here you may see Benedick the married man." (250–68)

Benedick here offers in succession three versions of his fate if he becomes subjected to a woman, if he "ever lose[s] more blood with love than [he] will get again with drinking"—a loss of vitality and virility like "Th' expense of spirit" of sonnet 129, perhaps suggesting also the bleeding wound of castration. What makes these three statements (of what would happen "if") roughly parallel is their recurrent images of vulnerability, mutilation, and exposure as legible signs. In the first case, loss of eyes suggests the lover's mutilation—and, obliquely, castration—but also enforces the particular humiliation of denying the victim the ability to witness his own condition.[2] Displayed publicly at the site of sexual degradation, the lover is fully objectified, seen but unseeing, subjected to the aggression of others' gazes. That the instrument of blinding is the satiric ballad maker's pen links the visual objectification through display with a textual objectification through language, as the emasculated cuckold is ridiculed and published in degrading fictions. In the second case, the lover is to be hung "in a bottle like a cat" and shot at by other men, who compete for the first hit. In his public exposure and vulnerability, the cuckold becomes the target for other men's "shots," their witty jibes.[3] Finally, Benedick picks up Don Pedro's aphorism about the yoking of the savage bull. The bull's horns are the manifestations of its savagery, its undomesticated masculine power, and by extension an image of virility in general. Should the sensible Benedick ever submit to the yoke, he says, "pluck off the bull's horns"—that is, turn them from signs of potency to signs of emasculation—"and set them in my forehead." The displacement motif here recalls the invisible baldrick, and again the emasculation of the lover is followed by public display—the sign designating the humiliated victim "Benedick the married man."

The cuckold joke partakes of all three categories of what Freud calls "tendentious jokes": the aggressive or hostile joke (the cuckold joke expresses masculine competition), the cynical joke (aimed at the institution of marriage itself), and the obscene or exposing joke. In discussing the last category, Freud makes a number of observations that are pertinent here. "Smut," he writes, in *Jokes*, or "the intentional bringing into prominence of sexual facts and relations by speech, is . . . originally directed toward women and may be equated with attempts at seduction" (97). Such sexual talk "is like an exposure of the sexually different person to whom it is directed" (98). If the woman does not respond sexually to the verbal overture—as is often the case at "the higher social levels," where sexual inhibitions are strongest—"the sexually exciting speech becomes an aim in itself" and "becomes hostile and cruel, and . . . thus summons to its help against the obstacle the sadistic components of the sexual instinct" (99). Denied its original aim of seduction, the sexual joking will be directed to a new audience: "The men save up this kind of entertainment, which originally presupposed the presence of a woman who was feeling ashamed, until they are 'alone together'" (99). The tendentious joke calls for three participants: "the one who makes the joke, . . . a second who is taken as the object of the hostile or sexual aggressiveness, and a third in whom the joke's aim of producing pleasure is fulfilled" (100).

Freud's diachronic analysis of the origin of "smut" can be more usefully understood here as an account of the different aims that a joke may simultaneously fulfill. As such, his model turns out to illuminate the cuckold jokes in *Much Ado*. Freud's paradigmatic joke teller is a man, speaking to a male audience, with women as the silent, absent objects of the jokes. The tendentious jokes work on several levels of direction and indirection. Thus, when Claudio aims a cuckold joke at Benedick for the benefit of Don Pedro ("Tush, fear not, man, we'll tip thy horns with gold . . ." [5.4.44]), the object of the joke is Benedick, imagined as a cuckold and hence as having lost his masculine status in the sexual hierarchy, but at another remove the object is also women, with their fearful power to cuckold men.

The cuckold joke expresses hostility and fear, but the relational structure of the joke-telling situation offers a compensation.[4] Cuckoldry occurs as a triangular relationship that the cuckold joke revises—and perhaps revenges. In the act of cuckolding, which dominates the imaginations of Messina's men, it is the husband who is the silent and absent butt of the joke, while a woman takes the active and powerful role (comparable to that of the teller of a joke), in complicity with a third party in whom, as Freud puts it, the "aim of producing pleasure is fulfilled." The telling of cuckold jokes, then, restores the male prerogative: it returns the woman to silence and absence, her absence authorizing the male raconteur to represent her in accordance with particular male fantasies, and produces pleasure through male camaraderie.

Thus, Benedick's lines figure emasculation, or the loss of masculine privilege, in two ways: as a literal, physical castration and as a concomitant loss of masculine prerogative in language. In becoming a cuckold, a man relinquishes his role as the teller of jokes, the manipulator, reader, and subject of language, and falls instead to the woman's position as the object of jokes, the silent, legible sign. It is the place of the woman to be the object, or referent, of language, a sign to be read and interpreted; silent herself, she becomes a cipher, the target of unconscious fantasies and fears, and is dangerously vulnerable to the representations and misrepresentations of men, as the main plot of *Much Ado* bears out. The woman is therefore doubly threatening, both in her imagined capacity to betray and cuckold men and as an image of what men fear to become: paradoxically, her very vulnerability is threatening.[5]

The social world of *Much Ado*'s Messina seems rather precariously founded on a denial of its most pervasive anxieties, and its potential for violence is triggered when the repressed fear of the feminine, and all that woman represents, is forced into consciousness by Don John's machinations. Messina, the most sophisticated and urbane society in all Shakespeare's comedies, is also the most confined. No moonlit wood or forest of Arden offers escape from Messina's social tensions, and the characters' romantic and sexual roles are not relieved by opportunities for sexual disguise. Social and sexual roles are firmly established, and the inhabitants are acutely conscious of them.

To note the rigidity of this world is not to suggest that Messina lacks charm. Its aristocratic characters demonstrate the most elaborate courtesy; formality does not make their manners less genial, and they move through their elegant social patterns with an almost choreographic grace. Yet beneath their easy charm, their wit and conviviality, the characters are evidently anxious, edgy, afraid of betraying spontaneous emotion, afraid of exposing themselves to one another. Messina is much concerned with its carefully preserved surfaces. The characters talk a good deal about how they dress. We hear about "cloth o' gold . . . down sleeves, side-sleeves, and skirts" (3.4.19–21); about Benedick's metamorphosis in "strange disguises" (3.2.32–33); about "slops" (3.2.36), doublets, rabatos, gloves, and vizards; about Dogberry's two gowns; and about "the deformed thief, fashion"—the rhetorical figure overheard by Messina's night watch, in whose minds "the thief, Deformed" takes on a remarkably vivid personality and criminal record (3.3.130–31). Just as the Messinans talk about dress, they talk about talking. They are highly conscious of verbal style. Benedick and Beatrice are known for their "skirmish of wit" (1.1.63); if they were married "but a week," Leonato predicts, "they would talk themselves mad" (2.1.353–54). We hear about the speed of Beatrice's tongue, about "quips and sentences and paper bullets of the brain," about the "ill word" that may "empoison liking," about Don John, who is "not of many words" (1.1.157).

Entering into the social intercourse of Messina entails dressing well and talking well, and in a way these modes of decorous behavior serve similar functions. Early in the play, Benedick withdraws from the banter of Don Pedro and Claudio saying: "Nay, mock not, mock not. The body of your discourse is sometimes guarded with fragments, and the guards are but slightly basted on neither" (1.1.285–87). Benedick here makes explicit a relation between discourse and dress that continues to be important throughout the play. The discourse of Claudio and Don Pedro (and perhaps of all the major characters except Hero) is guarded—that is, decorated (rhetorically) and also, in the now more common sense of the word, defensive. The characters use their wit to cover their emotional nakedness and to avoid exposure. Discourse in Messina is aggressive and witty; real wounds are dealt in the "merry war" between Benedick and Beatrice, in which Beatrice "speaks poiniards, and every word stabs" (2.1.247–48). Because of its capacity to inflict wounds, language—especially wit—is wielded both as weapon and as shield.

The metaphoric language of the play consistently figures speech as phallic and capable of violent penetration. Leonato tells Claudio that his slander, daggerlike, has "gone through and through" the heart of Hero (5.1.68). When Benedick meets Claudio to avenge that slander (5.1), he tells Claudio and Don Pedro that he wears his wit "in my scabbard" and will meet Claudio's "wit in the career and you charge it against me. . . . [Y]ou break jests as braggarts do their blades . . ." (134–35, 185). Margaret compares Benedick's wit to "fencer's foils," albeit dull ones (5.2.12)—a lame wit is one that cannot wound. Hero's image for Margaret's jabs at Beatrice—"there thou prick'st her with a thistle" (3.5.74)— is more benign, but "prick'st" enforces the phallic association. As Hero's line suggests, phallic language may be appropriated by women—Beatrice speaks poiniards—but remains nonetheless gendered as masculine. In exchanging quips with Margaret, Benedick describes her wit as a "greyhound's mouth" that "catches" (5.2.11–12), but he claims swordlike phallic wit as a masculine prerogative that women only wield through usurpation:

> *Marg.* Give us the swords; we have bucklers of our own.
> *Bene.* If you use them, Margaret, you must put in the pikes with a vice; and they are dangerous weapons for maids. (5.2.18–22)

To brandish phallic wit is to defend against others' castrating "swords" or to deny a castration already accomplished. Or rather it is both: for both male and female wits in this play use their repartee to disguise a lack or a weakness, a susceptibility or a wound already suffered.

II

The construction of femininity within an economy of representation governed by the phallus—a construction in which women mirror masculine identity by their own lack—obviates the possibility of "feminine values" or of a feminine alternative to the "predominately masculine ethos." Alternatives cannot be generated from within the binary structures by which patriarchy figures gender. The women in *Much Ado* demonstrate in their different ways their entrapment within the contradictions of this system of difference, for ironically it is the docile Hero, rather than her sharp-tongued cousin, who is the primary focus for masculine anxieties. The vocal Beatrice refuses the subjection of femininity, of castration, by placing herself among the men and wielding phallic wit as aggressively as they; it is the often silent Hero who figures the threat of difference for Messinan men.

Like Benedick, Beatrice adopts the role of "profess'd tyrant" to the opposite sex (1.1.169), satirizing masculine pretensions with agile wit. To Hero, she remarks tartly on paternal authority: "Yes, faith, it is my cousin's duty to make cursy and say, 'Father, as it please you.' But for all that, cousin, let him be a handsome fellow, or make another cursy, and say, 'Father, as it please me'" (2.1.52–56). And, like Benedick, she makes cynical pronouncements on romantic love and marriage:

> . . . wooing, wedding, and repenting, *is* as a Scotch jig, a measure, and a cinquepace; the first suit *is* hot and hasty like a Scotch jig, and full as fantastical; the wedding, mannerly-modest, as a measure, *full* of state and ancientry; and then comes repentance, and with his bad legs falls into the cinquepace faster and faster, till he sink into his grave. (2.1.73–80)

Beatrice's ironic comments on men and marriage, and her passionate outburst against Claudio in the first scene of act 4, have led some critics to regard her as the champion of a "feminine principle" and as a kind of protofeminist.[6] Yet Beatrice's ostentatious flouting of conventional sexual roles is often only a concession to them at another level, and instead of challenging Messina's masculine ethos, she participates in its assumptions and values. In the opening scene, she mocks Benedick's soldiership: "I pray you, how many hath he killed and eaten in these wars? But how many hath he killed? For indeed, I promised to eat all of his killing" (42–45). On the messenger's remarking that Benedick is a "good soldier too, lady," she quibbles "And a good soldier to a lady. But what is he to a lord?" (1.1.53–55). But her insinuation that "Signior Mountanto" is effeminate does not question the machismo value of soldiership itself.

Beatrice tacitly accepts her culture's devaluation of "feminine" characteristics— of weakness, dependence, vulnerability—and sees conventionally masculine behavior as the only defense against them. She usurps the masculine prerogatives of language and phallic wit, speaking poiniards as an escape from feminine silence or inarticulate expression of emotion.

Beatrice's audacious speech might seem a serious violation of Messina's conventions of gender, but it is significant how little she actually threatens Messina's men, who regard her generally as rather a good fellow. Though Benedick professes a hyperbolical terror of "My Lady Tongue" (2.1.262–75) and Leonato rebukes her mildly ("By my troth, niece, thou wilt never get thee a husband, if thou be so shrewd of thy tongue" [2.1.18–19]), she provokes nothing like the hysterical reactions to the quiet Hero's supposed transgressions against the social and sexual code. When Beatrice retracts a bit on her own impertinence—"But I beseech your Grace to pardon me. I was born to speak all mirth and no matter"—Don Pedro replies, "Your silence most offends me, and to be merry best becomes you . . ." (2.1.329–32). It is silence and the exposure of vulnerability that are the real threats to Messinan men, painful reminders of the sexual difference that is really a mirror.[7]

Beatrice is as aggressive and as guarded as the men in the play, and for the same reasons: she fears emotional exposure and vulnerability to the opposite sex. As the play begins she already seems to be nursing wounds from some abortive romance with Benedick, to which she alludes cryptically more than once.[8] Beatrice vacillates uneasily between self-exposure and affected indifference; she chafes at times against the constraints of her ironist's role, which consigns her to isolation and detachment when part of her desires love, but recognizing her susceptibility, she clings the more tenaciously to her role. The long first scene of act 2 reveals her contradictory impulses. Leonato chides her for being "so shrewd of [her] tongue" and tells her "So, by being too curst, God will send you no horns." "Just," she replies, "if he send me no husband, for the which blessing I am at him upon my knees every morning and evening" (27–29). At Hero's betrothal, however, she speaks in a different key: "Good Lord, for alliance! Thus goes everyone to the world but I, and I am sunburnt. I may sit in a corner and cry 'Heigh-ho for a husband!'" (318–20). If the tone is mock lament here, the sense of exclusion is real; yet each of her tentative gestures of self-exposure is followed by a nervous reassertion of ironic detachment. She alternately challenges others' misreadings of her humorist's mask and encourages them to take her as she appears. When Don Pedro seems too readily to accept her as "born in a merry hour," she replies, "No, sure, my lord, my mother cried; but then there was a star danc'd and under that was I born. Cousins, God give you joy!" (334–36).

Chafing at the reductiveness of Don Pedro's image of her as merely "merry," Beatrice offers a fleeting glimpse of a part of herself and a realm of experience that cannot be given expression in Messina, figured in the laboring mother whose only articulation is an ambiguous cry. But she compulsively banishes the image of the crying mother with that of the dancing star and quickly turns attention away from herself by congratulating her "cousins." She is thus perceived only as "a pleasant-spirited lady" (341) whose "merry heart . . . keeps on the windy side of care" (314–15). Leonato misses the significance of his own remark when he tells Don Pedro: "There's little of the melancholy element in her, my lord. She is never sad but when she sleeps, and not ever sad then; for I have heard my daughter say she hath often dreamt of unhappiness and waked herself with laughing" (342–46). Whatever unhappiness haunts Beatrice's dreams, her laughter is a conscious defense against it. She cannot in her waking moments articulate or address the conflicts inherent in her relation to her world.

Beatrice is a character of some complexity, a character whose contradictions, manifest in her own words and actions, we read as signs of interiority and ambivalence, as evidence of different levels of motivation. Hero presents another kind of problem. Here the contradictions consist of a tension between the manifest representation of her character (which is quite uncomplicated and one-dimensional) and her latent significance, which is evident in the effects she produces in others. Minimally drawn, with few lines, she is less a character than a cipher, or a mirror to the other characters. She is represented as conventionally feminine; meek, self-effacing, vulnerable, obedient, seen and not heard, she is a face without a voice. In the world of the play Hero's role is to meet or reflect others' expectations of what women are supposed to be (as Beatrice does not) and paradoxically, therefore, to represent a powerful threat.[9]

Hero's status as a character and the mode of her representation are peculiar enough to require special consideration. Crick characterizes Hero as "nebulous" (36), but he uses the word to dismiss rather than to analyze her. In fact, Hero's nebulousness is significant: she is the "nothing" that generates so much ado. The pun on *nothing* and *noting* in the play has frequently been remarked, but we might usefully pursue it in this connection. To note can mean to observe (to read) or to make note of (to inscribe); both involve acts of interpretation. A similar ambiguity arises in connection with the word *mark*. Benedick believes that he spies "some marks of love" in Beatrice once he falls in love with her (2.3.245–46). In the climactic church scene the friar, "by noting of the lady" (Hero), has "marked / A thousand blushing apparitions / To start into her face . . ." (4.1.158–60). Benedick's act of "marking" is clearly a projection, but the question then arises whether the friar's marking of Hero is not equally so.

Hero's nothing invites noting, her blankness produces marking, and the ambiguity of this action occurs not only in the play but also in the critical commentary. Marilyn French describes Hero this way: "As a noncharacter, the obedient and silent Hero exemplifies the inlaw [i.e., subordinate] feminine principle at its most acceptable: but like Bianca in *Taming*, she wears the disguise society demands of her, but harbors other thoughts under her impeccable exterior" (133). The equation of Hero with Bianca, a conscious hypocrite who wears a "disguise" and harbors a subversive will, blurs the distinction toward which

French seems to gesture with her initial suggestion that Hero is a "noncharacter." Without confronting her conflicting readings as a critical problem, French contradictorily treats Hero sometimes as a character whose hidden depths she can read and sometimes as a symbol that functions as pure surface; but in effect the play itself does the same thing. Ironically, the attempt to read Hero as a psychologically realized character, in this feminist approach to the play, leads French to adopt a notion of Hero's "seeming" that concurs with the one Claudio takes up in his most misogynistic moment (4.1). To avoid this difficulty, it seems to me, one must be willing to regard Hero as a kind of cipher or space, which other characters—and perhaps critics as well—fill with readings of their own.

In the opening scene, where the personalities, roles, and relations of the characters are largely established, Hero has only one line, seven words, and these are to explain a remark of Beatrice's. Though the actor playing the part has recourse to some nonverbal means of establishing the character for the audience (facial expressions, gestures, placement on stage, etc.), the text itself portrays Hero primarily through the effect she produces on Claudio. Typically, the exchange between Claudio and Benedick about Claudio's "soft and delicate desires" (303) reveals little about Hero but a good deal about the two speakers. Beside Benedick's energetic irony, Claudio's desires seem a little too delicate, his love a little bloodless. When he tremulously asks whether Benedick does not find Hero "a modest young lady" (165) and, gathering courage, pronounces her "the sweetest lady that ever I looked on" (187–88), his adjectives betray more propriety and sentiment than they do passion. When he demonstrates a penchant for romantic hyperbole ("Can the world buy such a jewel?" [181]), which Benedick neatly deflates, his extravagant praise expresses, not burning Petrarchan longings, but a kind of wistful acquisitiveness.

Benedick greets Claudio's desire to marry with a sardonic lament for the decline of bachelors: "hath not the world one man but he will wear his cap with suspicion?" (197–99). It becomes clear, however, that Claudio does wear his cap with suspicion—and a good deal of it, too. The cautious reticence of his confession of his love is self-protective: a desire to assess the lady's merit and other men's opinions of it before betraying too ardent a regard for her. He is edgy about the whole business and wary of his friend's responses. "Didst thou note the daughter of Signior Leonato? . . . Is she not a modest young lady?" he asks Benedick; and he then exhorts him, "I pray thee tell me truly how thou lik'st her" (161–63, 165, 177–78). Even when told what he wants to hear, Claudio has misgivings. When Don Pedro assures him that "the lady is very well worthy" Claudio responds "You speak this to fetch me in, my lord" (221–23). Claudio further reveals his anxieties in the first scene of act 2: anticipating his later behavior by believing without question Don John's assertion that Don Pedro has won Hero, Claudio gives vent to his sense of betrayal in a brief, telling soliloquy:

'Tis certain so. The Prince woos for himself.
Friendship is constant in all other things
Save in the office and affairs of love;
Therefore all hearts in love use their own tongues.
Let every eye negotiate for itself,
And trust no agent; for beauty is a witch
Against whose charms faith melteth into blood.
This is an accident of hourly proof,
Which I mistrusted not. Farewell therefore Hero!

    (174–82)

Abdicating the use of one's own tongue, Claudio laments bitterly, leaves one vulnerable to treachery; to be represented by another is to be wounded. What is perhaps more revealing, though, is the way in which the speech subtly shifts the blame for the supposed betrayal from its ostensible object, Don Pedro, to the "witch," female beauty.[10] Though not specifically accused, Hero is subsumed into an archetype of destructive female power—of the sorceress who deprives men of their wills and dissolves the solidarity of masculine bonds into the "blood" of passion and violence. Like Benedick, Claudio associates love with a loss of blood, not the woman's loss of hymenal blood but the loss a man suffers from the castrating wound love inflicts. Claudio's references to Hero here take on sexual overtones wholly lacking in his earlier "noting" of her modesty and sweetness. He perceives her as a sexual being only in her capacity to betray and then perceives her as a powerful threat, suggesting that in his imagination he has desexualized the Hero he wishes to marry. When he learns that Don Pedro has, in fact, honored their agreement and that Hero is to be his, he reverts to his romantic perception of her. The pattern established in this early episode is repeated, as we shall see, in the catastrophe of acts 4 and 5.

III

The first three acts of *Much Ado* clearly establish the capabilities and limitations of Messina's aristocratic milieu: its sophisticated, graceful, almost choreographic social forms; its brilliant language and aggressive wit; and the tight rein kept on emotions, making them difficult or dangerous to express. Whether we are more charmed or put off by Messina's genteel artificiality, the violent outburst in the catastrophic church scene comes as a shock (4.1). We have, of course, seen trouble brewing. Don John's malicious intentions are revealed early (1.3), and we know from his first attempt at sabotaging Claudio's love that Claudio's distrust of the witchlike powers of female beauty is close to the surface and easily triggered. In a scene paralleling that earlier deception (3.2), Don John comes to Claudio with his accusation that "the lady is disloyal" (104). He offers ocular proof, and Claudio, who had earlier resolved to "let every eye negotiate for itself," swallows the bait: "If I see anything to-night why I should not marry her, to–morrow in the congregation, where I should wed, there will I shame her" (123–25). It is not so much on Claudio's eye, however, as on his mind's eye that Don John practices deceit. Using subtly sexual language to describe what Claudio will see—"Go but with me to-night, and you shall see her chamber-window entered" (112–13)—Don John raises the figure of a witchlike, betraying, sexual Hero in Claudio's imagination, and the image of the "sweet" and "modest" Hero gives way before it. Claudio believes the ocular proof before he sees anything—"O mischief strangely thwarting!" he cries (132), as he goes off to spy on her window.

Critics dissatisfied with *Much Ado* have complained that its near tragic catastrophe violates the comic mood of the rest of the play (see, e.g., Pettet 132–35 and West). The naked emotions that erupt in act 4 among the hitherto highly civil characters are calculated, I think, to be startling. Yet what makes this behavior almost inevitable has been implicit from the first scene. The witty discourse that gives the play its vitality and the Messinans much of their charm consists mainly of tendentious jokes—covert expressions of aggression or sexual hostility. The polished behavior, the elegant courtesies, and the verbal sophistication of the characters have served through three acts of the play to cover or contain these energies. In the scene at the church, however, once the surface of decorous ritual has been stripped away, the violence of the emotion and the language, especially Claudio's, becomes explicit and shocking.

Though the manner Claudio displays here differs drastically from his reverence for Hero in the scenes of his courtship and betrothal, he is not inconsistent. The self-protective reserve and the conflicted perceptions of Hero underlying his earlier sentimental expressions now motivate his scathing castigation of her. Kerby Neill, writing an "acquittal" for Claudio, emphasizes Shakespeare's departure from his sources in "removing all trace of carnality from the hero's love" (97). "If anything," he argues, "the bitterness of Claudio's denunciation of Hero shows an abhorrence of . . . carnality. . . . The . . . effect is to idealize Claudio even as he denounces the innocent Hero. He remains a good man, although deceived . . ." (97). Neill, in effect, takes Claudio at his own valuation—claiming that he "sinned not but in mistaking," as Claudio says of himself (5.1.273–74)—and in so doing accepts implicitly the dualism inherent in Claudio's view of Hero: it is his "abhorrence of carnality" that allows his romantic idealism to coexist with a powerful misogyny. In the first scene of act 4 the thought that, despite his caution, he was nearly taken advantage of kindles in Claudio a hot, self-righteous resentment. The "witch" female beauty, he thinks, almost made him the victim of her "exterior shows." This time he is well guarded with elaborate language, wittier in his cruelty than he had ever been in jest:

O Hero! What a Hero hadst thou been,
If half thy outward graces had been placed
About thy thoughts and counsels of thy heart!
But fare thee well, most foul, most fair! farewell;
Thou pure impiety and impious purity! (100–04)

Claudio's radically divided sense of Hero's identity is most fully apparent in this scene. When Leonato suggests that Claudio himself might, in a bridegroom's natural impatience, have "made defeat of her virginity," Claudio denies it with priggish distaste:

I know what you would say: If I have known her,
You will say, she did embrace me as a husband,
And so extenuate the 'forehand sin.
No, Leonato,
I never tempted her with word too large,
But as a brother to his sister, show'd
Bashful sincerity and comely love. (48–54)

Either Hero must be the unthreatening sexless recipient of Claudio's "comely" fraternal love, or she becomes the treacherous beauty whose witchlike powers destroy men.[11] But where Claudio had previously responded to alternative possibilities for Hero's identity, he now imagines the dichotomy to be one between her surface and her hidden nature. He is most outraged by what he takes to be her "seeming":

She's but the sign and semblance of her honor.
Behold how like a maid she blushes here!
O, what authority and show of truth
Can cunning sin cover itself withal!
Comes not that blood as modest evidence
To witness simple virtue? Would you not swear,
All you that see her, that she were a maid,
By these exterior shows? But she is none.
She knows the heat of a luxurious bed;
Her blush is guiltiness, not modesty. (33–42)

In a sense Claudio is correct in calling Hero "the sign and semblance of her honor." Her place in the world of this play is most apparent in this scene, where, nearly silent and finally subsiding into unconsciousness under the onslaught of abuse, she becomes in effect a sign to be read and interpreted by others. Claudio sarcastically rejects her "authority" to be perceived as she presents herself. He has, he thinks, the clue that allows him to read her true worth and nature. It is particularly the "blood" visible in Hero's face that is taken to signify the state of her soul. "Comes not that blood as modest evidence / To witness simple virtue?" he asks with the ironic jubilance of a reader onto the meaning of a text, the truth that her "blush is guiltiness, not modesty." His descriptions of the polarities of Hero's identity become more and more elaborate and literary, and he returns to the significance of her "blood" in this depiction of opposing female archetypes:

> You seem to me as Dian in her orb,
> As chaste as is the bud ere it be blown;
> But you are more intemperate in your blood
> Than Venus, or those pamp'red animals
> That rage in savage sensuality. (57–61)

Having found the key to reading women, Claudio suggests as he exits, he will know how to apply it in the future:

> For thee I'll lock up all the gates of love,
> And on my eyelids shall conjecture hang,
> To turn all beauty into thoughts of harm,
> And never shall it more be gracious. (105–08)

Leonato, thrown into an anguish of uncertainty by Claudio's outburst, charges his daughter to answer her accusers, but he hardly hears her simple denial. Quickly persuaded when Claudio's claims are seconded by Don Pedro, and by Don John, who hints darkly at the unutterable nature of Hero's crimes ("There is not chastity enough in language / Without offense to utter them" [97–98]), Leonato grasps Claudio's method of reading his child. He believes that her surface has been stripped away to expose the secret foulness of her sexuality; her silence is a horrifying nakedness. When the friar ventures to suggest that her accusers may be mistaken, Leonato rejects the possibility:

> Friar, it cannot be.
> Thou see'st that all the grace that she hath left
> Is that she will not add to her damnation
> A sin of perjury; she not denies it.
> Why seek'st thou then to cover with excuse
> That which appears in proper nakedness? (170–75)

Leonato too rejects Hero's authority to voice her own nature, which he believes he can read. "[C]ould she here deny / The story that is printed in her blood?"

he demands. In her blood he reads the story of "her foul tainted flesh" and insists that "Death is the fairest cover for her shame / That may be wish'd for" (121–22, 143, 116–17). Ironically, thinking that they have exposed the "proper nakedness" of Hero's sin, her accusers expose only themselves.

It is in the wake of this scene of exposure that Benedick and Beatrice reveal their love for each other. Love, and the vulnerability that comes with it, has been a kind of exposure each has dodged through most of the play. Their resolutions to open themselves to love have been followed by physical illness (Benedick's toothache, Beatrice's cold), which, whether real or feigned, suggests the anxiety such exposure produces. Distracted from their anxieties about themselves for a moment by their preoccupation with Claudio's denunciation of Hero, Benedick and Beatrice are able to talk to each other without persiflage. The intimacy of the situation (255–88) quickly leads to revelation, and for a moment we watch what appears to be an alternative to the kind of self-protective emotional display witnessed in Claudio. Benedick initiates it with his sudden, apropos-of-nothing, unprecedentedly literal confession: "I do love nothing in the world so well as you—is not that strange?" (268–69). And though Beatrice has to be teased out of her evasiveness, she is brought to respond in kind:

> *Beat.* You have stayed me in a happy hour, I was about to protest I loved you.
> *Bene.* And do it with all thy heart.
> *Beat.* I love you with so much of my heart that none is left to protest.
> (283–87)

The warmth and simplicity of the language are like nothing we have heard before in the play (as was Claudio's unmasked brutality), and we are apt to watch this exchange with relief. At last the masks seem to be dropped; at last two characters seem to confront each other "in proper nakedness." But the intimacy of the moment is volatile, and it leads to something for which we are unprepared. "Come, bid me do anything for thee," Benedick jubilantly exclaims. And Beatrice quite unexpectedly responds, "Kill Claudio" (288–89).

Benedick's Claudio-like hyperbole perhaps recalls to Beatrice the whole preceding scene of Hero's rejection and humiliation by the man in whose power she had placed herself, and Beatrice hastily retreats from her emotional surrender. Her demand that Benedick kill Claudio is a double defense, placing Benedick in an impossible position and covering her exposed tenderness with a display of ferocity. She is both magnificent and absurd in her vigorous denunciation of Claudio:

> Is 'a not approv'd in the height a villain, that hath slander'd, scorned, dishonored my kinswoman? O that I were a man! What, bear her in hand

until they come to take hands; and then, with public accusation, uncovered
slander, unmitigated rancor—O God that I were a man! I would eat his
heart in the marketplace! (301–07)

Beatrice's explosion of moral outrage against Claudio is immensely satisfying,
partly because it gives vent to our own frustrated sense of justice (the release
of this pent-up emotion is also why we laugh at the scene). Her anger takes in
not only Claudio but men in general—the "princes and counties" (315), and
the fathers, who have united in persecuting Hero and against whom Beatrice is
powerless to act.

The critics quoted at the beginning of this essay emphasize particularly this
moment in designating Beatrice a champion of the "feminine principles" needed
to correct the evils of Messina's "predominantly masculine ethos" (Crick 36).
John Crick praises her "feminine charity," her "generosity and sympathy in a
world dominated by ultimately inhumane standards" (37), as Barbara Everett
does her "dogged, loyal, irrational femininity" (327). Although Beatrice's
outburst is extremely gratifying—the scene is constructed to make it so—it is
important to recognize that her fury imitates what we might call the dogged,
brutal, irrational masculinity just displayed by Claudio and Leonato: her rage is
generated by her inability to "be a man with wishing" and to do what men do.
She echoes the masculine revenge ethic voiced earlier by Leonato, who, brought
finally to consider the possibility of Hero's innocence, had vowed to have his
revenge on *somebody* (190–92). Far from proposing an alternative to masculine
values, Beatrice regrets their decline and upbraids Benedick for his unmanly
reluctance to exchange verbal aggression, which is common coin in Messina, for
real violence:

O that I were a man for his sake! Or that I had any friend who would
be a man for my sake! But manhood is melted into cursies, valor into
compliment, and men are only turned into tongue, and trim ones too. He is
now as valiant as Hercules that only tells a lie, and swears it. I cannot be a
man with wishing; and therefore I will die a woman with grieving. (317–23)

The last line of her tirade raises the question of what might be an adequate
"feminine" alternative to the "predominately masculine ethos" of Messina.
Beatrice longs to take arms against a sea of masculine troubles but, by opposing,
would only perpetuate them. The sole alternative that presents itself to her,
however, is to follow Hero's model of conventional femininity and "die a woman"
in silent grief.

The friar has proposed a somewhat different way of dealing with the crisis.
"By noting of the lady," he has "marked" signs of her innocence and has produced
a plan that he hopes will work changes in Claudio's poisoned imagination by
means of a fiction:

> So will it fare with Claudio.
> When he shall hear she died upon his words,
> Th' idea of her life shall sweetly creep
> Into his study of imagination,
> And every lovely organ of her life
> Shall come apparell'd in more precious habit,
> More moving, delicate, and full of life,
> Into the eye and prospect of his soul
> Than when she liv'd indeed. Then shall he mourn,
> If ever love had interest in his liver,
> And wish he had not so accused her.
> No, though he thought his accusation true. (222–33)

Many critics have seen the friar as the point of moral reference in the play and also as the instrument of its resolution.[12] His sensible resistance to the false evidence that has fooled Don Pedro and Claudio, his opposition to their outbursts of violent emotion, his attentions to Hero, and his proposal to educate Claudio in Christian forgiveness—all these actions seem to place the religious father outside Messina's masculine ethos and to confer on him a special moral authority. The tendency to see him in this light, whether we attribute it to indicators in the text (the friar's speech is rhetorically impressive) or to a powerful desire to see moral coherence in Shakespearean comedy, has led otherwise careful critics into a simple error of fact: the friar's plan fails.[13] The plan is specifically a response to Claudio's determination to "lock up all the gates of love" by hanging "conjecture" on his eyelids "To turn all beauty into thoughts of harm." The friar proposes to change the way Claudio sees, introducing a "moving" image of Hero "Into the eye and prospect of his soul" through the fiction of her death. The friar looks to do more than correct Claudio's "mistake" about Hero's virtue: he hopes that Claudio will change in a way that will induce remorse and love "*though he thought his accusation true.*" Shakespeare dramatized such a conversion much later in *Cymbeline*, when Posthumus, believing himself responsible for Imogen's death, laments his harsh judgment of her in a long soliloquy *before* he learns of her innocence (5.1.1–17).

The proposed resolution does not occur. Not only is Claudio not grief-stricken when we see him next (5.1), he is rather giddy. He shows no shame when Leonato accuses him of killing Hero through his villainy ("My villainy?" he asks indignantly [72]), and he describes the incident flippantly when Benedick arrives: "We had lik'd to have our two noses snapp'd off with two old men without teeth" (115–16). He then goads Benedick about Beatrice as though nothing had happened since the third scene of act 3. Don Pedro behaves with the same careless good humor, both of them apparently hoping that Hero's "death" will pass off as merely an unfortunate social awkwardness. It is not until

he learns of her innocence that Claudio's feeling changes; the issue is no longer
a matter of forgiveness now but only of getting the facts straight. Claudio does
not question his behavior or his assumptions, contending that he "sinned not
but in mistaking," and once in possession of the "truth" about Hero, he simply
reverts to his initial image of her: "Sweet Hero, now thy image doth appear /
In the rare semblance that I lov'd it first" (251–52). The image of the witch is
dispelled—and replaced by its opposite—but the sexual dualism that governs
Hero's "image" is not displaced or questioned.

It would perhaps be tendentious to refer this outcome to some moral or
tactical failure on the friar's part. The simpler explanation is that the plan to
reform Claudio fails because his callousness makes him incapable of responding
as predicted. Nonetheless, the friar's well-meaning intervention on Hero's
behalf may in some sense undercut its own power to effect changes in the world
of the play and may unconsciously reinforce the assumptions of which Hero is a
victim. The friar's plea on behalf of the prostrate Hero reverses but also imitates
the speeches of her accusers. Claudio had angrily denied the "authority" of her
"semblance" and had read her blush as the sign of her guilt. Leonato too had
insisted on his reading of "the story that is printed in her blood." The friar, in
opposing these interpretations of what is seen in Hero's face, also emphasizes his
authority to speak *for* the silent Hero:

> Trust not my reading, nor my observations,
> Which with experimental seal doth warrant
> The tenure of my book; trust not my age,
> My reverence, calling, nor divinity,
> If this sweet lady lie not guiltless here
> Under some biting error. (4.1.165–70)

The friar offers his own reading of Hero's blood:

> I have marked
> A thousand blushing apparitions
> To start into her face, a thousand innocent shames
> In angel whiteness beat away those blushes . . .
>
> (4.1.158–61)

The friar's plot to counter the "misprision" of Claudio and Don Pedro parallels in certain respects the plot by which Don John engineers the catastrophe.
Don John, though "not of many words," is a master of representation in the
play. Keeping aloof from the action himself, he commissions Borachio to stage
the scene in which Claudio will read Hero's guilt. "I will so fashion the matter
that Hero shall be absent," promises Borachio (2.2.46–47); and he then enlists

Margaret to represent Hero by dressing in her clothes. The representation succeeds in replacing in Claudio's imagination the image of Hero as chaste Dian with that of her as intemperate Venus. The friar too intends to make Hero's absence the occasion for a "moving" representation of her (4.1): "Let her awhile be secretly kept in, / And publish it that she is dead indeed . . ." (203–04). When the fiction of Hero's death reaches Claudio, the friar predicts, her image will present itself to him "apparll'd in more precious habit, / . . . Than when she liv'd indeed." Claudio will then see Hero's "angel whiteness," which the friar believes to represent her true character, "her maiden truth" (164). Though the friar intends the image to be "More moving, delicate, and full of life" than her physical presence ("Than when she liv'd indeed"), death is its essential feature: this representation of Hero is cleansed of carnality, of the blood that has been read as the sign of sexuality and guilt; the friar can interpret Hero's blood as the blush of innocence because "a thousand innocent shames / In angel whiteness beat away those blushes"—leaving her bloodless, white, and corpse-like in her swoon. He will represent her as "delicate," like the "soft and delicate desires" that Claudio claims to be "comely" and asexual; "every lovely organ of her life" will come to Claudio to be anatomized and read as evidence of chastity, so that the fluid, vital, ambiguous text of her face will be replaced by a petrified monument to her virginity. The displacement is achieved when the penitent Claudio goes in obedience to Leonato, to "Hang an epitaph upon her tomb" that declares her innocent and glorified by death.

IV

The ghost of Hero's ambiguity continues to haunt the play. In the scenes following Claudio's denunciation, her "death" has an uncanny force that far exceeds its limited status as a strategic fiction. Like the deformed-thief fashion, the fiction of Hero's death takes on a life of its own, independent of the circumstances for which it was invented. A striking peculiarity of the final act is the way in which the practicers seem taken in by their own device, becoming Hero's mourners and avengers in a plot that exercises a peculiar power over their emotions and imaginations: it is as though they—and somehow the play itself—need Hero to be dead for reasons that have nothing to do with Claudio.

Claudio's outburst against Hero has exposed the potential for cruelty and violence in Messina's masculine order so unequivocally that resolution would seem to depend on some kind of confrontation with the fears and assumptions of which Hero has been a victim. In the fiction of her death, however, the play finds a ritual resolution that reasserts Messina's stability without the need for painful questioning. Nonetheless, the play's attempt to move toward a comic conclusion and to evade what its plot has exposed places a strain on the fifth act, producing a peculiar shiftiness of tone and mode.

As the characters come under the sway of their fiction, they become increasingly enigmatic in a way that seems to mark a shift in the play's mode of representation. Act 5 begins with Antonio's grieving "counsel" and Leonato's formal lament:

> I pray thee cease thy counsel,
> Which falls into mine ears as profitless
> As water in a sieve. Give not me counsel,
> Nor let no comforter delight mine ear
> But such a one whose wrongs do suit with mine.
> Bring me a father that so lov'd his child,
> Whose joy of her is overwhelm'd like mine,
> And bid him speak of patience.... (3–10)

Leonato's language, with its past-tense references to Hero, has the emotional impact of a father's lament for his dead child; it carries a weight, a dignity and conviction, which nearly overshadows our own knowledge that the death is a fiction. Somehow this fiction has become the governing reality of the play, a fantasy more real than the "truth."

Benedick too, acting on his pledge to Beatrice, challenges Claudio and, like Leonato, becomes formalized and enigmatic as he solemnly maintains Hero's death and appears ready to make it good with his sword: "You have killed a sweet lady, and her death shall fall heavy on you" (148–49). The characters no longer seem to be in the same play, and the resolution cannot come about until Claudio enters the more formalized dramatic world in which the governing plot is the fiction of Hero's death.

The scene at Hero's "tomb" (5.3) marks Claudio's and Don Pedro's entrance into the fictional world created by the other characters. This is the play's most highly formal scene, governed in both its action and its language by the conventions of ritual. Even the few lines of dialogue that are not read from Claudio's prepared text are noticeably conventional in style. Don Pedro's dismissal of the mourners is hardly a return to natural speech:

> Good morrow, masters, put your torches out.
> The wolves have preyed, and look, the gentle day,
> Before the wheels of Phoebus, round about
> Dapples the drowsy east with spots of gray. (24–27)

Much of the critical worrying about *Much Ado* and its ending focuses on the question of whether this ritual signifies a change in Claudio sufficient to warrant his good fortune in the next scene, where Hero is restored to him. The question cannot be answered. The entire play has shifted its grounds in a way that makes such assessments impossible, if not irrelevant. Yet the ritual itself witnesses to the survival of the fundamental structures of Messina's masculine ethos—structures that the shift toward ritual has allowed the play to preserve.

As I have argued, the sequence of events in act 5 points explicitly to the practical gratuitousness of the fiction and the funeral. Early in the first scene the deception proves ineffectual as a means of softening Claudio, who remains unmoved by the news of Hero's death. Moments later Borachio confesses his crimes and clears Hero's name, leaving no effective reason why the characters cannot produce Hero and reveal her death as a lie. Instead, they complicate the fiction with details about a marriageable niece and engage Claudio to take part in mourning Hero. Hero's funeral is dramatically necessary as Claudio's ritual of expiation. Were Claudio not assimilable into the circle of Hero's family and friends, Messina would be confronted with a fundamental breakdown of its cultural assumptions, which Claudio reflects. Claudio's submission to the authority of Leonato, his agreement to lead Hero's obsequies and to take an unknown bride, permits the play to reach a kind of comic closure. The question is not whether Claudio is sincere—he is certainly that, insofar as a ritual mode allows for such a distinction. The question is what the ritual and Claudio's participation in it signify.

For the ritual itself is, if anything, a reassertion of Messina's old order in new terms. At this crucial moment Hero's exclusion is the condition on which Claudio's reintegration into Messina's social structure and the play's comic resolution depends. Hero's ambiguous blood has been purged away; she is now only "glorious fame" (5.3.8), a name placed unequivocally under the sign of chaste Dian, whose "virgin knight" (5.3.13) Hero is declared to be. The ritual exorcises the threat of Hero's body, whose intactness was so precariously in question, and the ambiguity of her face, which led to violently contradictory readings in act 4. When Hero becomes a monument, her signifying power is tamed. She is redefined so as to be reappropriated to the patriarchal order as a disembodied ideal: "the sign and semblance of her honor." Claudio's placement of the epitaph on her tomb explicitly dramatizes the silencing of the woman's voice, the substitution of the man's: "Hang thou there upon the tomb, / Praising her when I am dumb" (5.3.9–10). Claudio's text will always speak for Hero, even after Claudio himself is "dumb."

Besides the shift toward ritual, the play engages another strategy in moving toward its comic conclusion. This might be described as a centrifugal process that deflects emphasis from the central characters onto those who constitute the plot's machinery. Claudio's guilt is displaced onto Borachio and ultimately onto Don John, making it possible for Leonato to declare in the last scene that Claudio and Don Pedro are innocent, having accused Hero "upon the error" perpetrated by others (5.4.3).

The serviceable Borachio is most immediately behind Hero's undoing. It is he who first discovers Claudio's interest in Hero and relays the information to Don John (1.3). It is Borachio, again, who concocts the scheme to deceive Claudio with the amorous tableau at Hero's window. Borachio is also, in a sense, responsible for the denouement, as his confession reveals Hero's innocence and Claudio's "mistake." Autonomous as Borachio is in inventing and carrying out his plot, it is Don John who is the archvillain and the "author of all, who is fled and gone" (5.2.98–99). Don John remains behind the scenes, a shadow himself who causes Claudio to see in shadows the signs of Hero's guilt. Don John's motive is ostensibly resentment toward his legitimate brother; but just as guilt is transferred from Claudio to Borachio to Don John, so Don John's malice, aiming at Don Pedro, glances on Claudio but strikes Hero as its victim. As victim and villain, Hero and Don John serve Messina in the capacities of sacrifice and scapegoat, the one bringing about Messina's atonement through her death, the other carrying off its sins.

The ambiguity of Margaret's role in Borachio's plot has caused some consternation among critics.[14] Logically speaking, Margaret must have known of the accusations against Hero and would inevitably recognize the source of error, that she herself had been mistaken for Hero as she talked with Borachio from Hero's window. Margaret does not disclose any of this, nor does she show any signs of concern or uneasiness during her witty exchange with Benedick in the second scene of act 5. In absolving Claudio and Don Pedro of their "error" in humiliating Hero, however, Leonato transfers part of the blame to Margaret— "But Margaret was in some fault for this"—while paradoxically suggesting that she participated "against her will" (5.4.1–5). The sequence of Leonato's lines suggests, if somewhat vaguely, that Margaret is being made to bear Claudio's and Don Pedro's guilt, that she is guilty in their place, while at the same time denying her conscious, voluntary complicity. Margaret is, in a sense, Hero's double, wearing her clothes, speaking from her window, answering to her name; and the ambiguity of her innocence or guilt points to an ambiguity about Hero, an ambiguity not "in" her character but, rather, in others' perceptions of her.[15] The play simultaneously represents Hero as innocent and punishes her as guilty. Margaret both represents and carries off Hero's ambiguous taint.

"If you meet a thief," Dogberry instructs the watch, "you may suspect him, by virtue of your office, to be no true man; and for such a kind of men, the less you meddle or make them, why the more is for your honesty" (3.3.50–53). In a passing comment, Freud compares Dogberry's counsel to that of physicians who "implore us for heaven's sake not to meddle with the evil things that lurk behind a neurosis" (*Enlightenment* 179). Freud finds in Dogberry a convenient figure for avoidance or repression of the unconscious and does not pursue the comparison with reference to *Much Ado about Nothing*, but perhaps we might take up Freud's analogy in considering Dogberry's function in the play. Despite the admonition not to "meddle or make with" unsavory characters, the night watch does "comprehend" (at least in Dogberry's sense) the "false knaves" Borachio and Conrade (4.2.21). Yet Dogberry and his men do serve the plot as a means of avoiding what might otherwise be the crux of the play: Claudio's intractability in the face of Hero's death. By producing the malefactors and getting their "villainy . . . upon record" (5.1.239–40), Dogberry shifts the play's focus away from this violent and unsettling misogyny and into a more legalistic vein. By providing villains against whom the law can proceed, Dogberry allows the play to move toward its comic resolution without meddling further with the tensions that triggered its catastrophe.

Besides functioning as an avoidance mechanism, Dogberry serves in another way to mimic larger processes at work in the play: he participates in and parodies the masculine concern with controlling signification, particularly that which relates to himself. We have seen this masculine anxiety most conspicuously in Benedick's fantastic fear of being marked by, even of becoming, a sign of the cuckold, of losing his status as a subject of language and becoming instead its object, its victim, its fool. Dogberry attempts to impress his authority on others by means of his ponderous language, the inflated diction that leads him from one malapropism to the next. Because he cannot master his own meanings, he is continually over-mastered by a language that eludes his control and undercuts the authority he wishes to exert over it—and through it, over others.

The final scene restores something like the balance of formality and gaiety with which the play opens. Claudio and Don Pedro are absolved in a single line from Leonato, and our attention quickly turns to Benedick's mock-rueful request that the friar "bind [him], or undo [him]" (5.4.20) by marrying him to Beatrice. Benedick and Beatrice have left off the dangerous literalness of their mutual self-exposure in act 4; they resume their roles, knowing full well now how transparent they are, and their playfulness is perfectly winning. The critical consensus seems to be that this union of Benedick and Beatrice answers whatever dissatisfaction we continue to feel over Claudio and Hero, and in a sense this is right: we like these characters and the sense of euphoria their wit produces. But it is another question whether Benedick and Beatrice represent a challenge or an alternative to Messina's limitations. Different as they are in style from Claudio and Hero, Benedick and Beatrice are of a piece with their world; there is no world elsewhere in this play—even their irony cannot create one, for it participates in the assumptions that shape Messina.

In many ways the final scene reiterates what has been problematic from the play's beginning. The four ladies enter masked and remain, in effect, ciphers until called for by their betrothed husbands. (The text indicates no point at which Margaret or Ursula unmasks. Remaining perhaps a little behind Hero and Beatrice on the stage, the effaced women reinforce the status of women as ciphers until named by men.) In revealing herself and giving herself to Claudio, Hero repeats Claudio's dualistic notion of her identity: "One Hero died defiled; but I do live, / And surely as I live, I am a maid" (5.4.63–64). Her ritual death has purged Hero of intemperate Venus's sexuality, and she returns as Dian in her orb. Don Pedro's exclamation is telling: "The former Hero! Hero that is dead!" (65). Hero remains dead in her resurrection, as she is reappropriated to the mode of perception that killed her.

The circularity here is reinforced by the way this final scene repeats the play's beginning. Having avoided the violent confrontations that threatened to break out after Hero's "death," the male characters recur to their verbal aggression and particularly to their cuckold jokes (5.4.43–51, 121–22). That the jokes retain their original force indicates that Messina's masculine ethos survives unchanged. The play began with the defeat of Don John, and with his defeat it ends, leaving us to wonder, if we care to, when he will next escape.

* * *

The readings of *Much Ado* quoted at the beginning of this essay participate in the play's drive toward ritual transcendence—a movement invoked and sanctioned by the friar. To resist this movement, as my reading of the play does, is manifestly to read against the grain of the play's explicitly offered resolution: it is to recognize what the play's drive toward comic closure suppresses but simultaneously exposes. In his repeated exposure of the limits of his own authority, perhaps Dogberry suggests a way of reading the play as self-exposure: the play is partly the record of its own limitations. In presenting Hero as a kind of cipher, *Much Ado* reflects its patriarchal heritage; yet it is Hero's very blankness that allows the revealing explosion to occur. The play's explicit representation of masculine fantasy and delusion trades on, and partakes of, the process it explores. Or should we say it exposes the process it trades on? The mode of representation that makes possible the play's main plot—a mode in which women are ciphers—is implicated in that plot, obliquely revealing the underlying sexual values and assumptions that motivate the unfolding of the drama.

NOTES

1.

> *Leon.* So, by being too curst, God will send you no horns.
> *Beat.* Just, if he send me no husband. . . .
> (2.1.25–27)

The association of cuckoldry with castration and displacement is suggested by the derivation of the notion of the cuckold's horns, described in the *OED*:

> Cuckolds were fancifully said to wear horns on the brow. . . . [The origin of this, which appears in so many European tangs. . . . is referred to by Dunger (*Germania* XXIX, 39) to the practice formerly prevalent of planting or engrafting the spurs of a castrated cock on the root of the excised comb, where they

grew and become horns, sometimes several inches long. He shows that Ger. *hahnreh* or *hahnrei* 'cuckold,' originally meant 'capon.']

2. In his essay "The Uncanny," Freud writes, "A study of dreams, phantasies and myths has taught us that a morbid anxiety connected with the eyes and with going blind is often enough a substitute for the dread of castration" (36).

3. Benedick later describes undergoing one of Beatrice's verbal attacks: "I stood like a man at a mark, with a whole army shooting at me" (2.1.244–45).

4. Coppélia Kahn, taking her cue from Freud, offers another account of the relation between cuckoldry and compensation: "Regarded endopsychically, from the cuckold's point of view, horns are a defense formed through denial, compensation, and upward displacement. They say, 'It's not that I can't keep my wife because I don't have enough of a penis. I have two of them, in fact, right up where everyone can see them'" (122). For a related discussion of phallic imagery and compensation fantasies, see Freud's essay "The Medusa's Head."

5. The fear of women as castrated and as potentially castrating is a theme to which Freud frequently recurs. In "The Taboo of Virginity" (1918) he discusses certain beliefs and practices of "primitive races" that extend in some form into sophisticated culture. The essay begins by examining "the high value set upon . . . virginity" and the extensive taboos related to virginity and defloration and culminates in a discussion of the male dread of women:

> Wherever primitive man institutes a taboo, there he fears a danger; and it cannot be disputed that the general principle underlying all these regulations and avoidances is a dread of women. . . . Man fears that his strength will be taken away from him by woman, dreads becoming infected with her femininity and then proving himself a weakling. (78)

This essay is characteristic of Freud's writings on gender, both in its perspicacity and in its curious reflexiveness. He initially describes the premium placed on female virginity as something difficult to explain, only noting that it is "but a logical consequence of the exclusive right of possession over a woman which is the essence of monogamy. . . ." He then goes on to "justify what at first appeared to be a prejudice by referring to our ideas concerning the character of the erotic life in women" (70). It is clear that "our" ideas are those of male psychoanalysts, shared in an intuitive, less conscious way by all men, both "savage" and sophisticated. Yet it is not really to these "ideas" that Freud refers for his explanation but to "the character of the erotic life in women"; that is, he ceases to distinguish male fantasies and theories about women from female sexuality itself. The elaborate taboos concerning women make sense, Freud suggests, when we recognize them as a response to something real—to women's penis envy and vengeful desire to castrate men: "Now, upon this penis-envy follows the hostile embitterment displayed by women against men, never entirely absent in the relations between the sexes, the clearest indications of which are to be found in the writings and ambitions of 'emancipated women'" (83). Consistently in this essay, Freud refers what is paradoxical in practices and beliefs related to women and to sexuality, not to paradoxes of masculine psychology and patriarchal culture, but to "the paradoxical reaction of women to defloration . . ." (83), thus, in effect, reproducing the very phenomenon (dread of women) he set out to analyze.

6. See Barbara Everett and John Crick. Marilyn French, while noting that Beatrice "does not break decorum," describes her as "a Rosalind who has taken a step further into freedom . . . a force for anarchy—democracy—in Messina" (131).

7. It could be argued that Beatrice's aggressive tongue serves as a reassuring fetishistic substitute for the phallus: like all fetishes it signifies a denial of female (i.e., the mother's) castration, the denial by which a male child fends off the threat of his own castration. Castrated, the woman mirrors for the male child his own possible fate; the fetish revises the frightening image to figure back a phallicly endowed reflection of the male subject. See Freud's "Fetishism" (1927).

8. For example, Beatrice gives this account of Benedick: "He set up his bills here in Messina, and challeng'd Cupid at the flight, and my uncle's fool, reading the challenge, subscrib'd for Cupid, and challeng'd him at the burbolt" (1.1.37–40). Was Beatrice the "fool" who "subscribed for Cupid"? In her general slander of Benedick she represents him as faithless—"He wears his faith but as the fashion of his hat; it ever changes with the next block" (1.1.71–72)—and responds to Don Pedro's comment that she has "lost the heart of Signior Benedick" with "Indeed, my lord, he lent it me awhile, I gave him use for it, a double heart for his single one. Marry, once before he won it of me with false dice . . ." (2.1.274–78).

9. Linda Boose has pointed out to me that Hero becomes much more apt of speech during the masked-ball scene (2.1) and also in the orchard scene, where she and Ursula trick Beatrice with their stories of Benedick's desperate love for her (3.1). Given a mask or a role to play, Hero improvises well; but her speech serves, as does wit generally in the play, to disguise or deceive, and in the latter example Hero is explicitly playing a role scripted for her by a man, Don Pedro.

10. In Hayes's reading, Claudio regards Don Pedro as a kind of father figure and fears engaging in oedipal competition with him (84–85).

11. Hayes links these lines with "the incestuous root of Claudio's anxiety . . ." (86).

12. T. W. Craik refers to "the reasonableness of Friar Francis's plan for Claudio and Hero" (308), measures the other characters against the friar's "better judgment" (310), and writes, somewhat inaccurately, that "the effect [of the friar's plan] on Claudio is exactly as Friar Francis prophesied . . ." (312). W. R. Davis agrees that "the wisdom of the friar's plan is immediately attested" (9). Graham Storey praises "the Friar's wisdom" and his "calm sanity [which] admirably 'places' Leonato's hysteria" (27). While Storey's argument, which does not deal specifically with gender in the play, places the friar on the side of masculine cool-headedness in the face of "hysteria," Janice Hayes, who does address questions of gender in the play, places the friar on the side of the "expressive" qualities she associates with women: "as the spokesman for Christian grace, the priest is an asexual figure associated with expressive functioning, for the theology of Grace predicates a passive reception of unmerited favor rather than the active pursuit of an earned reward. . . . The resolution of the Claudio-Hero plot is thus contingent upon the intervention of a benign Providence that has placed a man who can function with both his head and his heart in the right place at the right time" (92, 93).

13. Hayes is ambiguous on this point, acknowledging that "the play's resolution does not come any more according to the priest's than to Don John's scheming . . ." but arguing that "ultimately the priest's faith is correct . . ." (93).

14. Allan Gilbert suggests that the peculiar contradictions in Margaret's role result from Shakespeare's having pieced together material from Bandello's story

of Timbreo and Fenicia and cantos 5 and 6 of Ariosto's *Orlando furioso*. Gilbert's discussion is both interesting and persuasive, but it leaves room for some account of how Margaret's doubleness affects the play.

15. In *The Interpretation of Dreams* Freud writes that "The form of a dream or the form in which it is dreamt is used with quite surprising frequency for representing its concealed subject matter" (367). That is, an ambiguity in a dream may have "no connection at all with the make-up of the dream itself but arises from the material of the dream thoughts and is a constituent of it" (366). This observation may provide a useful analogy for thinking about the ambiguity of Margaret's role—an ambiguity that points, I think, to the dualism that characterizes the play's representation of women.

WORKS CITED

Craik, T. W. "*Much Ado about Nothing*." *Scrutiny* 19 (1953): 297–316.

Crick, John. "*Much Ado about Nothing*." *The Use of English* 17 (1965): 223–27. Rpt. in Davis 33–38.

Davis, Walter R., ed. *Twentieth Century Interpretations of Much Ado about Nothing*. Englewood Cliffs: Prentice, 1969.

Everett, Barbara. "*Much Ado about Nothing*." *Critical Quarterly* 3 (1969): 319–35.

French, Marilyn. *Shakespeare's Division of Experience*. New York: Simon, 1981.

Freud, Sigmund. "Fetishism." Trans. Joan Riviere. *Sexuality and the Psychology of Love* 214–19.

———. *The Interpretation of Dreams*. Trans. James Strachey. New York: Avon, 1965.

———. *Jokes and Their Relation to the Unconscious*. Trans. and ed. James Strachey. New York: Norton, 1960.

———. "The Medusa's Head." Trans. James Strachey. *Sexuality and the Psychology of Love* 212–13.

———. *The Sexual Enlightenment of Children*. Ed. Philip Rieff. New York: Macmillan, 1963.

———. *Sexuality and the Psychology of Love*. Ed. Philip Rieff. New York: Macmillan, 1963.

———. "The Taboo of Virginity." Trans. Joan Riviere. *Sexuality and the Psychology of Love* 70–86.

———. "The Uncanny." Trans. Alix Strachey. *Studies in Parapsychology*. Ed. Philip Rieff. New York: Macmillan, 1963. 19–60.

Gilbert, Allan H. "Two Margarets: The Composition of *Much Ado about Nothing*." *Philological Quarterly* 41 (1962): 61–71.

Hayes, Janice. "Those 'soft and delicate desires': *Much Ado* and the Distrust of Women." *The Woman's Part. Feminist Criticism of Shakespeare*. Ed. Carolyn Ruth Swift Lenz, Gayle Greene, and Carol Thomas Neely. Chicago: U of Illinois P, 1980. 79–99.

Kahn, Coppélia. *Man's Estate: Masculine Identity in Shakespeare*. Berkeley: U of California P, 1981.

Neill, Kerby. "More Ado about Claudio: An Acquittal for the Slandered Groom." *Shakespeare Quarterly* 3 (1952): 91–107.

Pettet, E. C. *Shakespeare and the Romance Tradition*. London: Staples, 1949.

Shakespeare, William. *Much Ado about Nothing*. The Riverside Shakespeare. Ed. G. Blakemore Evans. 2 vols. Boston: Houghton, 1974. 1: 322–62.

Storey, Graham. "The Success of *Much Ado about Nothing*." *More Talking about Shakespeare*. Ed. John Garrett. London: Longmans; New York: Theatre Art, 1959. 128–43. Rpt. in Davis 18–32.

West, E. J. "Much Ado about an Unpleasant Play." *Shakespeare Association Bulletin* 22 (1947): 30–34.

1999—Nova Myhill. "Spectatorship in/of *Much Ado About Nothing*"

Nova Myhill (b. 1970) is an Elizabethan scholar and professor of English at the New College of Florida. In her article, Myhill argues that much of the action in *Much Ado about Nothing* hinges on differences based on perspective and the belief in what one has witnessed, despite the fact that perceptions can easily be mistaken, swayed by pre-existing prejudices, or deceived. Thus "seeing" is an action essential to the play, and what the characters "see," or how they are led to "see" others, is often distorted from the truth. Examples of this abound: in the scenes where Benedick and Beatrice are convinced of each other's love; in the scenes of Don John's deceptions; in the play's conclusion, when Claudio must swear his loyalty to a woman whose face is concealed. Myhill uses an early line to highlight these distinctions, when Claudio suggests to Benedick that Hero, "In mine eye, she is the sweetest lady that ever I looked on" (I.i.181–82). Benedick, ever ready with a quip, retorts, "I can see yet without spectacles, and I see no such matter" (I.i.183–84). Myhill reports that "eavesdropping, rather than conversation, is established as the accepted model for receiving credible information throughout the play." Eventually, Myhill concludes that what is seen—or, more distinctly, what is perceived to be seen—may ultimately be the reason for the "much ado about nothing" that hallmarks the play.

In the past twenty years, a great deal of criticism has focused on concerns about appearances in the early modern period, particularly in terms of "self-fashioning";[1] in this article, I want to look at the other side of this issue: the fashioning not of the self but of others through theatrical display. The debate over the stage in early modern England was also a debate over the ways in which audiences perceived and were affected by spectacles. This debate, at its most polemical, led the theater's detractors to claim that audiences would "learne howe . . . to beguyle, howe to betraye . . . howe to murther, howe to poyson, howe to disobey and rebell agaynst Princes," and its supporters to claim the theater "teach[es] the subjects obedience to their King . . . shew[s] the people the untimely ends of such as have moved tumults, commotions and insurrections . . . present[s] them with the flourishing estate of such as live in obedience, exhorting them to allegeance, dehorting them from all trayterous and fellonious stratagems."[2] These claims can easily be applied to the same plays; the "trayterous and fellonious stratagems" that Thomas Heywood claims the theater teaches its audience members to avoid are the same as those John Northbrooke claims it teaches them to perform. But playwrights recognized the power of the audience over the play as well as the converse that so agitated the theater's opponents.

For the antitheatrical tracts of the 1580s, the threatening power of the stage lies in the inevitable interpretive failure of its audience—in the way in which "straunge consortes of melody . . . costly apparel . . . effeminate gestures . . . and wanton speache . . . by the privie entries of the eare, slip downe into the hart, and . . . gaule the minde, where reason and vertue should rule the roste."[3] Playwrights seem to have shared the antitheatrical writers' interest in, though not their despair of, the ways in which their audiences perceived spectacles. *Much Ado about Nothing* is centrally concerned with problems of knowledge and perception. The representation of multiple deceptions reveals a mechanism of creating methods of interpretation—the process by which narratives ensure particular readings of spectacles, at times in the face of other equally possible interpretations. The theater audience's assumption of its own privileged position as eavesdropper is undercut by the frequency with which the play's characters are deceived by their assumptions that eavesdropping offers unproblematic access to truth.[4]

When Claudio denounces Hero at their abortive wedding, he asks as a means of confirming his accusation, "Leonato, stand I here? / Is this the prince? Is this the prince's brother? / Is this face Hero's? Are our eyes our own?"[5] If, as Leonato admits, "All this is so," then Hero is guilty of seeming unchastity and Claudio's denunciation and repudiation of her is acceptable within the social framework of the play (IV.i.66). But Leonato is wrong; all of this is *not* so. In supposing that our eyes are our own in the same unarguable way that he "stand[s] here," Claudio implies that only one interpretation of a spectacle is possible—a position the play is at some pains to dispute. Claudio sees Hero's face, but it is not the same face he saw the previous night at Hero's window because, in the deception of Claudio and Don Pedro, their eyes are extensions of Don John's vision, *not* their own. Moreover, the theater audience is denied direct access to the pivotal moments in Don Pedro and Claudio's courtship of Hero—Don Pedro's wooing of her at the masked ball and the scene of Margaret and Borachio at Hero's window—and instead must cope with multiple and contradictory narratives it can only measure against each other. In its dependence on frequently false narratives, the theater audience also sees with eyes that are not its own.

From the first scene, *Much Ado* presents a world of differing interpretations
which cannot be reconciled. Claudio says of Hero that "In mine eye, she is
the sweetest lady that ever I looked on," but Benedick "can see yet without
spectacles, and [sees] no such matter" (I.i.139–40). While a difference in taste
does not indicate a fundamental difference in perception, this emphasis on sight
reappears throughout the play in describing the assumptions that characters
bring to their observations. When Don Pedro asks Claudio about his feelings for
Hero, Claudio answers that he "looked upon her with a soldier's eye" (I.i.224)
before he went to the wars, but now that

> war-thoughts
> Have left their places vacant, in their rooms
> Come thronging soft and delicate desires,
> All prompting me how fair young Hero is,
> Saying I liked her ere I went to wars.

> (I.i.227–31)

The way Claudio saw Hero before he went to war and the way he sees her at
the start of the play seem to differ only situationally. In attributing his new
view of Hero to the promptings of his "delicate desires," which seem to function independently from the "me" they prompt, Claudio defines his vision as
involuntary and unquestionable. Benedick marvels at Claudio's new way of
seeing, wondering "may I be so converted and see with these eyes?" (II.iii.18).
Eyes in *Much Ado* are not what one sees with, but what one sees through—the
filters that lead characters to see people in particular, conventionalized ways. At
the play's end, Leonato claims that Benedick has "the sight" of his "eye of love
. . . from me, / From Claudio and the prince," and that Beatrice's "eye of favor"
for Benedick "my daughter lent her" through the false narratives of each other's
passion that Beatrice and Benedick overhear (V.iv.23–6). This essay examines
how characters in the play come to "see with these eyes."

The possibility that spectacles can "convert" their audiences against their wills
is the basis of a persistent anxiety in antitheatrical writing. In *Playes Confuted in
Five Actions* (1582), Stephen Gosson warns that "as long as we know ourselves to
be fleshy, beholding those examples in Theaters that are incident to flesh, we are
taught by other men's examples how to fall. And they that came honest to a play
may depart infected."[6] The language of infection, which appears frequently in
antitheatrical writings, implies an audience helpless to avoid the influence of the
plays. Gosson's final "action" of *Playes Confuted* is a discussion of "ye Effects yt
this poyson works amõg us . . . These outward spectacles effeminate and soften
ye hearte of men, vice is learned in beholding, sense is tickled, desire pricked,
& those impressions of mind are secretly conveyed over to ye gazers, which
ye players do counterfeit on ye stage."[7] He describes these "effects" as entirely

outside the playgoers' control. In his example of the effect of Bacchus's seduction of Ariadne on its spectators, Gosson claims that the audience reproduces what it sees: "when Bacchus rose up . . . the beholders rose up . . . when they sware, the company sware . . . when they departed to bedde; the company presently was set on fire, they that were married posted home to their wiues; they that were single vowed very solemnly to be wedded."[8] While the first set of imitations, rising up and swearing, are physically identical—imitation in the simplest and most literal sense—the second set involves a replication of the mental state, not the physical. "Vow[ing] very solemnly to be wedded" is not the same thing as having sex, but in this context it suggests that the effect of seeing Bacchus and Ariadne was to compel the audience to replicate not the physical action of seduction, but the mental state that enabled this action.

Gosson's example suggests that "we" will all have no choice but to learn from the same examples. His formulation implies a stable relationship between spectator and spectacle, in which the spectator is always at the mercy of his (for Gosson's spectator is always male) involuntary responses.[9] But John Northbrooke, in the earliest pamphlet directed specifically against the London public theaters, recognizes what Gosson attempts to deny—that members of the theater audience are simultaneously spectators and spectacles, and vulnerable on both accounts. His anxieties about female theatergoers stem from their positions as spectacles for and spectators of the male theatergoers and actors: "What safegarde of chastitie can there be, where the woman is desired with so many eyes, where so many faces look upon her and again she upon so many?"[10] For Gosson, whose spectators all become like Bacchus, not like Ariadne, spectatorship is a male province, and his expressed concern for female playgoers is that "you can forbid no man, that vieweth you, to note you and that noteth you to judge you."[11] In becoming spectators—a role that Gosson implicitly denies them—women make spectacles of themselves and are vulnerable to the judgment of the male spectators. But if spectacles shape the viewer, as Gosson and many other writers claim, does not the woman have as much threatening power as the play? And if the opposite is true, then is not the play threatened as much as the woman?

The "nothing" about which there is much ado in Shakespeare's play is simultaneously the female genital "nothing" and "noting"—habits of observation and interpretation.[12] "Noting" becomes a problem in the play because the male characters accept that women should be, as Hero is, silent and defined by the ways in which they are seen.[13] Hero is defined visually not only for Claudio, but for the theater audience, which has more access to her than her lover, but still cannot see or hear her response to Don Pedro's offstage wooing, cannot hear her response to Claudio's declaration of his own silence, "the perfectest herald of joy" (II.i.232). Hero characteristically lacks a voice and "becomes in effect a sign to be read and interpreted by others."[14]

The contested territory of *Much Ado about Nothing* is not action, but interpretation, and while the theater audience occupies a privileged position in relation to the action of the play, the play presents it with audiences that also believe their position privileged and shows how that assumption leaves them vulnerable to having their readings controlled by the play's internal dramatists Don John, Borachio, and Don Pedro.[15] The represented audience's perception of an event is based on both what it is allowed to see and hear and what it expects—an expectation created by a narrative like the one of Hero's falseness that Don John provides Don Pedro and Claudio or the narratives of the other's love and their own shortcomings to which Beatrice and Benedick are exposed. While much criticism examines the difference between Don Pedro's benevolent and Don John's malevolent deception, the similarity both of methods and of results is striking.[16] The represented audience's perception of its spectatorial power allows it to accept an externally imposed narrative over the evidence of its senses. By presenting the manipulation of interpretation and questioning the privileged status of the spectator, the play challenges the idea of omniscience in any spectator, or the possibility of any spectator having the sort of automatic access to truth that the position implies for both characters in the play and the theater audience.

Don Pedro, Claudio, Beatrice, and Benedick all observe and overhear scenes actually predicated on their presence, which they believe to be predicated on their absence; the deceptions are based on the victim's assumption that he or she is seeing and hearing a private scene. In conceiving of themselves as subjects making discoveries, they become the objects of deception; they are not simply spectators, but spectacles of their gullers. The gulling scenes emphasize how visible the supposed eavesdropper is; Benedick's access to Don Pedro, Claudio, and Leonato's conversation in the orchard is based not on his success in "hid[ing] me in the arbour," but his failure (II.iii.28). Three lines after Benedick conceals himself, Don Pedro asks Claudio "See you where Benedick hath hid himself?" (II.iii.32) and Claudio has, "very well, my lord" (II.iii.33). In the parallel scene involving Beatrice, Hero tells Ursula to "look where Beatrice like a lapwing runs / Close by the ground, to hear our conference" (III. i.24–5), and Borachio, describing the unrepresented scene at Hero's window, tells Conrade that "the prince, Claudio and my master planted, and placed, and possessed, by my master Don John, saw afar off in the orchard this amiable encounter" between himself and Margaret (III.iii.121–4). The discrepancy between their spectatorial position and the one they believe they occupy leads characters to accept what they hear as truth, and model themselves accordingly. With the sole exception of the watch's overhearing of Borachio and Conrade's conversation in act III, scene iii, all other represented eavesdropping occurs with the contrivance of those being overheard; the positions of performer and audience are reversed.

All of the upper-class male characters in Messina are quite aware of the possibility of deception; they recognize that the world around them is not transparent and that other characters may wish to show them a false version of events. Benedick twice considers and rejects the idea that he is being gulled, Borachio knows that Claudio and Don Pedro "will scarcely believe this [that Hero is false] without trial" (II.ii.30–1), and even the perennial dupe Claudio fears that Don Pedro praises Hero "to fetch me in" (I.i.165). But Claudio's very awareness that he may be deceived ensures that he will be, causing him to distrust his own experience of Don Pedro and Hero, and to accept both the news of Don Pedro's betrayal that he hears "in name of Benedick" and his observation spying on Hero's window (II.i.128). S. P. Cerasano claims that "the natural tendency of the residents of Messina is toward gullibility, inconstancy, unpredictability and slander," but this gullibility is less a "natural tendency" than a product of characters' awareness of their vulnerability to deception.[17]

Eavesdropping, rather than conversation, is established as the accepted model for receiving credible information throughout the play; to see or hear an action and believe yourself to be unobserved or unrecognized is to see that action as authentic and unstaged. Most characters in *Much Ado* believe that the awareness of audience is what creates "performance": people cannot act for an audience if they are unaware of it. Thus, assuming (correctly) that "Hero" is unaware that he is watching her window, Claudio reinterprets all of her previously displayed behavior as a staged action. The "exterior shows" cease to be an indicator of maidenhood and Claudio rereads Hero's blushes when he accuses her of unfaithfulness as "guiltiness, not modesty" (IV.i.35–7).

Claudio and his fellow eavesdroppers are correct in believing that the awareness of audience is what creates "performance," but not in the way that they, as audiences who believe themselves invisible, suppose. Don Pedro and Don John both take advantage of the belief that eavesdropping constitutes authentic experience. As Anthony Dawson observes, "for most of the characters, eavesdropping . . . is a natural, spontaneous gesture," a habit of placing themselves at one remove from conversation so that they can have the perspective that they believe guarantees access to truths that other characters would not tell them to their faces.[18] In the parallel scenes in which first Benedick and then Beatrice believe themselves to be secretly observing the discussion of the other's passion, they assume that since the spectatorial position is one of power, they know more than the characters they watch because only they know of their presence at this private conference.

In both cases, the gullers insist that their victim should not be told of the other's love because they would "make a sport of it" (II.iii.134, cf. III.i.58). In gulling Benedick, Don Pedro and his assistants raise the specter of deception in order to dispel it; Don Pedro suggests that Beatrice "doth but counterfeit" so that Leonato may describe her passion (II.iii.92). Benedick's judgment that "this can be no trick" is based on outward signs of reliability (II.iii.181); he "should think this a gull, but that the white-bearded fellow speaks it: knavery cannot sure hide himself in such reverence" (II.iii.106–7). His explicit consideration of what constitutes reliable evidence emphasizes that belief is not a default condition in *Much Ado*; everything is open to the accusation of "counterfeit," which must be explicitly refuted.

The circumstances of Benedick making his "discovery" convince him of its veracity, and lead him to reinterpret Beatrice and himself. Resolving to love Beatrice, Benedick explicitly reacts against the description he has heard of himself as a man who "hath a contemptible spirit" (II.iii.153–4), proclaiming that "happy are they that hear their detractions and can put them to mending" (II.iii.187–8). He constructs himself as a lover, resolving to be "horribly in love with her" (II.iii.191–2). Just as he redefines himself in opposition to the unflattering portrait he has overheard, Benedick reads in Beatrice's unaltered behavior toward him "some marks of love in her" (II.iii.199–200), reinterpreting her sentences to make their meaning consistent with what he has heard: "I took no more pains for those thanks than any pains you took to thank me: that's as much as to say any pains I take for you is as easy as thanks" (II.iii.209–11). Beatrice's language, like Hero's blush when Claudio refuses to marry her, is subject to reinterpretation to make it fit into the idea Benedick has received about her from outside agents. Benedick, having accepted Claudio, Don Pedro, and Leonato's narrative, reads Beatrice's avowed indifference as a form of acting which he, as an audience member with access to more information than she believes he has, can now penetrate and interpret correctly.

Benedick's labored reinterpretation of Beatrice's summons to dinner points not to the new clarity of his perception as he claims, but to his newfound determination to read her as Don Pedro, Leonato, and Claudio have suggested that he should. When Benedick, in asking Leonato for Beatrice's hand, tells him that he "with an eye of love requite[s] her," Leonato seems justified in answering, "The sight whereof I think you had from me, / From Claudio, and the prince" (V.iv.24–6). Benedick's reading of Beatrice is socially constructed, and his shift in vision is the one Don Pedro arranges.

Don Pedro's plan for winning Hero for Claudio assumes a less complex response from her than from either Beatrice or Benedick. While he expects both of them to react against a negative reading of themselves, Hero is to be won almost without her consent. Don Pedro proposes to "take her hearing prisoner with the force / And strong encounter of my amorous tale," implying that his speech will exercise absolute control over Hero (I.i.250–1); once he has taken her hearing prisoner, "the conclusion is, she shall be thine" (I.i.253). The possibility of failure, or even of a response from Hero, never crosses Don Pedro's mind. Hero, Don Pedro's audience, is to be molded by "the force / And strong encounter of my amorous tale" (I.i.250–1); her hearing, as separable from her reason as Claudio's "delicate desires" are from his, is to form her response (I.i.229). Don Pedro's confidence in the power of speech seems justified by the success of narratives throughout the play in changing their hearers' methods of interpretation. Benedick and Beatrice are persuaded to regard each other "with an eye of favor" (V.iv.21) through the conversations among their friends that they imagine they overhear by chance, and Claudio and Don Pedro accept the sight of Hero as "every man's Hero" after hearing Don John's account of what they will see (III.ii.78). But Don Pedro's success in winning Hero is not necessarily the testimony to his eloquence that he imagines; well before he takes her out to dance, Hero, as Leonato tells her, "know[s her] answer" to any proposal from the prince (II.i.49).

The theater audience, in the presence of Don Pedro and Claudio's explicitly "secret" communication onstage, supposes itself to have a more complete narrative than the play's other characters who are unaware of the scene (I.i.151). But this privilege is undermined throughout the first act, as Antonio's servant and Borachio, both invisible to the theater audience, Don Pedro, and Claudio, are retroactively introduced into the scene, and bring back varying reports to their masters. If Claudio and Don Pedro suppose their conversation secret, then so does the theater audience suppose its access to it unique. The two scenes following Don Pedro's revelation of his plot make the audience position progressively more crowded. By the time the first act has finished, the "secret" of Don Pedro's plan is known, in one form or another, to almost every character in the play, and the theater audience's position as privileged observer has come into question.

Despite Don Pedro's faith in his ability to manipulate perception through narrative, his impersonation of Claudio, which he believes will win Hero through "the force / And strong encounter of my amorous tale" wins her instead because of her obedience to her father (I.i.250–1). After Antonio tells Leonato what his servant has overheard, Leonato resolves to "acquaint my daughter withal, that she may be the better prepared for an answer, if peradventure this be true" (I.ii.17–8). Hero's response is determined before the performance begins, not by Don Pedro's eloquence in the role of Claudio but by Leonato and Antonio's instructions to Hero, based on the assumption that Don Pedro is her suitor. The wooing scene which Don Pedro wishes to enact becomes a scene in which his audience knows far more than he supposes, and the presence of multiple narratives of Don Pedro's "secret" conversation with Claudio, which was not to produce any, allows Don John and Borachio to suggest to Claudio, plausibly enough, that Don Pedro "is enamored on Hero," particularly when Don Pedro's performance of wooing Hero becomes a secret scene to which Hero alone, not Claudio and not the theater audience, has access (II.i.121–2).

When Don John and Borachio tell Claudio that Don Pedro woos for himself, the theater audience, although it can be sure of their motives, cannot have the immediate certainty that they are lying. Don John's claim that "Sure my brother is amorous on Hero, and hath withdrawn her father to break with him about it" (II. i.115–6) before he makes clear that he and Borachio are performing for Claudio causes editors to insert notes explaining that Don John does not actually believe this,[19] and "Garrick's text (1777) makes this explicit by inserting 'Now then for a trick of contrivance' at the beginning of the speech."[20] But the play text offers no such certainty; Don Pedro's courtship is inaccessible to any audience, including the paying one, until it is over. Claudio instantly believes, and Benedick later is willing to consider the possibility, that Don John and Borachio are telling the truth. The possibility of Don Pedro wooing for himself is at least voiced by every man at the ball except Don Pedro.[21] Don John's falseness is no guarantee of Don Pedro's truth.

Believing that Don John and Borachio mistake him for Benedick and are thus transparent conduits of information, Claudio accepts without question their claim that Don Pedro woos Hero for himself, reasoning that "beauty is a witch, / Against whose charms faith melteth into blood" (II.i.135–6). Claudio supposes that rather than taking "her hearing prisoner with the force / And strong encounter of my amorous tale," Don Pedro has himself been bewitched in looking at Hero (I.i.250–1). Hero's status suddenly and dangerously shifts, from the audience which can be controlled by what she hears, Don Pedro's words entering her ear, to the spectacle before which he is similarly powerless. But Hero's consistent position as a spectacle does not endow her with witchlike powers; it only allows the men who observe her to read her as having them.

Upon Don John's accusation, Claudio instantly reveals (or develops) a distrust of his own "agent" Don Pedro, claiming that "all hearts in love use their own tongues. / Let every eye negotiate for itself, / And trust no agent" (II.i.133–5). This is not only a disclaimer of the efficacy of wooing by proxy, but a distrust of proxies in general. The "negotiation" of the eye is the way in which the eye observes as well as the way in which it seduces. But in *Much Ado*, all eyes seem ultimately to "trust agents"; sights and sounds are filtered through the characters who first bring them to mind.

Although the characters of the play have great faith in their own abilities to "see a church by daylight" (II.i.59), the scene in which Claudio denounces Hero as "an approvèd wanton" (IV.i.39) is the most forceful reminder of how easily interpretation can be guided. The "eye of love" which Benedick claims he and Beatrice see each other with is something that can be "lent" (V.iv.23–4), as Leonato says. And it is lent in almost precisely the same way as "conjecture" is placed on Claudio, "to turn all beauty into thoughts of harm" so that "never shall it more be gracious" (IV.i.100–1). Borachio tells Conrade that Don Pedro and Claudio have been deceived "partly by [Don John's] oaths, which first possessed them, partly by the dark night which did deceive them, but chiefly, by my villainy, which did confirm any slander that Don John had made" (III.iii.127–30). The possession by the oaths is the necessary precondition to everything else: what makes Borachio's "villainy" serve as "confirmation" in the same way as Beatrice's statement that she was not Hero's bedfellow the previous night although she had been at all other times becomes confirmation for Leonato of Hero's falseness rather than of the impossibility of Borachio's confession of "the vile encounters they have had / A thousand times in secret" (IV.i.87–8).

When Borachio claims that he "can at any unseasonable instant of night, appoint [Margaret] to look out at her lady's chamber window" (II.ii.14–5), Don John sees this as an insignificant event, as Borachio agrees it is, but "the poison of that lies in you to temper" (II.ii.17).[22] The event will only have meaning that can "be the death of this marriage" if Don John provides Don Pedro and Claudio with that meaning (II.ii.16). Both Borachio and Don John recognize that their main problem is to get Don Pedro and Claudio to believe Don John's story—the production of "proof."

The visual proof that Borachio tells Don John to offer is identical to his narrative; the syntax of Borachio's sentence transforms Don John's promise of what Don Pedro and Claudio will see into what they will actually see:

> tell them that you know that Hero loves me, intend a kind of zeal to both the prince and Claudio ... who is thus like to be cozened with the semblance of a maid ... that you have discovered thus: they will scarcely believe this without trial: offer them instances which shall bear no less likelihood, than to see me at her chamber window, hear me call Margaret Hero, hear Margaret term me Claudio, and bring them to see *this* the very night before the intended wedding ... and there shall appear such seeming truth of Hero's disloyalty, that jealousy shall be called assurance and all the preparation overthrown.
>
> (II.ii.26–37, my italics)

The deictic "this" refers to a scene that exists only in Don John's accusation: the sight of Hero with Borachio. The verbal "instances" that Don John is to offer become precisely the same as what he is to "bring [Don Pedro and Claudio] to see," and what they, under the influence of his narrative, do see.

The absence of the theater audience from this scene prevents any knowledge of whether Margaret, in the guise of Hero, calls Borachio "Claudio" as the text insists, or not. The appearance of "Claudio" rather than the more logical (at least for Borachio and Don John's plan) "Borachio" can be explained, as the *Riverside Shakespeare* does, as "apparently a slip," but forcibly demonstrates that no matter how often the theater audience may hear the events of "the very night before the intended wedding" described, it cannot know what Don Pedro and Claudio saw and heard, only what they were prepared to see and hear (II.ii.33–4).[23] In this instance, description and preconception replace sight on the most literal level.

Indeed, the theater audience's conspicuous exclusion from the scene of Borachio and Margaret at Hero's window, combined with the seven distinct descriptions of the event that replace it, suggest both the uncertainty of the theater audience's position and the impossibility of any scene having a transparent meaning.

When Don John tells Don Pedro and Claudio of Hero's disloyalty, he does not, as Borachio instructs him, describe what they will hear, preferring to tell them what they will see: "go but with me tonight, you shall see her chamber window entered, even the night before her wedding day . . . If you dare not trust that you see, confess not that you know" (III.ii.82–8). Don John implies to Claudio and Don Pedro that "knowledge" is acquired through becoming a part of the same group of spectators, but what they see will be materially different from what Don John (or the theater audience, were the scene visually represented) sees.

Don John plays upon Don Pedro and Claudio's belief in their ability to understand what they see, to be in the position of power that eavesdropping implies. The deception works because he constructs it as a choice that they can make, based on the evidence of their senses, between himself and Hero. The choice offers Don Pedro and Claudio the chance to prove their own ability as observers, to see through the mask of Hero's "seeming" (IV.i.50). To see Hero's disloyalty is to confirm Don John's loyalty. Don John represents his speech as insufficient, insisting that Hero cannot be adequately represented in language: "she has been too long a-talking of," "the word [disloyal] is too good to paint out her wickedness" (III.ii.76, 80).[24] In promising to "disparage her [Hero] no further, till you are my witnesses," Don John claims that Don Pedro and Claudio's acuteness as spectators, rather than his suspect testimony, will prove Hero's unchastity (III.ii.95). As in the case of Don Pedro's plan to have Benedick "overhear" the discussion of Beatrice's love and his own misgovernment, the promise of the ability to see through a deception—Hero's chastity, Beatrice's indifference—assures the interpretation for which the spectator has been prepared.

In the first description the theater audience (and the watch, "stand[ing] close" in the play's only instance of successful eavesdropping [III.iii.88]) hear of the incident at the window after it has happened, Borachio tells Conrade that Claudio and Don Pedro are deceived "partly by [Don John's] oaths, which first possessed them, partly by the dark night which did deceive them, but chiefly, by my villainy, which did confirm any slander that Don John had made" (III. iii.127–30). The action only serves as confirmation; Don Pedro and Claudio have previously been possessed by Don John's story. Placed as they are "afar off in the orchard" in the dark night, Don Pedro and Claudio's senses are as unreliable as Don John's oaths, but their senses and his story, neither of which can be believed, confirm one another (III.iii.123).

In telling Conrade (and the watch) what has just occurred in Leonato's orchard, Borachio illustrates the shift from spectator to spectacle that threatens all of the play's audiences; he first tells Conrade that he has "tonight wooed Margaret, the Lady Hero's gentlewoman, by the name of Hero: she leans me out at her mistress' chamber-window, bids me a thousand times good night" (III. iii.118–21). To this point, he describes what he saw, but realizes this is insufficient to explain how he has earned a thousand ducats from Don John, and backs up to explain that "the Prince, Claudio, and my master planted, placed and possessed, by my master Don John, saw afar off in the orchard this amiable encounter" (III. iii.121–4). This is the unrealized perspective of the theater audience; Borachio speaks first as the object of scrutiny that Don Pedro and Claudio think him, the spectacle unaware of observers, then as the omniscient audience member, aware of how all of the characters involved in the scene see it.

The theater audience's exclusion from the scene at Hero's window insists that its members must, like the characters in the play, accept narratives which color their interpretation. The scene at the window is finally inaccessible, vanishing behind the screen of multiple narratives which are never quite in agreement.[25] The theater audience's relationship to Hero is established as one of observation; its position is established through its access to the information that will allow it to read Hero correctly—Don John and Borachio's plot to show Don Pedro and Claudio "Hero" at the window. But this is precisely the scene to which the theater audience is denied access. At other points in the play, the theater audience sees the same scene as the designated audience (Beatrice or Benedick, for instance), but is able to interpret it differently because it knows that the scene is staged only so that the designated audience will hear it. But the most crucial staged action is not staged for the theater audience—and as it is reported seven separate times for seven distinct audiences, the theater audience's knowing exactly what happened becomes increasingly impossible.

Almost all critical descriptions of the scene at Hero's window mention that Margaret is wearing Hero's clothes, as if this is the sign that explains Claudio's credulousness. And it may be; for an audience observing the action from "afar off," costume is an exceedingly useful indicator of who is who.[26] But this piece of information does not come to light until Borachio confesses to Leonato in act V, when the theater audience has already judged Don Pedro and Claudio's spectatorship. Claudio's immediate response to this revelation is to return to his original idea of Hero: "now thy image doth appear / In the rare semblance that I loved it first" (V.i.220–1). Hero remains a visual construct, now purified by her retroactive absence from the scene; Claudio simply switches from one way of seeing, which he now perceives as incorrect, to his earlier view.

Claudio's understanding of Hero in purely visual terms is obviously problematic in that it allows the success of Don John and Borachio's plot, but only Beatrice seems to have any other way of understanding her. Even at the very beginning of the play, when Leonato makes the old joke "Her mother hath many times told me so" in answer to Don Pedro's "I think this is your daughter" (I.i.76–8), Don Pedro takes Hero's physical appearance, not the word of Leonato's wife, as a guarantor of her paternity.[27] Despite Beatrice's best efforts to convince Hero to have some voice in choosing her husband, Hero seems to accept her father's choice: "if the prince do solicit you in that kind, you know your answer" (II.i.48–9). Despite Leonato and Beatrice's attempts to put words into her mouth, Hero never directly responds to the debate around her. The silence that leaves appearance as the only indication of female significance is established as culturally and socially desirable; Claudio praises Hero for being "modest" (I.i.121) and Benedick at first ignores Beatrice's beauty because he "cannot endure my Lady Tongue" (II.i.207–8).[28] But, in the absence of speech, and thus in the absence of narrative, interpretation becomes ever more important, particularly since female characters are then only to be looked on as spectacles. In this model, to be exclusively a spectacle is to have no power, to be completely subject to interpretation as Hero is at the wedding.

Hero's appearance, rather than her words, speaks for her; Claudio accuses her of being "but the sign and semblance of her honor: / Behold how like a maid she blushes here" (IV.i.28–9). Certain visual cues, outward appearances, are assumed to signify truth; when Benedick speaks of Leonato's credibility, he bases this not on personal knowledge of Leonato but on his white beard, the "reverence" in which knavery cannot hide itself (II.iii.106–7). Claudio's condemnation of Hero is particularly violent because he identifies her as "the sign and semblance of her honor," as being "like a maid" without being one. Hero cannot defend herself from this charge because only her physical exterior has been available; if this is a lie, no clear way to read her exists.

Readings of *Much Ado* that focus on right and wrong methods of interpretation generally find the model for proper interpretation in Beatrice's certainty of Hero's innocence and in Friar Francis's "noting of the lady" (IV.i.150). Richard Henze says that "this combination of intuitive trust and careful observation seems to be the one that the play recommends," but to whom and under what circumstances?[29] How is one to make judgments simultaneously based on faith and careful noting? According to Henze's argument, if Claudio is wrong about Hero, and Beatrice and Friar Francis are right, then they look in the right way and Claudio looks in the wrong way. But Friar Francis's "noting" consists of interpreting the meaning of Hero's blushes, just as Claudio's and Leonato's do. Until Friar Francis allows Hero to speak, quite late in the scene, her body is the only available object of interpretation.

All of Hero's accusers, but especially Claudio, are preoccupied with the disparity in what they have seen "Hero" do and what her outward appearance suggests. Claudio insists that she is "but the sign and semblance of her honor" and remains preoccupied with her exterior (IV.i.28): "Would you not swear / All you that see her, that she were a maid, / By these exterior shows?" (IV.i.33–5), "O Hero! What a hero hadst thou been, / If half thy outward graces had been placed / About thy thoughts and counsels of thy heart?" (IV.i.93–5). Claudio's experience outside Hero's bedroom window has led him, by accepting Don John's version of ocular proof, to distrust his sight and the appearances of those around him. As a result, he says that "on my eyelids shall conjecture hang, / To turn all beauty into thoughts of harm, / And never shall it more be gracious" (IV.i.99–101). Claudio has learned a new way of seeing, one in which appearance is now branded as seeming, and everything must be observed through the filter of "conjecture"; Don John is no longer necessary as an external creator of preconception because he has been replaced by "conjecture," a purely internal filter which assures that Claudio's eyes are no longer his own.

Even assuming that "any man with me [Hero] conversed, / At hours unmeet" (IV.i.175), Claudio's accusations that she is

> more intemperate in your blood,
> Than Venus, or those pampered animals,
> That rage in savage sensuality
>
> (IV.i.53–5)

and "knows the heat of a luxurious bed" seem to have little to do with what he saw (IV.i.36). Don Pedro, although much less hysterical, still accuses Hero of being "a common stale" (IV.i.59). Hero's supposed, and Margaret's actual, "crime" has been to place herself on view—to, as Borachio says when describing his plan in the most neutral way possible, "at any unseasonable instant of the night . . . look out at her lady's chamber window" (II.ii.14–5). Gosson's warning that "you can forbid no man, that vieweth you, to note you and that noteth you to judge you" becomes a threat in this context.[30] But while Hero cannot forbid the "noting of the lady" in which Claudio, Don Pedro, Don John, Friar Francis, and Leonato engage, and is as vulnerable to ill report as may be imagined, the play is not comfortable with this vulnerability of spectacle (IV.i.150). Claudio and Don Pedro's view of the situation seems skewed, especially for a theater audience that did not see any woman "talk with a ruffian at her chamber window" (IV.i.85).

Hero's accusers, particularly Claudio, are, as Beatrice forcefully insists, not only incorrect but cruel; their accusations are out of proportion with what they have actually seen. They respond not to their own observation but to Don John and Borachio's narratives, and to their own fears of being disgraced. In accusing Hero, Don John, Don Pedro, and Claudio provide very limited descriptions of what they saw the previous night; their focus on vituperation outweighs any desire to convince others of the justice of their accusation. Claudio spends nearly fifty lines abusing Hero before he provides a specific accusation, and Don Pedro only says that

> Myself, my brother, and this grievèd count
> Did see her, hear her, at that hour last night
> Talk with a ruffian at her chamber window
> Who hath indeed like a most liberal villain,
> Confessed the vile encounters they have had
> A thousand times in secret.
>
> (IV.i.83–8)

The final proof that Don Pedro offers is Borachio's confession, a confession unnecessary to confirm what they have seen, but necessary, as it confirms the implications of Hero speaking to a man outside her window. Once again, a narrative gives meaning to an ambiguous staged event, and Hero, who has never produced narratives except those Don Pedro told her to in the gulling of Beatrice, is faced with Claudio's, Don Pedro's, and Don John's readings of her—readings her own father accepts with startling readiness.

In accepting Claudio and Don Pedro's reading, Leonato asks, "Could she here deny / The story that is printed in her blood?" (IV.i.114–5). Like Claudio's rhetorical questions, "Leonato, stand I here? / Is this the prince? Is this the prince's brother? / Is this face Hero's? Are our eyes our own?" (IV.i.63–5), Leonato's questions establish his certainty, even as their possible answers establish the problems with his interpretation. The structure of the question whose speaker thinks it is rhetorical reveals the assumptions he will not question.[31] Despite Hero's insistence thirty-five lines previously that she "talked with no man at that hour," Leonato is sure that he can read "the story that is printed in her blood" (IV.i.80). Her characteristic silence becomes another reason for believing her accusers: "Thou seest that all the grace that she hath left, / Is that she will not add to her damnation / A sin of perjury, she not denies it" (IV.i.164–6). Hero's rescue in this scene comes when the friar speaks of his "noting of the lady" (IV. i.150); again, this is an observation of physical signs: the

> thousand blushing apparitions
> [that] start into her face, a thousand innocent shames,
> In angel whiteness beat away those blushes,
> And in her eye there hath appeared a fire,
> To burn the errors that these princes hold
> Against her maiden truth.
>
> (IV.i.152–7)[32]

Friar Francis is one of a group of men who read Hero's body, and that he is correct can be read as chance. Carol Cook observes that "Benedick's act of 'marking' [Beatrice] is clearly a projection, but the question then arises whether the friar's marking of Hero is not equally so."[33] Much can be said in Friar Francis's favor, but, if his observation is privileged, it is through his willingness to let Hero speak in her own defense, not his "careful observation."

The friar's reading of Hero's appearance ultimately leads him to question her after stating his belief in her innocence; and her answer, not Friar Francis's faith, is what finally removes Leonato's certainty of her guilt, although the certainty of her innocence does not immediately follow. Leonato's acceptance of the testimony of "the two princes" whose social position authorizes their accusation, exemplifies some of the most problematic viewing in the play, as he chooses to read Hero in light of their accusation although he has not seen the proof they have (IV.i.145). Leonato never asks for Hero's story; from the moment Don Pedro and Don John join Claudio in his accusation, Leonato sees her as having "fallen / Into a pit of ink, that the wide sea / Hath drops too few to wash her clean again" (IV.i.132–4), asking "Would the two princes lie, and Claudio lie" (IV.i.145). In the face of two opposing readings, Leonato is unable to decide:

> I know not: if they speak but truth of her,
> These hands will tear her, if they wrong her honour,
> The proudest of them shall well hear of it.
>   (IV.i.183–5)

Although his eventual determination to believe Hero is obvious in act V, his last word on the subject as he leaves the wedding scene is that the "smallest twine may lead me" (IV.i.243); belief in either version seems to him equally well, or poorly, grounded.

Comparing the ways in which Don Pedro and Claudio look at Hero with the ways in which Beatrice and Friar Francis do ultimately seems impossible because none of Hero's defenders has seen what Don Pedro and Claudio have, and, if Benedick and Beatrice will accept a less well-supported tale of the other's love, Don Pedro and Claudio's belief in Don John and their own eyes indicates more of a problem with the vulnerability of spectatorship in general than a fault particular to those two. Benedick's acceptance of the words of his friends (although his trust seems based on Leonato's participation rather than that of Don Pedro), describing a scene he has not seen and his rereading Beatrice's speech to conform to what he has heard, exemplifies the same problems as Leonato's initial acceptance of the accusations against Hero, in which he reinterprets Hero's silence as guilt.

In representing Margaret at the window only verbally, and in leaving the content of the dialogue that occurs at the window entirely obscure, *Much Ado* avoids a number of problems for the theater audience. To observe a staged action that one recognizes as such is to be complicit, voluntarily or involuntarily, with the character who produces that action, sharing knowledge that the represented audience does not possess. The position of shared superior knowledge defines the represented audience's position as credulous. The problem is acute in *Much Ado* because, if Margaret were represented at the window, the theater audience would be in a position to decide exactly how credulous Don Pedro and Claudio are and how good the deception is. Like Don Pedro's and Claudio's, the theater audience's view of Margaret will be from "afar off," and the question arises of exactly how much Margaret looks like Hero. Costumes are primary markers of identity on the early modern stage (hence the unbreakable disguise convention), and Margaret in Hero's clothes may look enough like Hero to convince an unprepared (or differently prepared) audience of Hero's guilt—or she may look enough unlike her to suggest that observation has no power over narrative.

The scene of Borachio and Margaret at Hero's window has not always remained inaccessible in production. Michael Friedman discusses Michael Langham's 1961 Stratford-upon-Avon production, which featured a dumbshow in which Don John, Don Pedro, and Claudio saw Borachio climb up to the balcony where he was joined "by 'Hero.'" In fact, the actress on stage was not Margaret disguised as Hero, but Hero herself, "heavily cloaked [promptbook's phrase], pretending to be Margaret pretending to be Hero."[34] This interpolation justifies Claudio to the point of making Don John's accusation accurate. But the absence of the chamber window scene from the play makes this sort of identification with, or sympathy for, Claudio's position at the wedding rather improbable. A slightly less determined, but probably more influential, attempt to excuse Claudio's behavior through the representation of the window scene, appears in Kenneth Branagh's 1993 film of *Much Ado*. Branagh explains his decision to include the scene on the grounds that "if we saw this occur on screen, it would add a new dimension to our understanding of Claudio," saving him from being dismissed for his gullibility.[35] But this anxiety about Claudio's gullibility seems to leave him peculiarly vulnerable to it; the actress playing Margaret in Branagh's film bears almost no physical resemblance to the actress playing Hero. And Claudio's gullibility is not unique to him but part of a larger range of issues of problematic forms of spectatorship.

If Margaret is represented as very similar to Hero, Claudio and Don Pedro's reaction at the wedding becomes understandable, although not laudable. More significantly, deception becomes impossible to detect visually, an uncomfortable position for a play whose resolution depends on Friar Francis's "noting of the lady" (IV.i.150), Claudio's willingness to accept Leonato's offer of his niece, "Almost the copy of my child that's dead" (V.i.256), and Beatrice and Benedick's seeing each other with the eyes of love Leonato says their gullers "lent" them (V.iv.23). One of the reasons Don Pedro and Claudio believe Don John is that "his lie . . . easily passes in Messina as a truthful reading of women,"[36] but if the visual proofs he gives them are irrefutable at the distance of a theater audience member from the acting area above the stage, then his lie will pass anywhere, and the position of spectator is no more one of control than that of spectacle.

NOTES

I am grateful to A. R. Braunmuller, Rebecca Jaffe, Claire McEachern, and Robert N. Watson for comments, advice, and encouragement on this article.

1. Stephen Greenblatt, *Renaissance Self-Fashioning: From More to Shakespeare* (Chicago: Univ. of Chicago Press, 1980).

2. John Northbrooke, *A Treatise wherein Dicing, Dauncing, Vaine Playes or Enterluds . . . Are Reproved by the Authoritie of the Word of God and Auntient Writers*, ed. Arthur Freeman (New York: Garland Publishing, 1974), pp. 67–8. Thomas Heywood, *An Apology for Actors*, ed. Richard H. Perkinson (New York: Scholars' Facsimilies and Reprints, 1941), sig. F4v.

3. Stephen Gosson, *The Schoole of Abuse* (London: T. Dawson, 1579), sig. B6v–B7.

4. The representation of audiences, rather than mirroring the behavior of theater audiences, presents reception codes in an exaggerated form for scrutiny in the same way that inset spectacle presents performance codes. For a discussion of performance code, see Keir Elam, *The Semiotics of Theatre and Drama* (London and New York: Methuen, 1980), pp. 49–97. Michèle Willems discusses how inset plays present performance code for scrutiny in "'They do but jest' or do they? Reflexions on the Ambiguities of the Space Within a Space," in *The Show Within: Dramatic and Other Insets, English Renaissance Drama (1550–1642)*, ed. François Laroque (Montpellier: Publications de Université Paul-Valéry, 1990), pp. 51–64, 53.

5. William Shakespeare, *Much Ado About Nothing*, ed. F. H. Mares (Cambridge: Cambridge Univ. Press, 1988), IV.i.63–5. Further references will appear parenthetically in the text.

6. Stephen Gosson, *Playes Confuted in Five Actions* (London: Thomas Gosson, 1582), sig. G4.

7. Gosson, sig. G4.

8. Gosson, sig. G5. Laura Levine argues that the Bacchus/Ariadne passage suggests not only that "watching leads inevitably to 'doing' . . . [b]ut . . . the more radical idea that watching leads inevitably to 'being'—to assuming the identity of the actor" (*Men in Women's Clothing: Anti-theatricality and Effeminization, 1579–1642* [Cambridge: Cambridge Univ. Press, 1994], p. 13).

9. Levine argues that the antitheatrical writers envision "a self which can always be altered not by its own playful shaping intelligence, but by malevolent forces outside its control" (p. 12).

10. Northbrooke, p. 63.

11. Gosson, *The Schoole of Abuse*, sig. F2. For a discussion of the letter "to the Gentlewoman Citizens of London" appended to the end of *The School of Abuse*, arguing that Gosson's anxiety is motivated as much by the possibility of women looking at their fellow theatergoers as by the way that male theatergoers look at

them, see Jean Howard, *The Stage and Social Struggle in Early Modern England* (London and New York: Routledge, 1994), pp. 76–80.

12. For some early discussions of this double meaning, see Dorothy Hockey, "Notes Notes, Forsooth . . . ," *SQ* 8, 3 (Summer 1957): 353–8, 355, and David Horowitz, "Imagining the Real," in *Twentieth Century Interpretations of "Much Ado About Nothing,"* ed. Walter R. Davis (Englewood Cliffs NJ: Prentice Hall, 1969), pp. 39–53, 39.

13. The only character in Messina to encourage female speech directly is Don Pedro, who tells Beatrice that "Your silence most offends me" (II.i.252). This response to Beatrice's "I was born to speak all mirth, and no matter" (II.i.251) suggests a sanctioned form of female speech, but one that cannot construct the narratives that shape perception. I am grateful to the anonymous reader for *SEL* for drawing my attention to this exchange.

14. Carol Cook, "'The Sign and Semblance of Her Honor': Reading Gender Difference in *Much Ado about Nothing*," *PMLA* 101, 2 (March 1986): 186–202, 194.

15. Laurie Osborne observes ("Dramatic Play in *Much Ado about Nothing*: Wedding the Italian Novella and English Comedy," *PQ* 69, 2 [Spring 1990]: 167–88) that "the purpose [of staged actions] is not to manipulate events so much as to control the way that others perceive them" (p. 184).

16. See, for instance, Richard Henze's "Deception in *Much Ado abut Nothing*," *SEL* 11, 2 (Spring 1971): 187–201. For a discussion of the way in which this argument naturalizes Don Pedro's deceptions as revelatory rather than constitutive, see Howard, pp. 59–65.

17. S. P. Cerasano, "Half a Dozen Dangerous Words" in *Gloriana's Face: Women, Public and Private, in the English Renaissance*, ed. S. P. Cerasano and Marion Wynne-Davies (New York: Harvester Wheatsheaf, 1992), pp. 167–83, 175.

18. Anthony Dawson, "Much Ado about Signifying," *SEL* 22, 2 (Spring 1982): 211–21, 215.

19. See, for instance, Mares's edition of the play, p. 72.

20. Mares, p. 72, n. 115–6.

21. Mark Taylor, "Presence and Absence in *Much Ado About Nothing*," *CentR* 33, 1 (Winter 1989): 1–12, 4.

22. Margaret is here represented as an observer herself, but to "look out at her lady's chamber window" is to be seen at that window (II.iii.15). As in Gosson's formulation of the female theatergoer, to be a spectator is to become a spectacle.

23. G. Blakemore Evans, ed. *The Riverside Shakespeare* (Boston: Houghton Mifflin Co., 1974), p. 341, n. 44.

24. For a discussion of Don John's use of and representation of language, see Dawson, p. 214.

25. Taylor argues that "the play focuses our attention on [the] blank space[s of Don Pedro's wooing and the scene at Hero's window] as a way of showing how various characters perceive themselves in that blank spot" (p. 5).

26. Beyond this, Stephen Orgel argues that costume on the early modern transvestite stage constitutes the identity of the characters that wear it; in *Twelfth Night* Viola cannot return to her original identity until she recovers her original costume. *Impersonations: The Performance of Gender in Shakespeare's England* (Cambridge: Cambridge Univ. Press, 1996), pp. 103–5.

27. Claire McEachern observes, "Hero's physical resemblance to her father guarantees her mother's fidelity, and with it her father's honor" ("'Fathering Herself': A

Source Study of Shakespeare's Feminism," *SQ* 39, 3 [Autumn 1988]: 269–90), but I think it significant that Hero must "father herself" with her body rather than her mother's words. Michael D. Friedman, in "'Hush'd on Purpose to Grace Harmony': Wives and Silence in *Much Ado About Nothing*," *TJ* 42, 3 (October 1990): 350–63, discusses the stage directions in both the quarto and folio texts which give an entrance in act I, scene i and act II, scene i to "Innogen [Leonato's] wife," and the possibilities of staging Hero's perfectly silent and unacknowledged mother.

28. For discussions of the relationship between silence and gender roles in *Much Ado*, see Howard, pp. 65–70 and Friedman.

29. Henze, p. 194.

30. Gosson, *The Schoole of Abuse*, sig. F2.

31. Many of the accusations against Hero are couched in terms of rhetorical questions. In addition to the examples above, Claudio asks, "Comes not that blood, as modest evidence, / To witness simple virtue? Would you not swear / All you that see her, that she were a maid, / By these exterior shows?" (IV.i.32–5). Leonato finds confirmation in asking, "Would the two princes lie, and Claudio lie, / Who loved her so, that speaking of her foulness, / Washed it in tears?" (IV.i.145–7). Hero's attempt to use this structure, asking "Is it [my name] not Hero? Who can blot that name / With any just reproach?" (IV.i.74–5), collapses when Claudio instantly answers her, "Marry, that can Hero" (IV.i.75).

32. For a discussion of the ambiguity of Hero's blushes and the multiple interpretations available, see David Bevington, *Action is Eloquence: Shakespeare's Language of Gesture* (Cambridge MA and London: Harvard Univ. Press, 1984), pp. 96–7.

33. Cook, p. 192.

34. Friedman, "The Editorial Recuperation of Claudio," *CompD* 25, 4 (Winter 1991–92): 369–86, 373. Friedman's account of the production comes from Pamela Mason's "'Much Ado' at Stratford-upon-Avon, 1949–1976," M. A. thesis (University of Birmingham, England, 1976). In his more recent "Male Bonds and Marriage in *All's Well* and *Much Ado*" (*SEL* 35, 2 [Spring 1995]: 231–49), Friedman also discusses the introduction of the scene of Margaret and Borachio at Hero's window into Kenneth Branagh's 1993 film (pp. 240–1).

35. Branagh, *"Much Ado about Nothing" by William Shakespeare: Screenplay, Introduction, and Notes on the Making of the Film* (London: Chatto and Windus, 1993), p. xv.

36. Howard, p. 61.

2000—Maurice Hunt. "The Reclamation of Language in *Much Ado About Nothing*"

Maurice Hunt (b. 1942) is on the faculty of Baylor University. He is the author/editor of numerous books on Shakespeare, including *Shakespeare's Romance of the Word* (1990), *Shakespeare's Labored Art* (1995), *Shakespeare's Religious Allusiveness: Its Play and Tolerance* (2004), and *Shakespeare's "As You Like It": Late Elizabethan Culture and Literary Representation* (2008). In the following essay, Hunt reacts to the common reading that *Much Ado about Nothing* is focused on the act of hearing and, to perhaps an even greater extent, overhearing. Hunt agrees with this assessment, but also urges that the act of communication itself is essential in understanding the play; to Hunt, Shakespeare "dramatize[s] the potential of speech to exasperate and resolve humankind's wishes and schemes, especially as they involve romantic love." Hunt proposes that the act of listening cannot be fulfilled without someone—or some speech—to listen to, and that while much of the communication in *Much Ado about Nothing* may be false, it is an essential part of the process of "noting" that critics have for more than a century seen as crucial in fully understanding the text. In examining the types of speech (such as Beatrice's more masculine speech patterns, as noted in Cook previously, or the effects of humorous speech) and the context behind it (such as the subterfuge that dominates much of the masked ball scene), Hunt demonstrates that the speaker is as significant—or perhaps even more so—than the listener. Benedick's supposition that "man is a giddy thing; and this is my conclusion" (5.4.107–08) suggests to Hunt that the intent behind the speech is as important as the content itself; and that falsity or inconstancy in one's speech can be forgiven if the speech itself is tempered with the knowledge that it is, in fact, only words. Thus the skirmish of words between Beatrice and Benedick can be more easily forgiven, while Claudio's belief in Don John's lies, for example, suggests that his behavior in shaming Hero at their wedding reflects not only what he has noted but what he, on some level, feels as well.

Interpreters of *Much Ado about Nothing* have often remarked that Shakespeare focuses in this middle comedy upon the faculty of hearing. And indeed "noting," in its senses of listening and eaves dropping, does much to complicate and unravel the play's fable.[1] What is rarely noted in accounts of *Much Ado* is the dependence of hearing upon speaking, the possibility that Shakespeare may also dramatize the potential of speech to exasperate and resolve humankind's wishes and schemes, especially as they involve romantic love. Repeatedly the language of *Much Ado* illustrates the fact that expression often becomes disjoined from meaning. "The body of your discourse is sometime guarded with fragments [trimmed with odds and ends]," Benedick tells jesting Don Pedro, "and the guards are but slightly basted on neither" (1.1.26,5–66).[2] Anne Barton takes Benedick's quip to mean that "the trimmings" of Don Pedro's speech "are very insecurely stitched on too (i.e. they have little connection with what is being said)."[3] A. P. Rossiter has remarked that in *Much Ado* Cupid does not work by slander, but by hearsay.[4] "Of this matter / Is little Cupid's crafty arrow made," Hero pronounces, "That only wounds by hearsay" (3.1.21–23). The word has two parts. In *Much Ado*, "[l]ove by *hearsay*," according to René Girard, "means love by another's voice."[5] Love arises when stratagems of eavesdropping make Benedick, Beatrice, and Claudio fall either in or out of love, but they do so only because of what other characters say, only because of the speech uttered and the attitude of members of the trio toward it. One would assume that a gap of some kind naturally exists between Beatrice's, Benedick's, and Claudio's original self-generated (in some cases faint) amorous inclinations and the romantic love created by others' speech and the speech of lovers molded by their utterances. It is another version of the disjunction between inward meaning and spoken words that we hear in Benedick's quip about the "slightly basted" rhetorical "trimmings" of Don Pedro's speech.

At stake in these examples is what we are accustomed to call the truth. Shakespeare unforgettably invites the question of the relation of spoken language to the truth by showing how easily the words of others cause Benedick and Beatrice to fall in and out of love. In *Much Ado*, Shakespeare suggests that the desire to exert power over another in a way that flatters or amuses the wielder often determines both the use of speech and the control of conversation and monologues. To achieve and exercise personal power, Don Pedro, Benedick, Claudio, and other male characters in *Much Ado* capitalize upon inherent disjunctions between expression and meaning, upon auditors' distrust of an interlocutor's words, and upon speakers' inability to govern their tongues (and thus the language they speak). In this process, patriarchal speech almost always triumphs by mandating its construction of the truth. Marked by irreverence, aggressiveness, and an authoritarian tone and content, Shakespearean patriarchal speech is designed to establish social dominance by twisting, dismissing, or oppressing the words and ideas of others. Moreover, it is not exclusively the property of men. In *Much Ado*, Beatrice's acerbic speech, compared to the qualities of patriarchal language, appears at times more conventionally male than conventionally female. Because the seekers after power in the play often cannot manage problematic language or rule their own tongues, they generally become the verbal and literal victims of someone else's power stratagems, and social prestige shifts distressingly within the community of Messina.

Early in *Much Ado*, Shakespeare represents a paradigmatic image of exemplary speech and speaker. In act 2, scene 1, Beatrice wittily conceives of authentic manhood in terms of moderate speech. "He were an excellent man," she quips, "that were made just in the mid-way between [Don John] and Benedick: the one is too like an image and says nothing, and the other too like my lady's eldest son, evermore tattling" (2.1.6–9). Beatrice's assertion sets up a standard of modulated, tempered speech that she herself cannot practice. "By my troth, niece," Leonato tells sharp-tongued Beatrice, "thou wilt never get thee a husband, if thou be so shrewd of thy tongue" (2.1.16–17). Nevertheless, Beatrice's linguistic analysis applies, strictly speaking, to the attainment of excellent manhood. Thus the tempering of speech that she recommends could possibly rectify certain absolutist traits of patriarchal speech. But self-destructive consequences entailed by the compulsion to acquire and exert social and physical power over others preclude the attainment of this temperance. At least they do so until, suffering adversity, characters such as Benedick learn to modulate significantly their quest for power and thus the speech associated with it. The relatively sanctified, integrated speech of the powerless Hero and that of Friar Francis, who has piously relinquished the pursuit of self-congratulatory power, become guides toward this end for Shakespeare's audience. An appreciation of the melding of their expression and intended meaning depends upon initially grasping the extent of Shakespeare's depiction of the manifold, subtle foibles of language.

Patriarchal speech is often edgy, distrustful, because male speakers frequently imagine that male interlocutors may have competitive designs upon them, or because they are hyperconscious of losing among men a masculine persona. When Claudio asks Benedick, "Is [Hero] not a modest young lady?" (1.1.153),[6] Benedick's response reveals his habitual distrust of the wholesome, straightforward meaning of a friend's speech: "Do you question me as an honest man should do, for my simple true judgement, or would you have me speak after my custom, as being a professed tyrant to their sex?" (1.1.154–57). Benedick implies that he has two kinds of speech—an honest, simple discourse, rarely spoken, and a customary caustic, witty idiom that (by the logic of his own question) is dishonest and false. Benedick has cultivated the reputation of being a tyrant to women in order to enhance his stature (his power) primarily among his male friends. Yet he has become an ironic victim of this strategy, a prisoner of his circulated, anti-feminist sayings. With a life of their own, these witty sayings have created a persona that he believes he must inhabit and maintain. To venture outside of it (as he here intimates he might) is to gamble the loss of a self-fashioned identity and imagined respect. In the present case, Benedick suggests that the risk of simple, relatively honest speech is too great. When Claudio protests, "I pray thee speak in sober judgement," Benedick jokes, "Why, i'faith, methinks she's too low for a high praise, too brown for a fair praise, and too little for a great praise: only this commendation I can afford her, that were she other than she is, she were unhandsome, and being no other but as she is, I do not like her" (1.1.158–64). Benedick's clever paradoxes are sufficiently ambiguous to keep Claudio uncertain of the speaker's feelings. "Thou thinkest I am in sport," the thoroughly frustrated Claudio complains; "I pray thee tell me truly how thou lik'st her" (1.1.165–66). Benedick's linguistic suspicion proves deep-seated, however. He asks Claudio, "But speak you this with a sad brow, or do you play the flouting Jack, to tell us Cupid is a good hare-finder, and Vulcan a rare carpenter? Come, in what key shall a man take you to go in the song?" (1.1.169–73). Benedick's concluding metaphor suggests his notion that talk with Claudio amounts to no more than a kind of duet valuable for its harmony rather than its content, a creation in which one finds one's part in conjunction with other *artistes* of language.

Benedick never does directly answer Claudio's question about Hero's modesty. (He says instead that he sees no sweetness in her.) His reluctance to conform to Claudio's expectation of the rules governing conversation constitutes a comic, poetically just punishment of Claudio. "God help the noble Claudio!" Beatrice has exclaimed concerning Benedick's company; "[i]f he have caught the Benedick, it will cost him a thousand pound ere a be cured" (1.1.80–82). In terms of our subject, Claudio can be said to have "caught the Benedick," for he himself shares his companion's distrust of forthright speech. Responding to Claudio's qualified declaration of love for Hero, Don Pedro pronounces, "Amen, if you love her, for the lady is very well worthy" (1.1.204–5). "You speak this to fetch me in, my lord" (1.1.206), Claudio anxiously replies. "By my troth, I speak my thought" (1.1.207), Don Pedro assures him. When Claudio responds, "And in faith, my lord, I spoke mine" (1.1.208), Benedick cannot resist joking about the extralinguistic guarantee of their words that Don Pedro and Claudio seek in Christian invocations: "And by my two faiths and troths, my lord, I spoke mine" (1.1.209–10).[7] Whatever effective communication Don Pedro and Claudio have achieved gets derailed by Benedick's ingenious witticism about his (and humankind's) double—deceitful—faith and truth. His joke—in his mind, at least—for the moment makes him the dominant speaker among male friends wary through speech of giving auditors an advantage.

The masked ball of *Much Ado* provides characters suspicious of direct speech an opportunity to speak without hesitation or subterfuge, simply because they believe that their visors absolve them from the responsibility of owning their utterances. No longer do they feel compelled to worry about how their words might gain or lose them respect. In such a context, they risk speaking imagined truths. Recognizing Benedick behind his mask (but thinking that he does not recognize her), Beatrice unleashes the aggression that her anxious feeling of vulnerability to men has created by directly, painfully telling him of the foolish ass his self-conceit makes him (2.1.127–33). In other words, she powerfully compensates for her usual secret sense of powerlessness in a decidedly patriarchal society. Admittedly, Beatrice's frustrated affection for Benedick contributes to her aggressiveness, her criticism a personally safe attempt to encourage him to reform himself and his language. But the painful extremity of her portrait of him reveals the deeper source of her aggression in the dynamics of power and powerlessness, which distort the truth of her utterances. "She speaks poniards," Benedick complains, "and every word stabs" (2.1.231–32). Benedick has his flaws, but her verbal portrait of him as "the Prince's jester, a very dull fool; [whose] only gift is in devising impossible slanders" (2.1.127–28) misrepresents—skews—the whole man. Beatrice's criticism of Benedick's "gift," moreover, could just as easily apply to her everyday, ridiculing self.

Characters' inability to control their speech, their failure to shape it to their wills, can be heard throughout *Much Ado*. Benedick's "double" faith reflects his "double tongue"; at least, it does so in Don Pedro's report of Beatrice's opinion of Benedick's verbal duplicity. When Don Pedro tells Benedick that he praised Benedick's knowledge of foreign languages to Beatrice ("'Nay,' said I, 'he hath the tongues'"), he says that she responded, "'That I believe . . . for he swore a thing to me on Monday night, which he forswore on Tuesday morning; there's a double tongue; there's two tongues'" (5.1.164–66). Benedick's double tongue, a characterization reminiscent of that of Demetrius in *A Midsummer Night's Dream*,[8] manifests itself not only in his swearing and forswearing of love for Beatrice, but also in his punning jests, which require the ability to speak two disruptive meanings at once. Swearing, forswearing, and punning in *Much Ado*, as in life, usually involve the imagined acquisition or consolidation of social prestige. The stress in this judgment falls upon the word "imagined." Often punning jokes escape the jester's control, wounding him in the poor opinion of others, even as his swearing and forswearing painfully work eventually against the swearer's image in others' eyes.

Few characters in the Messina of *Much Ado* consistently rule their tongues to their advantage. Underscoring this impression is that of Beatrice's and Benedick's runaway tongues. Both of these characters suffer from logorrhea. "I wonder that you will still be talking, Signior Benedick," Beatrice quips; "nobody marks you" (1.1.107–8). She, however, in Benedick's chauvinistic opinion, is "my Lady Tongue" (2.1.258), a "dish" whose garrulousness makes her unpalatable. Surprisingly, the play's memorable analysis of humankind's inability to govern its tongue belongs to its low-life personage, Borachio. Concerning Borachio's claim that he can tell a story of intrigue, Conrade, uttering a phrase repeated later in *The Tempest*, exclaims, "and now forward with thy tale" (3.3.99–100).[9] The pun latent in this statement—the notion of putting forward something naturally belonging to the rear ("tale" / "tail"—predicts the preposterousness (literally, the backward-firstness) of Borachio's narrative.[10] The beginning of Borachio's tale—"Therefore know, I have earned of Don John a thousand ducats" (3.3.106–7)—is actually its conclusion: the reward that the trick to be narrated brought him. Then, by holding forth on the truth that "the fashion of a doublet, or a hat, or a cloak, is nothing to a man" (3.3.114–34), Borachio makes Conrade complain, "But art not thou thyself giddy with the fashion too, that thou hast shifted out of thy tale into telling me of the fashion?" (3.3.136–38). Thus rebuked, Borachio explains that he has just wooed Margaret by the name of Hero and that she repeatedly bid him good night from the window of Hero's bedchamber. Despite this conformity to Conrade's request, Borachio catches himself up: "I tell this tale vilely—I should first tell thee how the Prince, Claudio, and my master, planted and placed and possessed by my master Don John, saw afar off in the orchard this amiable encounter" (3.3.143–47). Borachio has giddily gone forward with his tale, again telling a later part first. Throughout *Much Ado*, Shakespeare uses forms of the word "giddy" to refer to humankind's inveterate inconstancy (its defining trait, according to the Player King in act 3, scene 2 of *Hamlet*). "For man is a giddy thing, and this is my conclusion" (5.4.106–7), Benedick summarizes near the end of *Much Ado*.[11] Humankind (especially mankind), in this play, reveals its essential giddiness chiefly in inconstant, fickle speech, which often entails the loss of control over logical discourse. Giddy Borachio exemplifies this phenomenon with his wordy, backward-first tale.[12] His loss of linguistic control amounts to a semicomic instance of the flaw that Benedick and Beatrice mutually accuse each other of committing in the form of subversive, irrelevant jests.

The inevitable ambiguity of public speech complicates in *Much Ado* problems of linguistic distrust and loss of control. Beatrice's and Benedick's verbal cleverness allows them to both inject and read what they will into an inherently imprecise symbolic medium of communication.[13] Believing that Beatrice secretly loves him, Benedick often misinterprets her utterances. "Against my will I am sent to bid you come in to dinner," she tells Benedick; when he thanks her for her pains, she coldly replies, "I took no more pains for those thanks than you take pains to thank me" (2.3.238–42). Left alone, Benedick's fertile imagination falls prey to his self-conceit working on the mismatch between a speaker's apparent intention and the broad language that never exactly registers it:[14] "Ha! 'Against my will I am sent to bid you come in to dinner'—there's a double meaning in that. 'I took no more pains for those thanks than you took pains to thank me'—that's as much as to say, 'Any pains that I take for you is as easy as thanks.' If I do not take pity of her, I am a villain; if I do not love her, I am a Jew. I will go get her picture" (2.3.248–54).[15] The inherent imprecision of language thus serves an anxious need to magnify the self's importance. Having taken pleasure in his double tongue (see above, 1.1.209–10), Benedick suffers the poetic justice of misconstruing to his later embarrassment the radical double meaning of Beatrice's speech. At this point, my reader might object that Benedick has in fact not misconstrued the basic tenor of Beatrice's utterance; he or she might argue that Beatrice's hostile and neutral statements serve to mask her conflicted but nevertheless authentic attraction to Benedick and that he intuitively has picked up on this concealed resonance and somehow heard it for what it affectionately is. While this argument carries weight, I would point out that the inevitable ambiguity of Beatrice's and Benedick's dialogue, working with feelings of self-importance, causes each of them much more suffering and public embarrassment concerning their hidden feelings for each other than relatively unambiguous, trusted words of affection would. This is true simply because in the latter case a mode of communication which the world assumes, even if it does not usually practice, would allow their love to bloom naturally.

The physical and social contexts of utterances can significantly affect the designs of speakers intent on using ambiguous language to forge or strengthen social identities.[16] Antonio states that his servant, "in a thick-pleach'd alley in mine orchard" (1.2.9–10), overheard Don Pedro telling Claudio that he plans to propose to Hero. Evidently the density of the foliage warps or muffles Don Pedro's speech, permitting Antonio's man to hear only part of the truth (that Don Pedro woos Hero on behalf of Claudio). In this instance, the context of an utterance determines its meaning as much as the simple mode of hearing does. That the villain Borachio hears the whole truth about Don Pedro's wooing indicates that the arras behind which he hides in a musty room, unlike the garden's foliage, does not in this case significantly damage acoustics. Hero's gentlewoman Margaret demonstrates the extent to which a speaker sometimes goes to neutralize a distorting interpretive context and recover an imagined integrity of self. When Margaret jokes that Hero's heart will "be heavier soon by the weight of a man," Hero exclaims, "Fie upon thee, art not ashamed?" (3.4.25–26). Somewhat indignant, Margaret disavows the bawdy meaning of this jest: "Of what, lady? of speaking honorably? Is not marriage honorable in a beggar? Is not your lord honorable without marriage? I think you would have me say, saving your reverence, 'a husband.' And bad thinking do not wrest true speaking, I'll offend nobody. Is there any harm in 'the heavier for a husband'? None, I think, and it be the right husband, and the right wife; otherwise 'tis light, and not heavy" (3.4.29–36). Margaret tellingly makes the point that a jest's innocuousness lies in the ear of the auditor. If a wife genuinely loves and respects her husband, nothing necessarily salacious attaches to her expression of the thought of her husband's weight during sexual intercourse. "A jest's prosperity lies in the ear / Of him that hears it," Rosaline authoritatively pronounces in Love's Labour's Lost, "never in the tongue / Of him that makes it" (5.2.861–63).[17] Margaret revises this truth so as to suggest that the existential context of a speaker's and auditor's thinking invests the broad ambiguity of speech with relatively accurate meaning.

Still, Margaret has made an obscene jest (to Hero's and our ears, at least), and the troublesome instability of speech has allowed her to escape responsibility for a possibly coarse intention. That Margaret should articulate the above-described principle of language interpretation is heavily ironic. Her bidding Borachio "a thousand times good night" (3.3.142–43) in the name of Hero (given her by Borachio) corrupts Claudio's faith in his beloved. Language is so imprecise that an auditor, suspiciously hearing it in a vile context, can wrench it to conform to a fantasy. Margaret vainly takes pride in her linguistic virtuosity and ability to wiggle out of responsibility for her words' meaning, but she suffers the consequences of Borachio's duplicity when her honestly meant good night (she seems to care for Borachio) goes awry and Leonato later faults her for her part in Hero's slander (5.4.4–6).

Such a nonessential property is speech that socially empowered characters such as Don Pedro and Leonato can appropriate (steal) subordinates' voices, reducing Claudio and Hero to either ventriloquism or silence. In the patriarchal hierarchy of Messina, empowering voices tend to concentrate in the Prince of Aragon, Don Pedro, and Leonato, the governor of Messina and Hero's father.[18] Don Pedro autocratically wrenches Claudio's words of courtship away from the young lover. "Thou wilt be like a lover presently," he tells Claudio, "And tire the hearer with a book of words": "If thou dost love fair Hero, cherish it, / And I will break with her, and with her father, / And thou shalt have her" (1.1.286–90). Not only will Don Pedro conduct Claudio's suit to Leonato (a typically Elizabethan patriarchal arrangement), but he will also, unconventionally, speak Claudio's words of love to his beloved's own ears. Claudio's muteness includes the nonverbal signifier of his face, pale with love, which he thinks speaks his meaning far better than his own words could. "How sweetly you do minister to love," he gratefully tells Don Pedro, "That know love's grief by his complexion!" (1.1.292–93). Still, he would like to speak on his own behalf: "But lest my liking might too sudden seem, / I would have salv'd it with a longer treatise" (1.1.294–95). Don Pedro, however, peremptorily silences him: "What need the bridge much broader than the flood?" (1.1.296). The "flood," of course, is Claudio's imagined passion for Hero; by saying that the lover need not describe it, and that he might briefly "bridge" it, Don Pedro patronizingly suggests that Claudio's love is narrow, relatively unsubstantial. What Claudio could never have supposed when he agreed to Don Pedro's "gracious" offer is the prince's plan to woo Hero on Claudio's behalf from behind a mask, a situation that makes his words of love indistinguishable from Claudio's to Hero's ear. "And in her bosom I'll unclasp my heart," he tells Claudio, "And take her hearing prisoner with the force / And strong encounter of my amorous tale" (1.1.303–5). Don Pedro's powerful metaphor of the tyranny of speech includes as its victim not simply Hero, but Claudio too. Don Pedro has robbed Claudio of his voice in a way that neither Hero nor Claudio could ever have supposed.

Hero's father Leonato and her uncle Antonio generally dictate her speech and enforce her silence. Beatrice makes clear that Antonio's advice to Hero—"Well, niece, I trust you will be rul'd by your father" (2.1.46–47)—chiefly pertains to her speech. "Yes, faith," Beatrice sarcastically responds: "it is my cousin's duty to make curtsy and say, 'Father, as it please you': but yet for all that, cousin, let him be a handsome fellow, or else make another curtsy and say, 'Father, as it please me'" (2.1.48–52). Beatrice's facetious putting of words in silent, obedient Hero's mouth serves to stress the verbal dependency of Claudio's beloved in a patriarchal society. The second imputed utterance—"'Father, as it please me'"— strengthens this negative impression, mainly because no one, onstage or off, could imagine dutiful Hero voicing it.[19] Recognizing Beatrice's insubordination, Leonato coarsely tries to quell it: "Well, niece, I hope to see you one day fitted with a husband" (2.1.57–58). As the obscene connotation of the word later more extensively indicates in *Cymbeline*,[20] "fitted" implies a physical conformity of shape to the complementary male phallus that symbolizes female subordination in a patriarchy. In effect, Leonato crudely suggests that Beatrice's husband will one day, through the effect of his sexual power, reform her language.[21] Cast as a solicitous wish, Leonato's utterance is in fact a harsh threat. That Beatrice ignores this warning and continues her witty, mutinous protest in no way liberates Hero's speech. Ignoring Beatrice's rebellion, Leonato reminds Hero that he has scripted the language of her courtship: "Daughter, remember what I told you: if the Prince do solicit you in that kind, you know your answer" (2.1.61–62). That we never hear Hero's response to this reminder—Beatrice speaks up again, telling Hero that she should "dance out the answer" to Don Pedro (2.1.63–73)— confirms Leonato's linguistic supremacy and her voicelessness.

The presence of socially privileged speakers continues to mute Claudio and Hero even in their betrothal. After Don Pedro has told Claudio that he has "woo'd in thy name" and won both Hero's and her father's consent to the wedding (facts that Leonato immediately confirms) (2.1.298–304), Beatrice must prod the lover: "Speak, Count, 'tis your cue" (2.1.305). Claudio's all-important pledge of love, however, minimizes the agency of language: "Silence is the perfectest herald of joy; I were but little happy, if I could say how much! Lady, as you are mine, I am yours. I give away myself for you, and dote upon the exchange" (2.1.306–9). Regarded in light of his distrust of other speakers' words, Claudio's opting for silence in the midst of several potent, linguistically aggrandizing men is understandable. As is Hero's. She speaks not an audible word in reply to her lover's proposal. "Speak, cousin," irrepressible Beatrice urges, "or (if you cannot) stop his mouth with a kiss, and let not him speak neither" (2.1.310–11). All that shy, dutiful Hero can do is whisper; "My cousin tells him in his ear that he is in her heart" (2.1.315–16), Beatrice remarks. "And so she doth, cousin" (2.1.317), Claudio confirms. Suddenly Hero's silence, which has become a sign of patriarchal oppression in playgoers' minds, acquires positive value. Beatrice and Benedick's previously quoted dialogue indicates that Hero's unheard whispers constitute a private language whose privateness insures the communication of the purity of her thoughts and insulates them from the degradations of a totalitarian codification of verbal meaning. At this moment in the public context, Hero's language is, paradoxically, an eloquent silence. At the beginning of *King Lear*, Cordelia represents (and preserves) an integrity of speech in the midst of a rigged totalitarian discourse. But while attractive, her frank, public utterances begin a disastrous chain of events. Hero, in an admittedly different context, succeeds where Cordelia fails because she forgoes public speech. For the moment she escapes danger because she enfolds a fine private language within an expressive public silence, a strategy apparently unavailable to Cordelia.

Paradoxically Hero's clipped, unconventional language of the heart positively contrasts with the more attractive (because amusingly witty) effusive language of Beatrice that delivers her over to and imprisons her within a patriarchy.

After some "masculine" banter with Don Pedro, Beatrice begs his pardon for its license. "I was born to speak all mirth and no matter" (2.1.330), she explains. "Your silence most offends me, and to be merry best becomes you" (2.1.331–32), Don Pedro patronizingly replies. Beatrice's male banter paradoxically works to subordinate her in a male circle. Obviously the prince applies a double standard here. The socially presumptuous badinage that a woman like Beatrice engages in with men would be offensive in Hero, whereas a silent wiseacre like Beatrice would deprive him and his comrades of amusement. Leonato firmly puts Beatrice in her place when he abruptly says, "Niece, will you look to the things I told you of?" (2.1.337–38) Beatrice's submissive reply—"I cry you mercy, uncle. By your Grace's pardon" (2.1.339–40)—reveals that at this moment she adopts an early modern woman's idiom and accepts her socially and linguistically subordinate role.

The public nature of Hero's nuptials precludes an integrity-preserving private language; consequently, she finds herself forced to participate, with personally disastrous results, in a compromising public dialogue ruled by men with masculinist assumptions. Patriarchal attempts to control the wedding ceremony immediately become apparent. When Friar Francis asks Claudio, "You come hither, my lord, to marry this lady," and the groom abruptly answers "No" (4.1.4–5), the linguistic autocrat Leonato takes charge and reinterprets his blunt reply: "To be married to her, friar: you come to marry her" (4.1.6–7). Uncertainty about the relation of speech acts to one another, and the plausibility of hearing an utterance within related but different social contexts, make language interpretation ambiguous. This fact permits Leonato to hear Claudio's negative in an ingenious but incorrect way, prompting him to remind the friar that the speech act of marriage is properly the churchman's and not Claudio's. Rattled, Leonato appropriates Claudio's voice when the ceremony reaches a potentially dangerous requirement:

> *Friar:* If either of you know any inward impediment why you should not be conjoin'd, I charge you on your souls to utter it.
> *Claud:* Know you any, Hero?
> *Hero:* None, my lord.
> *Friar:* Know you any, count?
> *Leon:* I dare make his answer, none.
>
>   (4.1.11–17)

This patriarchal appropriation of speech sends Claudio into the rage that shatters the wedding ceremony and ends in his cruel claim that Hero has fornicated with Borachio. Claudio's following words incidentally describe Leonato's presumptuous theft of his own speech as much as they do Borachio's bold stealing Hero's honor: "O, what men dare do! What men may do! What men daily do, not knowing what they do!" (4.1.18–19). Leonato's appropriation makes Claudio feel powerless, and he compensates by redirecting his angry frustration onto Hero, who seems generally powerless and so someone lesser than himself at this moment. Thus he explodes against the supposed fornicator perhaps before he had planned to do so. In keeping with the play's emphasis on the appropriation of speech, even body language is seized upon and misconstrued. During their wedding ceremony, Claudio claims that Hero is "but the sign and semblance of her honour":

> Behold how like a maid she blushes here!
> O, what authority and show of truth
> Can cunning sin cover itself withal!
> Comes not that blood as modest evidence
> To witness simple virtue? Would you not swear,
> All you that see her, that she were a maid,
> By these exterior shows? But she is none:
> She knows the heat of a luxurious bed:
> Her blush is guiltiness, not modesty.
>
> (4.1.32–41)

Hero does not even get to translate the "speech" of her blushes—that she is shyly modest. Interpreted by angry Claudio, her vascular language proclaims blood corrupted by guilty lust. Likewise, disconsolate Leonato later exclaims, "Could she here deny / The [supposedly damning] story that is printed in her blood?" (4.1.121–22).[22] Privileged males rob mute Hero even of the speech of her body—yet it was that physical language, in the form of Margaret's embrace of Borachio, that they were all too ready to "hear" and credit, to Hero's demise.

Labeled a "rotten orange" (4.1.31), Hero manages only one utterance in the midst of Leonato's and Claudio's dialogue concerning her supposed promiscuity. When Claudio asserts that he loved Hero as a brother might, with "Bashful sincerity," she protests, "And seem'd I ever otherwise to you?" (4.1.54–55). Her remark, however, only serves to launch Claudio into a condemnation of her imputed seeming. Finally, Don John insists that Claudio's nasty allegations are true (4.1.67). Picking up Don John's last word, stunned Hero can only echo "'True'! O God!" (4.1.68). This three-word utterance captures the essence of Hero's integrity. Ironically, the exclamation "O God!" reflects the piety that makes Hero's utterances true. Her three words "speak" her nature as no other words could. And yet they include a man's word ("true") put in her mouth, in this case by false Don John.

Hero's discourse, even in this utterance that genuinely expresses her, thus partly derives from a socially privileged male statement (Don John's). More important, when heard within the public arena of masculinist prejudgment and condemnation, Hero's exclamation can be misheard as an admission of guilt. When the agonized Hero asks, "What kind of catechizing call you this?" (4.1.78), Claudio coldly replies, "To make you answer truly to your name" (4.1.79). Claudio would fit Hero with the name "common stale," but she protests that her name reflects her inner purity. Only in her name does Hero find a word her own, all her own: "Is it not Hero? Who can blot that name / With any just reproach?" (4.1.80–81). But even this apt, potentially ennobling word is reinterpreted and devalued by the malicious Claudio. "Marry, that can Hero," he snarls; "Hero itself can blot Hero's virtue" (4.1.81–82). It can do so because the name of Hero, in Claudio's estimation, is "now the name of an unchaste woman."[23] Viewed from one perspective, the Hero of Marlowe's *Hero and Leander* (1598) appears an idealized heroine of love (e.g., ll. 1–50, 117–30). But the celebrated Elizabethan epyllion took the representation of Ovidian eroticism to new extremes, and the on-a-pedestal heroine also appeared a gamesome young woman (e.g., ll. 494–96 502–16, 529–36). In fact, like the name Cressida, Hero in a matter of months during 1598 had come for Shakespeare's playgoers to denote a commonplace—a literary stereotype—of an idealized woman of surprisingly erotic behavior.[24] Shakespeare's Hero could be considered a "stale" in two senses: as Claudio's whorish woman and as a familiar commonplace of eroticism. In this latter case, Hero's very name (a staleness) conspires against her, muffling in Claudio's ears the singular integrity of her utterances.[25] Stripped finally of even the protective grace of her name, Hero in despair swoons in a death-like trance.[26] "Hath no man's dagger here a point for me?" (4.1.109), her father moans just before her collapse. Men's words, however, have amounted to seemingly lethal equivalents in his daughter's case. Hamlet's spoken daggers in the ear threaten to become an equally lethal metaphor in *Much Ado about Nothing*.[27]

Granted Shakespeare's portrayal in *Much Ado* of the several inadequacies and failures of speech analyzed in the preceding pages, the play's audience wonders how words, which after all constitute a primary medium of drama, can effect the prosperous outcome of comedy. The reification of language, first as a talismanic name and then as authoritative writing, appears to offer a solution. Throughout *Much Ado*, characters insist upon virtues inherent in name, initially understood to be that of reputation. Concerning Leonato's question about gentlemen lost in the recent battle, a messenger responds, "But few of any sort, and none of name" (1.1.6). Later, during the gulling of Beatrice, Ursula says that "For shape, for bearing, argument, and valour," Benedick "Goes foremost in report through Italy" (3.1.96–97)—a fact (rather than a fabrication) that urges Hero to say, "Indeed he hath an excellent good name" (3.1.98). The powerful condensation of reputation in name leads Claudio, albeit wrongheadedly, to try to make Hero, in the tradition of church catechism, "answer truly [in a negative spirit] to [her] name" (4.1.79).

Historically, the prince's name compresses many more efficacious virtues than simply that of his reputation. Most of these additional attributed virtues in late medieval/early modern cultures possessed quasi-supernatural properties.[28] At first Shakespeare in *Much Ado* skeptically dramatizes this dimension of the word. In the punchy dialogue of Dogberry with the Watch, the playwright appears intent on satirizing characters' stereotypic trust in the magical nature of the royal name. Told that they are to "comprehend" (apprehend) all vagrants, the Watch hears Dogberry conclude that they "are to bid any man stand, in the Prince's name" (3.3.25–26). But the supposed talismanic power of the prince's name disappears in the ridiculous dialogue which follows Dogberry's injunctions:

> *2. Watch*: How if a will not stand?
> *Dog*: Why then, take no note of him, but let him go, and presently call the rest of the watch together, and thank God you are rid of a knave.
> *Verg*: If he will not stand when he is bidden, he is none of the Prince's subjects.
>
> (3.3.27–32)

Here the Second Watchman, George Seacole, the literate neighbor, reveals a distrust of the purportedly essential force of the prince's name. This skeptical attitude gets reinforced by Dogberry's and Verges' absurd advice that the Watch should ignore a vagrant commanded to stop in the prince's name who instead walks away from them. Despite this skeptical staging, later, when Seacole "present[s] [represents] the Prince's own person" (3.3.73) and orders Conrade and Borachio, "in the Prince's name, stand!" (3.3.159), the villains obey his command. Since the Watch (Seacole included) immediately reveal to the villains their stupidity by believing that Deformed is a flesh-and-blood thief, and since Conrade and Borachio meekly obey the order to accompany the constable, playgoers deduce that the arresting force lies not in these obvious bumpkins, but in the prince's name. To the considerable degree that the play's comic resolution hinges on the apprehension of Borachio and his forthcoming recorded admission of guilt, the prince's name uttered by his deputy proves redemptive.[29]

Seacole's ability to reify a truth-producing word is not limited to his role as the prince's deputy. "To be a well-favoured man is the gift of fortune," Dogberry tells him, "but to write and read comes by nature" (3.3.14–16). By nurture—not nature—Shakespeare and his contemporaries would most likely say. By being able to freeze through writing the evanescent, shifting, unreliable word, Seacole adumbrates a remedy for the near-tragedy wrought in *Much Ado* by slander and inherently imprecise speech.[30] It is his "pen and inkhorn" (3.5.54) that fix the verbal testimony of Borachio and provide the record by which Leonato, Don Pedro, and Claudio conclusively learn that an innocent woman has been roundly slandered.[31] "Only get the learned writer to set down our excommunication [examination, communication]," Dogberry ebulliently commands Verges, "and meet me at the jail" (3.5.58–60). Shakespeare stresses the salvatory effect of the reified word by staging the written transcription of testimony in act 4, scene 2, the comic episode of the malefactors' examination.[32] Despite the egregious malapropisms of Dogberry and company on this occasion (a reminder of the play's several problems of language), the Watch's indictment is recorded (4.2.39–59).[33] And it is done so, appropriately enough, in the prince's efficacious name: "Masters," Dogberry addresses the Watch, "I charge you in the Prince's name accuse these men" (4.2.37–38). Nevertheless, one must realize that the pronouncement of the prince's name in *Much Ado* does not, strictly speaking, ideally state the truth or contain a truth; rather, it is an agent of secular power that helps discover or determine the truth. Shakespeare throughout his plays implies that the exercise of secular power to some degree always diminishes or impairs some kind of truth. The marks of physical abuse apparent on the pinioned Conrade's and Borachio's faces at the beginning of the interrogation scene in Kenneth Branagh's recent film version of the play tell audiences that the power of the prince's name may have limits, may need an even more powerful supplement for the complete revelation of a social or a romantic truth. Violated sadistically in this case is a truth about Christian charity (or one about humane treatment). More promising for the reclamation of language in *Much Ado* than the prince's name is the written poetic word.

The beneficial results of freezing unreliable, unconfirmable speech by writing it down also appear in Benedick's and Beatrice's tumultuous courtship. At play's end, Don Pedro's plot to cause the pair to fall irrevocably in love through hearsay comes to nothing when they tell one another that their reported and overheard protestations of love meant nothing. The unconfirmability of uttered speech, vanished into air without a trace, holds hostage the actually affectionate but once again distrustful pair. That is, it does so until Claudio and Hero produce stolen love sonnets of Benedick and Beatrice (5.4.85–90). Their secret writings arrest their words for all to read, conclusively trapping them and giving them the blessed relief of being able to acknowledge their genuine but hitherto denied love. "A miracle! here's our own hands against our hearts," Benedick exclaims; "Come, I will have thee, but by this light I take thee for pity" (5.4.91–93). Rather than showing their hands *against* their hearts, however, Beatrice's and Benedick's amorous handwriting complies with the hidden yearnings of their hearts. The concord that the written legal record creates for the community of Messina has its counterpart in the relatively integrated personalities that the written poetic word makes possible in Beatrice and Benedick. In keeping with its biblical—especially Johannine—power, the imaginative word in *Much Ado* can make a man and woman, in the sense that the lovers' poetry gives them the first basis for the ultimate confidence to recreate themselves through the sacrament of marriage into one sanctified flesh. If spoken slander undoes them, the written poetic word promises their recreation.

But does spoken language have any restorative capability in *Much Ado?* Answering this question involves the subject of physical language. Friar Francis' ability to read the "words" of silent Hero's face leads to a declaration that ultimately saves her marriage. Whereas Claudio misinterprets the message of Hero's blushes (4.1.33–41), the friar correctly "hears" what they "utter":

> I have mark'd
> A thousand blushing apparitions
> To start into her face, a thousand innocent shames
> In angel whiteness beat away those blushes,
> And in her eye there hath appear'd a fire
> To burn the errors that these princes hold
> Against her maiden truth. Call me a fool;
> Trust not my reading nor my observations,
> Which with experimental seal doth warrant
> The tenor of my book; trust not my age,
> My reverence, calling, nor divinity,
> If this sweet lady lie not guiltless here
> Under some biting error.

> (4.1.158–70)

Friar Francis silently reads the words "encoded" in the "book" of Hero's face.[34] Benedick was fooled by Leonato's white beard as the guarantor of Hero's father's words (2.3.118–20).[35] The friar, however, explicitly invokes the nonverbal signifiers of his own advanced age, his priesthood, and the facts of his scholarly, reverent life as validators of his uttered judgment. He, of all the principal male characters in the play, is least caught up in the power games that distort and falsify what is said and heard. Playgoers gather that his piety, his wise chastity of life, determines his ability to perceive and speak the truth. Leonato initially rejects the friar's conclusion, perhaps because the churchman's authority does not derive from the political/sexual patriarchy that Hero's father represents. Nevertheless, Leonato eventually credits the friar's scheme for either reviving Claudio's love for Hero or disposing of her among a religious sisterhood. This scheme entails the advice that Leonato broadcast Hero's "death," the report prompting Claudio's imagination to revalue what has been lost. Friar Francis' formulation of the dynamics of revaluing what has been lost amounts to the most eloquent, moving speech in *Much Ado* (4.1.210–43). It does, with Benedick's urging, win over Leonato, and it is a qualified success.[36] These facts testify to the source of the speech's authority, a learned, relatively pure speaker, disinterested in whether his scheme might bring him social prestige. In this respect, he contrasts sharply with his counterpart, Friar Lawrence in *Romeo and Juliet*, whose similar scheme is hatched partly to bring him credit for reconciling the Capulets and Montagues. Its failure theoretically is in keeping with the impurity—the vanity—of its conception.

The qualified success of Friar Francis' language contradicts Leonato's opinion about the ineffectuality of similar spoken advice. This opinion deserves quotation. Suffering from the imagined sin of his daughter and the ruin of his name, Leonato tells his brother Antonio that he could only credit the uttered counsel of a man exactly like himself, one who has been wronged by the sexual lapse of a daughter once dearly loved. "But there is no such man," Leonato moans,

> for, brother, men
> Can counsel and speak comfort to that grief
> Which they themselves not feel; but tasting it,
> Their counsel turns to passion, which before
> Would give preceptial medicine to rage,
> Fetter strong madness in a silken thread,
> Charm ache with air, and agony with words.
> No, no, 'tis all men's office to speak patience
> To those that wring under the load of sorrow,
> But no man's virtue nor sufficiency
> To be so moral when he shall endure
> The like himself. Therefore give me no counsel:
> My griefs cry louder than advertisement.
>
> (5.1.20–31)

Leonato has apparently forgotten that a man most unlike himself, Friar Francis, counseled patience in language so charged that Leonato agreed to defer immediate judgment and participate in the saving plan proposed. A relatively dispassionate priest who has never had a daughter successfully inculcates a patience within Leonato that gives the friar's plan time to work. In one sense, Friar Francis' sayings have proved medicinal.

Given the role of the friar's language in Leonato's ultimate rehabilitation, playgoers conclude that Hero's father's part in the subsequent linguistic process of Claudio's recreation of Hero is fitting. As part of the friar's stratagem for renovating Claudio's love, Leonato commands the young man to compose a poetic epitaph, hang it on Hero's tomb, and "sing it to her bones" (5.1.279), actions which amount to recompense for participating in potentially lethal slander. Act 5, scene 3 stages this ritual behavior. Claudio's epitaph immortalizes Hero through the proclaimed fame of her chastity, slandered by villains. Like those of Shakespeare's sonnets, the text of *Much Ado* has survived time's ravages. In both cases, the poetic word grants a kind of eternity—to the Young Man of the sonnets and to Hero, "praising her [even after the Renaissance Claudio is] dumb" (dead) (5.3.10). Claudio's recreative words compensate for his earlier destructive language. His song has an effect both cathartic (for the speaker) and resurrectional (for the subject):

> *Pardon, goddess of the night,*
> *Those that slew thy virgin knight;*
> *For the which, with songs of woe,*
> *Round about her tomb they go.*
>   *Midnight, assist our moan,*
>   *Help us to sigh and groan,*
>   *Heavily, heavily:*
> *Graves, yawn and yield your dead,*
> *Till death be uttered*
>   *Heavily, heavily.*
>
>   (5.3.12–21)

The notion that this song should be sung "Till *death be uttered*" has purgative overtones. While "*uttered*" may mean "fully expressed, i.e. adequately lamented,"[37] the word also connotes "finally articulated, finally expelled." The idea that speech can triumph over mortality gets reinforced by the proximate command that graves open to yield their dead. The conceit entails enlisting wraith-like mourners who can augment the volume of laments. By circling the tomb chanting the song and vowing to repeat the ceremony yearly (5.3.23), Claudio and Don Pedro, through incantatory means, intend to purge their sin and cast out (off) death. This last effect involves not so much a miracle as it does permanent release from feelings of morbidity and despair.

Nevertheless, metaphoric resurrection gets attached to Claudio's and Don Pedro's conceit in the suggestion of death's expulsion. Playgoers sense that privileged speech (elevated by being sung poetry) is beginning to work in Claudio's mind the resurrection of Hero. Intellectually, the charming effects of this self-begot language stimulate Claudio's imagination in the idealizing of Hero's image and the reclamation of his love. What was dead comes alive. And it does so through the force of poetic words, further empowered by their utterance in a ritual context. Late in the play, when Claudio and Don Pedro insist that Antonio's "daughter" is "Another Hero!" "The former Hero! Hero that is dead!" (5.4.62, 65), Leonato calmly explains, "She died, my lord, but whiles her slander liv'd" (5.4.66). His remark reemphasizes the main fact of the epitaph scene— that Hero was reborn when near-magical words of repentance and catharsis superseded (killed) the slander with which Hero's loss was synonymous.[38]

Likewise, adversity and the self-examination that arises from it reform, partially at least, Benedick's speech. Together they work to dissolve the self-importance that distorts and inflates language. Benedick experiences an uncharacteristic impoverishment of speech as a result of Claudio's brutal destruction of the marriage ceremony and slander of Hero: "For my part I am so attir'd in wonder," he admits, "I know not what to say" (4.1.144–45). Related to this inarticulateness, his love for Beatrice makes him realize, perhaps for one of the first times in his life, that he can have feelings that the most clever playing with language cannot convey. Attempting to express his passion for Beatrice in the form of a sonnet, he discovers, "Marry, I cannot show it in rhyme; I have tried. I can find out no rhyme to 'lady' but 'baby'—an innocent rhyme; for 'scorn,' 'horn,'—a hard rhyme; for 'school,' 'fool'—a babbling rhyme; very ominous endings! No, I was not born under a rhyming planet, nor I cannot woo in festival terms" (5.2.34–40). The "halting" sonnet that Benedick finally manages to write is valuable as inscribed public proof of his love rather than as an adequate conveyor of that love. In this respect, he contrasts with Claudio, renovated through the vehicle of poetry. Nevertheless, love—as it does in a somewhat different way for Claudio—joins with adversity to correct, that is to say, to chasten and simplify Benedick's speech.

Like Shakespeare's King Henry V with regard to Katherine Princess of France, Benedick eschews "festival terms" and becomes disposed to woo Beatrice in plain, direct, unequivocal language. This plain idiom is heard almost immediately in Benedick's unprecedented declining a match of jests with Beatrice. When he says that only foul words passed between himself and Claudio and demands a kiss, she jokes: "Foul words is but foul wind, and foul wind is but foul breath, and foul breath is noisome; therefore I will depart unkiss'd" (5.2.49–51). Benedick, however, protests, "Thou has frighted the word out of its right sense, so forcible is thy wit. But I must tell thee plainly, Claudio undergoes my challenge, and either I must shortly hear from him, or I will subscribe him a coward" (5.2.52–56). Significantly, Benedick objects for the first time in *Much Ado* to the disruptive, scornful jesting that has distinguished his language. The key phrase in Benedick's quoted protest is "tell thee plainly"—a mode of speech auditors would never have predicted from Benedick. His criticism of jesting necessarily entails an abatement of the vain need to call attention to himself through the supposedly amusing (but actually hostile) punning disruption of others' speech meanings. Don Pedro earlier foresaw Benedick's capacity for authentic speech. "He hath a heart as sound as a bell," Don Pedro asserted, "and his tongue is the clapper; for what his heart thinks, his tongue speaks" (3.2.11–13). While in its local context Don Pedro's remark has slightly negative overtones (Benedick lacks an internal censor of impulsive speech that consequently rings a bit brazenly), his judgment forecasts Benedick's ability to articulate genuine heart-felt speech that is not overly calculated.[39]

The negative connotations of Don Pedro's statement suggest that speech in *Much Ado* can be tempered but not wholly reformed. Benedick could be said, at play's end, to approximate roughly Beatrice's model of a tempered speaker midway between Don John's sullen silences and terseness and an uneducated Benedick's disruptive, oblique garrulousness. Benedick does not completely exorcise his jesting spirit after his criticism of Beatrice's punning word associations (see, for example, 5.2.82–86, 5.2.102–4, and 5.4.48–51), but his manifestation of a new confidence to withstand barbed witticisms without responding in kind reflects his tempering of a problematic speech trait. Hearing Don Pedro tease him with being "'Benedick, the married man'" (5.4.98), he steadfastly pronounces, "I'll tell thee what, Prince; a college of wit-crackers cannot flout me out of my humour. Dost thou think I care for a satire or an epigram? No: if a man will be beaten with brains, a shall wear nothing handsome about him. In brief, since I do purpose to marry, I will think nothing to any purpose that the world can say against it; and therefore never flout at me for what I have said against it; for man is a giddy thing, and this is my conclusion" (5.4.99–107).

Benedick realizes that a person may with genuine impunity contradict one of his or her previous statements, as long as the speaker understands that the fault lies not in language but in the essentially inconstant humanity of the speaker. This inconstancy—this "giddiness"—will always preclude the ideal tempering of one's speech. Nevertheless, a less-than-perfect tempering of speech and the kind of verbal contradiction represented by Benedick can be harmless and blameless as long as speakers' self-awareness of their own inconstancy breeds the humility in everyone not to make too much of a linguistic inconsistency or fault.[40] Coupled with this humility is the self-respect that allows scornful jests to never influence one's settled opinions and behavior, ridiculous though these attributes at times may be. Benedick, with these insights expressed in relatively unadorned, direct speech, fulfills in *Much Ado* the secondary etymology of his name: "Speak Well" ("Bene-Dic").[41] While Benedick's name will never achieve the talismanic power of the Prince of Messina's, it does at last truly capture and express a palpable new understanding refined in the crucible of hearsay and slander.

NOTES

1. See, for example, Paul A. Jorgensen, "*Much Ado about Nothing*," in *Redeeming Shakespeare's Words* (Berkeley: University of California Press, 1962), 22–42.

2. All quotations of *Much Ado about Nothing* are from the Arden text, ed. A. R. Humphreys (London: Methuen, 1981).

3. Anne Barton, introduction to *Much Ado about Nothing*, in *The Riverside Shakespeare*, ed. G. Blakemore Evans et al. (Boston: Houghton Mifflin, 1997), 369. Since the word "guarded" for Shakespeare's contemporaries could mean both "protected" and "ornamented," the secondary connotation of the word in Benedick's quip ironically conveys the speaker's use of puns and facetious speech to protect a vulnerable, straight-thinking, straight-talking self. Here he imagines that Don Pedro uses jests for the same purpose.

4. A. P. Rossiter, *Angel with Horns and Other Shakespeare Lectures*, ed. Graham Storey (New York: Theatre Arts Books, 1961), 65–81, esp. 68: "Cupid is not responsible for calumny; but 'hearsay' is a main force in both love-plots: each is about its effects on proud, self-willed, self-centered and self-admiring creatures."

5. René Girard, "Love by Hearsay: Mimetic Strategies in *Much Ado about Nothing*," in *A Theater of Envy: William Shakespeare* (New York: Oxford University Press, 1991), 82.

6. Carol Thomas Neely, in *Broken Nuptials in Shakespeare's Plays* (New Haven, CT: Yale University Press, 1985), notes that "Claudio protects himself from Hero's sexuality by viewing her as a remote, idealized love object who is not to be touched or even talked to: 'she is the sweetest lady that ever I looked on' (1.1.183)" (44).

7. For the extralinguistic properties of the speech act of a spoken oath, see Michel Foucault, *The Archaeology of Knowledge*, trans. A. M. Sheridan Smith (1969; reprint, New York: Harper and Row, 1976), 83; and John Searle, 'A Taxonomy of Illocutionary Acts,' in *Language, Mind, and Knowledge*, ed. Keith Gunderson (Minneapolis: University of Minnesota Press, 1975), 344–69, esp. 354.

8. See Maurice Hunt, "The Voices of *A Midsummer Night's Dream*," *Texas Studies in Literature and Language* 34 (1992): 218–38, esp. 222–23.

9. For the dramatic importance of this idea in *The Tempest*, see Maurice Hunt, *Shakespeare's Romance of the Word* (Lewisburg, PA: Bucknell University Press, 1990), 117–19.

10. For the centrality of preposterousness in this literal sense in the design of *Love's Labour's Lost*, See Patricia Parker, "Preposterous Reversals: *Love's Labor's Lost*," *Modern Language Quarterly* 54 (1993) 435–82.

11. That the theme of human "giddiness" (radical inconstancy) is central to the design of *Much Ado* has been argued by Ejner J. Jensen, *Shakespeare and the Ends of Comedy* (Bloomington: Indiana University Press, 1991), 71; and by Graham Storey, "The Success of *Much Ado about Nothing*," in *More Talking of Shakespeare*, ed. John Garrett (New York: Theatre Arts Books, 1959), 128–43, esp. 142.

12. Mark Taylor, in "Presence and Absence in *Much Ado about Nothing*," *Centennial Review* 33 (1989): 1–12, has argued that Borachio's violation of chronology in telling his tale merely betrays the Spanish etymology of his name—"borracho" (drunkard). But while Borachio may have just emptied several cans of ale, he remains sufficiently sober to make his purported digression on fashion illustrate humankind's propensity for giddiness, for inconstancy in all things. When impatient Conrade interjects, "But art not thou thyself giddy with the fashion too, that thou hast shifted out of thy tale into telling me of the fashion?" (3.3.136–38), Borachio carefully answers, "Not so, neither; but know that I have tonight wooed Margaret, the Lady Hero's gentlewoman, by the name of Hero" (3.3.139–41). Borachio's reply strongly implies that he calculated his anatomy of fashion to exemplify the universal trait of inconstancy that Margaret practices when she abandons loyalty to her mistress for participation in her lover's strange charade of switching names. In other words, Borachio's strategy may be partly designed to excuse Margaret's behavior. For other arguments that Borachio's account of fashion does not constitute a digression, see John A. Allen, "Dogberry," *Shakespeare Quarterly* 24 (1973): 35–53, esp. 40–43; and David Ormerod, "Faith and Fashion in *Much Ado about Nothing*," *Shakespeare Survey* 25 (1972): 93–105, esp. 93–95.

13. "In the sixteenth century," Margreta de Grazia argues, "it was assumed that defects in man brought about confused speech; in the seventeenth century, it became widely held that confused speech brings on many of the defects in man" ("Shakespeare's View of Language: An Historical Perspective," *Shakespeare Quarterly* 29 [1978]: 381). De Grazia's judgment is uncannily justified by the facts

that *Much Ado* most likely straddles the two centuries and that in it, Shakespeare depicts both of the relationships that De Grazia describes.

14. The definitive (and original) major study of this aspect of Shakespeare's art—the problematic difference between a character's singular intention and the less specific public, social language that necessarily distorts (or perverts) it to some degree—appears in Sigurd Burckhardt, *Shakespearean Meanings* (Princeton, NJ: Princeton University Press, 1968), esp. 22–46 and 260–84. Francis Bacon, in his well-known description of the Idols of the Market-Place in *Novum Organum* anticipates Burckhardt's linguistic thesis (see *The Works of Francis Bacon*, ed. James Spedding, Robert Ellis, and Douglas Denon Heath, 15 vols. [London, 1875], 4:54–55 and 61).

15. Anthony B. Dawson, in "Much Ado about Signifying," *Studies in English Literature* 22 (1982): 211–21, esp. 215, also claims that this dialogue is about Benedick's preoccupation with making others' words mean what he would have them signify. Dawson asserts that "[i]n general [in *Much Ado*], language, as a system of messages, is consistently, comically, called into question: further messages are intercepted, misinterpreted, overheard in a variety of ways that move the plot forward and pose problems of interpretation for the characters" (212).

16. See J. R. Firth, *Papers in Linguistics: 1934–51* (London: Oxford University Press, 1957), 27 and 182; M. A. K. Halliday, *Language as Social Semiotic: The Social Interpretation of Language and Meaning* (London: Edward Arnold, 1978), 27–35, passim; and Fernando Peñalosa, *Introduction to the Sociology of Language* (Rowley, MA: Newbury House, 1981), 23.

17. *The Riverside Shakespeare* (See note 3).

18. Camille Wells Slights has argued that *Much Ado* "*is* centrally concerned with the social nature of language—with the power of language and with language as an articulation of power" ("The Unauthorized Language of *Much Ado about Nothing*," in *The Elizabethan Theatre XII*, ed. A. L. Magnusson and C. E. McGee [Toronto: P. D. Meany, 1993], 116). Slights anticipates several of my points—such as that about this comedy's characters' "talk about the problematics of language" (114) in the play's opening scenes (113–15)—but her line of argument and evidence remain essentially different from mine.

19. Michael Taylor, in "*Much Ado about Nothing*: The Individual in Society," *Essays in Criticism* 23 (1973): 146–53, argues that the dialogue presently under analysis (2.1.46–52) joins with other passages in the play to associate certain traits of Beatrice with more extreme, pernicious counterparts in Don John: "Like Don John, she appears to be totally antagonistic to any compulsion from without, jealously guarding the freedom of her individual will" (146–47). I would add that in the present case, that freedom involves the right of a woman to speak and be heard in her own right, a deserved liberty that makes Beatrice's rebellion different in kind from Don John's.

20. See David Bergeron, "Sexuality in *Cymbeline*," *Essays in Literature* 10 (1983): 159–68, esp. 163.

21. David Ormerod alternatively judges that Leonato's harsh remark (2.1.57–58), "if we discount the lewd joke, is tantamount to saying that a man is no more than the clothes he wears" ("Faith and Fashion," 96)—in this case the "fashionable" woman "fitted" to him.

22. Citing these lines, John Drakakis claims that Leonato "transforms Hero's body into a 'writing' . . . lamenting her *loss of value* as a signifier in the masculine discourse of possession" ("Trust and Transgression: The Discursive Practices of

Much Ado about Nothing," in *Post-Structuralist Readings of English Poetry*, ed. Richard Machin and Christopher Norris [Cambridge: Cambridge University Press, 1987], 77).

23. The quoted opinion is that of Anne Barton in *The Riverside Shakespeare*, 386.

24. For this stereotyping of Cressida's name, see Maurice Hunt, "Shakespeare's *Troilus and Cressida* and Christian Epistemology," *Christianity and Literature* 42 (1993): 243–60, esp. 255–56.

25. Like Drakakis, Slights concludes that Hero, "dehumanized by being deprived of language . . . to her father's eyes becomes not a speaking subject but the objectified printed text of the story Claudio has told: 'the story that is printed in her blood'" ("Unauthorized Language," 121)—printed also, I would add, in a text written by Christopher Marlowe.

26. Jean Howard concludes that "when Hero hears herself named whore at her wedding, she does not contest that construction of herself; she swoons beneath its weight. It is as if there were no voice with which to contest the forces inscribing her in the order of fallen 'woman' women. . . . What Claudio gets [at play's end] is the still-silent Hero, the blank sheet upon which men write whore or goddess as their fears or desires dictate" ("Renaissance Antitheatricality and the Politics of Gender and Rank in *Much Ado about Nothing*," in *Shakespeare Reproduced: The Text in History and Ideology*, ed. Jean E. Howard and Marion F. O'Connor [New York: Methuen, 1987], 179 and 181).

27. The motif of imperfect speech in *Much Ado* symbolically condenses in Balthasar's claim that his "bad . . . voice" slanders the musical songs that he sings (2.3.44–45). After he sings "*Sigh no more, ladies, sigh no more*," Benedick jokes, "And he had been a dog that should have howled thus, they would have hanged him, and I pray God his bad voice bode no mischief" (2.3.79–81). Benedick confirms the notion of a bad voice ruining an exquisite message. The episode assumes an emblematic significance in the flawed Messinan world of words.

28. Focusing upon Genesis 2:19–20, wherein God parades the animals by Adam to encourage him to name them, early modern commentators such as Richard Mulcaster (1582) and Joshua Sylvester (1592) extrapolated the idea that Adam's intuitive naming the creatures instantaneously gave him knowledge of their essences. (For the historical development of this idea, see William C. Carroll, *The Great Feast of Language in "Love's Labour's Lost"* [Princeton, NJ: Princeton University Press, 1976], 12–13). *Richard II* constitutes Shakespeare's fullest analysis of the theory that the ruler's name (and his naming) have supernatural properties and effects. In respect to this, see James L. Calderwood, *Metadrama in Shakespeare's Henriad: "Richard II" to "Henry V"* (Berkeley: University of California Press, 1979), 13.

29. Phoebe S. Spinrad, in "Dogberry Hero: Shakespeare's Comic Constables in Their Communal Context," *Studies in Philology* 89 (1992): 161–78, judges that "[s]ince Dogberry invokes 'the Prince's name' when briefing his deputies, he is obviously aware of the bureaucratic channels to which he is responsible" (165). My analysis, however, indicates that this invocation involves much more than bureaucratic deference. Nevertheless, René Girard asserts that "there is one more reason for the general instability of opinion in *Much Ado about Nothing*. This is the prince himself, around whom everyone revolves, but who cannot provide a stable center for the very reason that he is just as decentered and mimetic as everybody else"

("Love by Hearsay," 88). My analysis concludes that while the Prince of Messina may to some degree be "decentered," his name becomes a central deed in the play. In this respect, he contrasts with Don John who, as John Drakakis has pointed out, lacks a legitimate name, a fact which precludes the lasting power to name socially or create verbally ("Trust and Transgression," 73).

30. Jonathan Goldberg, in *Writing Matter: From the Hands of the English Renaissance* (Stanford, CA: Stanford University Press, 1990), provides extensive evidence for the early modern English belief that the word inscribed by handwriting invests the oral word with diverse social energies and efficacies.

31. While 3.5.53–55 clearly indicates Shakespeare's intention to make Seacole the recorder of the malefactors' examination, the staging of that event (4.2) suggests that the Town Clerk (or sexton) may have performed the role in original performances. While Seacole is present in this latter episode, Dogberry exclaims, "where's the sexton? Let him write down 'the Prince's officer coxcomb'" and "O that he [the Town Clerk] were here to write me down an ass!" (4.2.67–68, 72–73). (Dogberry's second utterance occurs moments after the Town Clerk's exit, at 4.2.63.) Nevertheless, my point about the value of the written as opposed to the spoken word in *Much Ado*'s subplot stands irrespective of the identity of the transcriber in act 4, scene 2.

32. Spinrad remarks that Dogberry does not appear "to be liable to an unpopular constable's problem of having literate but malicious neighbors falsify what they are reading and writing for him. Dogberry's literate deputies obey his orders, and the Sexton (or Town Clerk) who transcribes the testimony in the examination of prisoners is careful to guide the testimony into the correct channels" ("Dogberry Hero," 164).

33. Throughout his career Shakespeare implies that truth in speech has something to do with rationality and then something to do with qualities beyond (or apart) from rationality: qualities such as the madness of King Lear, the stupidity of Bottom, and the piety, virtually muted in Hero's case, of Leonato's daughter and of Friar Francis in *Much Ado*. In his denseness and malapropisms, Dogberry invites comparison with Bottom, but a search of the text of *Much Ado* turns up no speech of Dogberry's comparable to Bottom's garbled yet nevertheless authoritative echo of passages from 1 Corinthians in his awestruck formulation of supernatural mysteries that he has experienced (*A Midsummer Night's Dream, The Riverside Shakespeare* 4.1.203–17). Shakespeare gives certain marginalized characters—the biblical last who will one day be first—an inside track on true speech (which is close to silence) because their authority appears guaranteed by something other than socially privileged male statements, in short, by God. Dogberry joins Friar Francis and Hero as one of the more pious characters in *Much Ado* (God's name is repeatedly on his lips), and he approaches the truth-speaking of the other two characters but he does not quite match their achievement, perhaps because a vain insistence on social prestige (power) afflicts his speech. The nature of Dogberry's comic malapropisms betrays his pitiful desire that auditors perceive him to be more educated and socially prominent than he will ever be (e.g., 4.2.75–83). Jean Howard has concluded that Dogberry's and Verges' "gift of intuition is bought at the price of speech and rationality. Dogberry and Verges exist almost outside of language, and this displacement denies them any real social power" ("Renaissance Antitheatricality," 177).

34. For the literary topoi of the human face as a "book" to be read, see Ernst R. Curtius, *European Literature and the Latin Middle Ages*, trans. Willard R. Trask (1953; reprint, New York: Harper and Row, 1963), 334–37.

35. Benedick receives comic poetic punishment for his engrained distrust of others' speech when, during the scene of the trick played upon him, Leonato's white beard seems to him to confirm the truth of the old man's actually deceitful words of Beatrice's amorous behavior. "I should think this a gull, but that the white-bearded fellow speaks it. Knavery cannot sure hide himself in such reverence" (2.3.118–20). But knavery does lurk behind this cliché of truthfulness. Despite his verbal acumen, Benedick labors under some mistaken stereotypes of kinds of speakers and their language, one of which is that elderly years and the whiteness of a beard always promise the truth of speech by a possessor of these attributes. In this respect, Benedick appears verbally naive.

36. The friar predicts that Claudio will revalue Hero when he hears that "she died upon his words" (4.1.223). In fact, he repairs his idea of her only after he learns from Borachio that she was the victim of Don John's slanderous plot (5.1.225–46). The report of her wronged innocence, not the narration of her death from his rejection, moves Claudio to reimagine her worth. "Sweet Hero!" Claudio concludes; "Now thy image doth appear / In the rare semblance that I lov'd it first" (5.1.245–46). This notorious discrepancy does not override Claudio's general conformity to the friar's psychological script. Among the many commentators on the play who have remarked this discrepancy are Barbara K. Lewalski, "Love, Appearance, and Reality: *Much Ado about Something*," *Studies in English Literature* 8 (1968): 235–51, esp. 249–50; Carol Cook, "'The Sign of Her Honor': Reading Gender Difference in *Much Ado about Nothing*," *PMLA* 101 (1986): 186–202, esp. 196–97; and Neely, *Broken Nuptials*, 51–53. Neely remarks that "only in *Antony and Cleopatra* and *Cymbeline* does the mock death by itself lead to the guilt, penitence, and forgiveness predicted by the Friar [of *Much Ado*]" (52).

37. *The Riverside Shakespeare*, 394.

38. My argument for the importance of the tomb/epitaph scene for the potential success of Claudio and Hero's later marriage questions the negative overtones of Neely's claim that "Claudio performs a ritualistic but impersonal penance" (*Broken Nuptials*, 55).

39. Several critics have charted a reformation of Benedick's character in the latter acts of *Much Ado*. Among them is Jensen, who notes that "[s]omewhere between Beatrice's account of Benedick as boaster, coward, trencherman, and affliction and the messenger's report of a good soldier' and one who 'hath done good service . . . in these wars' . . . exists the Benedick who will emerge later in the play" (*Shakespeare and the Ends of Comedy*, 50).

40. Lewalski identifies Benedick's play-ending assessment of humankind's "giddiness" as an insight comparable to the Neoplatonic mode of knowledge that love brings: "Benedick explicitly renounces foolish consistency, and his observation that 'man is a giddy thing' (V.iv.108) signals the lovers' new affirmation of the whole range of human life and activity" ("Love, Appearance, and Reality," 245).

41. Critics generally agree that the primary Latin etymology of Benedick's name is "'Benedictus,' he who is blessed" (Humphreys' Introduction of *Much Ado* 87), a counterpart to "'Beatrix,' she who blesses" (88). Considered in light of the two characters' painful mutual gibes, the complementary primary etymologies appear highly ironic.

BIBLIOGRAPHY

General Bibliography

Allen, John A. "Dogberry." *Shakespeare Quarterly* 24.1 (1973): 35–53.

Ansari, A. A. *"Much Ado about Nothing* and the Masks of Reality." *Aligarh Journal of English Studies* 5 (1980): 175–89.

Bache, William B. "The 'Eye of Love' in *Much Ado About Nothing.*" *Discourse* 11 (1968): 224–29.

Baker, David Weil. "'Surpris'd with All': Rereading Character in *Much Ado about Nothing.*" *Second Thoughts: A Focus on Rereading.* Ed. David Galef. Detroit, MI: Wayne State UP; 1998. 228–45.

Barber, C. L. *Shakespeare's Festive Comedy: A Study of Dramatic Form and Its Relation to Social Custom.* Princeton, NJ: Princeton University Press, 1959.

Barish, Jonas A. "Pattern and Purpose in the Prose of *Much Ado about Nothing.*" *Renaissance Studies in Honor of Carroll Camden.* Ed. J. A. Ward. Houston, TX: Rice University Press, 1974. 19–30.

Berry, Edward I. *Shakespeare's Comic Rites.* Cambridge: Cambridge University Press, 1984.

Berry, Ralph. *"Much Ado About Nothing*: Structure and Texture." *English Studies: A Journal of English Language and Literature* 52 (1971): 211–23.

Berry, Ralph. *Shakespeare's Comedies: Explorations in Form.* Princeton, NJ: Princeton University Press, 1972.

Bloom, Harold. *William Shakespeare: Comedies & Romances.* New York: Chelsea House, 1986.

Branagh, Kenneth, and William Shakespeare. *Much Ado About Nothing: Screenplay,Introduction, and Notes on the Making of the Film.* London: Chatto & Windus, 1993.

Brown, John Russell. *Shakespeare, Much Ado About Nothing and As You Like It: A Casebook.* London: Macmillan, 1979.

Burke, Robert R. "The Other Father in *Much Ado about Nothing.*" *Explorations in Renaissance Culture* 19 (1993): 85–96.

Champion, Larry S. *Evolution of Shakespeare's Comedy: A Study in Dramatic Perspective.* Cambridge: Harvard University Press, 1970.

Charney, Maurice. *Shakespearean Comedy.* New York: New York Literary Forum, 1980.

Cheney, Patrick. "Halting Sonnets: Poetry and Theater in *Much Ado about Nothing.*" *A Companion to Shakespeare's Sonnets.* Ed. Michael Schoenfeldt. Oxford: Blackwell, 2007.

Collington, Philip D. "'Stuffed with All Honourable Virtues': *Much Ado about Nothing* and *The Book of the Courtier.*" *Studies in Philology* 103.3 (2006): 281–312.

Crichton, Andrew B. "Hercules Shaven: A Centering Mythic Metaphor in *Much Ado about Nothing.*" *Texas Studies in Literature and Language* 16 (1975): 619–26.

Daalder, Joost . "The 'Pre-History' of Beatrice and Benedick in *Much Ado about Nothing.*" *English Studies* 85.6 (2004): 520–27.

Davenant, William. *The Law Against Lovers.* London: Cornmarket Press, 1970.

Dobranski, Stephen B. "Children of the Mind: Miscarried Narratives in *Much Ado about Nothing.*" *SEL: Studies in English Literature, 1500–1900* 38.2 (1998): 233–50.

Drakakis, John. "Trust and Transgression: The Discursive Practices of *Much Ado about Nothing.*" *Post-Structuralist Readings of English Poetry.* Ed. Richard Machin and Christopher Norris. Cambridge: Cambridge University Press, 1987. 59–84.

Draper, John W. "Benedick and Beatrice." *Journal of English and Germanic Philology* 41 (1942): 140–49.

Draper, John W. "Dogberry's Due Process of Law." *Journal of English and Germanic Philology* 42 (1943): 563–78.

Draper, John William. *Stratford to Dogberry: Studies in Shakespeare's Earlier Plays.* Pittsburgh: University of Pittsburgh Press, 1961.

Draper, Ronald P. *Shakespeare, the Comedies.* New York: St. Martin's Press, 2000.

Elam, Keir. *Shakespeare's Universe of Discourse: Language-games in the Comedies.* Cambridge: Cambridge University Press, 1984.

Evans, Bertrand. *Shakespeare's Comedies.* Oxford: Clarendon Press, 1960.

Evans, John X. "The Villainy of 'One Deformed': The Complex Word Fashion in *Much Ado About Nothing.*" *Literary Studies: Essays in Memory of Francis A. Drumm.* Ed. John H. Dorenkamp. Worcester, MA: College of the Holy Cross, 1974. 91–114.

Fleck, Andrew. "The Ambivalent Blush: Figural and Structural Metonymy, Modesty, and *Much Ado about Nothing.*" *ANQ* 19.1 (2006): 16–23.

Friedman, Michael D. "'For Man Is a Giddy Thing, and This Is My Conclusion': Fashion and *Much Ado About Nothing.*" *Text and Performance Quarterly* 13.3 (1993): 267–82.

————. "'Hush'd on Purpose to Grace Harmony': Wives and Silence in *Much Ado about Nothing.*" *Theatre Journal* 42.3 (1990): 350–63.

————. "Male Bonds and Marriage in *All's Well* and *Much Ado.*" *SEL: Studies in English Literature, 1500–1900* 35.2 (1995): 231–49.

Furness, Horace Howard. *Much Adoe About Nothing.* A New Variorum Edition. Philadelphia: J. B. Lippincott Company, 1899.

Gardner, C. O. "Beatrice and Benedick." *Theoria: A Journal of Studies in the Arts, Humanities and Social Sciences* 49 (1977): 1–17.

Garrett, John, ed. *More Talking of Shakespeare.* New York: Theatre Arts Books, 1959.

Gaw, Allison. "Is Shakespeare's *Much Ado* a Revised Earlier Play?" *PMLA* 50.3 (1935): 715–38.

Gay, Penny. *As She Likes It: Shakespeare's Unruly Women.* London: Routledge, 1994.

Gilbert, Allan. "Two Margarets: The Composition of *Much Ado about Nothing.*" *Philological Quarterly* 41 (1962): 61–71.

Gordon, George Stuart, and E. K. Chambers. *Shakespearian Comedy and Other Studies.* London: Oxford University Press, 1944.

Gough, Melinda J. "'Her Filthy Feature Open Showne' in Ariosto, Spenser, and *Much Ado about Nothing.*" *SEL: Studies in English Literature, 1500–1900* 39.1 (1999): 41–67.

Hammersmith, James P. "Villainy upon Record: The Dogberrian Method." *Interpretations: Studies in Language and Literature* 11 (1979): 13–23.

Hanley, R. "*Much Ado about Nothing*: Critical Realism Examined." *Philosophical Studies*: 115.2 (2003): 123–47.

Hartby, Eva. *Man-Figures in Much Ado about Nothing.* Copenhagen: Univ. of Copenhagen Press, 1988.

Hassel, R. Chris. *Faith and Folly in Shakespeare's Romantic Comedies.* Athens: University of Georgia Press, 1980.

Henderson, Archibald. *Much Ado About Nothing: A Scene-by-Scene Analysis with Critical Commentary.* New York: American R.D.M. Corp., 1966.

Howard, Jean E. "Renaissance Antitheatricality and the Politics of Gender and Rank in *Much Ado about Nothing.*" *Shakespeare Reproduced: The Text in History and Ideology.* Eds. Jean E. Howard, Marion F. O'Connor, and Margaret Ferguson. New York: Methuen, 1987. 163–87.

Hunter, G. K. *William Shakespeare: The Late Comedies: A Midsummer-Night's Dream, Much Ado About Nothing, As You Like It, Twelfth Night.* London: Longman, 1962.

Huston, J. Dennis. *Shakespeare's Comedies of Play.* New York: Columbia University Press, 1981.

Jenkins, Harold. "The Ball Scene in *Much Ado about Nothing.*" *Shakespeare: Text, Language, Criticism: Essays in Honour of Marvin Spevack.* Eds. Bernhard Fabioan and Kurt Tetzeli von Rosador. Hildesheim: Olms, 1987. 98–117.

Kállay, Géza. "'It Is Not So, Nor 'Twas Not So': Funny Words and the Role-Playing of 'Double-Tongues' in *Much Ado about Nothing*." *AnaChronist* 2003: 29–45.

Kiefer, Frederick. "Poems as Props in *Love's Labor's Lost* and *Much Ado about Nothing*." *Reading and Literacy in the Middle Ages and Renaissance*. Ed. Ian Frederick Moulton. Turnhout, Belgium: Brepols; 2004. 127–41.

King, Walter N. "Much Ado About Something." *Shakespeare Quarterly* 15.3 (1964): 143–55.

Lane, Robert. "'Foremost in Report': Social Identity and Masculinity in *Much Ado about Nothing*." *Upstart Crow* 16 (1996): 31–47.

Lee, Yong-eun. "The Interrelation of Reality, Language and Power in *Much Ado About Nothing*." *Journal of English Language and Literature/Yongo Yongmunhak* 49. 2 (2003): 393–418.

Lewalski, Barbara K. "Hero's Name—and Namesake—in *Much Ado About Nothing*." *English Language Notes* 7 (1970): 175–79.

Lucking, David. "Bringing Deformed Forth: Engendering Meaning in *Much Ado about Nothing*." *Renaissance Forum* 2.1 (1997).

Lyon, Katherine M. "Male Bonds in *Much Ado About Nothing* and *Othello*." *Journal of the Wooden O Symposium* 2 (2002): 161–73.

Mangan, Michael. *A Preface to Shakespeare's Comedies, 1594–1603*. London: Longman, 1996.

Martz, William J. *Shakespeare's Universe of Comedy*. New York: D. Lewis, 1971.

McCollom, William G. "The Role of Wit in *Much Ado About Nothing*." *Shakespeare Quarterly* 19.2 (1968): 165–74.

McGlynn, Mary. "Buyer Beware: The Business of Marriage Contracts in Shakespeare's *Much Ado about Nothing*." *Proceedings of the Seventh Northern Plains Conference on Early British Literature*. Ed. Jay Ruud. Aberdeen, SD: Northern State UP; 1999. 90–100.

McGrady, Donald. "The Topos of 'Inversion of Values' in Hero's Depiction of Beatrice." *Shakespeare Quarterly* 44.4 (1993): 472–76.

McPeek, James A. S. "The Thief 'Deformed' and Much Ado about 'Nothing'." *Boston University Studies in English* 4 (1960): 65–84.

Miller, James. *The Universal Passion*. London: Cornmarket Press, 1969.

Mosian, Thomas. "Deforming Sources: Literary Antecedents and Their Traces in *Much Ado about Nothing*." *Shakespeare Studies* 31 (2003): 165–83.

Mueller, Martin. "Shakespeare's Sleeping Beauties: The Sources of *Much Ado about Nothing* and the Play of Their Repetitions." *Modern Philology* 91.3 (1994): 288–311.

Mueschke, Paul. "Illusion and Metamorphosis in *Much Ado about Nothing*." *Shakespeare Quarterly* 18.1 (1967): 53–65.

Muir, Kenneth. *Shakespeare's Comic Sequence*. New York: Barnes & Noble Books, 1979.

Mulryne, J. R. *Shakespeare: Much Ado About Nothing.* London: E. Arnold, 1965.

Newman, Karen. *Shakespeare's Rhetoric of Comic Character: Dramatic Convention in Classical and Renaissance Comedy.* New York: Methuen, 1985.

Olson, Paul A. *Beyond a Common Joy: An Introduction to Shakespearean Comedy.* Lincoln, NE: University of Nebraska Press, 2008.

Owen, Charles A., Jr. "Comic Awareness, Style, and Dramatic Technique in *Much Ado About Nothing.*" *Boston University Studies in English* 5 (1961): 193–207.

Page, Nadine. "Beatrice: 'My Lady Disdain'." *Modern Language Notes* 50.8 (1935): 494–99.

———. "The Public Repudiation of Hero." *PMLA* 50.3 (1935): 739–44.

Partee, Morriss Henry. "The Comic Equilibrium of *Much Ado About Nothing.*" *Upstart Crow* 12 (1992): 60–73.

Pasicki, Adam. "Some Rhetorical Figures in *Much Ado About Nothing.*" *Kwartalnik Neofilologiczny* 15 (1968): 147–54.

Peterson, Douglas L. *Time, Tide, and Tempest: A Study of Shakespeare's Romances.* San Marino, CA: Huntington Library, 1973.

Phialas, Peter G. *Shakespeare's Romantic Comedies: The Development of their Form and Meaning.* Chapel Hill: University of North Carolina Press, 1966.

Piette, Adam. "Performance, Subjectivity and Slander in *Hamlet* and *Much Ado about Nothing.*" *Early Modern Literary Studies*: 7.2 (2001): 1–29.

Porter, Charlotte and Helen A. Clarke, eds. *Much Adoe About Nothing: First Folio Edition.* New York: Thomas Y. Crowell & Co., 1903.

Potts, Abbie F. "Spenserian 'Courtesy' and 'Temperance' in *Much Ado about Nothing.*" *Shakespeare Association Bulletin* 17 (1942): 103–11, 126–33.

Prouty, Charles Tyler and Peter Beverley. *The Sources of Much Ado About Nothing, a Critical Study, Together with the Text of Peter Beverley's Ariodanto and Ieneura.* New Haven: Yale University Press, 1950.

Reiff, Raychel Haugrud. "The Unsung 'Hero' in *Much Ado about Nothing.*" *Journal of the Wooden O Symposium* 4 (2004): 139–49.

Richman, David. *Laughter, Pain, and Wonder: Shakespeare's Comedies and the Audience in the Theater.* Newark: University of Delaware Press, 1990.

Rolfe, William J., ed. *Shakespeare's Comedy of Much Ado About Nothing.* New York: Harper & Brothers, Publishers, 1881.

Ross, Thomas W. "Maimed Rites in *Much Ado About Nothing.*: *Costerus: Essays in English and American Language and Literature* 5 (1972): 125–34.

St. Pierre, Ronald. "'God will send you no horns': The Banter of Cuckoldry in *Much Ado about Nothing.*" *Shoin Literary Review* 22 (1988): 129–40.

Sarkar, Shyamal Kumar. "The Structure of *Much Ado about Nothing.*" *Shakespeare Studies* 23 (1984–1985): 39–58.

Scheil, Katherine West. *The Taste of the Town: Shakespearian Comedy and the Early Eighteenth-Century Theater.* Lewisburg, PA: Bucknell University Press, 2003.

Sexton, Joyce Hengerer. "The Theme of Slander in *Much Ado about Nothing* and Garter's *Susanna*." *Philological Quarterly* 54 (1975): 419–33.

Shaw, George Bernard. *Shaw on Shakespeare: An Anthology of Bernard Shaw's Writings on the Plays and Productions of Shakespeare*. Ed. Edwin Wilson. New York: E. P. Dutton & Co., Inc., 1961.

Smith, Emma, ed. *Shakespeare's Comedies: A Guide to Criticism*. Hoboken, NY: Wiley-Blackwell, 2003.

Snuggs, Henry L. "The Act-Division of *Much Ado about Nothing*." *Renaissance Papers*. Ed. A. H. Gilbert. Columbia: University of South Carolina Press, 1955. 65–74.

Spinrad, Phoebe S. "Dogberry Hero: Shakespeare's Comic Constables in Their Communal Context." *Studies in Philology* 89.2 (1992): 161–78.

Stafford, Tony J. "Benedick's Cure in *Much Ado*." *Artes Liberales* 4.2 (1971): 43–56.

———. "*Much Ado* and Its Satiric Intent." *Arlington Quarterly* 2.4 (1970): 164–74.

Straznicky, Marta. "Shakespeare and the Government of Comedy: *Much Ado about Nothing*." *Shakespeare Studies* 22 (1994): 141–71.

Swinden, Patrick. *An Introduction to Shakespeare's Comedies*. New York: Barnes & Noble, 1973.

Swisher, Clarice. *Readings on the Comedies*. San Diego: Greenhaven Press, 1997.

Taylor, Mark. "Presence and Absence in *Much Ado about Nothing*." *The Centennial Review* 33.1 (1989): 1–12.

Thaler, Alwin. "Spenser and *Much Ado about Nothing*." *Studies in Philology* 37 (1940): 225–35.

Thompson, Ann and Sasha Roberts, eds. *Women Reading Shakespeare: 1660–1900*. Manchester: Manchester UP, 1997.

Thompson, J. B. "'The Only Love-Gods'?: The Manipulation of Feeling in *Much Ado about Nothing*." *Shakespeare in Southern Africa: Journal of the Shakespeare Society of Southern Africa* 5 (1992): 33–42.

Tobin, J. J. M. "On the Asininity of Dogberry." *English Studies: A Journal of English Language and Literature* 59 (1978): 199–201.

Todokoro, Hiroyuki, and Josai Jinbun Kenkyu. "Dynamics of Deception in *Much Ado about Nothing*." *Studies in the Humanities* 7 (1980): 113–31.

Traugott, John. "Creating a Rational Rinaldo: A Study in the Mixture of the Genres of Comedy and Romance in *Much Ado about Nothing*." *Genre: Forms of Discourse and Culture* 15.2–3 (1982): 157–81.

Vaughn, Jack A. *Shakespeare's Comedies*. New York: F. Ungar, 1980.

Vickers, Brian, ed. *Shakespeare: The Critical Heritage*. London: Routledge and Kegan Paul, 1974.

Wain, John. "The Shakespearean Lie-Detector: Thoughts on *Much Ado About Nothing.*" *Critical Quarterly* 9 (1967): 27–42.

Wales, Julia G. "Shakespeare's Use of English and Foreign Elements in the Setting of *Much Ado about Nothing.*" *Transactions of the Wisconsin Academy of Sciences, Arts, and Letters* 28 (1933): 363–98.

Waller, Gary F. *Shakespeare's Comedies.* London: Longman, 1991.

Weil, Herbert. "'Be Vigilant, I Beseech You': A Fantasia on Dogberry and Doubling in *Much Ado about Nothing.*" *Ben Jonson Journal* 6 (1999): 307–17.

Weiss, Tanja. *Shakespeare on the Screen: Kenneth Branagh's Adaptations of Henry V, Much Ado About Nothing, and Hamlet.* New York: P. Lang, 1999.

West, E. J. "Much Ado about an Unpleasant Play." *Shakespeare Association Bulletin* 22 (1947): 30–34.

Westfall, Alfred Van Rensselaer. *American Shakespearean Criticism 1697–1865.* New York: H. W. Wilson Company, 1939.

Westlund, Joseph. *Shakespeare's Reparative Comedies: A Psychoanalytic View of the Middle Plays.* Chicago: University of Chicago Press, 1984.

Williamson, Marilyn L., ed. *Much Ado About Nothing: With New and Updated Critical Essays and a Revised Bibliography.* New York: Penguin, 1998.

———. *The Patriarchy of Shakespeare's Comedies.* Detroit: Wayne State University Press, 1986.

———. *Pegasus Shakespeare Bibliographies: As You Like It, Much Ado About Nothing, and Twelfth Night, or What You Will.* Fairview, NC: Pegasus Press, 2003.

Wilson, John Dover. *Shakespeare's Happy Comedies.* Evanston, IL: Northwestern University Press, 1962.

Wolfensperger, Peter. *Shakespeare, Impartial and Partial: Strategies of Persuasion in the Comedies.* Tübingen: Francke, 1994.

Wright, Nancy E. "Legal Interpretation of Defamation in Shakespeare's *Much Ado about Nothing.*" *Ben Jonson Journal* 13 (2006): 93–108.

Much Ado about Nothing Through the Ages: Bibliography

Anderson, Linda. *A Kind of Wild Justice: Revenge in Shakespeare's Comedies.* Newark: University of Delaware Press, 1987.

Auden, W. H. *Lectures on Shakespeare.* Ed. Arthur Kirsch. Princeton, NJ: Princeton UP, 2000.

Berger, Harry, Jr. "Against the Sink-a-Pace: Sexual and Family Politics in *Much Ado about Nothing.*" *Shakespeare Quarterly* 33.3 (1982): 302–13.

Bloom, Harold. *Modern Critical Interpretations: William Shakespeare's Much Ado About Nothing.* New York: Chelsea House, 1988.

———. *Shakespeare's Comedies: Comprehensive Research and Study Guide.* Broomall, PA: Chelsea House Publishers, 2000.

————, ed. *William Shakespeare's Much Ado About Nothing.* New York: Chelsea House Publishers, 1988.

Cook, Carol. "'The Sign and Semblance of Her Honor': Reading Gender Difference in *Much Ado About Nothing.*" *PMLA* 101.2 (Mar 1986): 186–202.

Cook, David. "'The very temple of delight': The Twin Plots of *Much Ado about Nothing.*" *Poetry and Drama, 1570–1700: Essays in Honour of Harold F. Brooks.* Eds. Anthony Coleman and Antony Hammond. London: Methuen, 1981. 32–46.

Cookson, Linda and Bryan Loughrey. *Critical Essays on Much Ado About Nothing: William Shakespeare.* Harlow: Longman, 1989.

Davis, Walter R., ed. *Twentieth Century Interpretations of Much Ado About Nothing.* Englewood Cliffs, N.J.: Prentice-Hall, 1969.

Dawson, Anthony B. "Much Ado about Signifying." *SEL: Studies in English Literature, 1500–1900* 22.2 (1982): 211–21.

Edwards, Gavin. "Anticipation and Retrospect in *Much Ado about Nothing.*" *Essays in Criticism: A Quarterly Journal of Literary Criticism* 41.4 (1991): 277–90.

Everett, Barbara. "*Much Ado about Nothing*: The Unsociable Comedy." *English Comedy.* Ed. Michael Cordner, Peter Holland, and John Kerrigan. Cambridge: Cambridge University Press, 1994. 68–84.

Friedman, Michael D. "The Editorial Recuperation of Claudio." *Comparative Drama* 25.4 (1991–1992): 369–86.

————. *The World Must Be Peopled: Shakespeare's Comedies of Forgiveness.* Madison, NJ: Fairleigh Dickinson University Press, 2002.

Hartley, Lodwick. "Claudio and the Unmerry War." *College English* 26.8 (1965): 609–14.

Hays, Janice. "Those 'soft and delicate desires': *Much Ado* and the Distrust of Women." *The Woman's Part: Feminist Criticism of Shakespeare.* Eds. Carolyn Lenz, Ruth Swift, Gayle Greene, Carol Thomas Neely. Urbana: University of Illinois Press, 1980.

Henze, Richard. "Deception in *Much Ado about Nothing.*" *SEL: Studies in English Literature, 1500–1900* 11.2 (1971): 187–201.

Krieger, Elliot. "Social Relations and the Social Order in *Much Ado about Nothing.*" *Shakespeare Survey* 32 (1979): 49–61.

Leggatt, Alexander. *Shakespeare's Comedy of Love.* London: Methuen & Co Ltd, 1974.

Lewalski, B. (Barbara) K. "Love, Appearance and Reality: *Much Ado about Something.*" *SEL: Studies in English Literature, 1500–1900* 8.2 (1968): 235–51.

Myhill, Nova. "Spectatorship in/of *Much Ado About Nothing.*" *Studies in English Literature 1500–1900* 39.2 (Spring 1999): 291–311.

Neill, Kerby. "More Ado About Claudio: An Acquittal for the Slandered Groom." *Shakespeare Quarterly* 3.2 (1952): 91–107.

Richmond, Hugh Macrae. "The Two Sicilies: Ethnic Conflict in *Much Ado*." *Shakespeare Newsletter* 57.1 (2007): 17–18.

Rose, Steven. "Love and Self-Love in *Much Ado About Nothing*." *Essays in Criticism: A Quarterly Journal of Literary Criticism* 20 (1970): 143–50.

Slights, Camille Wells. "The Unauthorized Language of *Much Ado about Nothing*." *The Elizabethan Theatre, XII*. Ed. A. L. Magnusson and C. E. McGee. Toronto: Meany; 1993. 113–33.

Weil, Herbert. "'Be Vigilant, I Beseech You': A Fantasia on Dogberry and Doubling in *Much Ado about Nothing*." *Ben Jonson Journal* 6 (1999): 307–17.

Williams, Mary C. "Much Ado about Chastity in *Much Ado about Nothing*." *Renaissance Papers* (1984): 37–45.

Wynne-Davies, Marion, ed. *Much Ado About Nothing and The Taming of the Shrew*. New York: Palgrave, 2001.

ACKNOWLEDGMENTS
❧

Much Ado about Nothing in the Twentieth and Twenty-first Centuries

W. H. Auden, "Much Ado About Nothing." From *Lectures on Shakespeare*, edited by Arthur Kirsch, pp. 113–23. Princeton University Press, Copyright © 2001 by the estate of W. H. Auden. Reprinted by permission of Curtis Brown, Ltd.

Graham Storey, "The Success of *Much Ado About Nothing*." From *More Talking of Shakespeare*, edited by John Garrett, pp. 128–43. Copyright © 1959 by Longman.

Marvin Felheim, "Comic Realism in *Much Ado About Nothing*." From *Philologica Pragensia* 7: 213–25. Copyright © 1964.

Carl Dennis, "Wit and Wisdom in *Much Ado About Nothing*." From *Studies in English Literature* 13:2 (Spring 1973): 223–37. Reprinted with permission from SEL, *Studies in English Literature 1500–1900*.

Carol Cook, "'The Sign and Semblance of Her Honor': Reading Gender Difference in *Much Ado About Nothing*." *PMLA*, vol. 101, no. 2 (March 1986): 186–202. Reprinted by permission of the Modern Language Association of America.

Nova Myhill, "Spectatorship in/of *Much Ado About Nothing*." From *Studies in English Literature* 39:2 (Spring 1999): 291–311. Reprinted with permission from *SEL, Studies in English Literature* 1500–1900.

Maurice Hunt, "The Reclamation of Language in *Much Ado About Nothing*." From *Studies in Philology*, vol. 97, no. 2 (Spring 2000): 165–91. Copyright © 2000 by the University of North Carolina Press. Used by permission of the publishers, www.uncpress.unc.edu

INDEX

❧

Characters in literary works are indexed by first name (if any), followed by the name of the work in parentheses